MW00510366

MAJESTY IN MISERY

3: CALVARY'S MOURNFUL MOUNTAIN

MAJESTY IN MISERY

3: CALVARY'S MOURNFUL MOUNTAIN

*Select Sermons on the
Passion of Christ from*

C. H. SPURGEON

THE BANNER OF TRUTH TRUST

THE BANNER OF TRUTH TRUST
3 Murrayfield Road, Edinburgh EH12 6EL, UK
P.O. Box 621, Carlisle, PA 17013, USA

*

© The Banner of Truth Trust 2005
ISBN 0 85151 916 4

*

Typeset in 11.5 /13 pt Sabon MT at the
Banner of Truth Trust, Edinburgh
Printed in the USA by
Versa Press, Inc.,
East Peoria, IL.

CONTENTS

CALVARY'S MOURNFUL MOUNTAIN CLIMB;
There, adoring at His feet,
Mark that miracle of time,
God's own sacrifice complete.
'It is finished!' – hear him cry:
Learn of Jesus Christ to die.
James Montgomery, 1771–1854

We here behold the Saviour in the depths of his agonies and sorrows. No other place so well shows the griefs of Christ as Calvary, and no other moment at Calvary is so full of agony as that in which this cry rends the air, 'My God, my God, why hast thou forsaken me?' At this moment, physical weakness, brought upon him by fasting and scourging, was united with the acute mental torture which he endured from the shame and ignominy through which he had to pass; and as the culmination of his grief, he suffered spiritual agony which surpasses all expression, on account of the departure of his Father from him. This was the blackness and darkness of his horror; then it was that he penetrated the depths of the caverns of suffering.

'My God, my God, why hast thou forsaken me?' There is something in these words of our Saviour always calculated to benefit us. When we behold the sufferings of men, they afflict and appal us; but the sufferings of our Saviour, while they move us to grief, have about them something sweet, and full of consolation. Here, even here, in this black spot of grief, we find our heaven, while gazing upon the cross. This, which might be thought a frightful sight, makes the Christian glad and joyous. If he laments the cause, yet he rejoices in the consequences.

C. H. SPURGEON, 1834–92

vii

I

THE PROCESSION OF SORROW[1]

And they took Jesus, and led him away.
JOHN 19:16

NEXT SATURDAY ALL EYES will be fixed on a great Prince who shall ride through our streets with his Royal Bride. Today I invite your attention to another Prince, marching in another fashion through his metropolis. London shall see the glory of the one: Jerusalem beheld the shame of the other. Come hither, ye lovers of Immanuel, and I will show you this great sight – the King of sorrow marching to his throne of grief, the cross.

I claim for the procession of my Lord an interest superior to the pageant you are now so anxiously expecting. Will your Prince be sumptuously arrayed? Mine is adorned with garments crimsoned with his own blood. Will your Prince be decorated with honours? Behold, my King is not without his crown – alas, a crown of thorns set with ruby drops of blood! Will your thoroughfares be thronged? So were the streets of Jerusalem; for great multitudes followed him. Will ye raise a clamour of tumultuous shouting? Such a greeting had the Lord of glory, but alas, it was not the shout of welcome, but the yell of 'Away with him! away with him.' High in the air ye bid your banners wave about the heir of England's throne, but how shall ye rival the banner of the sacred cross, that day for the first time borne among the sons of men. For the thousands of eyes which shall gaze upon the youthful Prince, I offer the gaze of men and angels. All nations gathered about my Lord, both great and

[1] Sermon No. 497. Preached at the Metropolitan Tabernacle on Sunday morning, 1 March 1863.

mean men clustered around his person. From the sky the angels viewed him with wonder and amazement; the spirits of the just looked from the windows of heaven upon the scene, yea, the great God and Father watched each movement of his suffering Son. But ye ask me where is the spouse, the king's daughter fair and beautiful? My Lord is not altogether without his espoused one. The church, the bride of Christ, was there conformed to the image of her Lord; she was there, I say, in Simon, bearing the cross, and in the women weeping and lamenting. Say not that the comparison is strained, for in a moment I will withdraw it and present the contrast.

Grant me only thus much of likeness: we have here a Prince with his bride, bearing his banner, and wearing his royal robes, traversing the streets of his own city, surrounded by a throng who shout aloud, and a multitude who gaze with interest profound. But how vast was the disparity! The most careless eye discerns it. Yonder young Prince is ruddy with the bloom of early youth and health; my Master's visage is more marred than that of any man. See, it has been blackened with bruises, and stained with the shameful spittle of them that derided him. Your heir of royalty is magnificently drawn along the streets in his stately chariot, sitting at his ease: my princely sufferer walks with weary feet, marking the road with crimson drops; not borne, but bearing; not carried, but carrying his cross. Your Prince is surrounded by a multitude of friends; hark how they joyously welcome him! And well they may; the son of such noble parents deserves a nation's love.

But my Prince is hated without a cause. Hark how their loud voices demand that he should be hastened to execution! How harshly grate the cruel syllables, 'Crucify him! crucify him! Your noble Prince is preparing for his marriage: mine is hastening to his doom. Oh, shame that men should find so much applause for Princes and none for the King of kings. Yet, dear friends, to some eyes there will be more attraction in the procession of sorrow, of shame, and of blood, than in yon display of grandeur and joy. Oh! I pray you, lend your ears to such faint words as I can utter on a subject all too high for me, the march of the world's Maker along the way of his great sorrow; your Redeemer traversing the rugged path of suffering, along which he went with heaving heart and heavy footsteps, that he might pave a royal road of mercy for his enemies.

I. After our Lord Jesus Christ had been formally condemned by Pilate, our text tells us he was led away. I invite your attention to CHRIST AS LED FORTH.

Pilate, as we reminded you, scourged our Saviour according to the common custom of Roman courts. The lictors executed their cruel office upon his shoulders with their rods and scourges, until the stripes had reached the full number. Jesus is formally condemned to crucifixion, but before he is led away he is given over to the Praetorian guards that those rough legionaries may insult him. It is said that a German regiment was at that time stationed in Judea, and I should not wonder if they were the lineal ancestors of those German theologians of modern times who have mocked the Saviour, tampered with revelation, and cast the vile spittle of their philosophy into the face of truth.

The soldiery mocked and insulted him in every way that cruelty and scorn could devise. The platted crown of thorns, the purple robe, the reed with which they smote him, and the spittle with which they disfigured him, all these marked the contempt in which they held the King of the Jews. The reed was no mere rush from the brook, it was of a stouter kind, of which easterns often make walking-staves, the blows were cruel as well as insulting; and the crown was not of straw but thorn, hence it produced pain as well as pictured scorn. When they had mocked him they pulled off the purple garment he had worn, this rough operation would cause much pain. His wounds unstaunched and raw, fresh bleeding from beneath the lash, would make this scarlet robe adhere to him, and when it was dragged off, his gashes would bleed anew. We do not read that they removed the crown of thorns, and therefore it is most probable, though not absolutely certain, that our Saviour wore it along the *Via Dolorosa,* and also bore it upon his head when he was fastened to the cross. Those pictures which represent our Lord as wearing the crown of thorns upon the tree have therefore at least some scriptural warrant. They put his own clothes upon him, because they were the perquisites of the executioner; as modern hangmen take the garments of those whom they execute, so did the four soldiers claim a right to his raiment. They put on him his own clothes that the multitudes might discern him to be the same man, the very man who had professed to be the Messiah. We all know that a different dress will often raise a doubt about the identity of an individual; but lo! the people saw him in the street, not arrayed in the purple robe, but wearing his garment without seam, woven from the top throughout, the common smock-frock, in fact, of the countrymen of Palestine, and they said at once, 'Yes, 'tis he, the man who healed the sick, and raised the dead; the mighty teacher who was wont to sit upon the mountain-top, or stand in the temple courts and preach with authority, and not as the Scribes.' There can be no shadow of doubt but that our Lord was really crucified, and no one substituted for him.

How they led him forth we do not know. Romish expositors, who draw upon their prolific fancy for their facts, tell us that he had a rope about his neck with which they roughly dragged him to the tree; this is one of the most probable of their surmises, since it was not unusual for the Romans thus to conduct criminals to the gallows. We care, however, far more for the fact that he went forth carrying his cross upon his shoulders. This was intended at once to proclaim his guilt and intimate his doom. Usually the crier went before with an announcement such as this, 'This is Jesus of Nazareth, King of the Jews, who for making himself a King, and stirring up the people, has been condemned to die.' This cross was a ponderous machine; not so heavy, perhaps, as some pictures would represent it, but still no light burden to a man whose shoulders were raw with the lashes of the Roman scourge. He had been all night in agony, he had spent the early morning at the hall of Caiaphas, he had been hurried, as I described to you last Sunday, from Caiaphas to Pilate, from Pilate to Herod, and from Herod back again to Pilate; he had, therefore, but little strength left, and you will not wonder that by-and-bye we find him staggering beneath his load, and that another is called to bear it with him. He goes forth, then, bearing his cross.

What learn we here as we see Christ led forth? Do we not see here the truth of that which was set forth in shadow by *the scape-goat?* Did not the high-priest bring the scape-goat, and put both his hands upon its head, confessing the sins of the people, that thus those sins might be laid upon the goat? Then the goat was led away by a fit man into the wilderness, and it carried away the sins of the people, so that if they were sought for, they could not be found. Now we see Jesus brought before the priests and rulers, who pronounce him guilty; God himself imputes our sins to *him*; he was made sin for us; and, as the substitute for our guilt, bearing our sin upon his shoulders – for that cross was a sort of representation in wood of our guilt and doom – we see the great Scapegoat led away by the appointed officers of justice. Bearing upon his back the sin of all his people, the offering goes without the camp. Beloved, can you say he carried *your* sin? As you look at the cross upon his shoulders does it represent *your* sin?

Oh! raise the question, and be not satisfied unless you can answer it most positively in the affirmative. There is one way by which you can tell whether he carried your sin or not. Hast thou laid thy hand upon his head, confessed thy sin, and trusted in him? Then thy sin lies not on thee; not one single ounce or drachma of it lies on thee; it has all been transferred by blessed imputation to Christ, and he bears it on his shoulder in the form of yonder heavy cross. What joy, what satisfaction this will give if we can sing –

> My soul looks back to see
> The burden thou didst bear,
> When hanging on the accursed tree,
> And knows her guilt was there!

Do not let the picture vanish till you have satisfied yourselves once for all that Christ was here the substitute for you.

Let us muse upon the fact that Jesus was conducted without the gates of the city. It was *the common place of death*. That little rising ground, which perhaps was called Golgotha, the place of a skull, from its somewhat resembling the crown of a man's skull, was the common place of execution. It was one of Death's castles; here he stored his gloomiest trophies; he was the grim lord of that stronghold. Our great hero, the destroyer of Death, bearded the lion in his den, slew the monster in his own castle, and dragged the dragon captive from his own den. Methinks Death thought it a splendid triumph when he saw the Master impaled and bleeding in the dominions of destruction; little did he know that the grave was to be rifled, and himself destroyed, by that crucified Son of man.

Was not the Redeemer led thither *to aggravate his shame?* Calvary was like our Old Bailey; it was the usual place of execution for the district. Christ must die a felon's death, and it must be upon the felon's gallows, in the place where horrid crimes had met their due reward. This added to his shame; but, methinks, in this, too, he draws the nearer to us, 'He was numbered with the transgressors, and bare the sin of many, and made intercession for the transgressors.'

But further, my brethren; this, I think, is the great lesson from Christ's being slaughtered without the gate of the city – *let us go forth, therefore, without the camp, bearing his reproach.* You see there the multitude *are leading him forth from the temple.* He is not allowed to worship with them. The ceremonial of the Jewish religion denies him any participation in its pomps; the priests condemn him never again to tread the hallowed floors, never again to look upon the consecrated altars in the place of his people's worship. He is exiled from *their friendship*, too.

No man dare call him friend now, or whisper a word of comfort to him. Nay more; he is banished from their *society*, as if he were a leper whose breath would be infectious, whose presence would scatter plague. They force him without the walls, and are not satisfied till they have rid themselves of his obnoxious presence. For him they have no tolerance. Barabbas may go free; the thief and the murderer may be spared; but for Christ there is no word, but 'Away with such a fellow from the earth! It is not fit that he should live.' Jesus is therefore hunted out of the city, beyond the gate, with the will and force of his own nation, but he journeys not against his own will; even as the lamb goeth as willingly to the shambles as to the meadow, so doth Christ cheerfully take up his cross and go without the camp.

See, brethren, here is a picture of what we may expect from men if we are faithful to our Master. It is not likely that we shall be able to worship with their worship. They prefer a ceremonial pompous and gaudy; the swell of music, the glitter of costly garments, the parade of learning – all these must minister grandeur to the world's religion, and thus shut out the simple followers of the Lamb. The high places of earth's worship and honour are not for us. If we be true to our Master we shall soon lose the friendship of the world. The sinful find our conversation distasteful; in our pursuits the carnal have no interest; things dear to us are dross to worldlings, while things precious to them are contemptible to us. There have been times, and the days may come again, when faithfulness to Christ has entailed exclusion from what is called 'society'. Even now to a large extent the true Christian is like a pariah, lower than the lowest caste, in the judgment of some. The world has in former days counted it God's service to kill the saints. We are to reckon upon all this, and should the worst befall us, it is to be no strange thing to us.

These are silken days, and religion fights not so stern a battle. I will not say it is because we are unfaithful to our Master that the world is more kind to us, but I half suspect it is, and it is very possible that if we were more thoroughly Christians the world would more heartily detest us, and if we would cleave more closely to Christ we might expect to receive more slander, more abuse, less tolerance, and less favour from men. You young believers, who have lately followed Christ, should father and mother forsake you, remember you were bidden to reckon upon it; should brothers and sisters deride, you must put this down as part of the cost of being a Christian. Godly working-men, should your employers or your fellow-workers frown upon you; wives, should your husbands threaten to cast you out, remember, without the camp was Jesus' place, and without the camp is yours.

Oh! ye Christian men, who dream of trimming your sails to the wind, who seek to win the world's favour, I do beseech you cease from a course so perilous. We are in the world, but we must never be of it; we are not to be secluded like monks in the cloister, but we are to be separated like Jews among Gentiles; men, but not of men; helping, aiding, befriending, teaching, comforting, instructing, but not sinning either to escape a frown or to win a smile. The more manifestly there shall be a great gulf between the church and the world, the better shall it be for both; the better for the world, for it shall be thereby warned; the better for the church, for it shall be thereby preserved. Go ye, then, like the Master, expecting to be abused, to wear an ill-name, and to earn reproach; go ye, like him, without the camp.

II. Let us now gaze for awhile upon CHRIST CARRYING HIS CROSS.

I have shown you, believer, your position; let me now show you your *service*. Christ comes forth from Pilate's hall with the cumbrous wood upon his shoulder, but through weariness he travels slowly, and his enemies urgent for his death, and half afraid, from his emaciated appearance, that he may die before he reaches the place of execution, allow another to carry his burden. The tender mercies of the wicked are cruel, they cannot spare him the agonies of dying on the cross, they will therefore remit the labour of carrying it. They place the cross upon Simon, a Cyrenian, coming out of the country. We do not know what may have been the colour of Simon's face, but it was most likely black. Simon was an African; he came from Cyrene. Alas poor African, thou hast been compelled to carry the cross even until now. Hail, ye despised children of the sun, ye follow first after the King in the march of woe. We are not sure that Simon was a disciple of Christ; he may have been a friendly spectator; yet one would think the Jews would naturally select a disciple if they could. Coming fresh from the country, not knowing what was going on, he joined with the mob, and they made him carry the cross. Whether a disciple then or not, we have every reason to believe that he became so afterwards; he was the father, we read, of Alexander and Rufus, two persons who appear to have been well known in the early Church; let us hope that salvation came to his house when he was compelled to bear the Saviour's cross.

Dear friends, we must remember that, although no one died on the cross with Christ, for atonement must be executed by a solitary Saviour, yet another person did carry the cross for Christ; for this world, while redeemed by price by Christ, and by Christ alone, is to be redeemed by divine power manifested in the sufferings and labours of the saints as well as those of Christ. Mark you, the *ransom* of men was all paid by Christ; that was redemption *by price*. But power is wanted to dash down those idols, to overcome the hosts of error; where is it to be found? In the Lord of hosts, who shows his power in the sufferings of Christ and of his church. The Church must suffer, that the gospel may be spread by her means. This is what the apostle meant when he said, 'I fill up that which is behind of the afflictions of Christ in my flesh for his body's sake, which is the church.' There was nothing behind in the price, but there is something behind in the manifested power, and we must continue to fill up that measure of revealed power, carrying each one of us the cross with Christ, till the last shame shall have been poured upon his cause, and he shall reign for ever and ever. We see in Simon's carrying the cross a picture of what the church is to do throughout all generations. Mark then, Christian, Jesus does not suffer so as to exclude your suffering. He bears a cross, not that you may escape it, but that you may endure it. Christ does exempt you from sin, but not from sorrow; he does take the curse of the cross, but he does not take the cross of the curse away from you. Remember that, and expect to suffer.

Beloved, let us comfort ourselves with this thought, that in our case, as in Simon's, *it is not our cross, but Christ's cross which we carry.* When you are molested for your piety; when your religion brings the trial of cruel mockings upon you; then remember, it is not *your* cross, it is *Christ's* cross; and how delightful is it to carry the cross of our Lord Jesus?

You carry the cross after him. You have blessed company; your path is marked with footprints of your Lord. If you will look, there is the mark of his blood-red shoulder upon that heavy cross. 'Tis his cross, and he goes before you as a shepherd goes before his sheep. Take up your cross daily and follow him.

Do not forget, also, *that you bear this cross in partnership.* It is the opinion of some commentators that Simon only carried one end of the cross, and not the whole of it. That is very possible; Christ may have carried the heavier end, against the transverse beam, and Simon may have borne the lighter end. Certainly it is so with you; you do but carry the light end of the cross; Christ bore the heavier end.

> His way was much rougher and darker than mine;
> Did Christ, my Lord, suffer, and shall I repine?

Samuel Rutherford says, 'Whenever Christ gives us a cross, he cries, "Halves, my love."' Others think that Simon carried the whole of the cross. If he carried all the cross, yet he only carried the wood of it; he did not bear the sin which made it such a load. Christ did but transfer to Simon the outward frame, the mere tree; but the curse of the tree, which was our sin and its punishment, rested on Jesus' shoulders still. Dear friend, if you think that you suffer all that a Christian can suffer; if all God's billows roll over you, yet, remember, there is not one drop of wrath in all your sea of sorrow. Jesus took the wrath; Jesus carried the sin; and now all that you endure is but for his sake, that you may be conformed unto his image, and may aid in gathering his people into his family.

Although Simon carried Christ's cross, *he did not volunteer to do it, but they compelled him.* I fear me, beloved, I fear me that the most of us if we ever do carry it, carry it by compulsion, at least when it first comes on to our shoulders we do not like it, and would fain run from it, but the world compels us to bear Christ's cross. Cheerfully accept this burden, ye servants of the Lord. I do not think we should seek after needless persecution. That man is a fool and deserves no pity, who purposely excites the disgust of other people. No, no; we must not make a cross of our own. Let there be nothing but your religion to object to, and then if that offends them let them be offended, it is a cross which you must carry joyfully.

Though Simon had to bear the cross for a very little while, it gave him lasting honour. I do not know how far it was from Pilate's house to the Mount of Doom. Romanists pretend to know; in fact they know the very spot where Veronica wiped the blessed face with her handkerchief, and found his likeness impressed upon it; we also know very well where that was *not* done; in fact they know the very spot where Jesus fainted, and if you go to Jerusalem you can see all these different places if you only carry enough credulity with you; but the fact is the city has been so razed, and burned, and ploughed, that there is little chance of distinguishing any of these positions, with the exception, it may be, of Mount Calvary, which being outside the walls may possibly still remain. The *Via Dolorosa,* as the Romanists call it, is a long street at the present time, but it may have been but a few yards. Simon had to carry the cross but for a very little time, yet his name is in this Book for ever, and we may envy him his honour. Well, beloved, the cross we have to carry is only for a little while at most. A few times the sun will go up and down the hill; a few more moons will wax and wane, and then we shall receive the glory. 'I reckon that these light afflictions, which are but for a moment, are not worthy to be compared with the glory which shall be revealed in us.' We should love the cross, and count it very dear, because it works out for us a far more exceeding and eternal weight of glory. Christians, will you refuse to be cross-bearers for Christ?

I am ashamed of some professed Christians, heartily ashamed of them! Some of them have no objection to worship with a poor congregation till they grow rich, and then, forsooth, they must go with the world's church, to mingle with fashion and gentility. There are some who in company hold their tongues, and never say a good word for Christ. They take matters very gently; they think it unnecessary to be soldiers of the cross. 'He that taketh not up his cross and followeth not after me,' says Christ, 'is not worthy of me.'

Some of you will not be baptized because you think people will say, 'He is a professor; how holy he ought to be.' I am glad the world expects much from us, and watches us narrowly. All this is a blessed clog upon us, and a means of keeping us more near the Lord. Oh! you that are ashamed of Christ, how can you read that text, 'He that is ashamed of me, and of my words, of him will I be ashamed when I come in the glory of my Father, and all my holy angels with me.' Conceal your religion? Cover it with a cloak? God forbid! Our religion is our glory; the Cross of Christ is our honour, and, while not ostentatiously parading it, as the Pharisees do, we ought never to be so cowardly as to conceal it. 'Come ye out from among them, and be ye separate, and touch not the unclean thing.' Take up your cross, and go without the camp, following your Lord, even until death.

III. I have now a third picture to present to you – CHRIST AND HIS MOURNERS.

As Christ went through the streets, a great multitude looked on. In the multitude there was a sparse sprinkling of tender-hearted women, probably those who had been healed, or whose children had been blessed by him. Some of these were persons of considerable rank; many of them had ministered to him of their substance; amidst the din and howling of the crowd, and the noise of the soldiery, they raised an exceeding loud and bitter cry, like Rachel weeping for her children, who would not be comforted, because they were not. The voice of sympathy prevailed over the voice of scorn.

Jesus paused, and said, 'Daughters of Jerusalem, weep not for me; but weep for yourselves and for your children.' The sorrow of these good women was a very proper sorrow; Jesus did not by any means forbid it, he only recommended another sorrow as being better; not finding fault with this, but still commending that. Let me show what I think he meant. Last Sunday the remark was made to me – 'If the story of the sufferings of Christ had been told of any other man, all the congregation would have been in tears.' Some of us, indeed, confess that, if we had read this narrative of suffering in a romance, we should have wept copiously, but the story of *Christ's* sufferings does not cause the excitement and emotion one would expect.

Now, I am not sure that we ought to blame ourselves for this. If we weep for the sufferings of Christ in the same way as we lament the sufferings of another man, our emotions will be only natural, and may work no good. They would be very proper, very proper; God forbid that we should stay them, except with the gentle words of Christ, 'Daughters of Jerusalem, weep not for me.' The most Scriptural way to describe the sufferings of Christ is not by labouring to excite sympathy through highly-coloured descriptions of his blood and wounds. Romanists of all ages have wrought upon the feelings of the people in this manner, and to a degree the attempt is commendable, but if it shall all end in tears of pity, no good is done. I have heard sermons, and studied works by Romish writers upon the passion and agony, which have moved me to copious tears, but I am not clear that all the emotion was profitable. I show unto you a more excellent way.

What, then, dear friends, should be the sorrows excited by a view of Christ's sufferings? They are these – *Weep not because the Saviour bled, but because your sins made him bleed.*

'Twere you my sins, my cruel sins,
   His chief tormentors were;
   Each of my crimes became a nail,
   And unbelief the spear.

When a brother makes confession of his transgressions, when on his knees before God he humbles himself with many tears, I am sure the Lord thinks far more of the tears of repentance than he would do of the mere drops of human sympathy. 'Weep for yourselves,' says Christ, 'rather than for me.'

The sufferings of Christ *should make us weep over those who have brought that blood upon their heads.* We ought not to forget the Jews. Those once highly favoured people of God who cursed themselves with, 'His blood be upon us and upon our children,' ought to make us mourn when we think of their present degradation. There are no passages in all the public ministry of Jesus so tender as those which have regard to Jerusalem. It is not sorrow over Rome, but Jerusalem. I believe there was a tenderness in Christ's heart to the Jew of a special character. He loved the Gentile, but still Jerusalem was the city of the Great King. It was, 'O Jerusalem, Jerusalem, how often would I have gathered thy children together as a hen gathereth her chickens under her wings, but ye would not!' He saw its streets flowing like bloody rivers; he saw the temple flaming up to heaven; he marked the walls loaded with Jewish captives crucified by command of Titus; he saw the city razed to the ground and sown with salt, and he said, 'Weep not for me, but for yourselves and for your children, for the day shall come when ye shall say to the rocks, Hide us, and to the mountains, Fall upon us.'

Let me add, that when we look at the sufferings of Christ, *we ought to sorrow deeply for the souls of all unregenerate men and women.* Remember, dear friends, that what Christ suffered for us, these unregenerate ones must suffer for themselves, except they put their trust in Christ. The woes which broke the Saviour's heart must crush theirs. Either Christ must die for me, or else I must die for myself the second death; if he did not carry the curse for me, then on me must it rest for ever and ever. Think, dear friends, there are some in this congregation who as yet have no interest in Jesu's blood, some sitting next to you, your nearest friends who, if they were now to close their eyes in death, would open them in hell! Think of that! Weep not for him, but for these. Perhaps they are your children, the objects of your fondest love, with no interest in Christ, without God and without hope in the world! Save your tears for them; Christ asks them not in sympathy for himself. Think of the millions in this dark world! It is calculated that one soul passes from time into eternity every time the clock ticks! So numerous has the family of man now become, that there is a death every second; and when we know how very small a proportion of the human race have even nominally received the cross – and there is none other name given under heaven among men whereby we must be saved – oh! what a black thought crosses our mind! What a cataract of immortal souls dashes downwards to the pit every hour! Well might the Master say, 'Weep not for me, but for yourselves.' You have, then, no true sympathy for Christ if you have not an earnest sympathy with those who would win souls for Christ. You may sit under a sermon, and feel a great deal, but your feeling is worthless unless it leads you to weep for yourselves and for your children. How has it been with you? Have you repented of sin? Have you prayed for your fellow men? If not, may that picture of Christ fainting in the streets lead you to do so this morning.

IV. In the fourth place, one or two words upon CHRIST'S FELLOW-SUFFERERS.

There were two other cross-bearers in the throng; they were malefactors; their crosses were just as heavy as the Lord's, and yet, at least, one of them had no sympathy with him, and his bearing the cross only led to his death, and not to his salvation. This hint only. I have sometimes met with persons who have suffered much; they have lost money, they have worked hard all their lives, or they have laid for years upon a bed of sickness, and they therefore suppose that because they have suffered so much in this life, they shall thus escape the punishment of sin hereafter. I tell you, sirs, that yonder malefactor carried his cross and died on it; and you will carry your sorrows, and be damned with them, except you repent. That impenitent thief went from the cross of his great agony – and it was agony indeed to die on a cross – he went to that place, to the flames of hell; and you, too, may go from the bed of sickness, and from the abode of poverty, to perdition, quite as readily as from the home of ease and the house of plenty. No sufferings of ours have anything to do with the atonement of sin. No blood but that which *he* has spilt, no groans but those which came from *his* heart, no suffering but that which was endured by *him*, can ever make a recompense for sin. Shake off the thought, any of you who suppose that God will have pity on you because you have endured affliction. You must consider Jesus, and not yourself; turn your eye to Christ, the great substitute for sinners, but never dream of trusting in yourselves. You may think that this remark is not needed; but I have met with one or two cases where it was required; and I have often said I would preach a sermon for even one person, and, therefore, I make this remark, even though it should rebuke but one.

V. I close with THE SAVIOUR'S WARNING QUESTION – '*If they do these things in the green tree, what will they do in the dry?*' Among other things methinks he meant this – 'If I, the innocent substitute for sinners, suffer thus, what will be done when the sinner himself – the dry tree – whose sins are his own, and not merely imputed to him, shall fall into the hands of an angry God.' Oh! ye unregenerate men and women, and there are not a few such here now, remember that when God saw Christ in the sinner's place he did not spare him, and when he finds you without Christ, he will not spare *you*. You have seen Jesus led away by his enemies; so shall you be dragged away by fiends to the place appointed for you. 'Deliver him to the tormentors,' was the word of the king in the parable; it shall be fulfilled to you – 'Depart ye cursed into everlasting fire, prepared for the devil and his angels.' Jesus was deserted of God; and if he, who was only imputedly a sinner, was deserted, how much more shall you be? '*Eloi, Eloi, lama sabachthani,*' – what an awful shriek! But what shall be your cry when you shall say, 'Good God! good God! why hast thou forsaken me?' and the answer shall come back, 'Because I have called, and ye refused; I have stretched out my hand, and no man regarded; but ye have set at nought all my counsel, and would none of my reproof: I also will laugh at your calamity; I will mock when your fear cometh.' These are awful words, but they are not mine; they are the very words of God in Scripture. Oh! sinner, if God hides his face from Christ, how much less will he spare you! He did not spare his Son the stripes.

Did I not describe last Sabbath the knotted scourges which fell upon the Saviour's back? What whips of steel for you, what knots of burning wire for you, when conscience shall smite you, when the law shall scourge you with its ten-thonged whip! Oh! who would stand in your place, ye richest, ye merriest, ye most self-righteous sinners – who would stand in your place when God shall say, 'Awake O sword against the rebel, against the man that rejected me; smite him, and let him feel the smart for ever!' Christ was spit upon with shame; sinner, what shame will be yours! The whole universe shall hiss you; angels shall be ashamed of you; your own friends, yes, your sainted mother, shall say 'Amen' to your condemnation; and those who loved you best shall sit as assessors with Christ to judge you and condemn you! I cannot roll up into one word all the mass of sorrows which met upon the head of Christ who died for us, therefore it is impossible for me to tell you what streams, what oceans of grief must roll over *your* spirit if you die as you now are.

You may die so, you may die now. There are more unlikely things than that you will be dead before next Sunday. Some of you will! It does not often happen that five or six thousand people meet together twice; it never does, I suppose; the scythe of death must cut some of you down before my voice shall warn you again! Oh! souls, I do beseech you, by the agonies of Christ, by his wounds and by his blood, do not bring upon yourselves the curse; do not bear in your own persons the awful wrath to come! May God deliver you! Trust in the Son of God and you shall never die.

The Lord bless you, for Jesu's own sake. Amen.

2

THE GREAT CROSS-BEARER AND HIS FOLLOWERS[1]

And when they had mocked him, they took off the purple from him,
and put his own clothes on him, and led him out to crucify him.
MARK 15:20

And he bearing his cross went forth.
JOHN 19:17

And they compel one Simon a Cyrenian who passed by, coming out
of the country, the father of Alexander and Rufus, to bear his cross.
MARK 15:21

WHEN OUR LORD had been condemned to die, the execution
of his sentence was hurried. The Jews were in great haste to shed
his blood: so intense was the enmity of the chief priests and
Pharisees that every moment of delay was wearisome to them.
Besides, it was the day of the Passover, and they wished to have
this matter finished before they went with hypocritical piety to
celebrate the festival of Israel's deliverance. We do not wonder at
their eagerness, for they could not bear themselves while he lived,
since his very presence reproved them for their falsehood and
hypocrisy. But at Pilate we do wonder, and herein he is much to be
blamed. In all civilized countries there is usually an interval
between the sentencing of the prisoner and the time of his putting
to death. As the capital sentence is irreversible, it is well to have a
little space in which possible evidence may be forthcoming, which
may prevent the fatal stroke. In some countries we have thought
that there has been a cruelly long delay between the sentence and

[1] Sermon No. 1,683. Preached at the Metropolitan Tabernacle on Sunday
morning, 8 October 1882.

17

the execution, but with the Romans it was usual to allow the reasonable respite of ten days. Now, I do not say that it was incumbent upon Pilate according to Roman law to have allowed ten days to a Jew, who had not the rights of Roman citizenship; but I do say that he might have pleaded the custom of his country, and so have secured a delay, and afterwards he might have released his prisoner. It was within his reach to have done so, and he was culpable, as he was all along, in thus yielding to the clamour for an immediate execution for no other reason than this, that he was 'willing to content the people.' When once we begin to make the wishes of other men our law we know not to what extremity of criminality we may be led; and so the Saviour's hasty execution is due to Pilate's vacillating spirit, and to the insatiable blood-thirstiness of the scribes and Pharisees.

Being given over to death, our Saviour was led away; and I suppose the painters are right when they put a rope about his neck or his loins; for the idea of being *led* in an open street would seem to imply some sort of bond: 'He was led as a sheep to the slaughter.' Alas, that the Emancipator of our race should be led forth as a captive to die!

The direction in which he is led is outside the city. He must not die in Jerusalem, though multitudes of prophets had perished there. Though the temple was the central place of sacrifice, yet must not the Son of God be offered there, for he was an offering of another kind, and must not lie upon their altars. Outside the city, because by the Jews he was treated as a flagrant offender who must be executed at the Tyburn of the city, in the appointed place of doom known as Calvary or Golgotha. When Naboth was unjustly condemned for blasphemy, they carried him forth out of the city, and stoned him with stones that he died; and afterwards Stephen – when they cried out against him as a blasphemer, they cast him out of the city, and there they stoned him. Our Saviour therefore must die in the ordinary place of execution, that in all respects he might be numbered with the transgressors. The rulers of the city so loathed and detested their great Reprover that they rejected him, and would not suffer him to die within their city walls. Alas, poor Jerusalem, in casting out the Son of David, thou didst cast out thy last hope: now art thou bound over to desolation.

He was led outside of the city because from that time no acceptable sacrifice could be offered there. They might go on with their offering of daily lambs, and they might sacrifice their bullocks, and burn the fat of fed beasts; but from that day the substance of the sacrifice had gone away from them, and Israel's offerings were vain oblations. Because the true sacrifice is rejected of them the Lord leaves them nothing but a vain show.

Still more forcible is the fact that our Lord must die outside the city because he was to be consumed as a sin-offering. It is written in the law, 'And the skin of the bullock, and all his flesh, with his head, and with his legs, and his inwards, and his dung, even the whole bullock shall he carry forth without the camp unto a clean place, where the ashes are poured out, and burn him on the wood with fire.' There were several sorts of offerings under the law: the sweet-savour offerings were presented upon the altar, and were accepted of God, but sin-offerings were burnt without the camp or gate, because God can have no fellowship with sin. Once let sin be imputed to the sacrifice and it becomes abhorrent to God, and must not be presented in the tabernacle or the temple, but burned outside the circle wherein his people have their habitations. And here let our hearts gratefully contemplate how truly our Lord Jesus became a sin-offering for us, and how in every point he followed out the type.

With his face turned away from his Father's house he must go to die: with his face turned away from what were once his Father's people he must be led forth to be crucified. Like a thing accursed, he is to be hung up where felons suffer condign punishment. Because we were sinners, and because sin had turned our backs to God, and because sin had broken our communion with God's accepted ones, therefore must he endure this banishment. In that sorrowful march of the cross-bearing Saviour my soul with sorrow sees herself represented as deserving thus to be made to depart unto death; and yet joy mingles with this emotion, for the glorious Sin-bearer hath thus taken away our sin, and we return from our exile: his substitution is infinitely effectual, Well may those live for whom Jesus died. Well may those return in whose place the Son of God was banished. There is entrance into the holy city now, there is entrance into the temple now, there is access unto God himself now, because the Lord bath put away our sin through him who was led to be crucified outside the city gate.

Nor do I think that even this exhausts the teaching. Jesus dies outside Jerusalem because he died, not for Jerusalem alone, nor for Israel alone. The effect of his atonement is not circumscribed by the walls of a city nor by the bounds of a race. In him shall all the nations of the earth be blessed. Out in the open he must die, to show that he reconciled both Jews and Gentiles unto God. For 'he is the propitiation for our sins', saith John, who was himself a Jew, 'and not for ours only, but also for the sins of the whole world' (1 John 2:2) Had he been the Saviour of Jews only, seclusion in the place of his offering would have been appropriate, but as he dies for all nations, he is hung up without the city.

And yet, once more, he suffered outside the gate that we might go forth unto him without the camp, bearing his reproach. 'Come ye out from among them; be ye separate, touch not the unclean thing,' henceforth becomes the command of God to all his sons and daughters: behold the Son of sons, his Only-begotten, leads the way in nonconformity to this present evil world, being himself officially severed from the old Jewish church, whose elders seek his life. He dies in sacred separation from the false and corrupt corporation which vaunted itself to be the chosen of God. He protested against all evil, and for this he died, so far as his murderers were concerned. Even so must his followers take up their cross and follow him withersoever he goeth, even though it be to be despised and rejected of men. See what instruction is found in the choice of the place wherein our great Redeemer offers himself unto God.

I. Let us draw near to our Lord for awhile, and carefully observe each instructive detail. Our imagination pictures the Blessed One standing outside the gate of Herod's palace in the custody of a band of soldiers with a centurion at their head, and we begin at once to observe HIS DRESS. That may seem a small matter, but it is not without instruction. How is he dressed? Our text tells us that when they had mocked him they took off the purple from him and put his own clothes on him; but we are not told that they took off *the crown of thorns,* and hence it has been currently believed that he continued to wear it to the cross and on the cross.

Is not this highly probable? Surely if the thorny crown had been withdrawn this would have been the place to have said, 'They took off the purple from him and removed the crown of thorns;' but it is not so written, and therefore we may believe that the sorrowful coronet remained upon him. Pilate wrote upon his accusation 'the King of the Jews,' and it was not unfitting that he should continue to wear a crown. Jesus died a crowned monarch, king of the curse. The Lord God in justice said to rebel man, 'Cursed is the ground for thy sake: thorns also and thistles shall it bring forth to thee;' and lo, the man by whom we are redeemed is crowned with that product of the earth which came of the curse.

> O sacred head surrounded
>   By crown of piercing thorn;
> O bleeding head, so wounded,
>   Reviled and put to scorn.

Probably also, as I have said, he was *bound;* for they led him as a sheep to the slaughter; but this binding was probably more abundant than that which we have hinted at, if it be indeed true that by Roman custom criminals were bound with cords to the cross which they were doomed to carry. If this was the case, you may picture our Lord with his cross bound to himself, and hear him say, 'Bind the sacrifice with cords, even to the horns of the altar.'

But the chief point to be noted is that Jesus *wore his own clothes,* the usual garments which he was accustomed to wear, and this no doubt for identification, that all who looked on might know that it was the same person who had preached in their streets and had healed their sick. They were under no misapprehension; they knew that it was Jesus of Nazareth: the keen hate of the scribes and Pharisees would not have permitted any substitution of another. It was none other than he, and his garments were the ensigns of that truth. He wore his own clothes also for another reason, namely, that there might be a fulfilment of prophecy. It may not strike you at first, but you will soon see it. Our Lord must not go to die in the purple: he must march to the cross in that vestment which was without seam and woven from the top throughout, or else the word could not have been fulfilled, 'They parted my garments among them, and upon my vesture did they cast lots.' Other raiment could readily have been rent and divided, but this garment, which was peculiar to the Saviour, could not have been so rent without destroying it, and therefore the soldiers cast lots for it. Little did they who put it on him dream that they were thus accessory to the fulfilment of a prophecy. Does it not strike you as strange that the Pharisees, who were so full of hatred to Christ, did not carefully draw back from the fulfilment of so many types and prophecies? Their rabbis and teachers knew the prophecy of Zechariah, that the Messiah should be sold for thirty pieces of silver: why did it not occur to them to make their bribe to Judas twenty-nine or thirty-one silver pieces? Why, again, did they cast the price unto the potter by buying of him the field of blood? Could they not, so to speak, have baulked the prophecy thereby? Here were voluntarily fulfilled by themselves prophecies which condemned them. I shall have to show you the same thing further on; but meanwhile observe that if it had been their object to fulfil type and prophecy they could not have acted more carefully than they did. So they put his own garments on him, and unwittingly they furnished the possibility for the fulfilment of the prophet's word: 'They parted my garments among them, and cast lots upon my vesture.'

To me there occurs one other thought touching his wearing his own garments. I do not know if I can express it, but it seems to me to indicate that our Lord's passion was a true and natural part of his life; he died as he lived. His death was not a new departure, but the completion of a life of self-sacrifice, and so he had no need to put on a fresh garb. Look! He goes to die in his ordinary everyday garments! Does not it almost seem as if people put on their Sunday clothes because they regard religion as something quite distinct from their common life? Do you not wish to see godliness in work-day clothes? religion in its shirt-sleeves? grace in a smock-frock? Do you not almost cry concerning some loud talkers – 'Put his own clothes on him, and then lead him out and let us see him'? It should be an integral part of our life to live and to die for our God. Must we become other men if we are to be God's men? Can we not wear our own clothes, habits, charac- teristics, and peculiarities and serve the Lord? Is there not some suspicion of unnaturalness in services which require men to put on a strange, outlandish dress? Surely they find their worship to be on another level than their life; they must step out of their way and dress up to attend to it. It is ill for a man when he cannot lead his fellows in prayer till he has gone to the wardrobe. Time was when vestments meant something; but ever since our great High-priest went up to his one sacrifice wearing his common clothes, all types are fulfilled and laid aside.

Now, we pray not officially, or we should need the robe; but we pray personally, and our own clothes suit us well. Jesus continued the unity of his life as he approached its close, and did not even in appearance change his way; he lived to die a sacrifice; this was the climax of his life, the apex of the towering pyramid of his perfect obedience. No mark is set, no line is drawn between his passion and all the rest of his life; nor should there be a screen between our life and death. Somehow, I dread a death which is meant to be pictorial and exhibitional. I am not an admirer of Addison's death, as some are, who praise him because he sent for a young lord, and cried, 'Come, see how a Christian can die!' I like better Bengel's wish when he desired to die just as a person would slip out from company because some one beckoned him outside. Such a person modestly thinking his presence or absence to be of small account in a great world, quietly withdraws, and friends only observe that he is gone. Death should be part of the usual curriculum, the close of the day's work, the entrance into harbour which ends the voyage. It is well to feel that you can die easily, because you have done it so many times before. He who dies daily will not fear to die. Bathe in the Jordan often, and you will not dread the fording of it when your hour has come. Our blessed Lord lived such a dying life that he made no show of death, he did not change his tone and spirit any more than his garments, but died as he lived. They put his own clothes on him: he had not himself taken them off; it was no wish of his to wear the purple even for an hour either in reality or in mockery. He was evermore the same, and his own vesture best beseemed him.

Truly, blessed Master, we may well say, 'All thy garments smell of myrrh, and aloes, and cassia;' even though they take thee not out of 'the ivory palaces wherein they have made thee glad;' but out of the common guard-room, where they had made thee to be despised and mocked and spit upon. Come from whence thou mayest, thy vesture hath a fragrant smell about it, and all thy brethren rejoice therein.

II. Brethren, I beg you for a few minutes to look at HIS COMPANY. Who were they that were with our Lord when he came to die? First and nearest to him were *the rough Roman soldiers,* strong, muscular, unfeeling men, ready to shed blood at any moment. In them human affection was kept down by stern discipline, they were the iron instruments of an empire of iron. They would do what they were bidden, and feeling and sympathy were not allowed to interfere. I do but bid you look at these guards to remind you that from beneath their eagle our Saviour won a trophy; for their centurion at our Lord's death uttered the confession, 'Certainly this was the Son of God.' This was a blessed confession of faith, and I delight to think of our Lord as thus becoming the conqueror of his conquerors by taking one out of them to be his disciple and witness, as we would fain believe he was. Surely after openly making the clear confession which the evangelist has recorded we may number him with believers.

Next to these guards were *two malefactors,* led out with him to execution. That was intended to increase his scorn, he must not be separated from the basest of men, but he must be led forth between two thieves, having previously had a murderer preferred to him. They seem to have been very hardened scoundrels, for they reviled him.

I mention them because our Lord won a trophy by the conversion of one of them, who dying said, 'We suffer justly, but this man hath done nothing amiss,' and then prayed, 'Lord, remember me when thou comest into thy kingdom.' This dying thief has brought more glory to Christ than hundreds of us, for in every place wherever this gospel has been preached this has been told as a memorial of him, and as a comfort to the guiltiest to look to Jesus. In the act of death he believed in Christ, and believed when the Lord himself was in the act of death, and that day he was with him in paradise. How hast thou conquered, O thou despised of men! How hast thou won by thy gentleness both Roman legionaries and Jewish thieves.

Beyond the prisoners were the *scribes and Pharisees, and high priests.* I could not picture their faces, but surely they must have been about the worst lot of human physiognomies that were ever seen, as with a fiendish delight they stared at Jesus. He had called them 'hypocrites': he had spoken of them as 'making clean the outside of the cup and platter', while their inner part was very wickedness, and now they are showing their venom, and silencing his reproofs. But their hate was so insatiable that it was accompanied with fear, and that night it was seen that Christ had conquered them, for they crouched before Pilate and begged a guard to prevent their victim from leaving the tomb. In their heart of hearts they feared that after all he might be the Son of God. Thus were they also vanquished: though to them the Lord Jesus was a savour of death unto death, yet they could not but be affected by him and vanquished by his death. Their hate brought with it alarm, and fear, and agitation: they trembled before the Nazarene. Look at the scene! Though the despised and sorrowful One is bowed down beneath his cross you can see at a glance the majesty which dwells in him; but as you look at *them*, the mean, wretched seed of the serpent, they seem to go upon their bellies, and dust is their meat. He is all truth and openness, and they are all cunning and craft. You can see at a glance that as an angel is to the fiends of hell, so is the Christ to his persecutors. That face distained with spittle, and blackened with blows, and encinctured with thorns wears a more than imperial glory, while their faces are as the countenances of slaves and criminals.

Around these there is a *great rabble,* and if you look into the mob you see with surprise that they are the same crowd, who a week ago shouted 'Hosanna! Hosanna!' They have changed their note and cry, 'Crucify him: crucify him;' for a few pence they were bribed to do so: they were an ignorant, fickle mob. When such do hiss at you for doing right, forgive them. When they point the finger of scorn at you for being a Christian, regard them not. It little boots what they may say or do; they yelled at him who was their best Benefactor and ours. The Lord Christ endured the popular scorn as he had once received the popular acclamation. He lived above it all, for he knew that men of low degree are vanity. Vanity of vanities; all that cometh of vain man is vanity.

Ay, but there was a little change for the better in the company: there was just a streak of light in that cloud, for *kindly women* were in the throng. These were not all his disciples, perhaps few of them were such for otherwise he would not have bidden them weep over a woe which his disciples escaped; but they were tender-hearted women who could not look upon him without tears: it is said by Luke that they bewailed and lamented him. They knew how innocent he was, and how kind he had been. Perhaps some of them had received favours at his hands, and therefore they wept sore that he should die. It was well done of them. In all the Evangelists there is no instance of a woman that had any hand in the death of Christ. As far as they are connected with the matter they are guiltless, they rather oppose his death than promote it. Woman was last at the cross and first at the sepulchre, and therefore we can never say a word about her being the first in the transgression. Oh, kindly eyes that gave the Lord of love the tribute of their pity! Blessed be ye of compassionate heaven! But the Saviour desired not at that time that human sympathy should be spent upon him, for his great heart was big with sorrows not his own. He knew that when the children of those women had grown up, and while yet some of the younger women would still be alive, their awful woe would make them exclaim, 'Blessed are the barren and the wombs that never bear, and the paps that never gave suck.' When they saw the slain of the Romans, and the slain of their own contending factions then would they mourn. The Master therefore said –

> Weep not for me! Oh! weep not, Salem's daughters,
> Faint though ye see me, stay the bursting tear;
> Turn the sad tide – the tide of bitter waters –
> Back on yourselves for desolation near.

It was well on the woman's part; it was better still on his, that he gently set the draught of sympathy on one side, because their coming sorrow oppressed him more deeply than his own.

We must now leave the company, but not till we have asked, Where are his disciples? Where is Peter? Did he not say, 'I will go with thee to prison and to death'? Where is John? Where are they all? They have fled, and have not yet returned to speak a word to him or for him. Holy women are gathering, but where are the men? Though the women are brave and act like men, the men are fearful and act as women. We are poor helpers to our Master. Had we been there, we should have done the same as they did, if not worse, for they were the flower of our Israel. Ah me!, how little worth are we for whom the Ever-blessed paid so much! Let us give clearer proof of loyalty, and follow our Prince more closely.

III. But now, come closer to the Saviour: break through the company, and hear my third talk with you while you look a little on HIS BURDEN. May the good Spirit teach me how to depict my Lord. We are told by John that our Saviour 'went forth bearing his cross'. We might have supposed, so far as the other three evangelists are concerned, that Simon the Cyrenian had carried the cross all the way, but John fills up the blank space in their accounts. Our Lord carried his own cross at the commencement of the sorrowful pilgrimage to Calvary.

This was done, first, by way of increasing his *shame*. It was a custom of the Romans to make felons bear their own gibbet, and there is a word in the Latin, *furcifer*, which signifies 'gallows bearer', which was hissed at men in contempt, just as nowadays a despised individual might be called a 'gallows-bird'. Nothing was more disgraceful, and therefore that must be added to the Redeemer's load of shame. He made himself of no reputation for our sakes.

Note, next, its *weight*. Usually only one beam of the cross was carried: it may have been so now. It does not look so, however; for the expression, 'bearing his cross', would naturally mean the whole of it. It is highly probable that, although that load could easily be borne by the rough, coarse criminals who ordinarily suffered, yet not so readily by the tender and more exquisite frame of our divine Lord. It is difficult to find any other reason why they should have laid the cross on Simon, unless it be true, as tradition says, that he fainted beneath the burden. I care nothing for tradition, nor even for conjecture; but still there must have been a reason, and as we cannot believe that these people had any real mercy for Christ, we think they must have acted upon the cruel wish that he might not die on the road, but might at least live to be nailed to the tree. 'The tender mercies of the wicked are cruel.' This I leave.

And now I call your attention to the fact that there was a *typical evidence* about this. If Simon had carried Christ's cross all the way, we should have missed the type of Isaac, for Isaac when he went to Mount Moriah to be offered up by his father carried the wood for his own sacrifice. I think if I had been a Jew, full of hate to Jesus Christ, I would have said, 'Do not let him carry his cross: that will be too much like Isaac carrying the wood.' No; but knowing the type, they wantonly fulfil it. It is their own will that does it, and yet the predestination of the Eternal is fulfilled in every jot and tittle, and our great Isaac carries the wood with which he is to be offered up by his Father. How marvellous it is that there should be a fixed decree and yet an altogether unlimited free agency.

The *spiritual meaning* of it, of course, was that Christ in perfect obedience was then carrying the load of our disobedience. The cross, which was the curse, for 'Cursed is every one that hangeth on a tree,' is borne on those blessed shoulders which were submissive to the will of God in all things. Our Lord's cross-bearing is the representation of his bearing all our sin, and therefore in it we rejoice.

It also has a *prophetic meaning:* that cross which he carried through Jerusalem shall go through Jerusalem again. It is his great weapon with which he conquers and wins the world: it is his sceptre with which he shall rule, governing the hearts of his people by no more forceful means than by the love manifested on his cross. 'The government shall be upon his shoulder;' that which he bore on his shoulder shall win obedience, and they that take his yoke upon them shall find rest unto their souls.

IV. I wish I had an hour during which I might speak upon the last head, which bristles with points of interest; but I must give its lessons to you rather in rough remarks than in studied observations.

The last thing to consider is HIS CROSS-BEARER. We are not told why the Roman soldiers laid the cross on Simon. We have made a conjecture; but we leave it as a conjecture, although a highly probable one. If it be true, it lets us see how truly human our Master was. He had been all night in the garden, sweating as it were great drops of blood in his anguish: he had been before the Sanhedrin, he had been before Pilate, then before Herod, then before Pilate again; he had endured scourging; he had been mocked by the soldiery; and it would have been a great wonder if the human frame had not shown some sign of exhaustion. Holy Scripture, by its example, teaches us great reticence about the sufferings of Jesus. Some of the mediaeval writers and certain good people who write devotional books are too apt to dilate upon every supposed grief of our Master, so as to harrow up your feelings; but it is the part of wisdom to imitate the ancient painter who, when he depicted Agamemnon as sacrificing his daughter, veiled the father's face. It is indelicate and almost indecent to write as some have done who would seem to be better acquainted with anatomy than awed by divinity. Much that Jesus endured must for ever remain veiled to us; whether he fainted once or twice or thrice, or did not faint at all, we are not informed; and therefore we leave the idea in the obscurity of probability, and reverently worship him who was tender in body and soul, and suffered even as we do. Oh, love surpassing knowledge which could make him suffer so!

There was a great singularity in the providence which brought Simon upon the scene just when he appeared. The right man came forward at the right moment. That Simon did not come at first, and that they did not place the cross on him from the beginning was for the fulfilment of the type of Isaac to which allusion has been made: thus providence arranges all things wisely.

Observe that *Simon was pressed into this duty.* The word used signifies that the person is impressed into the royal service. Simon was a pressed man, and probably not a disciple of Christ at the time when he was loaded with the cross. How often has a burden of sorrow been the means of bringing men to the faith of Jesus! He was coming in from the country about some business or other, and him they compelled to bear his cross, impressing him into the service which else he would have shunned, for 'he passed by', and would have gone on if he could. Roman soldiers were not accustomed to make many bones about what they chose to do. It was sufficient for them that he came under their notice, and carry the cross he must.

His name was Simon: and where was that other Simon? What a silent, but strong rebuke this would he to him. Simon Peter, Simon son of Jonas, where wast thou? Another Simon has taken thy place.

Sometimes the Lord's servants are backward where they are expected to be forward, and he finds other servitors for the time. If this has ever happened to us it ought gently to rebuke us as long as we live. Brothers and sisters, keep your places, and let not another Simon occupy your room. It is of Judas that it is said, 'his bishopric shall another take;' but a true disciple will retain his office. Remember that word of our Lord, 'Hold that fast which thou hast, that no man take thy crown.' Simon Peter lost a crown here, and another head wore it.

Simon was a Cyrenian – an African – I wonder if he was a black man. In the Acts of the Apostles, at the thirteenth chapter, we find mention of a Simeon that was called Niger, or black. We do not know whether he was the same man or no, but anyhow he was an African, for Cyrene lies just to the west of Egypt, on the southern coast of the Mediterranean. Surely the African has had his full share of cross-bearing for many an age. Oh that the pangs of his sorrow may bring forth a birth of joy! Blessed be he, whether African or Englishman, or who he may, that has the honour of bearing the cross after Christ.

He was coming in from the country. How often the Lord takes into his service the unsophisticated country people who as yet are untainted by the cunning and the vice of the city. Some young man is just come up from the country this very week, and is commencing his apprenticeship in London. How I wish my Master would impress him at the city gates, and do it in that divine way of his to which the will of the impressed person yields a sweet consent. Would God you would come at once and take up the cross of Jesus just at the city gate, before you learn the city's sin and plunge into its dangers. Happy is the Simon coming in from the country who shall this day be led to bear Christ's cross. Good Master, fulfil our heart's desire, and lay thy cross on some unaccustomed shoulder even now.

We are told he was *the father of Alexander and Rufus*. Which, my brethren, is the greater honour to a man, to have a good father, or to be the father of good sons? Under the Old Testament rule we usually read of a man that he is the son of such an one, but here we come to another style, and find it to a man's honour that he is the father of certain well-known brethren – 'the father of Alexander and Rufus'. Surely, Mark knew these two sons, or he would not have cared to mention them; they must have been familiar to the church, or he would not have thus described their father. It was their father who carried the cross. It is exceedingly likely that this Rufus was he of whom Paul speaks in the last chapter of his epistle to the Romans, for Mark was with Paul, and by this means knew Simon and Rufus. Paul writes, 'Salute Rufus chosen in the Lord, and his mother and mine.' His mother was such a motherly person that she had been a mother to Paul as well as to Rufus. Surely, if she was a mother to Paul, she was another disciple of Jesus, and it would look as if this man, his wife, and his two sons all became converts to our Lord after he had carried his cross. It is certainly not the most unlikely circumstance that has been accepted by us on the ground of probability. Oh, what a blessing to a man to be known by his sons! Pray, dear Christian friends, you that have an Alexander and a Rufus, that it may be an honour to you to be known as their father.

'Him they compelled to bear his cross' – perhaps the heavier end of it, if it was really bound to Christ, as they say; or as I judge, the whole of it. It matters little how it was; but Simon is the representative of the church which follows Christ bearing his cross. Here we may recall the language of Paul: 'I fill up that which is behind,' may I paraphrase it? – I take the hinder end – 'of the sufferings of Christ for his body's sake, that is the church.' Everyone that will live godly in Christ Jesus must suffer persecution. Jesus said, 'Whosoever doth not bear his cross, and come after me, cannot be my disciple.' Here is a representative, then, of all the godly – this Simon bearing Christ's cross.

Mark, it was not a cross of his own making, like those of monks and nuns who put themselves to pains of their own inventing. It was Christ's cross; and he carried it not before Christ, as some do who talk of their poverty as though it would get them to heaven, instead of resting on Christ's cross. He carried it after Christ in its right place. This is the order – Christ in front bearing all our sin, and we behind enduring shame and reproach for him, and counting it greater riches than all the treasures of Egypt.

There is Simon, and we will view him as a lesson to ourselves. First, let Simon be an example to us all, and let us readily take up the cross after Christ. Whatever is involved in being a Christian, rejoice at it. If there be any shame, if there be any contumely, if there be any loss, if there be any suffering, even if it were martyrdom, yet gladly take up the cross. Behold, the Father lays it upon you for Christ's sake.

The next is advice to any of you that have been compelled to suffer as Christians though you are not Christians. I wonder whether there is anybody here who is only a press-man and yet has to bear the cross. A working man became a teetotaller: he did not mean to be a Christian, but when he went to work his mates tempted him to drink, and as he would not join them they attacked him as a Christian, and said, 'You are one of those canting hypocrites, those Wesleyans, those Presbyterians, or those Spurgeonites!' This is not true of you: but thus you see the cross is forced on you: had you not better take it up and bear it joyfully? They have pressed you into this service: take it as an index of the will of providence, and say, 'I will not be a press-man only; I will be a volunteer, and I will cheerfully carry Christ's cross.' I know a man who merely comes to this place of worship because he is somewhat interested with the preaching, though he has no idea of being a converted man; yet in the street where he lives nobody ever goes to a place of worship, and therefore they set him down as a pious man, and some have even ridiculed him for it. Friend, you are in for it because you attend here, and you put me in for it too, for if you do anything wrong they are sure to lay all the blame on me. They say – 'That is one of Spurgeon's people.' You are not: I do not own you as yet; but the outsiders have pushed you into the responsibilities of a religious profession, and you had better go in for its privileges. They have laid the cross upon you, do not throw it off. Come on, and bring that dear motherly wife with you, and Alexander and Rufus too. The church will be glad to take you all in, and then as a volunteer you shall bear Christ's cross. It is, however, a remarkable thing that some should first of all be forced into it and then become willing followers.

Last of all, if you and I are cross-bearers, here is a sweet thought. Are we carrying a cross which presses us heavily just now? You know you are to be like your Master, and if so there will be someone found to help you bear your cross. They found Simon to bear the cross of Jesus, and there is a Simon somewhere to help you. Only cry to the Lord about it, and he will find you a friend. If Simon is not forthcoming I will tell you what to do. Imitate Simon. If Simon was what I think he was, he became a converted man, and before long found himself in trouble through it, and he at once went to the Lord in prayer, and said, 'Lord Jesus I am resting in thee alone. Thou didst give me the honour to carry thy cross once, now, I beseech thee, carry mine!' This is what I want you to do with your crosses at this time. You that have to endure hardness for Christ, and are glad to do it, ask him to bear your burden for you. He has borne your sins, and if you will but commit your troubles to him, joy and peace through believing shall stream into your souls by his Holy Spirit.

God bless you, for Christ's sake.

3

UP FROM THE COUNTRY, AND PRESSED INTO SERVICE[1]

*And they compel one Simon a Cyrenian, who passed
by, coming out of the country, the father of
Alexander and Rufus, to bear his cross.*
MARK 15:21

JOHN TELLS US that our Saviour went forth bearing his cross (*John* 19:17). We are much indebted to John for inserting that fact. The other evangelists mention Simon the Cyrenian as bearing the cross of Christ; but John, who often fills up gaps which are left by the other three, tells us that Jesus set out to Calvary carrying his own cross. Our Lord Jesus came out from Pilate's palace laden with his cross, but he was so extremely emaciated and so greatly worn by the night of the bloody sweat, that the procession moved too slowly for the rough soldiers, and therefore they took the cross from their prisoner and laid it upon Simon; or possibly they laid the long end upon the shoulder of the strong countryman, while the Saviour still continued to bear in part his cross till he came to the place of doom. It is well that we should be told that the Saviour bore his cross; for if it had not been so, objectors would have had ground for disputation. I hear them say: You admit that one of the most prominent types, in the Old Testament, of the sacrifice of the Son of God, was Abraham's offering up his son Isaac; now, Abraham laid the wood upon Isaac his son, and not upon a servant. Should not therefore the Son of God bear the cross

[1] Sermon No. 1,853. Preached at the Metropolitan Tabernacle on Sunday morning, 2 August 1885.

himself? Had not our Lord carried his cross, there would have been a flaw in his fulfilment of the type; therefore, the Saviour must bear the wood when he goes forth to be offered up as a sacrifice. One of the greatest of English preachers has well reminded us that the fulfilment of this type appeared to have been in eminent jeopardy, since, at the very first, our Lord's weakness must have been apparent, and the reason which led to the laying of the cross upon the Cyrenian might have prevented our Lord's carrying the cross at all. If the soldiers had a little earlier put the cross upon Simon, which they might very naturally have done, then the prophecy had not been fulfilled; but God has the minds of men so entirely at his control, that even in the minutest circumstance he can order all things so as to complete the merest jots and tittles of the prophecy. Our Lord was made to be, in all points, an Isaac, and therefore we see him going forth bearing the wood of the burnt-offering. Thus you see that it was important that Jesus should for a while bear his own cross.

But it was equally instructive that some one else should be made a partaker of the burden; for it has always been part of the divine counsel that for the salvation of men from sin the Lord should be associated with his church. So far as atonement is concerned, the Lord hath trodden the winepress alone, and of the people there was none with him; but as far as the conversion of the world is concerned, and its rescue from the power of error and wickedness, Christ is not alone. We are workers together with God. We are ourselves to be in the hands of God part bearers of the sorrow and travail by which men are to be delivered from the bondage of sin and Satan, and brought into the liberty of truth and righteousness. Hence it became important that in the bearing of the cross, though not in the death upon it, there should be yoked with the Christ one who should follow close behind him. To bear the cross after Jesus is the office of the faithful. Simon the Cyrenian is the representative of the whole church of God, and of each believer in particular.

Often had Jesus said, 'Except a man take up his cross daily, and follow me, he cannot be my disciple;' and now at last he embodies that sermon in an actual person. The disciple must be as his Master: he that would follow the Crucified must himself bear the cross: this we see visibly set forth in Simon of Cyrene with the cross of Jesus laid upon his shoulder.

> Shall Simon bear the cross alone,
>   And all the rest go free?
> No, there's a cross for every one,
>   And there's a cross for me.

The lesson to each one of us is to take up our Lord's cross without delay, and go with him; without the camp, bearing his reproach. That many among this vast and mixed congregation may imitate Simon is the anxious desire of my heart. With holy expectancy I gaze upon this throng collected from all parts of the earth, and I long to find in it some who will take my Lord's yoke upon them this day.

I. I will begin with this first remark, that UNEXPECTED PERSONS ARE OFTEN CALLED TO CROSS-BEARING. Like Simon, they are impressed into the service of Christ. Our text says: 'They compel one Simon a Cyrenian, who passed by, coming out of the country, the father of Alexander and Rufus, to bear his cross.' Simon did not volunteer, but was forced into this work of cross-bearing. It would seem from another evangelist that he speedily yielded to the impressment, and lifted the burden heartily; but at first he was compelled. A rude authority was exercised by the guard; who being upon the Governor's business acted with high-handed rigour, and forced whomsoever they pleased to do their bidding. By the exercise of such irresponsible power they compelled a passing stranger to carry Christ's cross. It was specially singular that the man to have this honour was not Peter, nor James, nor John, nor any one of the many who had for years listened to the Redeemer's speech; but it was a stranger from North Africa, who had been in no way connected with the life or teachings of Jesus of Nazareth.

Notice, first, that *he was an unknown man*. He was spoken of 'as one Simon'. Simon was a very common name among the Jews, almost as common as John in our own country. This man was just 'one Simon' – an individual who need not be further described.

But the providence of God had determined that this obscure individual, this certain man, or I might better say, this uncertain man, should be selected to the high office of cross-bearer to the Son of God. I have an impression upon my mind that there is 'one Simon' here this morning, who has to bear Christ's cross from this time forward. I feel persuaded that I am right. That person is so far unknown that most probably he does not recognize a single individual in all this throng, neither does anybody in this assembly know anything of *him*: certainly the preacher does not. He is one John, one Thomas, or one William; or perhaps, in the feminine, she is one Mary, one Jane, one Maggie. Friend, nobody knows you save our Father who is in heaven, and he has appointed you to have fellowship with his Son. I shall roughly describe you as 'one Simon', and leave the Holy Spirit to bring you into your place and service. But this 'one Simon' was a very particular '*one* Simon'. I lay the emphasis where there might seem to be no need of any: he was one whom God knew, and chose, and loved, and set apart for this special service. In a congregation like the present, there may be somebody whom our God intends to use for his glory during the rest of his life. That person sits in the pew and listens to what I am saying, and perhaps as yet he does not begin to enquire whether he is that 'one Simon', that one person; and yet it is so, and ere this sermon is ended, he shall know that the call to bear the cross is for him.

Many more unlikely things than this have happened in this house of prayer. I pray that many a man may go out from this house a different man from the man he was when he entered it an hour ago. That man Saul, that great persecutor of the church, afterwards became such a mighty preacher of the gospel that people exclaimed with wonder, 'There is a strange alteration in this man.' 'Why,' said one, 'when I knew him he was a Pharisee of the Pharisees. He was as bigoted a man as ever wore a phylactery, and he hated Christ and Christians so intensely that he could never persecute the church sufficiently.' 'Yes,' replied another, 'it was so; but he has had a strange twist. They say that he was going down to Damascus to hunt out the disciples, and something happened; we do not know exactly what it was, but evidently it gave him such a turn that he has never been himself since. In fact, he seems turned altogether upside down, and the current of his life is evidently reversed: he lives enthusiastically for that faith which once he destroyed.' This speedy change happened to 'one Saul of Tarsus.' There were plenty of Sauls in Israel, but upon this one Saul electing love had looked in the counsels of eternity; for that Saul redeeming love had shed its heart's blood, and in that Saul effectual grace wrought mightily. Is there another Saul here today? The Lord grant that he may now cease to kick against the pricks, and may we soon hear of him, 'Behold he prayeth.' I feel convinced the counterpart of that 'one Simon' is in this house at this moment, and my prayer goes up to God, and I hope it is attended with the prayers of many thousands besides, that he may at once submit to the Lord Jesus.

It did not seem likely that Simon should bear the cross of Christ, for *he was a stranger who had newly come up from the country.* He probably knew little or nothing of what had been taking place in Jerusalem; for he had come from another continent. He was 'one Simon a Cyrenian'; and I suppose that Cyrene could not have been less than eight hundred miles from Jerusalem. It was situated in what is now called Tripoli, in North Africa, in which place a colony of Jews had been formed long before. Very likely he had come in a Roman galley from Alexandria to Joppa, and there had been rowed through the surf, and landed in time to reach Jerusalem for the Passover. He had long wanted to come to Jerusalem; he had heard the fame of the temple and of the city of his fathers; and he had longed to see the great Assembly of the tribes, and the solemn Paschal feast. He had travelled all those miles, he had hardly yet got the motion of the ship out of his brain, and it had never entered into his head that he should be impressed by the Roman guard, and made to assist at an execution. It was a singular providence that he should come into the city at the moment of the turmoil about Jesus, and should have crossed the street just as the sad procession started on its way to Golgotha. He passed by neither too soon nor too late; he was on the spot as punctually as if he had made an appointment to be there; and yet, as men speak, it was all by mere chance. I cannot tell how many providences had worked together to bring him there at the nick of time, but so the Lord would have it, and so it came about. He, a man there in Cyrene, in North Africa, must at a certain date, at the tick of the clock, be at Jerusalem, in order that he might help to carry the cross up to Mount Calvary; *and he was there*. Ah! my dear friend, I do not know what providences have been at work to bring you here today; perhaps very strange ones. If a little something had occurred you had not taken this journey; it only needed a small dust to turn the scale, and you would have been hundreds of miles from this spot, in quite another scene from this. Why you are here you do not yet know, except that you have come to listen to the preacher, and join the throng. But God knoweth why he hath brought you here. I trust it will be read in the annals of the future:

> Thus the eternal mandate ran,
> Almighty grace arrest that man.

God has brought you here, that on this spot, by the preaching of the gospel, you may be compelled to bear the cross of Jesus. I pray it may be so. 'One Simon a Cyrenian, coming out of the country,' is here after a long journey, and this day he will begin to live a higher and a better life.

Further, notice, *Simon had come for another purpose*. He had journeyed to Jerusalem with no thought of bearing the cross of Jesus. Probably Simon was a Jew far removed from the land of his fathers, and he had made a pilgrimage to the holy city to keep the Passover. Every Jew loved to be present at Jerusalem at the Paschal feast. So, to put it roughly, it was holiday-time; it was a time for making an excursion to the capital; it was a season for making a journey and going up to the great city which was 'beautiful for situation, the joy of the whole earth.' Simon from far off Cyrene must by all means keep the feast at Jerusalem. Mayhap he had saved his money for months, that he might pay his fare to Joppa; and he had counted down the gold freely for the joy which he had in going to the city of David, and the temple of his God.

He was come for the Passover, and for that only; and he would be perfectly satisfied to go home when once the feast was over, and once he had partaken of the lamb with the tribes of Israel. Then he could say throughout the rest of his life, 'I, too, was once at the great feast of our people, when we commemorated the coming up out of Egypt.' Brethren, we propose one way, but God hath other propositions. We say, 'I will step in and hear the preacher,' but God means that the arrows of his grace shall stick fast in our hearts. Many and many a time with no desire for grace men have listened to the gospel, and the Lord has been found of them that sought him not. I heard of one who cared little for the sermon till the preacher chanced to use that word 'eternity', and the hearer was taken prisoner by holy thoughts, and led to the Saviour's feet. Men have stepped into places of worship even with evil designs, and yet the purpose of grace has been accomplished; they came to scoff, but they remained to pray. Some have been cast by the providence of God into positions where they have met with Christian men, and a word of admonition has been blessed to them. A lady was one day at an evening party, and there met with Caesar Malan, the famous divine of Geneva, who, in his usual manner, enquired of her whether she was a Christian. She was startled, surprised, and vexed, and made a short reply to the effect that it was not a question she cared to discuss; whereupon, Mr Malan replied with great sweetness, that he would not persist in speaking of it, but he would pray that she might be led to give her heart to Christ, and become a useful worker for him. Within a fortnight she met the minister again, and asked him how she must come to Jesus. Mr Malan's reply was, 'Come to him just as you are.' That lady gave herself up to Jesus: it was Charlotte Elliott, to whom we owe that precious hymn –

> Just as I am – without one plea
> But that thy blood was shed for me
> And that thou bidd'st me come to thee –
> O Lamb of God, I come.

It was a blessed thing for her that she was at that party, and that the servant of God from Geneva should have been there, and should have spoken to her so faithfully. Oh for many a repetition of the story 'of one Simon a Cyrenian', coming, not with the intent to bear the cross, but with quite another mind, and yet being enlisted in the cross-bearing army of the Lord Jesus!

I would have you notice, once more, that this man was at this particular time not thinking upon the subject at all, for *he was at that time merely passing by.* He had come up to Jerusalem, and whatever occupied his mind he does not appear to have taken any notice of the trial of Jesus, or of the sad end of it. It is expressly said that he 'passed by'. He was not even sufficiently interested in the matter to stand in the crowd and look at the mournful procession. Women were weeping there right bitterly – the daughters of Jerusalem to whom the Master said, 'Weep not for me, but weep for yourselves, and for your children;' but this man passed by. He was anxious to hurry away from so unpleasant a sight, and to get up to the temple. He was quietly making his way through the crowd, eager to go about his business, and he must have been greatly surprised and distressed when a rough hand was laid upon him, and a stern voice said, 'Shoulder that cross.' There was no resisting a Roman centurion when he gave command, and so the countryman meekly submitted, wishing, no doubt, that he were back in Cyrene tilling the ground. He must needs stoop his shoulder and take up a new burden, and tread in the footsteps of the mysterious personage to whom the cross belonged. He was only passing by, and yet he was enlisted and impressed by the Romans, and, as I take it, impressed by the grace of God for life; for whereas Mark says he was the father of Alexander and Rufus, it would seem that his sons were well known to the Christian people to whom Mark was writing. If his son was the same Rufus that Paul mentions, then it would seem that Simon's wife and his sons became believers and partakers of the sufferings of Christ. His contact with the Lord in that strange compulsory way probably wrought out for him another and more spiritual contact which made him a true cross-bearer.

O ye that pass by this day, draw nigh to Jesus! I have no wish to call your attention to myself, far from it; but I do ask your attention to my Lord. Though you only intended to slip into this tabernacle and slip out again, I pray that you may be arrested by a call from my Lord. I speak as my Lord's servant, and I would constrain you to come to him. Stand where you are a while, and let me beg you to yield to his love, which even now would cast the bands of a man around you. I would compel you, by my Lord's authority, to take up his cross and bear it after him. It would be strange, say you. Ay, so it might be, but it would be a glorious event. I remember

Mr Knill, speaking of his own conversion, used an expression which I should like to use concerning one of you. Here it is: 'It was just a quarter past twelve, August 2nd, when twang went every harp in Paradise; for a sinner had repented.' May it be so with you. Oh that every harp in Paradise may now ring out the high praises of sovereign grace, as you now yield yourself to the great Shepherd and Bishop of souls! May that divine impressment which is imaged in the text by the compulsion of the Roman soldier take place in your case at this very moment; and may it be seen in your instance that unexpected persons are often called to be cross-bearers!

II. My second observation is – CROSS-BEARING CAN STILL BE PRACTISED. Very briefly let me tell you in what ways the cross can still be carried.

First, and chiefly, *by your becoming a Christian.* If the cross shall take you up, you will take up the cross. Christ will be your hope, his death your trust, himself the object of your love. You never become a cross-bearer truly till you lay your burdens down at his feet, who bore the cross and curse for you.

Next, you become a cross-bearer *when you make an open avowal of the Lord Jesus Christ.* Do not deceive yourselves – this is expected of each one of you if you are to be saved. The promise as I read it in the New Testament is not to the believer alone, but to the believer who confesses his faith. 'He that with his heart believeth and with his mouth maketh confession of him shall be saved.' He saith, 'He that confesseth me before men, him will I confess before my Father; but he that denieth me' – and from the connection it should seem to mean, he that does not confess me – 'him will I deny before my Father which is in heaven.' To quote the inspired Scripture, 'He that believeth and is baptized shall be saved.' There should be, there must be, the open avowal in Christ's own way of the secret faith which you have in him. Now this is often a cross.

Many people would like to go to heaven by an underground railway – secrecy suits them. They do not want to cross the channel; the sea is too rough; but when there is a tunnel made they will go to the fair country. My good people, you are cowardly, and I must quote to you a text which ought to sting your cowardice out of you: 'But the fearful and unbelieving shall have their part in the lake which burneth with fire and brimstone.' I say no more, and make no personal applications; but, I beseech you, run no risks. Be afraid to be afraid. Be ashamed of being ashamed of Christ. Shame on that man who counts it any shame to say before assembled angels, and men, and devils, 'I am a follower of Christ.' May you who have hitherto been secret followers of the crucified Lord become manifest cross-bearers! Do you not even now cry out, 'Set down my name, sir'?

Further, some have to take up their cross by *commencing Christian work*. You live in a village where there is no gospel preaching: preach yourself. You are in a backwoods town where the preaching is very far from being such as God approves of: begin to preach the truth yourself. 'Alas!' say you, 'I should make a fool of myself.' Are you ashamed to be a fool for Christ? 'Oh, but I should break down.' Break down: it will do you good, and perhaps you may break somebody else down. There is no better preaching in the world than that of a man who breaks down under a sense of unworthiness: if that breakdown communicates itself to other people, it may begin a revival. If you are choked by your earnestness others may become earnest too. Do you still murmur, 'But I should get the ill-will of everybody'? For Christ's sake could you not bear that? When the good monk said to Martin Luther, 'Go thou home to thy cell and keep quiet,' why did not Martin take the advice? Why, indeed? 'It is very bad for young people to be so forward; you will do a great deal of mischief, therefore be quiet, young Martin. Who are you to interfere with the great authorities? Be holy for yourself, and don't trouble others. If you stir up a reformation thousands of good people will be burnt through you. Do be quiet.'

Bless God, Martin did not go home, and was not quiet, but went about his Master's business, and raised heaven and earth by his brave witness-bearing. Where are you, Martin, this morning? I pray God to call you out, and as you have confessed his name, and are his servant, I pray that he may make you bear public testimony for him, and tell out the saving power of the Saviour's precious blood. Come, Simon, I see you shrink; but the cross has to be carried;

therefore bow your back. It is only a wooden cross, after all, and not an iron one. You can bear it: you must bear it. God help you.

Perhaps, too, some brother may have to take up his cross by *bearing witness against the rampant sin which surrounds him.* 'Leave all those dirty matters alone; do not say a word about them. Let the people go to the devil, or else you will soil your white kid gloves.' Sirs, we will spoil our hands as well as our gloves, and we will risk our characters, if need be; but we will put down the devilry which now defiles London. Truly the flesh does shrink, and the purest part of our manhood shrinks with it, when we are compelled to bear open protest against sins which are done of men in secret. But, Simon, the Master may yet compel you to bear his cross in this respect, and if so, he will give you both courage and wisdom, and your labour shall not be in vain in the Lord.

Sometimes, however, the cross-bearing is of another and more quiet kind, and may be described as *submission to providence.* A young friend is saying, 'For me to live at home I know to be my duty; but father is unkind, and the family generally impose upon me. I wish I could get away.' Ah! dear sister, you must bear Christ's cross, and it may be the Lord would have you remain at home. Therefore bear the cross. A servant is saying, 'I should like to be in a Christian family. I do not think I can stop where I am.' Perhaps, good sister, the Lord has put you where you are to be a light in a dark place. All the lamps should not be in one street, or what will become of the courts and alleys? It is often the duty of a Christian man to say, 'I shall stop where I am and fight this matter through. I mean by character and example, with kindness and courtesy and love, to win this place for Jesus.'

Of course the easy way is to turn monk and live quietly in a cloister, and serve God by doing nothing; or to turn nun and dwell in a convent, and expect to win the battle of life by running out of it. Is not this absurd? If you shut yourself away from this poor world, what is to become of it? You men and women that are Christians must stand up and stand out for Jesus where the providence of God has cast you: if your calling is not a sinful one, and if the temptations around you are not too great for you, you must 'hold the fort' and never dream of surrender. If your lot is hard, look upon it as Christ's cross, and bow your back to the load. Your shoulder may be raw at first, but you will grow stronger before long, for as your day your strength shall be. 'It is good for a man that he bear the yoke in his youth;' but it is good for a man to bear the cross in his old age as well as in his youth; in fact, we ought never to be quit of so blessed a burden. What wings are to a bird, and sails to a ship, that the cross becomes to a man's spirit when he fully consents to accept it as his life's beloved load. Truly did Jesus say, 'My yoke is easy, and my burden is light.' Now, Simon, where are you? Shoulder the cross, man, in the name of God!

III. Thirdly, TO CROSS-BEARING THERE ARE NOBLE COMPULSIONS. Simon's compulsion was the rough hand of the Roman legionary, and the gruff voice in the Latin tongue, 'Shoulder that cross;' but we hear gentler voices which compel us this day to take up Christ's cross.

The first compulsion is this – *'the love of Christ constraineth us.'* He has done all this for you; therefore by sweet but irresistible compulsion you are made to render him some return of love. Does not Jesus appear to you in a vision as you sit in this house? Do you not see that thorn-crowned head, that visage crimsoned with the bloody sweat, those hands and feet pierced with the nails? Does he not say to you pointedly, 'I did all this for thee; what hast thou done for me'? Startled in your seat, you cover your face, and inwardly reply, 'I will answer that question by the rest of my life. I will be first and foremost a servant of Jesus: not a trader first and a Christian next, but a Christian first and a business man afterwards.' You, my sister, must say, 'I will live for Christ as a daughter, a wife, or a mother. I will live for my Lord; for he has given himself for me, and I am not my own, but bought with a price.'

The true heart will feel a compulsion arising from a second reflection, namely, *the glory of a life spent for God and for his Christ.* What is the life of a man who toils in business, makes money, becomes rich, and dies? It winds up with a paragraph in the *Illustrated London News*, declaring that he died worth so much: the wretch was not worth anything himself; his estate had value, he had none. Had he been worth anything he would have sent his money about the world doing good; but as a worthless steward he laid his Master's stores in heaps to rot. The life of multitudes of men is self-seeking. It is ill for a man to live the life of swine. What a poor creature is the usual ordinary man! But a life spent for Jesus, though it involve cross-bearing, is noble, heroic, sublime. The mere earth-worm leads a dunghill life. A life of what is called pleasure is a mean, beggarly business. A life of keeping up respectability is utter slavery – as well be a horse in a pug-mill. A life wholly consecrated to Christ and his cross is life indeed; it is akin to the life of angels; ay, higher still, it is the life of God within the soul of man. O ye that have a spark of true nobility, seek to live lives worth living, worth remembering, worthy to be the commencement of eternal life before the throne of God.

Some of you ought to feel the cross coming upon your shoulders this morning when you think of *the needs of those among whom you live.* They are dying, perishing for lack of knowledge, rich and poor alike ignorant of Christ; multitudes of them wrapped up in self-righteousness. They are perishing, and those who ought to warn them are often dumb dogs that cannot bark. Do you not feel that you ought to deliver the sheep from the wolf? Have you no bowels of compassion? Are your hearts turned to steel? I am sure you cannot deny that the times demand of you earnest and forceful lives. No Christian man can now sit still without incurring awful guilt. Whether you live in London or in any other great town amidst reeking sin, or dwell in the country amidst the dense darkness which broods over many rural districts, you are under bonds to be up and doing. It may be a cross to you, but for Jesus' sake you must uplift it, and never lay it down till the Lord calls you home.

Some of you should bear the cross of Christ *because the cause of Christ is at a discount where you dwell.* I delight in a man in whom the lordlier chivalry has found a congenial home. He loves to espouse the cause of truth in the cloudy and dark day. He never counts heads, but weighs arguments. When he settles down in a town he never enquires, 'Where is the most respectable congregation? Where shall I meet with those who will advantage me in business?' No, he studies his conscience rather than his convenience. He hears one say, 'There is a Nonconformist chapel, but it is down a back street. There is a Baptist church, but the members are nearly all poor, and no gentlefolk are among them. Even the evangelical church is down at the heel: the best families attend the high church.' I say he hears this, and his heart is sick of such talk. He will go where the gospel is preached, and nowhere else. Fine architecture has scant charms for him, and grand music is no part of his religion: if these are substitutes for the gospel, he abhors them. It is meanness itself for a man to forsake the truth for the sake of respectability. Multitudes who ought to be found maintaining the good old cause are recreant to their convictions, if indeed they ever had any. For this cause the true man resolves to stick to truth through thick and thin, and not to forsake her because her adherents are poor and despised. If ever we might temporize, that time is past and gone. I arrest yonder man this morning, who has long been a Christian, but has concealed half his Christianity in order to be thought respectable, or to escape the penalties of faithfulness. Come out from those with whom you are numbered, but with whom you are not united in heart. Be brave enough to defend a good cause against all comers; for the day shall come when he shall have honour for his guerdon who accepted dishonour that he might be true to his God, his Bible, and his conscience. Blessed be he that can be loyal to his Lord, cost him what it may – loyal even in those matters which traitors call little things. We would compel that Simon the Cyrenian this day to bear the cross, because there are so few to bear it in these degenerate days.

Besides, I may say to some of you, you ought to bear the cross because you know you are not satisfied; *your hearts are not at rest*. You have prospered in worldly things, but you are not happy; you have good health, but you are not happy; you have loving friends, but you are not happy. There is but one way of getting rest to the heart and that is, to come to Jesus. That is his word: 'Come unto me, all ye that labour and are heavy laden, and I will give you rest.' If after this you need a further rest for other and higher longings, then you must come again to the same Saviour, and hearken to his next word: 'Take my yoke upon you, and learn of me; for I am meek and lowly in heart: and ye shall find rest unto your souls. For my yoke is easy, and my burden is light.' Some of you professors have not yet found perfect rest, and the reason is because you have looked to the cross for pardon, but you have never taken to cross-bearing as an occupation. You are hoping *in* Christ but not living *for* Christ. The finding of rest unto your soul will come to you in having something to do or to bear for Jesus. 'Take my yoke upon you: and ye shall find rest unto your souls.'

There are many ways, then, of bearing the cross for Christ, and there are many reasons why some here present should begin at once to carry the load.

IV. To close: bear with me a minute or two while I say that CROSS-BEARING IS A BLESSED OCCUPATION. I feel sure that Simon found it so. Let me mention certain blessings which must have attended the special service of Simon. First, *it brought him into Christ's company.* When they compelled him to bear his cross, he was brought close to Jesus. If it had not been for that compulsion he might have gone his way, or might have been lost in the crowd; but now he is in the inner circle, near to Jesus. For the first time in his life he saw that blessed form, and as he saw it I believe his heart was enamoured with it. As they lifted the cross on his shoulders he looked at that sacred Person, and saw a crown of thorns about his brow; and as he looked at his fellow-sufferer, he saw all down his cheeks the marks of bloody sweat, and black and blue bruises from cruel hands. As for those eyes, they looked him through and through! That face, that matchless face, he had never seen its like. Majesty was therein blended with misery, innocence with agony, and love with sorrow. He had never seen that countenance so well, nor marked the whole form of the Son of man so clearly if he had not been called to bear that cross. It is wonderful how much we see of Jesus when we suffer or labour for him. Believing souls, I pray that this day you may be so impressed into my Lord's service, that you may have nearer and dearer fellowship with him than in the past. If any man will do his will he shall know of the doctrine. They see Jesus best who carry his cross most.

Beside, *the cross held Simon in Christ's steps.* Do you catch it? If Jesus carried the front part of the cross and Simon followed behind, he was sure to put his feet down just where the Master's feet had been before. The cross is a wonderful implement for keeping us in

49

the way of our Lord. As I was turning this subject over I was thinking how often I had felt a conscious contact between myself and my Lord when I have had to bear reproach for his sake; and how at the same time I have been led to watch my steps more carefully because of that very reproach. Brethren, we do not want to slip from under the cross. If we did so, we might slip away from our Lord and from holy walking. If we can keep our shoulder beneath that sacred load, and see our Lord a little on before, we shall be making the surest progress. This being near to Jesus is a blessed privilege, which is cheaply purchased at the price of cross-bearing. If you would see Jesus, bestir yourselves to work for him. Boldly avow him, cheerfully suffer for him, and then you shall see him, and then you shall learn to follow him step by step. O blessed cross, which holds us to Jesus and to his ways!

Then Simon had this honour, that *he was linked with Christ's work*. He could not put away sin, but he could assist weakness. Simon did not die on the cross to make expiation, but he did live under the cross to aid in the accomplishment of the divine purpose. You and I cannot interfere with Jesus in his passion, but we can share with him in his compassion; we cannot purchase liberty for the enslaved, but we can tell them of their emancipation. To have a finger in Christ's work is glory. I invite the man that seeks honour and immortality, to seek it thus. To have a share in the Redeemer's work is a more attractive thing than all the pomp and glitter of this world, and the kingdoms thereof. Where are the men of heavenly mind who will covet to be joined unto the Lord in this ministry? Let them step out and say, 'Jesus, I my cross have taken. Henceforth I will follow thee. Come life or death, I will carry thy cross till thou shalt give me the crown.'

While Simon was carrying the cross through the crowd, I doubt not that the rough soldiery would deal him many a kick or buffet – but I feel equally sure that the dear Master sometimes stole a glance at him. *Simon enjoyed Christ's smile.* I know the Lord so well that I feel sure he must have done so: he would not forget the man who was his partner for the while. And oh, that look! How Simon must have treasured up the remembrance of it. 'I never carried a load that was so light,' says he, 'as that which I carried that morning; for when the Blessed One smiled at me amidst his woes, I felt myself to be strong as Hercules.' Alexander, his first-born, and that red-headed lad Rufus, when they grew up both felt it to be the honour of the family that their father carried the cross after Jesus. Rufus and Alexander had a patent of nobility in being the sons of such a man. Mark recorded the fact that Simon carried the cross, and that such and such persons were his sons. Methinks when the old man came to lie upon his death-bed he said: 'My hope is in him whose cross I carried. Blessed burden! Lay me down in my grave. This body of mine cannot perish, for it bore the cross which Jesus carried, and which carried *him*. I shall rise again to see him in his glory, for his cross has pressed me, and his love will surely raise me.' Happy are we if we can while yet we live be co-workers together with him, that when he cometh in his kingdom we may be partakers of his glory. 'Blessed is the man that endureth temptation: for when he is tried, he shall receive the crown of life, which the Lord hath promised to them that love him.' God bless you, and especially you who have come out of the country. God bless you. Amen and amen.

4

THE DETERMINATION OF CHRIST TO SUFFER FOR HIS PEOPLE[1]

And they gave him to drink wine mingled with myrrh:
but he received it not.
MARK 15:23

OUR SAVIOUR, before he was nailed to the cross, and on the cross, several times had drinks of different sorts offered to him. Whilst they were nailing him to the cross, they endeavoured to make him drink wine, or vinegar as it is called, mingled with gall; and when he had tasted of it – he did taste it – he would not drink it. When he was on the cross, the soldiers, mocking him, offered him vinegar, or their weak drink of which they ordinarily partook, pledging him in their cups with scorn. And once more, when he said, 'I thirst,' they took a sponge filled with vinegar, dipped it in hyssop, and put it to his lips.

This occasion of offering the wine mingled with myrrh is, I believe, different from all the rest. This wine mingled with myrrh was given to him as an act of mercy. Matthew Henry seems to think that it was prepared by those holy women who were wont to attend to the necessities of our Lord. They had followed him in all his footsteps whithersoever he went; it was by their bounty that the bag which Judas kept was generally as full as it was required to be, so that out of the store they could go and buy meat for their Master and for his disciples. It was these holy women who

[1] Sermon No. 2,443. Preached at New Park Street Chapel, date not known.

prepared the spices to embalm him at his burial; and Matthew Henry thinks that these women, prompted by their compassion for him, got ready this cup of wine mingled with myrrh, that he might be strengthened for his miseries, and that those miseries might in some degree be alleviated by the partial stupefaction which a strong draught of wine and myrrh would give to him. This time, our Saviour positively declined the cup: 'He received it not.' The wormwood he tasted, but this he received not at all; he would have nothing to do with it. Why? The answer is not to be found in our Saviour's abstemiousness, for he was not abstemious; he was never self-indulgent, but he certainly was never abstemious. He was 'the Son of man' who 'came eating and drinking;' he felt no repugnance to wine; he himself made it, he himself drank it; he even earned for himself the name, 'a gluttonous man and a wine-bibber'; not deservedly, but because, in contrast to John, who abstemiously refrained from ordinary food, Jesus Christ sat down with publicans and sinners, feasted with the feasters, and ate and drank like other men.

Nor do I think the reason is to be found in any love of pain that Christ had, nor in any heartless bravado, which would lead him to say, 'I will suffer, and I will put the cup away from me.' Far be that from Christ; he never thrust himself in the way of suffering when it was unnecessary; he did not go to give himself up into the hands of his enemies before his hour was come; he avoided persecution when the avoidance of the persecution would not be an injury to his cause; he withdrew out of Judea, and would not walk in that land, because of Herod, who sought to slay him. I believe that, if our Saviour had not been the atoning sacrifice, if his sufferings had been merely those of a martyr, he would have quaffed to the very dregs the cup that was offered him, and would not have left any of it. The reason why he refused the cup, I think, is to be found in another thing altogether.

There is a glorious idea couched in the fact that the Saviour put the myrrhed wine-cup entirely away from his lips. On the heights of heaven the Son of God stood of old, and he looked down and measured how far it was to the utmost depths of misery; he cast up the sum total of all the agonies which a man must endure to descend to the utmost depths of pain and misery. He determined that, to be a faithful High Priest, and also to be a suffering one, he would go the whole way, from the highest to the lowest, 'from the highest throne in glory to the cross of deepest woe'. This myrrhed cup would just have stopped him within a little of the utmost limit of misery; therefore, he said, 'I will not stop half-way, but I will go all the way; and if this cup can mitigate my sorrow, that is just the reason why I will not drink it, for I have determined that to the utmost lengths of misery I will go, that I will do, and bear, and suffer all that Incarnate God can bear for my people, in my own mortal body.'

Now, beloved, it is this fact that I wish to bring out before you – the fact that Jesus Christ came into the world to suffer, and that because the myrrhed cup would have prevented him from reaching the lowest step of misery, 'he received it not'. I shall have to show you, first, that this was very frequently the case throughout his life, that he would not take a step which would have diminished his miseries, because *he was determined to go the whole length of suffering*. Secondly, I shall try to show you *the reason for this determination*. Then, thirdly, I shall close up by speaking of *the lesson that we may learn from it*.

I. OUR SAVIOUR WOULD GO THE WHOLE LENGTH OF MISERY; he would suffer in every respect like as we suffer; he would bear the whole of the tortures of atonement, without even the slightest shadow of mitigation or alleviation. Now, I think I can show you that, on many occasions in Christ's life, he determined to be tempted in every point in which men are tempted, and to be tempted to the utmost limit of the power of temptation; nor would he even accept anything which would have limited the force of the temptation upon man. I will give you some proofs of this.

First, *Christ knew that you and I would be exposed to peril;* he therefore determined that he would be exposed to peril, too, and that he would not by any means, when it was in his power, escape from the peril. Let me show him to you high up there, on the pinnacle of the temple; there stands our Master, and a fiend by his side, on a giddy eminence, with but little beneath his feet; he stands poised aloft, he looks down the hill on which the temple is built, into the depths below; and the enemy says, 'Cast thyself down, commit thyself to the care of the angels.' It was like this myrrhed cup – 'Do not stand in this peril; cast thyself upon that promise, and risk thyself upon the angels' wings, for they shall bear thee up in their hands, lest thou dash thy foot against a stone.' But like as he would not receive this cup, so neither would he receive this deliverance from his peril; but there he stood erect, confident in his God, not using the means of deliverance which the tempter wished him to exercise, even as he would not drink this cup.

Take another case: *Jesus Christ knew that many of his people would have to suffer bodily wants, and poverty, and woe.* He therefore hungered; after forty days' fast, when he might have delivered himself from his hunger by turning stones into bread, one would have said, 'It would have been a very innocent act to turn stones into bread, and feed himself;' but, 'No,' says Christ to the gnawing pangs of hunger, 'I will let you go as far as you can; I will not turn these stones into bread; I will let hunger exercise all its power upon me; I will let my body be gnawed by its fierce teeth; I will not mitigate its misery.' He would not receive that wine mingled with myrrh that the devil offered him in the wilderness, when he tempted him to make the stones into bread; he would not take the mitigation of his misery.

I will tell you another case. Many men have attempted to have their lives cut short because they have so much misery, and no more hope of being happy, therefore they have wished for death; they have wished that they might be as the untimely birth, that they might be shut up in the bowels of the earth for ever. *They have longed for death, and desired it;* and if an opportunity had cast itself in their way in which they might have died with honour, without having even the disgrace of suicide, how many would have accepted the alternative of death! Here is our Saviour in the same condition; for he is dragged to the brow of the hill of Nazareth. O Son of man, thy wisest choice is to be dashed down the sides of the hill on which the city is built! If thou art wise, thou wilt let them hurl thee headlong; there would be an end of all thy misery, for there are years before thee through which thou wilt be roasted at the slow fire of persecution, and afterwards thou wilt have to pass through floods of deepest misery. Do you not think the temptation started up in his mind, 'Let yourself be cast down'? He knew all about it. Had he been cast down, he would have died an honourable death, like the death of a prophet slain in his own country; but no, 'passing through the midst of them, he went his way,' because, as he refused the wine-cup, so he refused a hasty death, which would have delivered him from his miseries.

Do you not observe that I have only just given you specimens? You will find that *all through the Saviour's life it was just the same.* You will not find him in one instance working a miracle to lessen his own bodily fatigue, or to alleviate his own bodily wants and necessities, but always letting the ills of this life wreak themselves upon him with all their fury. He hushed the winds once, but it was for his disciples, not for himself; he lay in the ship asleep, and let the waves toss him up and down as much as they pleased. He multiplied the loaves and fishes but it was for the multitude, not for himself. He could find money in a fish's mouth: but it was to pay the tribute, not for himself. He could scatter mercies wherever he went – open men's eyes, and deliver many of them from pains: he never exercised any of his skill upon himself. If the wind blew, he let it spend itself upon his cheeks, and crack them; if the cold was bitter, he let the cold come round him, as it did in the garden of Gethsemane; if journeying was troublesome, he journeyed where he might have travelled as his Father did; as old Thomas Sternhold says in his fine translation of the Psalms –

> The Lord descended from above,
>   And bow'd the heavens most high,
> And underneath his feet he cast
>   The darkness of the sky.
>
> On cherub and on cherubim
>   Full royally he rode,
> And on the wings of mighty winds
>   Came flying all abroad.

So might Jesus, if he pleased, but he journeyed on in weariness. He might have made the water leap out of the well to his hand, but there he sat and thirsted, while he had power to make fountains gush even from the stone on which he sat. On the cross, 'I thirst,' was his cry; and yet, if he pleased, he might have opened in himself rivers of living water; he had them for others, but he had none for himself. You will observe this fact that, in all the history of Christ, never once did he take anything which could have lessened his miseries, but he went the whole length; and as on this occasion he refused the wine drugged with myrrh, so never did he receive anything that had a tendency to prevent him from going to the requisite lengths of suffering.

II. Now let me show you THE REASON FOR THIS. Was it out of any love to suffering that he thus refused the wine-cup? Ah, no; Christ had no love of suffering. He had a love of souls, but like us he turned away from suffering, he never loved it. We see he did not, for even in the garden he said, 'Father, if it be possible, let this cup pass from me.' It was his human nature struggling against suffering, as human nature rightfully does: God has made us so that we do not naturally love suffering, and it is not wrong for us to feel some repugnance to it, for God has implanted that repugnance in us. Christ did not suffer because he loved suffering. Why, then, did he suffer? For two reasons: because this suffering to the utmost was necessary to the completion of the atonement, which saves to the utmost; and because this suffering to the utmost was necessary to perfect his character as 'a merciful High Priest' who has to have compassion for souls that have gone to the utmost of miseries themselves; that he might know how to succour them that are tempted.

First, I say it was *necessary to make the atonement complete.* I do think that, if our Saviour had drunk this myrrhed cup, the atonement would not have been valid. It strikes me that, if he had drunk this wine mingled with myrrh, he could not have suffered to the extent that was absolutely necessary. We believe Christ did, on the cross, suffer just enough, and not one particle more than was necessary for the redemption of his people. If, then, this wine-cup had taken away a part of his sufferings, the ransom price would not have been fully complete, it would not have been fully paid. And if it had but taken away so much as a grain, the atonement would not have been sufficiently satisfactory. If a man's ransom is to be paid, it must be all paid; for though but one single farthing be left unpaid, the man is not fully redeemed, and he is not yet totally free. If, then, this drinking of the wine-cup had taken out the smallest amount from that fearful price of agony which our Saviour paid, the atonement would have been insufficient – insufficient only to a degree, but even insufficiency to a degree, however small, would have been enough to have caused perpetual despair, yea, enough to have shut the gates of heaven against all believers. The utmost farthing must be paid; inexorable justice never did yet omit so much as a fraction of its claim. Nor would it in this case have exonerated in any measure; Christ must pay it all. The wine-cup would have prevented his doing that, therefore he would suffer and go the whole length of suffering; he would not stop, but would go through it all.

Again, I say it was *that he might be made a compassionate High Priest*. Someone might have said, 'When my Master died, he did not suffer much. He suffered somewhat, but the wine-cup pre-vented much suffering. I dare not touch the wine-cup; at least, I dare not take it so as to alleviate my sufferings at all; then I must suffer more than he, for that drugged wine I must not drink. Surely, then, my Master cannot sympathize with me, if I for conscientious motives bear suffering without accepting alleviations which some think are wrong.' 'Nay,' said the Master, 'nay, you shall never say that. If you have to suffer without a comfort, I will let you know that I suffered without a comfort, too.' You say, 'Oh, if I had some myrrh given me which could mitigate my woe, it were well!' 'Ah!' says the Saviour, 'but I have had it offered to me, and I will not drink it, in order that you may see that I suffered woe without the comfort, without the cordial, without the consolation, which you think would enable you to endure it.' O blessed Lord Jesus, thou wast 'tempted in all points like as we are'! Blessed be thy name! This myrrh-cup could have put a plate of steel upon thy breast, it would have blunted many darts of suffering; therefore thou didst put it aside that thou mightest, naked, suffer every shaft to find its target in thy heart. This myrrh-cup would have steeled thy feelings, so that thou couldst not be rent by the whips of anguish; therefore thou wouldst not take its steeling influence, its hardening qualities. Thou, who didst stoop to become a poor, weak worm, 'a worm and no man,' didst bear the agony, without making the agony less, or strengthening thine own body to bear it. O blessed High Priest! Go to him, ye tried and tempted ones; go to him, and cast your burdens on him; he can bear them, he has borne burdens heavier than yours before. Cast your burden on the Lord, as his shoulders can sustain it; and his shoulders, that have borne trouble without comfort, can bear your troubles, though they be comfortless ones, too. Do but tell them to your Master, and you shall never find a lack of sympathy in him.

III. And now, what have we to say by way of A LESSON for this short discourse?

When Christ was offered this cup, he would not receive it. Sometimes, beloved, it is in your power to escape from sufferings for Christ's sake; and you may rightly do so, if you can escape from them without injuring the mission upon which your Father has sent you; for as he sent his Son into the world, even so has he sent you into the world. You have your mission; and there are times when the acceptance of a cordial, or the reception of an escape from peril, would be a degradation to your high dignity, an injury to your office; and therefore there are times when you should decline even the cup of consolation itself. You and I are called to hold fellowship with Christ in his sufferings; perhaps our business places us where we have to hold fellowship with Christ in the suffering of contempt. The finger is pointed at us; the lip is sometimes protruded in derision; sometimes an expression is used towards us, calling us a hypocrite, a cant, a formalist. You may be apt to think, 'Oh, that I could avoid all this! I wish I could escape.' Can you avoid it, and serve your Master as well? If you can, then drink the myrrh-cup, and avoid the misery; but if you cannot, and if it is proven that your position is one of duty, and one in which you can honour your Master, it is at your peril that you exchange your situation for an easier one, if you exchange it for one less useful.

'Oh!' says one, 'I work among wicked men, and I have to bear a testimony for truth in their midst; may I not leave the place at once? I feel that I am doing good there; but the jeers and taunts are so hard to bear, that the good I do seems to be always counterbalanced by the misery I suffer.' Take care, take care, lest you let the flesh prevail over the spirit. It would be like a myrrh-cup to you, for you to leave your situation, and go to another; it would be the removal of your pain; ponder a long time before you do it, weigh it well. If your Maker has put you there, to suffer for his name's sake, come not down from the cross to which he has nailed you by a daily crucifixion, till you have suffered all; and take not the myrrh-cup of an escape until you have borne all for Christ. I think it was holy Polycarp who, when the soldiers came to him to take him to prison, made his escape; but when he found afterwards that his doing so had dispirited some Christians, and had been attributed to his cowardice, when next the soldiers presented themselves, and he had an opportunity to escape, 'No,' he said, 'let me die.' It had been foolhardy of him, if he had run into the teeth of men the first time, in order to be put to death; but when he saw that he would serve his Master better by his death than by his life, it would have been an unrighteous thing if he had drunk of the wine-cup, if he had made his escape, and not died for his Master's sake.

O my brethren, I do think that there are many cordials which the world, too, has to offer to the Christian which he must not drink at all, because if his Master wishes him to have fellowship with him in his suffering, it is his to suffer so far as his Master wills. You are perhaps a man or a woman of a sorrowful spirit; you are given to solitude and loneliness. There are certain amusements, which some men say are harmless; they tell you that they are meant for you, and ask you to go and take them. You think, 'Well, in my low state, surely I might take these things. If I were happy and joyous, I should not need them; but surely, my Father, 'like as a father pitieth his children,' will pity me; and if I do these things, and do them merely for temporary comfort, my heart seems as though it would break if I had not this little temporary excitement.' Take care, take care, that it is not the wine-cup that prevents you, my friends. If your Master gives you the wine-cup, the golden wine-cup filled with the precious wine of the covenant, the strong promises, and sweet fellowship in Christ, drink it without a moment's hesitation. Drink it and be glad, for God has said, 'Give strong drink unto him that is ready to perish;' and this is the strong drink he gives to you in the golden wine-cup of the Saviour's fellowship. Drink it, and be happy. But if men would offer it to you, look many a time before you drink it. It may be, you may be right in drinking it, it may not be a wrong thing; but it may be, too, that even a thing that is innocent to others, may be wrong to you; and the taking of that amusement and pleasure into your hand, might be like our Saviour's taking the myrrh-cup and drinking it. It would stultify you, preventing you from learning all the lessons of your misery, from going in all the steps of your Redeemer, who wishes us to follow him through all the miseries which he has ordained for us, that they may be the means of fellowship with him in his suffering.

This is the only lesson I desire to give you at this time. If the Lord impress it on our minds, it may be of use to us. Only let me say, how many there are who would have drunk this wine-cup, if it had been offered to them! Your Saviour has taken from you the desire of your eyes with a stroke; he has robbed you of one who is dear and near to you. Say, Christian, if you had had the myrrh-cup put before you, if it had been said, 'If you like, that loved one of yours shall live,' if it had been offered to you that the life that has been taken away should be spared, could you with fortitude have said, 'Not my will, but thine, be done'? Could you have put it away, and said, 'No, my Master, if this cup may not pass from me except I drink it, thy will be done. And what is more, if it may pass from me, if I need not suffering, yet if I can honour thee more by suffering, and if the loss of my beloved one will serve thee and please thee, then so let it be, I refuse the comfort, when it comes in the way of thine honour; I reject the favoured mercy if it comes in the teeth of thy glory. I am willing to suffer; thy consolations I care not for; if I can honour thee better without them, I will do without them?'

There are some among you in the garments of mourning. Let me just, in conclusion, note a very beautiful thought of a good man on a passage of Scripture. Jesus says in his prayer, 'Father, I will that they also, whom thou hast given me, be with me where I am.' Do you know why good men die? Do you know why the righteous die? Shall I tell you what it is that kills them? It is Christ's prayer – 'Father, I will that they be with me.' It is that that fetches them up to heaven. They would stop here, if Christ did not pray them to death. Every time a believer mounts from this earth to heaven, it is caused by Christ's prayer. Now, says this good old divine, many times Christ and his people pull against one another in prayer. You bend your knee in prayer, and say, 'Father, I will that they whom thou hast given me be with me where *I* am;' Christ bends his knee, and says, 'Father, I will that they whom thou hast given me be with me where *I* am.' So, you see, one gets hold of him, and the other, too. He cannot be in both places; the beloved one cannot be with Christ and with you, too. Now, what shall be the answer? Put the prayers side by side; you are praying, 'Father, I will that they whom thou hast given me be with me where I am;' and there is your Saviour, praying that they may be with him where he is. Now, if you had your choice; if the King should step from his throne, and say, 'Here are two supplicants; they are praying opposite to one another; their prayers are clearly contrary to each other; I cannot answer them both'; oh, I am sure, though it were agony, you would start from your feet, and say, 'Jesus, not my will, but thine, be done.' You would give up your prayer for your sick husband's life, for your sick wife's life, for your dying child's life, if you could realize the thought that Christ was praying in the opposite direction, 'Father, I will that they whom thou hast given me be with me where I am.'

And now we come to the supper of our Master; oh, may the Master give us fellowship with him! Poor sinners that know not Christ, I have hardly a moment in which to address you; but remember, the separation which will be made between you and the church tonight is but a picture of an awful separation which shall be made between you and the church at the last great day. You will sit upstairs, some of you, to look down upon the solemnity: remember, you may look upon it here, but you will not look upon it in heaven, unless your hearts be made new by Christ, and unless you be washed in his precious blood.

5

CHRIST'S PLEA FOR IGNORANT SINNERS[1]

Then said Jesus, Father, forgive them;
for they know not what they do.
LUKE 23:34.

WHAT TENDERNESS we have here; what self-forgetfulness; what almighty love! Jesus did not say to those who crucified him, 'Begone!' One such word, and they must have all fled. When they came to take him in the garden, they went backward, and fell to the ground, when he spoke but a short sentence; and now that he is on the cross, a single syllable would have made the whole company fall to the ground, or flee away in fright. Jesus says not a word in his own defence. When he prayed to his Father, he might justly have said, 'Father, note what they do to thy beloved Son. Judge them for the wrong they do to him who loves them, and who has done all he can for them.' But there is no prayer against them in the words that Jesus utters. It was written of old, by the prophet Isaiah, 'He made intercession for the transgressors;' and here it is fulfilled. He pleads for his murderers, 'Father, forgive them.'

He does not utter a single word of upbraiding. He does not say, 'Why do ye this? Why pierce the hands that fed you? Why nail the feet that followed after you in mercy? Why mock the Man who loved to bless you?' No, not a word even of gentle upbraiding, much less anything like a curse. 'Father, forgive them.' You notice,

[1] Sermon No. 2,263. Preached at the Metropolitan Tabernacle on Sunday evening, 5 October 1890.

Jesus does not say, 'I forgive them,' but you may read that between the lines. He says that all the more because he does not say it in words. But he had laid aside his majesty, and is fastened to the cross; and therefore he takes the humble position of a suppliant, rather than the more lofty place of one who had power to forgive. How often, when men say, 'I forgive you,' is there a kind of selfishness about it! At any rate, self is asserted in the very act of forgiving. Jesus take the place of a pleader, a pleader for those who were committing murder upon himself. Blessed be his name!

This word of the cross we shall use tonight, and we shall see if we cannot gather something from it for our instruction; for, though we were not there, and we did not actually put Jesus to death, yet we really caused his death, and we, too, crucified the Lord of glory; and his prayer for us was, 'Father, forgive them; for they know not what they do.'

I am not going to handle this text so much by way of exposition, as by way of experience. I believe there are many here, to whom these words will be very appropriate. This will be our line of thought. First, *we were in measure ignorant;* secondly, *we confess that this ignorance is no excuse;* thirdly, *we bless our Lord for pleading for us;* and fourthly, *we now rejoice in the pardon we have obtained.* May the Holy Spirit graciously help us in our meditation!

I. Looking back upon our past experience, let me say, first, that WE WERE IN MEASURE IGNORANT. We who have been forgiven, we who have been washed in the blood of the Lamb, we once sinned, in a great measure, through ignorance. Jesus says, 'They know not what they do.' Now, I shall appeal to you, brothers and sisters, when you lived under the dominion of Satan, and served yourselves and sin, was there not a measure of ignorance in it? You can truly say, as we said in the hymn we sang just now –

Alas! I knew not what I did.

It is true, first, that we were ignorant of *the awful meaning of sin.* We began to sin as children; we knew that it was wrong, but we did not know all that sin meant. We went on to sin as young men;

peradventure we plunged into much wickedness. We knew it was wrong; but we did not see the end from the beginning. It did not appear to us as rebellion against God. We did not think that we were presumptuously defying God, setting at naught his wisdom, defying his power, deriding his love, spurning his holiness; yet we were doing that. There is an abysmal depth in sin. You cannot see the bottom of it. When we rolled sin under our tongue as a sweet morsel, we did not know all the terrible ingredients compounded in that deadly bittersweet. We were in a measure ignorant of the tremendous crime we committed when we dared to live in rebellion against God. So far, I think, you go with me.

We did not know, at that time, *God's great love to us.* I did not know that he had chosen me from before the foundation of the world; I never dreamed of that. I did not know that Christ stood for me as my Substitute, to redeem me from among men. I did not know that he had espoused himself to me in righteousness and in faithfulness, to be one with him for ever. You, dear friends, who now know the love of Christ, did not understand it then. You did not know that you were sinning against eternal love, against infinite compassion, against a distinguishing love such as God had fixed on you from eternity. So far, we knew not what we did.

I think, too, that we did not know all that we were doing in *our rejection of Christ, and putting him to grief.* He came to us in our youth; and impressed by a sermon we began to tremble, and to seek his face; but we were decoyed back to the world, and we refused Christ. Our mother's tears, our father's prayers, our teacher's admonitions, often moved us; but we were very stubborn, and we rejected Christ. We did not know that, in that rejection, we were virtually putting him away and crucifying him. We were denying his Godhead, or else we should have worshipped him. We were denying his love, or else we should have yielded to him. We were practically, in every act of sin, taking the hammer and the nails, and fastening Christ to the cross; but we did not know it. Perhaps, if we had known it, we should not have crucified the Lord of glory. We did know we were doing wrong; but we did not know all the wrong that we were doing.

Nor did we know fully *the meaning of our delays.* We hesitated; we were on the verge of conversion; we went back, and turned again to our old follies. We were hardened, Christless, prayerless still; and each of us said, 'Oh, I am only waiting a little while till I have fulfilled my present engagements, till I am a little older, till I have seen a little more of the world!' The fact is, we were refusing Christ, and choosing the pleasures of sin instead of him; and every hour of delay was an hour of crucifying Christ, grieving his Spirit, and choosing this harlot world in the place of the lovely and ever blessed Christ. We did not know that.

I think we may add one thing more. *We did not know the meaning of our self-righteousness.* We used to think, some of us, that we had a righteousness of our own. We had been to church regularly, or we had been to the meeting-house whenever it was open. We were christened; we were confirmed; or, peradventure, we rejoiced that we never had either of those things done to us. Thus, we put our confidence in ceremonies, or the absence of ceremonies.

We said our prayers; we read a chapter in the Bible night and morning; we did – oh, I do not know what we did not do! But there we rested; we were righteous in our own esteem. We had not any particular sin to confess, nor any reason to lie in the dust before the throne of God's majesty. We were about as good as we could be; and we did not know that we were even then perpetrating the highest insult upon Christ; for, if we were not sinners, why did Christ die; and, if we had a righteousness of our own which was good enough, why did Christ come here to work out a righteousness for us? We made out Christ to be a superfluity, by considering that we were good enough without resting in his atoning sacrifice.

Ah, we did not think we were doing that! We thought we were pleasing God by our religiousness, by our outward performances, by our ecclesiastical correctness; but all the while we were setting up anti-Christ in the place of Christ. We were making out that Christ was not wanted; we were robbing him of his office and glory! Alas! Christ would say of us, with regard to all these things, 'They know not what they do.' I want you to look quietly at the time past wherein you served sin, and just see whether there was not a darkness upon your mind, a blindness in your spirit, so that you did not know what you did.

II. Well now, secondly, WE CONFESS THAT THIS IGNOR-ANCE IS NO EXCUSE. Our Lord might urge it as a plea; but we never could. We did not know what we did, and so we were not guilty to the fullest possible extent; but we were guilty enough, therefore let us own it.

For first, remember, *the law never allows this as a plea*. In our own English law, a man is supposed to know what the law is. If he breaks it, it is no excuse to plead that he did not know it. It may be regarded by a judge as some extenuation; but the law allows nothing of the kind. God gives us the law, and we are bound to keep it. If I erred through not knowing the law, still it was a sin. Under the Mosaic law, there were sins of ignorance, and for these there were special offerings. The ignorance did not blot out the sin. That is clear in my text; for, if ignorance rendered an action no longer sinful, they why should Christ say, 'Father, forgive them'? But he does; he asks for mercy for what is sin, even though the ignorance in some measure be supposed to mitigate the criminality of it.

But, dear friends, *we might have known*. If we did not know, it was because we would not know. There was the preaching of the Word; but we did not care to hear it. There was this blessed Book; but we did not care to read it. If you and I had sat down, and looked at our conduct by the light of the Holy Scripture, we might have known much more of the evil of sin, and much more of the love of Christ, and much more of the ingratitude which is possible in refusing Christ, and not coming to him.

In addition to that, *we did not think*. 'Oh, but,' you say, 'young people never do think!' But young people should think. If there is anybody who need not think, it is the old man, whose day is nearly over. If he does think, he has but a very short time in which to improve; but the young have all their lives before them. If I were a carpenter, and had to make a box, I should not think about it after I had made the box; I should think, before I began to cut my timber, what sort of box it was to be. In every action, a man thinks before he begins, or else he is a fool. A young man ought to think more than anybody else, for now he is, as it were, making his box. He is beginning his life-plan; he should be the most thoughtful of all men. Many of us, who are now Christ's people, would have known much more about our Lord if we had given him more careful consideration in our earlier days. A man will consider about taking a wife, he will consider about making a business, he will consider about buying a horse or a cow; but he will not consider about the claims of Christ, and the claims of the Most High God; and this renders his ignorance wilful, and inexcusable.

Beside that, dear friends, although we have confessed to ignorance, *in many sins we did not know a great deal.* Come, let me quicken your memories. There were times when you knew that such an action was wrong, when you started back from it. You looked at the gain it would bring you, and you sold your soul for that price, and deliberately did what you were well aware was wrong. Are there not some here, saved by Christ, who must confess that, at times, they did violence to their conscience? They did despite to the Spirit of God, quenched the light of heaven, drove the Spirit away from them, distinctly knowing what they were doing. Let us bow before God in the silence of our hearts, and own to all of this. We hear the Master say, 'Father, forgive them; for they know not what they do.' Let us add our own tears as we say, 'And forgive us, also, because in some things we did know; in all things we might have known; but we were ignorant for want of thought, which thought was a solemn duty which we ought to have rendered to God.'

One thing more I will say on this head. When a man is ignorant, and does not know what he ought to do, what should he do? Well, he should do nothing till he does know. But here is the mischief of it, that *when we did not know, yet we chose to do the wrong thing.* If we did not know, why did we not choose the right thing? But, being in the dark, we never turned to the right; but always blundered to the left from sin to sin. Does not this show us how depraved our hearts are? Though we are seeking to be right, when we were let alone, we go wrong of ourselves. Leave a child alone; leave a man alone; leave a tribe alone without teaching and instruction; what comes of it? Why, the same as when you leave a field alone. It never, by any chance, produces wheat or barley. Leave it alone, and there are rank weeds, and thorns, and briars, showing that the natural set of the soil is towards producing that which is worthless. O friends, confess the innate evil of your hearts as well as the evil of your lives, in that, when you did not know, yet, having a perverse instinct, you chose the evil, and refused the good; and, when you did not know enough of Christ, and did not think enough of him to know whether you ought to have him or not, you would not come unto him that you might have life. You needed light; but you shut your eyes to the sun. You were thirsty; but you would not drink of the living spring; and so your ignorance, though it was there, was a criminal ignorance, which you must confess before the Lord. Oh, come ye to the cross, ye who have been there before, and have lost your burden there! Come and confess your guilt over again; and clasp that cross afresh, and look to him who bled upon it, and praise his dear name that he once prayed for you, 'Father forgive them; for they know not what they do.'

Now, I am going a step further. We were in a measure ignorant; but we confess that that measurable ignorance was no excuse.

III. Now, thirdly, WE BLESS OUR LORD FOR PLEADING FOR US.

Do you notice when it was that Jesus pleaded? It was, *while they were crucifying him*. They had not just driven in the nails, they had lifted up the cross, and dashed it down into its socket, and dislocated all his bones, so that he could say, 'I am poured out like water, and all my bones are out of joint.' Ah, dear friends, it was then that instead of a cry or groan, this dear Son of God said, 'Father, forgive them; for they know not what they do.' They did not ask for forgiveness for themselves, Jesus asked for forgiveness for them. Their hands were imbrued in his blood; and it was then, even then, that he prayed for them. Let us think of the great love wherewith he loved us, even while we were yet sinners, when we rioted in sin, when we drank it down as the ox drinketh down water. Even then he prayed for us. 'While we were yet without strength, in due time Christ died for the ungodly.' Bless his name tonight. He prayed for you when you did not pray for yourself. He prayed for you when you were crucifying him.

Then think of his plea, *he pleads his Sonship*. He says, 'Father, forgive them.' He was the Son of God, and he puts his divine Sonship into the scale on our behalf. He seems to say, 'Father, as I am thy Son, grant me this request, and pardon these rebels. Father, forgive them.' The filial rights of Christ were very great. He was the Son of the Highest. 'Light of light, very God of very God', the second Person in the Divine Trinity; and he puts that Sonship here before God and says, 'Father, Father, forgive them.' Oh, the power of that word from the Son's lip when he is wounded, when he is in agony, when he is dying! He says, 'Father, Father, grant my one request; O Father, forgive them; for they know not what they do;' and the great Father bows his awful head, in token that the petition is granted.

Then notice, that Jesus here, silently, but really *pleads his sufferings*. The attitude of Christ when he prayed this prayer is very noteworthy. His hands were stretched upon the transverse beam; his feet were fastened to the upright tree; and there he pleaded. Silently his hands and feet were pleading, and his agonized body from the very sinew and muscle pleaded with God. His sacrifice was presented there before the Father's face; not yet complete, but in his will complete; and so it is his cross that takes up the plea, 'Father, forgive them.' O blessed Christ! It is thus that we have been forgiven, for his Sonship and his cross have pleaded with God, and have prevailed on our behalf.

I love this prayer, also, because of the *indistinctness* of it. It is 'Father, forgive them.' He does not say, 'Father, forgive the soldiers who have nailed me here.' He includes them. Neither does he say, 'Father, forgive sinners in ages to come who will sin against me.' But he means them. Jesus does not mention them by any accusing name: 'Father, forgive my enemies. Father, forgive my murderers.' No, there is no word of accusation upon those dear lips. 'Father, forgive them.' Now into that pronoun 'them' I feel that I can crawl. Can you get in there? Oh, by a humble faith, appropriate the cross of Christ by trusting in it; and get into that big little word 'them'! It seems like a chariot of mercy that has come down to earth into which a man may step, and it shall bear him up to heaven. 'Father, forgive them.'

Notice, also, what it was that Jesus asked for; to omit that, would be to leave out the very essence of his prayer. *He asked for full absolution for his enemies:* 'Father, forgive them. Do not punish them; forgive them. Do not remember their sin; forgive it, blot it out; throw it into the depths of the sea. Remember it not, my

Father. Mention it not against them any more for ever. Father, forgive them.' Oh, blessed prayer, for the forgiveness of God is broad and deep! When man forgives, he leaves the remembrance of the wrong behind; but when God pardons, he says, 'I will forgive their iniquity, and I will remember their sin no more.' It is this that Christ asked for you and me long before we had any repentance, or any faith; and in answer to that prayer, we were brought to feel our sin, we were brought to confess it, and to believe in him; and now, glory be to his name, we can bless him for having pleaded for us, and obtained the forgiveness of all our sins.

IV. I come now to my last remark. Which is this, WE NOW REJOICE IN THE PARDON WE HAVE OBTAINED.

Have you obtained pardon? Is this your song?

> Now, oh joy! My sins are pardon'd,
> Now I can, and do believe.

I have a letter, in my pocket, from a man of education and standing, who has been an agnostic; he says that he was a sarcastic agnostic, and he writes praising God, and invoking every blessing upon my head for bringing him to the Saviour's feet. He says, 'I was without happiness for this life, and without hope for the next.' I believe that that is a truthful description of many an unbeliever. What hope is there for the world to come apart from the cross of Christ? The best hope such a man has is that he may die the death of a dog, and there may be an end of him. What is the hope of the Romanist, when he comes to die? I feel so sorry for many devout and earnest friends, for I do not know what their hope is. They do not hope to go to heaven yet, at any rate; some purgatorial pains must be endured first. Ah, this is a poor, poor faith to die on, to have such a hope as that to trouble your last thoughts. I do not know of any religion but that of Christ Jesus which tells us of sin pardoned, absolutely pardoned. Now, listen. Our teaching is not that, when you come to die, you may, perhaps, find out that it is all right, but, 'Beloved, now we are the sons of God.' 'He that believeth on the Son hath everlasting life.' He has it now, and he knows it, and he rejoices in it. So I come back to the last head of my discourse, we rejoice in the pardon Christ has obtained for us. We are pardoned. I hope that the larger portion of this audience can say, 'By the grace of God, we know that we are washed in the blood of the Lamb.'

Pardon has come to us through Christ's plea. Our hope lies in the plea of Christ, and specially in his death. If Jesus paid my debt, and he did if I am a believer in him, then I am out of debt. If Jesus bore the penalty of my sin, and he did if I am a believer, then there is no penalty for me to pay, for we can say to him –

> Complete atonement thou hast made,
> And to the utmost farthing paid
>   Whate'er thy people owed:
> Nor can his wrath on me take place,
> If shelter'd in thy righteousness,
>   And sprinkled with thy blood.
>
> If thou hast my discharge procured,
> And freely in my room endured
>   The whole of wrath divine:
> Payment God cannot twice demand,
> First at my bleeding Surety's hand,
>   And then again at mine.

If Christ has borne my punishment, I shall never bear it. Oh, what joy there is in this blessed assurance! Your hope that you are pardoned lies in this, that Jesus died. Those dear wounds of his bleed life for you.

We praise him for our pardon because *we do know now what we did.* Oh, brethren, I know not how much we ought to love Christ, because we sinned against him so grievously! Now we know that sin is 'exceeding sinful.' Now we know that sin crucified Christ. Now we know that we stabbed our heavenly Lover to his heart. We slew, with ignominious death, our best and dearest Friend and Benefactor. We know that now; and we could almost weep tears of blood to think that we ever treated him as we did. But, it is all forgiven, all gone. Oh, let us bless that dear Son of

God, who has put away even such sins as ours! We feel them more now than ever before. We know they are forgiven, and our grief is because of the pain that the purchase of our forgiveness cost our Saviour. We never knew what our sins really were till we saw him in a bloody sweat. We never knew the crimson hue of our sins till we read our pardon written in crimson lines with his precious blood. Now, we see our sin, and yet we do not see it; for God has pardoned it, blotted it out, cast it behind his back for ever.

Henceforth *ignorance*, such as we have described, *shall be hateful to us*. Ignorance of Christ and eternal things shall be hateful to us. If, through ignorance, we have sinned, we will have done with that ignorance. We will be students of his Word. We will study that masterpiece of all the sciences, the knowledge of Christ crucified. We will ask the Holy Spirit to drive far from us the ignorance that gendereth sin. God grant that we may not fall into sins of ignorance any more; but may we be able to say, 'I know whom I have believed; and henceforth I will seek more knowledge, till I comprehend, with all saints, what are the heights, and depths, and lengths, and breadths of the love of Christ, and know the love of God, which passeth knowledge!'

I put in a practical word here. If you rejoice that you are pardoned, *show your gratitude by your imitation of Christ*. There was never before such a plea as this, 'Father, forgive them; for they know not what they do.' Plead like that for others. Has anybody been injuring you? Are there persons who slander you? Pray tonight, 'Father, forgive them; for they know not what they do.' Let us always render good for evil, blessing for cursing; and when we are called to suffer through the wrongdoing of others, let us believe that they would not act as they do if it were not because of their ignorance. Let us pray for them; and make their very ignorance the plea for their forgiveness: 'Father, forgive them; for they know not what they do.'

I want you to think of the millions of London just now. See those miles of streets, pouring out their children this evening; but look at those public houses with the crowds streaming in and out. Go down our streets by moonlight. See what I almost blush to tell. Follow men and women, too, to their homes, and be this your prayer: 'Father, forgive them; for they know not what they do.' That silver bell – keep it always ringing. What did I say? That silver bell? Nay, it is the *golden* bell upon the priest's garments. Wear it on your garments, ye priests of God, and let it always ring out its golden note, 'Father, forgive them; for they know not what they do.' If I can set all God's saints imitating Christ with such a prayer as this, I shall not have spoken in vain.

Brethren, I see *reason for hope in the very ignorance that surrounds us.* I see hope for this poor city of ours, hope for this poor country, hope for Africa, China, and India. 'They know not what they do.' Here is a strong argument in their favour, for they are more ignorant than we were. They know less of the evil of sin, and less of the hope of eternal life, than we do. Send up this petition, ye people of God! Heap your prayers together with cumulative power, send up this fiery shaft of prayer, straight to the heart of God, while Jesus from his throne shall add his prevalent intercession, 'Father, forgive them; for they know not what they do.'

If there be any unconverted people here, and I know that there are some, we will mention them in our private devotion, as well as in the public assembly; and we will pray for them in words like these, 'Father, forgive them; for they know not what they do.'

May God bless you all, for Jesus Christ's sake! Amen.

6

THE FIRST CRY FROM THE CROSS[1]

Then said Jesus, Father, forgive them;
for they know not what they do.
LUKE 23:34

OUR LORD was at that moment enduring the first pains of crucifixion; the executioners had just then driven the nails through his hands and feet. He must have been, moreover, greatly depressed, and brought into a condition of extreme weakness by the agony of the night in Gethsemane, and by the scourgings and cruel mockings which he had endured all through the morning, from Caiaphas, Pilate, Herod, and the Praetorian guards. Yet neither the weakness of the past, nor the pain of the present, could prevent him from continuing in prayer. The lamb of God was silent to men, but he was not silent to God. Dumb as a sheep before her shearers, he had not a word to say in his own defence to man, but he continues in his heart crying unto his Father, and no pain and no weakness can silence his holy supplications. Beloved, what an example our Lord herein presents to us! Let us continue in prayer so long as our heart beats; let no excess of suffering drive us away from the throne of grace, but rather let it drive us closer to it.

Long as they live should Christians pray,
For only while they pray they live.

---

[1] Sermon No. 897. Preached at the Metropolitan Tabernacle on Sunday morning, 24 October 1869.

To cease from prayer is to renounce the consolations which our case requires. Under all distractions of spirit, and overwhelmings of heart, great God, help us still to pray, and never from the mercy-seat may our footsteps be driven by despair. Our blessed Redeemer persevered in prayer even when the cruel iron rent his tender nerves, and blow after blow of the hammer jarred his whole frame with anguish; and this perseverance may be accounted for by the fact that he was so in the habit of prayer that he could not cease from it; he had acquired a mighty velocity of intercession which forbade him to pause. Those long nights upon the cold mountain side, those many days which had been spent in solitude, those perpetual sudden prayerful utterances which he was wont to dart up to heaven, all these had formed in him a habit so powerful, that the severest torments could not stay its force. Yet it was more than habit.

Our Lord was baptized in the spirit of prayer; he lived in it, it lived in him, it had come to be an element of his nature. He was like that precious spice, which, being bruised, doth not cease to give forth its perfume, but rather yieldeth it all the more abundantly because of the blows of the pestle, its fragrance being no outward and superficial quality, but an inward virtue essential to its nature, which the pounding in the mortar did but fetch from it, causing it to reveal its secret soul of sweetness. So Jesus prays, even as a bundle of myrrh gives forth its smell, or as birds sing because they cannot do otherwise. Prayer enwrapped his very soul as with a garment, and his heart went forth in such array. I repeat it, let this be our example – never, under any circumstances, however severe the trial, or depressing the difficulty, let us cease from prayer.

Observe, further, that our Lord, in the prayer before us, remains in the vigour of faith as to his Sonship. The extreme trial to which he now submitted himself could not prevent his holding fast his Sonship. His prayer begins, 'Father'. It was not without meaning that he taught us when we pray to say, 'Our Father', for our prevalence in prayer will much depend upon our confidence in our relationship to God. Under great losses and crosses, one is apt to think that God is not dealing with us as a father with a child, but rather as a severe judge with a condemned criminal; but the cry of Christ, when he is brought to an extremity which we shall never reach, betrays no faltering in the spirit of sonship. In Gethsemane, when the bloody sweat fell fast upon the ground, his bitterest cry commenced with, '*My Father*', asking that if it were possible the cup of gall might pass from him; he pleaded with the Lord as his Father, even as he over and over again had called him on that dark and doleful night. Here, again, in this, the first of his seven expiring cries, it is 'Father.' O that the Spirit that makes us cry, 'Abba, Father', may never cease his operations! May we never be brought into spiritual bondage by the suggestion, 'If thou be the Son of God'; or if the tempter should so assail us, may we triumph as Jesus did in the hungry wilderness. May the Spirit which crieth, 'Abba, Father', repel each unbelieving fear. When we are chastened, as we must be (for what son is there whom his father chasteneth not?) may we be in loving subjection to the Father of our spirits, and live; but never may we become captives to the spirit of bondage, so as to doubt the love of our gracious Father, or our share in his adoption.

More remarkable, however, is the fact that our Lord's prayer to his Father was not for himself. He continued on the cross to pray for himself, it is true, and his lamentable cry, 'My God, my God, why hast thou forsaken me?', shows the personality of his prayer; but the first of the seven great cries on the cross has scarcely even an indirect reference to himself. It is, 'Father, forgive *them*.' The petition is altogether for others, and though there is an allusion to the cruelties which they were exercising upon himself, yet it is remote; and you will observe, he does not say, 'I forgive them' – that is taken for granted – he seems to lose sight of the fact that they were doing any wrong to himself, it is the wrong which they were doing to the Father that is on his mind, the insult which they are paying to the Father, in the person of the Son; he thinks not of himself at all. The cry, 'Father, forgive them,' is altogether un-selfish. He himself is, in the prayer, as though he were not; so complete is his self-annihilation, that he loses sight of himself and his woes. My brethren, if there had ever been a time in the life of the Son of man when he might have rigidly confined his prayer to himself, without any one cavilling thereat, surely it was when he was beginning his death throes. We could not marvel, if any man here were fastened to the stake, or fixed to a cross, if his first, and even his last and all his prayers, were for support under so arduous a trial. But see, the Lord Jesus began his prayer by pleading for others. See ye not what a great heart is here revealed! What a soul of compassion was in the Crucified! How Godlike, how divine! Was there ever such a one before him, who, even in the very pangs of death, offers as his first prayer an intercession for others? Let this unselfish spirit be in you also, my brethren. Look not every man upon his own things, but every man also on the things of others. Love your neighbours as yourselves, and as Christ has set before you this paragon of unselfishness, seek to follow him, treading in his steps.

There is, however, a crowning jewel in this diadem of glorious love. The Sun of Righteousness sets upon Calvary in a wondrous splendour; but amongst the bright colours which glorify his departure, there is this one – the prayer was not alone for others, but it was for his cruellest enemies. His enemies, did I say, there is more than that to be considered. It was not a prayer for enemies who had done him an ill deed years before, but for those who were there and then murdering him. Not in cold blood did the Saviour pray, after he had forgotten the injury, and could the more easily forgive it, but while the first red drops of blood were spurting on the hands which drove the nails; while yet the hammer was bestained with crimson gore, his blessed mouth poured out the fresh warm prayer, 'Father, forgive them, for they know not what they do.' I say, not that that prayer was confined to his immediate executioners. I believe that it was a far-reaching prayer, which included Scribes and Pharisees, Pilate and Herod, Jews and Gentiles – yea, the whole human race in a certain sense, since we were all concerned in that murder; but certainly the immediate persons, upon whom that prayer was poured like precious nard, were those who there and then were committing the brutal act of fastening him to the accursed tree. How sublime is this prayer if viewed in such a light! It stands alone upon a mount of solitary glory. No other had been prayed like it before. It is true, Abraham, and Moses, and the prophets had prayed for the wicked; but not for wicked men who had pierced their hands and feet. It is true, that Christians have since that day offered the same prayer, even as Stephen cried, 'Lay not this sin to their charge;' and many a martyr has made his last words at the stake words of pitying intercession for his persecutors; but you know where they learnt this, let me ask you where did *he* learn it? Was not Jesus the divine original? He learnt it nowhere; it leaped up from his own Godlike nature. A compassion peculiar to himself dictated this originality of prayer; the inward royalty of his love suggested to him so memorable an intercession, which may serve us for a pattern, but of which no pattern had existed before. I feel as though I could better kneel before my Lord's cross at this moment than stand in this pulpit to talk to you. I want to adore him; I worship him in heart for that prayer; if I knew nothing else of him but this one prayer, I must adore him, for that one matchless plea for mercy convinces me most overwhelmingly of the deity of him who offered it, and fills my heart with reverent affection.

Thus have I introduced to you our Lord's first vocal prayer upon the cross. I shall now, if we are helped by God's Holy Spirit, make some use of it. First, we shall view it as *illustrative of our Saviour's intercession;* secondly, we shall regard the text as *instructive of the church's work;* thirdly, we shall consider it as *suggestive to the unconverted.*

I. First, my dear brethren, let us look at this very wonderful text as ILLUSTRATIVE OF OUR LORD'S INTERCESSION.

He prayed for his enemies then, he is praying for his enemies now; the past on the cross was an earnest of the present on the throne. He is in a higher place, and in a nobler condition, but his occupation is the same; he continues still before the eternal throne to present pleas on the behalf of guilty men, crying, 'Father, O forgive them.' All his intercession is in a measure like the intercession on Calvary, and Calvary's cries may help us to guess the character of the whole of his intercession above.

The first point in which we may see the character of his intercession is this – it is *most gracious.* Those for whom our Lord prayed, according to the text, did not deserve his prayer. They had done nothing which could call forth from him a benediction as a reward for their endeavours in his service; on the contrary, they were most undeserving persons, who had conspired to put him to death. They had crucified him, crucified him wantonly and malignantly; they were even then taking away his innocent life. His clients were persons who, so far from being meritorious, were utterly undeserving of a single good wish from the Saviour's heart. They certainly never asked him to pray for them – it was the last thought in their minds to say, 'Intercede for us, thou dying King! Offer petitions on our behalf, thou Son of God!' I will venture to believe the prayer itself, when they heard it, was either disregarded, and passed over with contemptuous indifference, or perhaps it was caught at as a theme for jest. I admit that it seems to be too severe upon humanity to suppose it possible that such a prayer could have been the theme for laughter, and yet there were other things enacted around the cross which were quite as brutal, and I can imagine that this also might have happened. Yet our Saviour prayed for persons who did not deserve the prayer, but, on the contrary, merited a curse – persons who did not ask for the prayer, and even scoffed at it when they heard it. Even so in heaven there stands the great High Priest, who pleads for guilty men – for *guilty* men, my hearers. There are none on earth that deserve his intercession. He pleads for none on the supposition that they do deserve it. He stands there to plead as the just One on the behalf of the unjust. Not if any man be righteous, but 'if any man sin, we have an advocate with the Father.'

Remember, too, that our great Intercessor pleads for such as never asked him to plead for them. His elect, while yet dead in trespasses and sins, are the objects of his compassionate intercessions, and while they even scoff at his gospel, his heart of love is entreating the favour of heaven on their behalf. See, then, beloved, if such be the truth, how sure you are to speed with God who earnestly ask the Lord Jesus Christ to plead for you. Some of you, with many tears and much earnestness, have been beseeching the Saviour to be your advocate? Will he refuse you? Stands it to reason that he can? He pleads for those that reject his pleadings, much more for you who prize them beyond gold. Remember, my dear hearer, if there be nothing good in you, and if there be everything conceivable that is malignant and bad, yet none of these things can be any barrier to prevent Christ's exercising the office of Intercessor for you. Even for you he will plead. Come, put your case into his hands; for you he will find pleas which you cannot discover for yourselves, and he will put the case to God for you as for his murderers, 'Father, forgive them.'

A second quality of his intercession is this – its *careful spirit*. You notice in the prayer, 'Father, forgive them, for they know not what they do.' Our Saviour did, as it were, look his enemies through and through to find something in them that he could urge in their favour; but he could see nothing until his wisely affection-ate eye lit upon their ignorance: 'they know not what they do.' How carefully he surveyed the circumstances, and the characters of those for whom he importuned! Just so it is with him in heaven. Christ is no careless advocate for his people. He knows your precise condition at this moment, and the exact state of your heart with regard to the temptation through which you are passing; more than that, he foresees the temptation which is awaiting you, and in his intercession he takes note of the future event which his prescient eye beholds. 'Satan hath desired to have thee, that he may sift thee as wheat; but I have prayed for thee that thy faith fail not.' Oh, the condescending tenderness of our great High Priest! He knows us better than we know ourselves. He understands every secret grief and groaning. You need not trouble yourself about the wording of your prayer, he will put the wording right. And even the understanding as to the exact petition, if you should fail in it, he cannot, for as he knoweth what is the mind of God, so he knoweth what is your mind also. He can spy out some reason for mercy in you which you cannot detect in yourselves, and when it is so dark and cloudy with your soul that you cannot discern a foothold for a plea that you may urge with heaven, the Lord Jesus has the pleas ready framed, and petitions ready drawn up, and he can present them acceptable before the mercy-seat. His intercession, then, you will observe is very gracious, and in the next place it is very thoughtful.

We must next note its *earnestness*. No one doubts who reads these words, 'Father, forgive them, for they know not what they do,' that they were heaven-piercing in their fervour. Brethren, you are certain, even without a thought, that Christ was terribly in earnest in that prayer. But there is an argument to prove that. Earnest people are usually witty, and quick of understanding, to discover anything which may serve their turn. If you are pleading for life, and an argument for your being spared be asked of you, I will warrant you that you will think of one when no one else might. Now, Jesus was so in earnest for the salvation of his enemies, that he struck upon an argument for mercy which a less anxious spirit would not have thought of: 'They know not what they do.' Why, sirs, that was in strictest justice but a scant reason for mercy; and indeed, ignorance, if it be wilful, does not extenuate sin, and yet the ignorance of many who surrounded the cross was a wilful ignorance. They might have known that he was the Lord of glory. Was not Moses plain enough? Had not Isaiah been very bold in his speech? Were not the signs and tokens such that one might as well doubt which is the sun in the firmament as the claims of Jesus to be the Messiah? Yet, for all that, the Saviour, with marvellous earnestness and consequent dexterity, turns what might not have been a plea into a plea, and puts it thus: 'Father, forgive them, *for* they know not what they do.' Oh, how mighty are his pleas in heaven, then, in their earnestness! Do not suppose that he is less quick of understanding there, or less intense in the vehemence of his entreaties. No, my brethren, the heart of Christ still labours with the eternal God. He is no slumbering intercessor, but, for Zion's sake, he doth not hold his peace, and for Jerusalem's sake, he doth not cease, nor will he, till her righteousness goes forth as brightness, and her salvation as a lamp that burneth.

It is interesting to note, in the fourth place, that the prayer here offered helps us to judge of his intercession in heaven as to its *continuance,* perseverance, and perpetuity. As I remarked before, if our Saviour might have paused from intercessory prayer, it was surely when they fastened him to the tree; when they were guilty of direct acts of deadly violence to his divine person, he might then have ceased to present petitions on their behalf. But sin cannot tie the tongue of our interceding Friend. Oh, what comfort is here! You have sinned, believer, you have grieved his Spirit, but you have not stopped that potent tongue which pleads for you. You have been unfruitful, perhaps, my brother, and like the barren tree, you deserve to be cut down; but your want of fruitfulness has not withdrawn the Intercessor from his place. He interposes at this moment, crying, 'Spare it yet another year.' Sinner, you have provoked God by long rejecting his mercy and going from bad to worse, but neither blasphemy nor unrighteousness, nor infidelity, shall stay the Christ of God from urging the suit of the very chief of sinners. He lives, and while he lives he pleads; and while there is a sinner upon earth to be saved, there shall be an intercessor in heaven to plead for him. These are but fragments of thought, but they will help you, I hope, to realize the intercession of your great High Priest.

Think yet again, this prayer of our Lord on earth is like his prayer in heaven, because of its *wisdom*. He seeks the best thing, and that which his clients most need, 'Father, *forgive them*.' That was the great point in hand; they wanted most of all there and then forgiveness from God. He does not say, 'Father, enlighten them, for they know not what they do,' for mere enlightenment would but have created torture of conscience and hastened on their hell; but he crieth, 'Father, forgive;' and while he used his voice, the precious drops of blood which were then distilling from the nail wounds were pleading too, and God heard, and doubtless did forgive. The first mercy which is needful to guilty sinners is forgiven sin. Christ wisely prays for the boon most wanted. It is so in heaven; he pleads wisely and prudently. Let him alone, he knows what to ask for at the divine hand. Go you to the mercy-seat, and pour out your desires as best you can, but when you have done so always put it thus, 'O my Lord Jesus, answer no desire of mine if it be not according to thy judgment; and if in anything that I have asked I have failed to seek for what I need, amend my pleading, for thou art infinitely wiser than I.' Oh, it is sweet to have a friend at court to perfect our petitions for us before they come unto the great King. I believe that there is never presented to God anything but a perfect prayer now; I mean, that before the great Father of us all, no prayer of his people ever comes up imperfect; there is nothing left out, and there is nothing to be erased; and this, not because their prayers were originally perfect in themselves, but because the Mediator makes them perfect through his infinite wisdom, and they come up before the mercy-seat moulded according to the mind of God himself, and he is sure to grant such prayers.

Once more, this memorable prayer of our crucified Lord was like to his universal intercession in the matter of its *prevalence*.

Those for whom he prayed were many of them forgiven. Do you remember that he said to his disciples when he bade them preach, 'beginning at Jerusalem', and on that day when Peter stood up with the eleven, and charged the people that with wicked hands they had crucified and slain the Saviour, three thousand of these persons who were thus justly accused of his crucifixion became believers in him, and were baptised in his name. That was an answer to Jesus' prayer. The priests were at the bottom of our Lord's murder, they were the most guilty; but it is said, 'a great company also of the priests believed.' Here was another answer to the prayer. Since all men had their share representatively, Gentiles as well as Jews, in the death of Jesus, the gospel was soon preached to the Jews, and within a short time it was preached to the Gentiles also.

Was not this prayer, 'Father, forgive them,' like a stone cast into a lake, forming at first a narrow circle, and then a wider ring, and soon a larger sphere, until the whole lake is covered with circling waves? Such a prayer as this, cast into the whole world, first created a little ring of Jewish converts and of priests, and then a wider circle of such as were beneath the Roman sway; and today its circumference is wide as the globe itself, so that tens of thousands are saved through the prevalence of this one intercession 'Father, forgive them.' It is certainly so with him in heaven, he never pleads in vain. With bleeding hands, he yet won the day; with feet fastened to the wood, he was yet victorious; forsaken of God and despised of the people, he was yet triumphant in his pleas; how much more so now the tiara is about his brow, his hand grasps the universal sceptre, and his feet are shod with silver sandals, and he is crowned King of kings, and Lord of lords! If tears and cries out of weakness were omnipotent, even more mighty if possible must be that sacred authority which as the risen Priest he claims when he stands before the Father's throne to mention the covenant which the Father made with him. O ye trembling believers, trust him with your concerns! Come hither, ye guilty, and ask him to plead for you. O you that cannot pray, come, ask him to intercede for you. Broken hearts and weary heads, and disconsolate souls, come ye to him who into the golden censer will put his merits, and then place your prayers with them, so that they shall come up as the smoke of perfume, even as a fragrant cloud into the nostrils of the Lord God of hosts, who will smell a sweet savour, and accept you and your prayers in the Beloved. We have now opened up more than enough sea-room for your meditations at home this afternoon, and, therefore we leave this first point. We have had an illustration in the prayer of Christ on the cross of what his prayers always are in heaven.

II. Secondly, the text is INSTRUCTIVE OF THE CHURCH'S WORK.

As Christ was, so his church is to be in this world. Christ came into this world not to be ministered unto, but to minister, not to be honoured, but to save others. His church, when she understands her work, will perceive that she is not here to gather to herself wealth or honour, or to seek any temporal aggrandisement and position; she is here unselfishly to live, and if need be, unselfishly to die for the deliverance of the lost sheep, the salvation of lost men. Brethren, Christ's prayer on the cross I told you was altogether an unselfish one. He does not remember himself in it. Such ought to be the church's life-prayer, the church's active interposition on the behalf of sinners. She ought to live never for her ministers or for herself, but ever for the lost sons of men. Imagine you that churches are formed to maintain ministers? Do you conceive that the church exists in this land merely that so much salary may be given to bishops, and deans, and prebends, and curates, and I know not what? My brethren, it were well if the whole thing were abolished if that were its only aim. The aim of the church is not to provide out-door relief for the younger sons of the nobility; when they have not brains enough to win anyhow else their livelihood, they are stuck into family livings. Churches are not made that, men of ready speech may stand up on Sundays and talk, and so win daily bread from their admirers. Nay, there is another end and aim from this. These places of worship are not built that you may sit here comfortably, and hear something that shall make you pass away your Sundays with pleasure. A church in London, which does not exist to do good in the slums, and dens, and kennels of the city, is a church that has no reason to justify its longer existing. A church that does not exist to reclaim heathenism, to fight with evil, to destroy error, to put down falsehood, a church that does not exist to take the side of the poor, to denounce injustice and to hold up righteousness, is a church that has no right to be. Not for thyself, O church, dost thou exist, any more than Christ existed for himself. His glory was that he laid aside his glory, and the glory of the church is when she lays aside her respectability and her dignity, and counts it to be her glory to gather together the outcasts, and her highest honour to seek amid the foulest mire the priceless jewels for which Jesus shed his blood. To rescue souls from hell and lead to God, to hope, to heaven, this is her heavenly occupation. O that the church would always feel this! Let her have her bishops and her preachers, and let them be supported, and let everything be done for Christ's sake decently and in order, but let the end be looked to, namely, the conversion of the wandering, the teaching of the ignorant, the help of the poor, the maintenance of the right, the putting down of the wrong, and the upholding at all hazards of the crown and kingdom of our Lord Jesus Christ.

Now the prayer of Christ had a *great spirituality of aim*. You notice that nothing is sought for these people but that which concerns their souls, 'Father *forgive* them.' And I believe the church will do well when she recollects that she wrestles not with flesh and blood, nor with principalities and powers, but with spiritual wickedness, and that what she has to dispense is not the law and order by which magistrates may be upheld, or tyrannies pulled down, but the spiritual government by which hearts are conquered to Christ, and judgments are brought into subjection to his truth. I believe that the more the church of God strains after, before God, the forgiveness of sinners, and the more she seeks in her life prayer to teach sinners what sin is, and what the blood of Christ is, and what the hell that must follow if sin be not washed out, and what the heaven is which will be ensured to all those who are cleansed from sin, the more she keeps to this the better.

Press forward as one man, my brethren, to secure the root of the matter in the forgiveness of sinners. As to all the evils that afflict humanity, by all means take your share in battling with them; let temperance be maintained, let education be supported; let reforms, political and ecclesiastical, be pushed forward as far as you have the time and effort to spare, but the first business of every Christian man and woman is with the hearts and consciences of men as they stand before the everlasting God. O let nothing turn you aside from your divine errand of mercy to undying souls. This is your one business. Tell to sinners that sin will damn them, that Christ alone can take away sin, and make this the one passion of your souls, 'Father, forgive them, forgive them! Let them know how to be forgiven. Let them be actually forgiven, and let me never rest except, as I am the means of bringing sinners to be forgiven, even the guiltiest of them.'

Our Saviour's prayer teaches the church that while her spirit should be unselfish, and her aim should be spiritual, *the range of her mission is to be unlimited.* Christ prayed for the wicked, what if I say the most wicked of the wicked, that ribald crew that had surrounded his cross! He prayed for the ignorant. Doth he not say, 'They know not what they do'? He prayed for his persecutors; the very persons who were most at enmity with him, lay nearest to his heart. Church of God, your mission is not to the respectable few who will gather about your ministers to listen respectfully to their words; your mission is not to the *élite* and the eclectic, the intelligent who will criticise your words and pass judgment upon every syllable of your teaching; your mission is not to those who treat you kindly, generously, affectionately, not to these I mean alone, though certainly to these as among the rest; but your great errand is to the harlot, to the thief, to the swearer and the drunkard, to the most depraved and debauched. If no one else cares for these, the church always must, and if there be any who are first in her prayers it should be these who alas! are generally last in our thoughts. The ignorant we ought diligently to consider. It is not enough for the preacher that he preaches so that those instructed from their youth up can understand him; he must think of those to whom the commonest phrases of theological truth are as meaningless as the jargon of an unknown tongue; he must preach so as to reach the meanest comprehension; and if the ignorant many come not to hear him, he must use such means as best he may to induce them, nay, compel them to hear the good news. The gospel is meant also for those who persecute religion; it aims its arrows of love against the hearts of its foes. If there be any whom we should first seek to bring to Jesus, it should be just these who are the farthest off and most opposed to the gospel of Christ.

'Father, forgive *them;* if thou dost pardon none besides, yet be pleased to forgive *them.'*

So, too, the church should be *earnest* as Christ was; and if she be so, she will be quick to notice any ground of hope in those she deals with, quick to observe any plea that she may use with God for their salvation.

She must be *hopeful* too, and surely no church ever had a more hopeful sphere than the church of this present age. If ignorance be a plea with God, look on the heathen at this day – millions of them never heard Messiah's name. Forgive them, great God, indeed they know not what they do. If ignorance be some ground for hope, there is hope enough in this great city of London, for have we not around us hundreds of thousands to whom the simplest truths of the gospel would be the greatest novelties? Brethren, it is sad to think that this country should still lie under such a pall of ignorance, but the sting of so dread a fact is blunted with hope when we read the Saviour's prayer aright – it helps us to hope while we cry, 'Forgive them, for they know not what they do.'

It is the church's business to seek after the most fallen and the most ignorant, and to seek them perseveringly. She should never stay her hand from doing good. If the Lord be coming tomorrow, it is no reason why you Christian people should subside into mere talkers and readers, meeting together for mutual comfort, and forgetting the myriads of perishing souls. If it be true that this world is going to pieces in a fortnight, and that Louis Napoleon is the Apocalyptic beast, or if it be not true, I care not a fig, it makes no difference to my duty, and does not change my service. Let my Lord come when he will, while I labour for him I am ready for his appearing. The business of the church is still to watch for the salvation of souls. If she stood gazing, as modern prophets would have her; if she gave up her mission to indulge in speculative interpretations, she might well be afraid of her Lord's coming; but if she goes about her work, and with incessant toil searches out her Lord's precious jewels, she shall not be ashamed when her Bridegroom cometh.

My time has been much too short for so vast a subject as I have undertaken, but I wish I could speak words that were as loud as thunder, with a sense and earnestness as mighty as the lightning. I would fain excite every Christian here, and kindle in him a right idea of what his work is as a part of Christ's church. My brethren, you must not live to yourselves; the accumulation of money, the bringing up of your children, the building of houses, the earning of your daily bread, all this you may do; but there must be a greater object than this if you are to be Christlike, as you should be, since you are bought with Jesus' blood. Begin to live for others, make it apparent unto all men that you are not yourselves the end-all and be-all of your own existence, but that you are spending and being spent, that through the good you do to men God may be glorified, and Christ may see in you his own image and be satisfied.

III. Time fails me, but the last point was to be a word SUGGESTIVE TO THE UNCONVERTED.

Listen attentively to these sentences. I will make them as terse and condensed as possible. Some of you here are not saved. Now, some of you have been very ignorant, and when you sinned you did not know what you did. You knew you were sinners, you knew that, but you did not know the far-reaching guilt of sin. You have not been attending the house of prayer long, you have not read your Bible, you have not Christian parents. Now you are beginning to be anxious about your souls. Remember your ignorance does not excuse you, or else Christ would not say, 'Forgive them;' they must be forgiven, even those that know not what they do, hence they are individually guilty; but still that ignorance of yours gives you just a little gleam of hope. The times of your ignorance God winked at, but now commandeth all men everywhere to repent. Bring forth, therefore, fruits meet for repentance. The God whom you have ignorantly forgotten is willing to pardon and ready to forgive. The gospel is just this, trust Jesus Christ who died for the guilty, and you shall be saved. O may God help you to do so this very morning, and you will become new men and new women, a change will take place in you equal to a new birth; you will be new creatures in Christ Jesus.

But ah! my friends, there are some here for whom even Christ himself could not pray this prayer, in the widest sense at any rate, 'Father, forgive them; for they know not what they do,' for you have known what you did, and every sermon you hear, and especially every impression that is made upon your understanding and conscience by the gospel, adds to your responsibility, and takes away from you the excuse of not knowing what you do. Ah! sirs, you know that there is the world and Christ, and that you cannot have both. You know that there is sin and God and that you cannot serve both. You know that there are the pleasures of evil and the pleasures of heaven, and that you cannot have both. Oh! in the light which God has given you, may his Spirit also come and help you to choose that which true wisdom would make you choose. Decide today for God, for Christ, for heaven.

The Lord decide you for his name's sake. Amen.

7

CRIES FROM THE CROSS[1]

My God, my God, why hast thou forsaken me?
Why art thou so far from helping me, and from
the words of my roaring?
PSALM 22:1

WE HERE BEHOLD the Saviour in the depths of his agonies and sorrows. No other place so well shows the griefs of Christ as Calvary, and no other moment at Calvary is so full of agony as that in which this cry rends the air, 'My God, my God, why hast thou forsaken me?' At this moment, physical weakness, brought upon him by fasting and scourging, was united with the acute mental torture which he endured from the shame and ignominy through which he had to pass; and as the culmination of his grief, he suffered spiritual agony which surpasses all expression, on account of the departure of his Father from him. This was the blackness and darkness of his horror; then it was that he penetrated the depths of the caverns of suffering.

'My God, my God, why hast thou forsaken me?' There is something in these words of our Saviour always calculated to benefit us. When we behold the sufferings of men, they afflict and appal us; but the sufferings of our Saviour, while they move us to grief, have about them something sweet, and full of consolation. Here, even here, in this black spot of grief, we find our heaven, while gazing upon the cross. This, which might be thought a frightful sight, makes the Christian glad and joyous. If he laments the cause, yet he rejoices in the consequences.

[1] Sermon No. 2,562. Preached at New Park Street Chapel on Sunday evening, 2 November 1856.

I. First, in our text, there are THREE QUESTIONS to which I shall call your attention.

The first is, *'My God, my God, why hast thou forsaken me?'* By these words we are to understand that our blessed Lord and Saviour was at that moment forsaken by God in such a manner as he had never been before. He had battled with the enemy in the desert, but thrice he overcame him, and cast him to the earth. He had striven with that foe all his life long, and even in the garden he had wrestled with him till his soul was 'exceeding sorrowful.' It is not till now that he experiences a depth of sorrow which he never felt before. It was necessary that he should suffer, in the stead of sinners, just what sinners ought to have suffered. It would be difficult to conceive of punishment for sin apart from the frown of Deity. With crime we always associate anger, so that, when Christ died, 'the Just for the unjust, that he might bring us to God' – when our blessed Saviour became our Substitute, he became, for the time, the victim of his Father's righteous wrath, seeing that our sins had been imputed to him, in order that his righteousness might be imputed to us. It was necessary that he should feel the loss of his Father's smile – for the condemned in hell must have tasted of that bitterness – and therefore the Father closed the eye of his love, put the hand of justice before the smile of his face, and left his Son to cry, 'My God, my God, why hast thou forsaken me?'

There is no man living who can tell the full meaning of these words; not one in heaven or on earth – I had almost said, in hell; there is not a man who can spell these words out with all their depth of misery. Some of us think, at times, that we could cry, 'My God, my God, why hast thou forsaken me?' There are seasons when the brightness of our Father's smile is eclipsed by clouds and darkness. But let us remember that God never does really forsake us. It is only a seeming forsaking with us, but in Christ's case it was a real forsaking. God only knows how much we grieve, sometimes, at a little withdrawal of our Father's love; but the real turning away of God's face from his Son – who shall calculate how deep the agony which it caused him when he cried, 'My God, my God, why hast thou forsaken me?'

In our case, this is the cry of unbelief; in his case, it was the utterance of a fact, for God had really turned away from him for a time. O thou poor, distressed soul, who once lived in the sunshine of God's face, but art now in darkness – thou who art walking in the valley of the shadow of death, thou hearest noises, and thou art afraid; thy soul is startled within thee, thou art stricken with terror if thou thinkest that God has forsaken thee! Remember that he has not really forsaken thee, for –

> Mountains, when in darkness shrouded,
> Are as real as in the day.

God in the clouds is as much our God as when he shines forth in all the lustre of his benevolence; but since even the *thought* that he has forsaken us gives us agony, what must the agony of the Saviour have been when he cried, 'My God, my God, why hast thou forsaken me?'

The next question is, *'Why art thou so far from helping me?'* Hitherto, God had helped his Son, but now he must tread the winepress alone, and even his own Father cannot be with him. Have you not felt, sometimes, that God has brought you to do some duty, and yet has apparently not given you the strength to do it? Have you never felt that sadness of heart which makes you cry, 'Why art thou so far from helping me?' But if God means you to do anything, you can do it, for he will give you the power. Perhaps your brain reels; but God has ordained that you must do it, and you shall do it. Have you not felt as if you must go on even while, every step you took, you were afraid to put your foot down for fear you should not get a firm foothold? If you have had any experience of divine things, it must have been so with you. We can scarcely guess what it was that our Saviour felt when he said, 'Why art thou so far from helping me?' His work is one which none but a Divine Person could have accomplished, yet his Father's eye was turned away from him! With more than Herculean labours before him, but with none of his Father's might given to him, what must have been the strain upon him! Truly, as Hart says, he –

> Bore all incarnate God could bear,
> With strength enough, and none to spare.

The third enquiry is, '*Why art thou so far from the words of my roaring?*' The word here translated 'roaring' means, in the original Hebrew, that deep, solemn groan which is caused by serious sickness, and which suffering men utter. Christ compares his prayers to those roarings, and complains that God is so far from him that he does not hear him. Beloved, many of us can sympathize with Christ here. How often have we on our knees asked some favour of God, and we thought we asked in faith, yet it never came! Down we went upon our knees again. There is something which withholds the answer; and, with tears in our eyes, we have wrestled with God again; we have pleaded, for Jesu's sake, but the heavens have seemed like brass. In the bitterness of our spirit, we have cried, 'Can there *be* a God?' And we have turned round, and said, '"My God, my God, why hast thou forsaken me? Why art thou so far from the words of my roaring?" Is this like thee? Dost thou ever spurn a sinner? Hast thou not said, "Knock, and it shall be opened unto thee?" Art thou reluctant to be kind? Dost thou withhold thy promise?' And when we have been almost ready to give up, with everything apparently against us, have we not *groaned*, and said, 'Why art thou so far from the words of my roaring?' Though we know something, it is not much that we can truly understand of those direful sorrows and agonies which our blessed Lord endured when he asked these three questions, 'My God, my God, why hast thou forsaken me? why art thou so far from helping me, and from the words of my roaring?'

II. Let as now, in the second place, ANSWER THESE THREE QUESTIONS.

The answer to the first question I have given before. Methinks I hear the Father say to Christ, '*My Son, I forsake thee because thou standest in the sinner's stead.* As thou art holy, just, and true, I never would forsake *thee*; I would never turn away from *thee*; for, even as a man, thou hast been holy, harmless, undefiled, and separate from sinners; but on thy head doth rest the guilt of every penitent, transferred from him to thee; and thou must expiate it by thy blood. Because thou standest in the sinner's stead, I will not look at thee till thou hast borne the full weight of my vengeance. *Then*, I will exalt thee on high, far above all principalities and powers.'

O Christian, pause here, and reflect! Christ was punished in this way for thee! Oh, see that countenance so wrung with horror; those horrors gather there for thee! Perhaps, in thine own esteem, thou art the most worthless of the family; certainly, the most insignificant; but the meanest lamb of Christ's flock is as much the object of purchase as any other. Yes, when that black darkness gathered round his brow, and when he cried out, *'Eloi, Eloi,'* in the words of our text, for the Lord Omnipotent to help him; when he uttered that awfully solemn cry, it was because he loved *thee*, because he gave himself for *thee*, that thou mightest be sanctified here, and dwell with him hereafter. God forsook him, therefore, first, because he was the sinner's Substitute.

The answer to the second question is, *'Because I would have thee get all the honour to thyself;* therefore I will not help thee, lest I should have to divide the spoil with thee.' The Lord Jesus Christ lived to glorify his Father, and he died to glorify himself, in the redemption of his chosen people. God says, 'No, my Son, thou shalt do it alone; for thou must wear the crown alone; and upon thy person shall all the regalia of thy sovereignty be found. I will give thee all the praise, and therefore thou shalt accomplish all the labour.' He was to tread the winepress alone, and to get the victory and glory alone to himself.

The answer to the third question is essentially the same as the answer to the first. *To have heard Christ's prayers at that time, would have been inappropriate.* This turning away of the Divine Father from hearing his Son's prayer, is just in keeping with his condition; as the sinner's Surety, his prayer must not be heard; as the sinner's Surety, he could say, 'Now that I am here, dying in the sinner's stead, thou sealest thine ears against my prayer.' God did not hear his Son, because he knew his Son was dying to bring us near to God, and the Son therefore cried, 'My God, my God, why hast thou forsaken me?'

III. In conclusion, I shall offer you A WORD OF EARNEST EXPOSTULATION AND OF AFFECTIONATE WARNING.

Is it nothing to some of you that Jesus should die? You hear the tale of Calvary; but, alas! you have dry eyes. You never weep concerning it. Is the death of Jesus nothing to you? Alas! it seems to be so with many. Your hearts have never throbbed in sympathy with him. O friends, how many of you can look on Christ, thus agonising and groaning, and say, 'He is *my* Ransom, *my* Redeemer'? Could you say, with Christ, '*My* God'? Or is God another's, and not yours? Oh, if you are out of Christ, hear me speak one word, it is a word of *warning!* Remember, *to be out of Christ, is to be without hope;* if you die unsprinkled with his blood, you are lost. *And what is it to be lost?* I shall not try to tell you the meaning of that dreadful word *'lost'.* Some of you may know it before another sun has risen. God grant that you may not! Do you desire to know how you may be saved? Hear me. 'God so loved the world, that he gave his only begotten Son, that whosoever believeth in him should not perish, but have everlasting life.' 'He that believeth and is baptized shall be saved.' To be baptized is to be buried in water in the name of the Father, and of the Son, and of the Holy Ghost. Have you believed in Christ? Have you professed faith in Christ? Faith is the grace which rests alone on Christ. Whosoever will be saved, before all things it is necessary that he should feel himself to be lost – that he should know himself to be a ruined sinner, and then he should believe this: 'It is a faithful saying, and worthy of all acceptation, that Christ Jesus came into the world to save sinners,' even the very chief. You want no mediator between yourselves and Christ. You may come to Christ just as you are – guilty, wicked, poor; just as you are, Christ will take you. There is no necessity for washing beforehand. You want no riches; in him you have *all* you require, will you bring anything to *'all'?* You want no garments; for in Christ you have a seamless robe which will amply suffice to cover even the biggest sinner upon earth, as well as the least.

Come, then, to Jesus at once. Do you say you do not know *how* to come? Come just as you are. Do not wait to *do* anything. What you want is to leave off doing, and let Christ do all for you. What do you want to do, when he has done all? All the labour of your hands can never fulfil what God commands. Christ died for sinners, and you must say, 'Sink or swim, I will have no other Saviour but Christ.' Cast yourself wholly upon him.

> And when thine eye of faith is dim,
> Still trust in Jesus, sink or swim;

Still at his footstool humbly bow,
O sinner! sinner! *prostrate now!*

He is able to pardon you at this moment. There are some of you who know you are guilty, and groan concerning it. Sinner, why tarriest thou? 'Come, and welcome!' is my Master's message to you. If you feel you are lost and ruined, there is not a barrier between you and heaven; Christ has broken it down. If you know your own lost estate, Christ has died for you; believe, and come! Come, and welcome, sinner, come! O sinner, come! Come! Come! Jesus bids thee come; and as his ambassador to thee, I bid thee come, as one who would *die* to save your souls if it were necessary – as one who knows how to groan over you, and to weep over you – one who loves you even as he loves himself – I, as his minister, say to you, in God's name, and in Christ's stead, 'Be ye reconciled to God.' What say you? Has God made you willing? Then rejoice! Rejoice, for he has not made you willing without giving you the power to do what he has made you willing to do. Come! Come! This moment thou mayest be as sure of heaven as if thou wert there, if thou castest thyself upon Christ, and hast nothing but Jesus for thy soul's reliance.

8

FAITH AMONG MOCKERS[1]

'He trusted on the Lord that he would deliver him:
let him deliver him, seeing he delighted in him.'
PSALM 22:8

DAVID EXPERIENCED what Paul afterwards so aptly described as 'cruel mockings'. Note the adjective *cruel*: it is well chosen. Mockings may not cut the flesh, but they tear the heart; they may shed no blood, but they cause the mind to bleed internally. Fetters gall the wrists, but the iron of scorn entereth into the soul. Ridicule is a poisoned bullet which goes deeper than the flesh, and strikes the centre of the heart. David in the wilderness hunted by Saul, and on the throne abused by Shimei, knew what it was to be the butt of scorn, the football of contempt. Many a time and oft was he the song of the drunkard, and the byword of the scoffer.

But what have I to do with the son of Jesse? my heart remembers the Son of man. What if David suffered despising and scorn? He knew it but in small measure compared with our blessed Lord. Well is it said, 'The disciple is not above his master, nor the servant above his lord.' It is not wonderful that such an one as David should have to cry, 'My soul is among lions,' when the Lord of all, the perfectly pure and Holy One, was driven to utter the same cry, saying, 'All they that see me laugh me to scorn: they shoot out the lip, they shake the head, saying, He trusted on the Lord that he would deliver him: let him deliver him, seeing he delighted in him.' My brethren and sisters in Christ, if you have to pass through a like painful experience, count it no strange thing, for a strange

[1] Sermon No. 1,767. Preached at the Metropolitan Tabernacle, date not known.

thing it is not. Reproach is the common heritage of the godly. Do not think that this fire which you suffer is the first that ever burned a saint. Others have had to bear the enmity of the world long before you. Remember that, of old, from the first moment when sin came into the world, there were two seeds, the seed of the woman and the seed of the serpent; and between these two seeds there is an enmity of the most deadly kind, which will never cease. It may assume different forms, and it may be held in check by many forces, but it will always continue for ever the same while men are men, and sin is sin, and God and the devil are opposed. It was so, you know, in the house of Abraham: he was a man that walked before God, and was perfect in his generation, and yet in his family there were the two opposing powers: Ishmael, born after the flesh, mocked him that was born after the Spirit. When Rebekah had brought forth twin sons, yet the fact of their being twin sons of holy Isaac did not prevent the enmity that arose between Jacob and Esau. Nothing will prevent the seed of the serpent from exhibiting its spite towards the seed of the woman; even kinship and brotherhood go for little in this strife, in fact a man's foes full often are they of his own household.

Count it no marvel, then, if you are derided! It seems to be a necessity of the holy nature of God that it should incur the enmity of the evil nature of fallen man, and that this evil nature should show itself by direct and bitter attack. Remember 'him that endured such contradiction of sinners against himself, lest ye be wearied and faint in your minds.' Henceforth, bow your shoulders to the yoke; expect that if you follow the Crucified you will have to bear the cross, for so it will be. I trust that our present meditation may be useful to any of God's servants who are feeling the sharp lash of envious tongues, that they may not be driven from their steadfastness thereby. If any in their hearts are bowed down because they are conscious that possibly they have given the scoffers some opportunity to mock at them, may they even in this take heart, for David had done so, and yet he was not crushed by the blasphemies of the wicked.

The first thing to which I shall call your attention at this time is, that a truly gracious man is like David and like the Lord Jesus, in that HIS TRUST IN GOD IS KNOWN. Even the enemies of this holy man who is mentioned in the text, and, as I interpret it, even the enemies of our divine Lord and Master, never denied that he trusted in God. This, indeed, is the commencement of their scoff: 'He trusted on the Lord that he would deliver him.' From which I gather that every gracious man should have an apparent, manifest, public trust in God. He should not merely trust him in his heart alone, but that trust should so enter into his entire nature that he does not conceal it nor think of concealing it. He should be so open in the avowal of his confidence that his enemies, before whom he is naturally restrained and on his guard, nevertheless are able to spy out this precious thing within him, and are forced to bear their witness, though it be mockingly and jestingly, that 'He trusted on the Lord.' Such a testimony is all the more valuable as coming from an enemy. You know our character is not likely to be drawn too prettily by those who hate us; the utmost will be sure to be said against us; but if even our enemies say of us, 'He trusted on the Lord,' we may be very thankful that we have so lived as to extort this testimony from their lips.

What, then, ought a child of God to do in order to show that he really does trust in the Lord? How did Jesus do this? Well, I think that in our Lord's case it was *his wonderful calmness* which compelled everybody to see that 'he trusted on the Lord.' You never find him in a flurry; he is never worried nor confused. He is beset behind and before with men who try to catch him, but he is as self-possessed as if he spoke among friends. He does not appear to be the least upon his guard, and yet instead of their catching him, before long he either catches them, or else they retire saying, 'Never man spake like this man.' He was always cool, peaceful, ready, self-composed. You notice his inward quietude not only when enemies are round about him, but when he is surrounded by a great mob of people all hungry, starving, famishing: he breaks the bread and multiplies it; but not before he has made them all sit down on the green grass by hundreds and by fifties. He will have them in companies, arranged in ranks, for convenient distribution; and when they are all placed in order, as if it had been a well-marshalled royal entertainment, then it is that he takes the bread, and, looking up to heaven, with all deliberation asks a blessing, and breaks and gives the food to the disciples. The disciples make no scramble of it: it is an orderly festival, and the thousands are all fed in order due, in majestic decorum; for Christ was calm, and therefore master of the situation. He never looks as if he had fallen into difficulties, and then adopted expedients to get out of them; but his whole life is pre-arranged and ordered in the most prudent and peaceful manner. Nothing upon this earth, although he was so reduced that he had nowhere to lay his head, although he was sometimes so weary that he sat down upon a well to rest, could put him out of the way, or disarrange his perfect collectedness. He was always ready for every emergency; in fact, nothing was an emergency to him.

What a beautiful picture that is of Christ on board ship in a storm! While they that are with him are afraid that they will go down, that the wind will blow them into the water, or blow the water over them, so that they will certainly be drowned, what is he doing? Why, he is asleep: not because he forgot them – no; but because he knew that the vessel was in the great Father's hands. It was his time for sleep; he was weary and needed it, and so he carried out that which was the nearest duty, and in all peacefulness laid his head on a pillow, and slumbered. His sleep ought to have made them feel at ease. Whenever the captain can afford to go to sleep, the passengers may go to sleep too. Depend upon it, he that manages everything would not have gone to bed if he had not felt that it was all right in the hands of the Highest, who at any moment could stay the raging storm.

I wish we could be similarly restful; for then even our enemies would say of us, 'He trusted on the Lord.' I wish we could have that steadfast, imperturbable frame of mind, in which our Lord untied the knots wherewith his foes would have bound him; for then our assailants would marvel at our quiet confidence. Jesus knew no hurry, but calmly and deliberately he met each matter as it came, and grandly kept himself free from all entanglement. Oh, for the holy quiet which would prevent our going about our business in haste! 'He that believeth shall not make haste,' but do everything as in the infinite leisure of the Eternal, who never is before his time, and never is behind. If we could do that, and did not get so flurried and worried, and tossed about and driven to our wit's end, then our enemies would say with astonishment, 'He trusted on the Lord.'

Brethren, this ought also to come out not merely in our calm and quiet manner, but also *by our distinct avowal*. I do not think that any man has a right to be a secret believer in the Lord Jesus Christ at this time. You will tell me that Nicodemus was so, that Joseph of Arimathaea was so, and I answer 'Yes;' but therein they are not our exemplars. These weak brethren were forgiven and strengthened; but we may not therefore presume. Times, however, are different now: by the death of Christ the thoughts of many hearts were revealed, and from that day those secret disciples were among the foremost to avow their faith. Nicodemus brought the spices, and Joseph of Arimathaea went in boldly and begged the body of Jesus. Since that day when the Christ was openly revealed upon the cross, the thoughts of other men's hearts are revealed too; and it is not now permissible for us to play hide-and-seek with Christ. No; 'He that believeth *and is baptized* shall be saved;' 'He that with his heart believeth and *with his mouth maketh confession of him,* shall be saved.' The open confession is constantly, in Scripture, joined with the secret faith. The Lord Jesus Christ puts it, 'He that denieth me before men, him will I deny;' and if you read it, the text sets denying in opposition to confession, so that it really means, 'He that does not confess me before men, him will I not confess when I come in the glory of the Father.' Our Lord does not reckon upon leading a body of followers who will always keep behind the hedge, hiding themselves in holes and corners whenever there is anything to be done for his glory, and only running out at meal-times when there is something to be got for themselves. I know some professors of that sort, but I have very little to say to their credit: they are a cowardly crew.

No, no. We ought distinctly to declare that we believe in God, and we should take opportunities, as prudence dictates, of telling to our friends and neighbours what our experience has been about trusting in God, telling them of deliverances we have received, of prayers which have been answered, and of many other tokens for good which have come to us as the result of our faith in God. To trust in man is a thing of which we may be ashamed, for we find man to be as a broken reed; or as a spear that pierces us to our heart when we lean thereon; but blessed are they that trust in the Lord, for they shall be as trees planted by the rivers of water, they shall bring forth their fruit in their season, and even their leaf shall not wither. God, in whom they trust, will honour their faith, and bless them yet more and more; let them therefore honour their God, and never hesitate to speak well of his name. So, then, I say first a calm belief, and, secondly, an open avowal should cause even our adversaries to know that we have trusted in the Lord.

And, then, I will add to that, that *our general conduct should reveal our faith*. The whole of our life should show that we are men who rejoice in the Lord, for trusting the Lord, as I understand it, is not a thing for Sundays and for places of worship alone: we are to trust in the Lord about everything. If I trust the Lord about my soul I must trust him about my body, about my wife, about my children, and all my domestic and business affairs. It would have been a terrible thing if the Lord had drawn a black line around our religious life, and had said, 'You may trust me about that, but with household matters I will have nothing to do.' We need the whole of life to be within the ring-fence of divine care. The perfect bond of divine love must tie up the whole bundle of our affairs, or the whole will slip away. Faith is a thing for the closet, and the parlour, and the counting-house, and the farmhouse; it is a light for dark days, and a shade for bright days: you may carry it with you everywhere, and every-where it shall be your help. Oh, that we did so trust in the Lord that people noticed it as much as they notice our temper, our dress, or our tone. The pity is that too often we go forward helter-skelter, following our own wisdom, whereas we ought to say, 'No, I must wait a little while, till I ask counsel of the Lord.' It should be seen and known that we are distinctly waiting upon God for guidance. What a stir this would make in some quarters! I wish that without any desire to be Pharisaical, or to display our piety, we nevertheless did unconsciously show the great principle which governs us. Just as one man will say, 'Excuse me, I must consult a friend,' or, 'I must submit the case to my solicitor,' so it ought to be habitual with a Christian before he replies to an important matter, to demand a moment wherein he may wait upon God and obtain direction. In any case I wish that it may be so usual with us to ask guidance from above that it may be noticed as our habit to trust on the Lord.

Once more, I think this ought to come out most distinctly *in our behaviour during times of trouble;* for then it is that our adversaries are most likely to notice it. You, dear sister, have lost a child. Well now, remember that you are a Christian woman, and sorrow not as those that are without hope. Do let the difference be real and true, and do not be ashamed that others should observe it. When your neighbour lost her child it occasioned a quarrel between her and God, but it is not so with you, is it? Will you quarrel with God about your baby? Oh, no; you love him too well. And you, brother, you are perplexed in business, and you know what a worldling does: if he has nothing more than outward religion, he complains bitterly that God deals hardly with him, and he quarrels with God; or, perhaps, to make things better, he does what he ought not to do in business, and makes them a great deal worse. Many a man has plunged into rash speculations until he has destroyed himself commercially; but you, as a Christian man, must take matters calmly and quietly: it is not yours to specu-late, but to confide. Your strength lies in saying – 'The Lord gave, and the Lord hath taken away; blessed be the name of the Lord.' You must not be so eager to be rich that you would put forth your hand to do iniquity in order to seize the golden apples: that is the reverse of faith.

You are now to play the man, and in the power of the Holy Ghost you are now with resignation – with more than that – with a sweet acquiescence in the Divine will – to show men how a Christian can behave himself. I have never admired Addison's words as some have done, who, when he came to die, sent for a lord of his acquaintance, and said, 'See how a Christian can *die*.' There is a little parade about *that;* but I do desire that every Christian should say in his soul, 'I will show men how a Christian can *live*. I will let them see what it is to live by faith in the Son of God who loved me, and gave himself for me. Those who do not believe there is a God shall yet be led to feel there must be a God, because my faith in him doth speed so well, and I obtain such unnumbered blessings as the result of it.' I say, most earnestly, that especially in the time of sorrow and bereavement, when other people are sore put to it because they have lost their joy, and the light of their house is quenched, it is the believer's duty and privilege by his holy calm of heart to show his trust in God. If religion cannot help you in trouble, it is not worth having; if the Spirit of God does not sustain you when you lose your dearest friend, you ought to question whether it is the Spirit of God; you ought to ask, 'Can this be the Spirit which bore up the martyrs at the stake?' if now that you are passing through these waters you are carried away by them? If our faith shines out in dark times, even as the stars are seen by night, then is it well with us.

Oh, that you and I might in all these ways so live that all who see us should know that we are believers in the Lord Jesus Christ! It would be ridiculous if a man went into society with a label on his breast, '*This man trusts in God*', and it would be a pretty clear sign that he needed to be thus ticketed. I would have you shun all distinctive phylacteries in matters of religion as too much flavoured with the leaven of the Pharisees; but when the possession of godliness proclaims its own self, even as a box of precious spikenard tells its own tale, you need not be ashamed of it. Display and ostentation are vicious, but the unrestrained use of influence and example is commendable. In these days when men glory in their unbelief, let us not be bashful with our faith. If, in a free country, men should not persecute an infidel, they certainly ought not to silence a believer. We do not intend to smuggle our religion through the land. It is not contraband, and therefore we shall bear it with us openly in the sight of all men, and let them say if they please, 'He trusted on the Lord.'

II. Secondly, THIS TRUST ON THE PART OF BELIEVING MEN IS NOT UNDERSTOOD BY THE WORLD. 'He trusted on the Lord that he would deliver him.' Observe that they restricted the Saviour's trust to that point – 'He trusted on the Lord *that he would deliver him.*' But now, in the first place, *our faith is not confined to merely receiving from God.* No, brethren, if the Lord does not deliver us we will trust him. See how firmly Shadrach, Meshach, and Abednego stood to it that they would not bow before the image which Nebuchadnezzar had set up: 'Our God whom we serve is able to deliver us from the burning fiery furnace, and he will deliver us out of thine hand, O king. But *if not*, be it known unto thee, O king, that we will not serve thy gods, nor worship the golden image which thou hast set up.' There was great faith in that 'if not'. We must not live and wait upon God with a kind of cupboard love, just as a stray dog might follow a man for bones; but we must speak well of our God even if he scourge us, for therein lies both the truth and the strength of faith. Job has put it – 'Shall we receive good at the hand of God, and shall we not receive evil?' 'The Lord gave, and the Lord hath taken away; blessed be the name of the Lord.' Whatever happens to us, if our faith is the work of the Holy Spirit we shall hold on to our trust in God.

Neither is our faith limited to what men call deliverance. It is a misrepresentation when his enemies say, 'He trusted on the Lord that he would deliver him;' because though it is the truth, it is not the whole truth. Our blessed Lord continued to trust in the Father though the cup did not pass from him, and though no legions of angels were sent to deliver him from Pilate. Though the enemy was permitted to exercise all his malice upon him until his blessed body was nailed to the accursed tree, yet the faith of our divine Lord and Master was not moved from its steadfastness. He trusted in God for something higher than deliverance from death, for he looked beyond the grave, and said, 'Thou wilt not leave my soul in hell, neither wilt thou suffer thine Holy One to see corruption.' In all his pains his heart said, 'It is the Lord, let him do what seemeth him good.'

The blind world cannot understand this. They say, like their father, 'Doth Job fear God for nought?' They insinuate that Christian people trust God for what they get out of him. Now I have often thought that if the devil could have put it the other way he would have been very rejoiced to do so. Suppose he could have said, 'Job serves God for nought,' then the ungodly world would have shouted, 'We told you so. God is a bad Paymaster: his servants may serve him as perfectly as Job, but he never gives them any reward.' Happily the accuser's grumble is of quite the opposite kind. Neither one way nor another is there any pleasing the devil, and it is not a thing we desire to do. Let him put it as he likes. We serve God and we have our reward; but if the Lord does not choose to give us exactly what we look for, still will we trust in him, for it is our delight. It is a misrepresentation to say of a believer that 'he trusted on the Lord *that he would deliver him,'* if he is supposed to trust for no other reason.

And, dear friends, *our faith is not tied to time.* That is the mistake of the statement in the text. They said, 'He trusted on the Lord that he would deliver him' – as much as to say, 'If God does not deliver him *now* his trust will have been a folly, and God will not have answered to his confidence.' But it is not so. Brethren, if we are in the fire tonight, and we are trusting in God, our faith does not mean that we expect to come forth from the furnace at this very hour. Nay, we may not come out tonight, nor tomorrow, nor next month, it may be not for years. We do not tie God down to conditions, and expect him to do this and that, and then if he does not in his wisdom see fit to do it, threaten that we will trust him no more. The very worst we could do would be to make the Eternal God a slave to time, as though he must do everything at our bidding, and measure his divine movements by the ticking of a clock. The Lord did deliver his Son Jesus Christ, but he suffered him to die first; he was put into the grave before he was uplifted from the power of death; and if it had not been that he died and lay in the tomb he could not have had that splendid deliverance which his Father did vouchsafe him when he raised him again from the dead, had he not yielded to death there could have been no resurrection for him or for us.

So, beloved, it may be God has not effected his purpose with you yet, nor has he quite prepared you for the height of blessing to which he has ordained you. Receive what he is going to give you, and take gratefully the painful preliminaries. High palaces must have deep foundations, and it takes a long time to excavate a human soul so deep that God can build a gorgeous palace of grace therein. If it be a mere cottage that the Lord is to build in you, you may escape with small troubles; but if he is going to make you a palace to glorify himself withal, then you may expect to have long trials. Coarse pottery needs not the laborious processes which must be endured by superior vessels. Iron which is to become a sword for a hero must know more of the fire than the metal which lies upon the road as a rail. Your eminence in grace can only come by affliction. Will you not have trust in God if severe trials are ordained for you? Yes, of course you will. The Holy Spirit will be the all-sufficient helper of your infirmities. I say it is misrepresentation if we limit the Holy One of Israel to any form for our deliverance, or to any time for our deliverance. Let not the Lord of love be treated like a child at school, as if he could be taught anything by us!

So, also, *our faith must not judge at all by present circumstances.* The ungodly world judges that God has not delivered us because we are now in trouble, and are at present distressed by it. Oh, how wrongly the world judged of Christ when it judged of him by his condition! Covered with a bloody sweat and groaning out his soul to God beneath the olives at midnight – why, they that passed by who did not know him must have judged him to be a man accursed of God. 'See,' they would have said, 'we never heard of a man that sweat blood before – sweat blood in prayer; and yet listen to his groaning; he is not heard by God, for evidently the cup does not pass from him.' If any man had looked at our Lord Jesus when he was on the cross and had heard him cry, 'My God, my God, why hast thou forsaken me?' they would have certainly concluded that he was the most ungracious and undeserving of men; for had he been a saint, surely, they say, God would not have forsaken him. Yes, but you see they only saw a little of our blessed Master's career; they only looked upon a span of his existence, what a grievous error it was to have estimated his life by his brief passion, knowing nothing of its grand intent!

See him now while harps unnumbered sound his praises and all heaven rejoices to behold his glory, and the Father looks upon him with ineffable delight! This is the same Jesus who was crucified! What think you of him now? You must not measure a man by a little bit of his life, nor even by the whole of his earthly career; for it is nothing compared with the hidden future of his life in eternity. These men measured David's faith, and measure our faith by what they see of us on one day: we are sick, we are sorry, we are poor, we are troubled, and then they say, 'We told you so! This faith of theirs is not worth having, or else they would not fare so roughly or be found in so much heaviness.' Faith and feeling are in contrast. Outward circumstances must never be made the tests of the value of pious trust in our God. We must not judge God by his dealings with us nor judge ourselves thereby; but let us still hold on to this pure, simple faith that the Lord is good to Israel. Let us love the Lord for a whole eternity of his love, and then for everything, for every turn of his hand, for every frown and stroke and rebuke; for he is good in everything, unalterably good. If with this faith of ours we are praying and pleading and God does not answer us, does not help us, but leaves us in the dark, yet still let not our trust waver. If any man walk in darkness and see no light, let him trust and trust on until the light shall come.

So, then, we have just touched upon two points – that a true man's faith is soon made known, but that, though it be known, it is usually misunderstood. We live among blind men; let us not be angry because they cannot see.

III. Thirdly, THIS TRUE FAITH WILL, IN ALL PROBABILITY, BE MOCKED AT SOME TIME OR OTHER. It is a great honour to a man to trust in God, and so to have his name written upon the Arch of Triumph which Paul has erected in the eleventh chapter of the Hebrews, where you see name after name of the heroes who served God by faith. It is a glorious thing to mingle our bones with those who are buried in that mausoleum which bears this epitaph, 'These all died in faith.' It is an honourable thing to be a believer in God, but there are some who think the very reverse, and these begin to scoff at the believer. Sometimes *they scoff at faith itself*: they count faith itself to be a folly of weak minds. Or else they insult over one particular Christian's faith. 'Oh,' they say, 'he professes to trust in God. This man talks after this mad fashion! Why, he is a working man like other people – works in a shop along with me. What has he to do with trusting God any more than I have? He is conceited and fanatical.' Or in other circles they cry, 'This is a man of business, he keeps a shop, and I dare say he knows as much of the tricks of the trade as we do, and yet he talks about trusting in God. No doubt he pretends to this faith to win religious customers.'

Sometimes the mockery comes from one of your own family, for faith's foes live in the same house with her. The husband has been known to say to his wife, 'Ridiculous nonsense, your trusting in God!' Ay, and parents have said the like to holy children; and, alas! children have grown up to speak in like fashion to their parents to the wounding of their hearts. As if faith in God were a thing that could be scoffed at, instead of being the most wise, and proper, and rational thing under heaven. Faith in God is a thing to be reverenced rather than reviled. True religion is sanctified common-sense. It is the most common-sense thing in the world to put your trust in One that cannot lie. If I trust myself, or trust my fellow man, I am thought to be in the first case self-reliant, and in the second case I am judged to have a charitable disposition; yet in either case I shall, sooner or later, prove my folly; but if I trust God, who can bring a reason against my confidence? What is there to be ridiculed in a man's trusting his Maker? Can HE fail that created the blue heavens, that settled the foundations of the earth and poured out the waters of the great sea? Can the Almighty retract his promise because he is unable to fulfil it? Can he break his word because circumstances master him and prevent his performance of it? 'Trust ye in the Lord for ever: for in the Lord Jehovah is everlasting strength.' The day shall come when it will be known by all intelligent beings that unbelief of God is folly, but that faith in the Eternal is essential wisdom. God give us more faith in himself. No doubt we may expect to have all the more of the laughter of the ungodly, who will make a spectacle of us for our faith: but what of that? We can bear mockery and much more for his sake who died for us.

And then *men scoff at the very idea of divine interposition.* They judge the Lord's deliverance to be the main point of our faith. 'He trusted God that he would deliver him.' 'Look,' they say, 'he fancies that God will deliver *him*, as if the Creator had not something else to do besides looking after *him*, poor miserable creature that he is! He is nothing to God – a mere speck – the insect of an hour, and yet he trusts in God to interfere on his behalf.' The philosophers laugh whenever you speak of divine interposition, and count that we must be in the last stage of lunacy to expect anything of the kind. They believe in laws, they say – irreversible, immutable laws, that grind on, like the great cogs of a machine which, when once they are set in motion, tear everything to pieces that comes in their way. They do not believe that God fulfils promises, or answers prayers, or delivers his people. Their God is a dead force, without mind, or thought, or love, or care. He who in nature acts according to law is yet believed to have no power to carry out his own word, which must always be law to a truthful being. Why, some of us are as sure that God has interposed for us as if he had rent the heavens and thrust forth his right hand visibly before the eyes of all beholders. The wise ones laugh at us for this, but we are not abashed; rather do we reply, 'Laugh if you like, and as long as you like; but we daily receive unnumbered blessings from God in answer to our cries, and your laughter no more affects us than the noise of the dogs by the Nile disturbs the flow of the river. We shall believe for all your merriment, and if it please you to go on with your laughter we also will go on with our faith.' The object of the ungodly man's scorn is the idea that God should ever interfere to help his people in human affairs, but do you stand to it, O true believers; for he does still show himself strong on the behalf of them that trust in him. Let them say, and laugh at you as they say it, 'He trusted on the Lord that he would deliver him;' but let none of these things move you.

Further, we have known this mockery to extend to *all kinds of faith in the divine love.* 'Let him deliver him,' they say, 'seeing that he delighted in him.' Perhaps you have unwisely told out the tale of God's special love to those who are now making merriment of you; you have cast your pearls before swine, and they turn again to rend you. They say, 'This man says God loves him above others; that he chose him before the world began; that he redeemed him from among men with the blood of Christ; that he has called him by his Holy Spirit; that he has admitted him into his secrets and made him his child,' and then they laugh again right lustily, as if it were a rare jest.

How the world rages against electing love! It cannot endure any speciality in grace. The idea that one man should be more beloved of heaven than another it scouts as horrible. The heathen could not make out a certain brave saint because he called himself Theophorus, or 'Godbearer'; but he stuck to it that he was so, and this made his foes the more wrathful. God dwelt in him, he said, and he would not give up his happy belief, therefore they ceased not to mock. It was a carrying out of our text, 'Let him deliver him, seeing he delighteth in him.' Well, well; we can afford to bear these mockings; for if we are beloved by a king it will not much matter if we are sneered at by his subjects; if we are beloved by God it is a small concern though all men should make us the subject of their jest.

Ungodly men are exceedingly apt to find *amusement in the trials involved in the life and walk of faith*. Their cry of 'Let him deliver him' implies that their victim was in serious difficulty from which he could not extricate himself. This is no novelty to the believer, but it makes rare fun for the ungodly. What is the good of faith if the believer suffers like others, and endures the same pains, and losses and diseases as others? So the men of the world argue. They would be believers too if it would bring them in a fortune, or a handsome salary, or at least a loaded table and a full cup. But when they see a saint on the dunghill with Job, or in the pit with Joseph, or in the dungeon with Jeremiah, or among the dogs with Lazarus, they sneer and cry, Is this the reward of piety? Is this the recompense of godliness? They like to spy us out in our time of trouble and taunt us with our confidence in God; and, alas, there is so much unbelief in us that we are all too prone in such seasons to question the justice and faithfulness of the Lord, and to say with David, 'Verily I have cleansed my heart in vain, and washed my hands in innocency.' It seems hard for us to be mocked by the base ones of the earth, to become the song and the byword of the ungodly; yet this has happened to the excellent of the earth and will happen yet again. Set your account that this is a part of the covenanted heritage, and accept it with joy for Christ's sake.

IV. Now, I must close with this point (though there is much more to be said): THE TIME SHALL COME WHEN THE FAITH OF THE MAN WHO HAS TRUSTED IN GOD SHALL BE ABUNDANTLY JUSTIFIED. I think it is no small thing to have *the ungodly bearing witness* that 'He trusted in God that he would deliver him.' I have known what it is to be exceedingly grateful to ungodly men for helping me to believe that I am truly a child of God. Somebody, years ago, uttered an atrocious lie against me – an abominable slander. I was very low and heavy of spirit at the time, but when I read it I clapped my hands for joy, for I felt, 'Now I have one of the marks and seals of a child of God, for it is written, "Blessed are ye, when men shall revile you, and persecute you, and shall say all manner of evil against you falsely, for my sake."' The love of the Lord's brethren and the hatred of the Lord's enemies are two things to be desired. We may gather that we are not of the wicked when they will not endure us in their company, when our very presence irritates them, and they begin to rail and jeer. It has happened unto us even as Jesus said: 'If ye were of the world, the world would love his own: but because ye are not of the world, but I have chosen you out of the world, therefore the world hateth you.' So that there is justification, as it were, of our faith even from the lips of adversaries, and we ought to be thankful for it instead of being downcast about it.

Another justification awaits us, and in due season it will come. Brethren, the day will come when *God will deliver his people.* You will be brought out of your trouble – it may not be immediately, but it will be seasonably. You may most wisely in the meantime learn to glory in your tribulation; your bitters shall turn into sweets, and your losses into gains; your sorrows shall be your joys, your struggles your triumphs – perhaps in this life this trans-formation may occur, even as the Lord gave to Job twice as much as he had before; but certainly in the life to come you will find the tables turned. Then, what will the ungodly say? They say now, 'He trusted on God that he would deliver him;' but they will be compelled to say as they gnash their teeth, 'God has delivered him.'

Whereas the ungodly ridicule the idea that God delights in his people, the day shall come when they shall be made to see that he does delight in them. When the Lord appears on behalf of his people, and gives them 'beauty for ashes, the oil of joy for mourning', the wicked shall gnash their teeth, and be filled with confusion. When the Lord shall turn again our captivity, even our most desperate foes shall be made to say, 'The Lord hath done great things for them.' They shall wonder and be sore vexed to see how the Lord hath a favour to his chosen. If they do not see it in this life, oh, what an exhibition ungodly men will see of his delight in his people in the world to come! Dives sees Lazarus in Abraham's bosom: what a sight for him! They that scoff at God's poor people here, shall see them exalted to be kings and priests, to reign with Christ for ever and ever, and what will they say then? What can they say but be compelled to bear witness that their faith was justified.

Brethren, at the last great day ungodly men will be witnesses on behalf of the saints. If any doubt whether the saints trusted in God, the wicked will be compelled to come forward and say, 'They did trust, for we laughed at them for it.' Of this and that man they shall say, 'He trusted on God that he would deliver him.' In that day the unbelieving will be swift witnesses against themselves; for as they ridiculed the children of God here, they will have it read out before them as evidence of their enmity against the Lord: and how will they answer it? A man is generally much grieved with any one who injures his children. I have known a man behave patiently to his neighbours, and put up with a great deal from them; but when one of them has struck his child I have seen him incensed to the last degree. He has said, 'I cannot stand that, I will not look on and see my own children ill-used.' The Lord says, 'He that touches you touches the apple of my eye.' Jesus rises from his throne in glory and stands up indignantly while his servant Stephen is being stoned. If I had no other amusement whatever, I would not for merriment sake mock the people of God; for it will go hard with those who make unhallowed mirth out of the saints of the Host High. If any of you have ever done so – if you have done so ignorantly – the Lord forgive you, and bring you to be numbered among his people, as was Saul of Tarsus; and if any of you have done so knowingly, be humble and penitent, and the Lord will forgive you and receive you amongst his people.

But whether ye revile or flatter, it is all one to us. We are at a pass with you: we do trust in God that he will deliver us, and we cannot be removed from this confidence. O ye mockers, we will not be fooled out of our hope, nor jested out of our peace. We cannot find any one like our God to trust to, and so we will not depart from him in life or death, but will rest in him, come what may, even till we see him face to face.

9

'LET HIM DELIVER HIM NOW'[1]

He trusted in God; let him deliver him now, if he will
have him: for he said I am the Son of God.
MATTHEW 27:43

THESE WORDS are a fulfilment of the prophecy contained in
the twenty-second Psalm. Read from the seventh verse – 'All they
that see me laugh me to scorn: they shoot out the lip, they shake
the head, saying, He trusted on the Lord that he would deliver
him: let him deliver him, seeing he delighted in him.' Thus to the
letter doth our Lord answer to the ancient prophecy.

It is very painful to the heart to picture our blessed Master in
his death-agonies, surrounded by a ribald multitude, who watched
him and mocked him, made sport of his prayer and insulted his
faith. Nothing was sacred to them: they invaded the Holy of holies
of his confidence in God, and taunted him concerning that faith
in Jehovah which they were compelled to admit. See, dear friends,
what an evil thing is sin, since the Sin-bearer suffers so bitterly to
make atonement for it! See, also, the shame of sin, since even the
Prince of Glory, when bearing the consequences of it, is covered
with contempt! Behold, also, how he loved us! For our sake he
'endured the cross, despising the shame.' He loved us so much that
even scorn of the most cruel sort he deigned to bear, that he might
take away our shame and enable us to look up unto God.

Beloved, the treatment of our Lord Jesus Christ by men is the
clearest proof of total depravity which can possibly be required or
discovered. Those must be stony hearts indeed which can laugh at

---

[1] Sermon No. 2,029. Preached at the Metropolitan Tabernacle on Sunday
morning, 17 June 1888.

a dying Saviour, and mock even at his faith in God! Compassion would seem to have deserted humanity, while malice sat supreme on the throne. Painful as the picture is, it will do you good to paint it. You will need neither canvas, nor brush, nor palette, nor colours. Let your thoughts draw the outline, and your love fill in the detail; I shall not complain if imagination heightens the colouring. The Son of God, whom angels adore with veiled faces, is pointed at with scornful fingers by men who thrust out the tongue and mockingly exclaim, 'He trusted on the Lord that he would deliver him: let him deliver him, seeing he delighted in him.'

While thus we see our Lord in his sorrow and his shame as our substitute, we must not forget that he also is there as our representative. That which appears in many a psalm to relate to David is found in the Gospels to refer to Jesus, our Lord. Often and often the student of the Psalm will say to himself, 'Of whom speaketh the prophet this?' He will have to disentangle the threads sometimes, and mark off that which belongs to David and that which relates to the Son of God; and frequently he will not be able to disentangle the threads at all, because they are one, and may relate both to David, and to David's Lord. This is meant to show us that the life of Christ is an epitome of the life of his people. He not only suffers for us as our substitute, but he suffers before us as our pattern. In him we see what we have in our measure to endure. 'As he is, so are we also in this world.' We also must be crucified to the world, and we may look for somewhat of those tests of faith and taunts of derision which go with such a crucifixion. 'Marvel not if the world hate you.' You, too, must suffer without the gate. Not for the world's redemption, but for the accomplishment of divine purposes in you, and through you to the sons of men, you must be made to know the cross and its shame. Christ is the mirror of the church. What the head endured every member of the body will also have to endure in its measure. Let us read the text in this light, and come to it saying to ourselves, 'Here we see what Jesus suffered in our stead, and we learn hereby to love him with all our souls. Here, too, we see, as in a prophecy, how great things we are to suffer for his sake at the hands of men.' May the Holy Spirit help us in our meditation, so that at the close of it we may more ardently love our Lord, who suffered for us, and may the more carefully arm ourselves with the same mind which enabled him to endure such contradiction of sinners against himself.

Coming at once to the text, first, *observe the acknowledgment* with which the text begins: 'He trusted in God.' The enemies of Christ admitted his faith in God. Secondly, consider *the test which is the essence of the taunt:* 'Let him deliver him, if he will have him.' When we have taken those two things into our minds, then let us for a while consider *the answer* to that test and taunt: God does assuredly deliver his people: those who trust in him have no reason to be ashamed of their faith.

I. First, then, my beloved brethren, you who know the Lord by faith and live by trusting in him, let me invite you to OBSERVE THE ACKNOWLEDGMENT which these mockers made of our Lord's faith: 'He trusted in God.' Yet the Saviour did not wear any peculiar garb or token by which he let men know that he trusted in God. He was not a recluse, neither did he join some little knot of separatists, who boasted their peculiar trust in Jehovah. Although our Saviour was separate from sinners, yet he was eminently a man among men, and he went in and out among the multitude as one of themselves. His one peculiarity was that 'he trusted in God.' He was so perfectly a man that, although he was undoubtedly a Jew, there were no Jewish peculiarities about him. Any nation might claim him; but no nation could monopolize him. The characteristics of our humanity are so palpably about him that he belongs to all mankind. I admire the Welsh sister who was of opinion that the Lord Jesus must be Welsh. When they asked her how she proved it, she said that he always spoke to her heart in Welsh. Doubtless it was so, and I can, with equal warmth, declare that he always speaks to me in English. Brethren from Germany, France, Sweden, Italy – you all claim that he speaks to you in your own tongue. This was the one thing which distinguished him among men – 'He trusted in God', and he lived such a life as naturally grows out of faith in the Eternal Lord. This peculiarity had been visible even to that ungodly multitude who least of all cared to perceive a spiritual point of character. Was ever any other upon a cross thus saluted by the mob who watched his execution? Had these scorners ever mocked anyone before for such a matter as this? I believe not. Yet faith had been so manifest in our Lord's daily life that the crowd cried out aloud, 'He trusted in God.'

How did they know? I suppose they could not help seeing that *he made much of God* in his teaching, in his life, and in his miracles. Whenever Jesus spoke it was always godly talk; and if it was not always distinctly about God, it was always about things that related to God, that came from God, that led to God, that magnified God. A man may be fairly judged by that which he makes most of. The ruling passion is a fair gauge of the heart. What a soul-ruler faith is! It sways the man as the rudder guides the ship. When a man once gets to live by faith in God, it tinctures his thoughts, it masters his purposes, it flavours his words, it puts a tone into his actions, and it comes out in everything by ways and means most natural and unconstrained, till men perceive that they have to do with a man who makes much of God. The un-believing world says outright that there is no God, and the less impudent, who admit his existence, put him down at a very low figure, so low that it does not affect their calculations; but to the true Christian, God is not only much, but all. To our Lord Jesus, God was all in all; and when you come to estimate God as he did, then the most careless onlooker will soon begin to say of you, 'He trusted in God.'

In addition to observing that Jesus made much of God, men came to note that he was *a trusting man, and not self-confident*. Certain persons are very proud because they are self-made men. I will do them the credit to admit that they heartily worship their maker. Self made them, and they worship self. We have among us individuals who are self-sufficient, and almost all-sufficient; they sneer at those who do not succeed, for *they* can succeed anywhere at anything The world to them is a football which they can kick where they like. If they do not rise to the very highest eminence it is simply out of pity to the rest of us, who ought to have a chance. A vat of sufficiency ferments within their ribs! There was nothing of that sort of thing in our Lord. Those who watched him did not say that he had great self-reliance and a noble spirit of self-confidence. No, no! They said, 'He trusted in God.' Indeed it was so. The words that he spake he spake not of himself, and the great deeds that he did he never boasted of, but said 'the Father that dwelleth in me, he doeth the works.' He was a truster in God, not a boaster in self. Brethren and sisters, I desire that you and I may be just of that order. Self-confidence is the death of confidence in God; reliance upon talent, tact, experience, and things of that kind, kills faith. Oh that we may know what faith means, and so look out of ourselves and quit the evil confidence which looks within!

On the other hand, we may wisely remember that, while our Lord Jesus was not self-reliant, *he trusted, and was by no means despondent:* he was never discouraged. He neither questioned his commission, nor despaired of fulfilling it. He never said, 'I must give it up: I can never succeed.' No; 'He trusted in God.' And this is a grand point in the working of faith, that while it keeps us from self-conceit, it equally preserves us from enfeebling fear. When our blessed Lord set his face like a flint; when, being baffled, he returned to the conflict; when, being betrayed, he still persevered in his love, then men could not help seeing that he trusted in God. His faith was not mere repetition of a creed, or profession of belief, but it was childlike reliance upon the Most High. May ours be of the same order!

It is evident that the Lord Jesus *trusted in God openly,* since even yonder gibing crowd proclaimed it. Some good people try to exercise faith on the sly: they practice it in snug corners, and in lonely hours, but they are afraid to say much before others, for fear their faith should not see the promise fulfilled. They dare not say, with David, 'My soul shall make her boast in the Lord: the humble shall hear thereof, and be glad.' This secrecy robs God of his honour. Brethren, we do not glorify our God as he ought to be glorified. Let us trust in him, and own it. Wherefore should we be ashamed? Let us throw down the gauge of battle to earth and hell. God, the true and faithful, deserves to be trusted without limit. Trust your all with him, and be not ashamed of having done so. Our Saviour was not ashamed of trusting in his God. On the cross he cried, 'Thou didst make me hope when I was upon my mother's breast.' Jesus lived by faith. We are sure that he did, for in the Epistle to the Hebrews he is quoted as saying, 'I will put my trust in him.' If so glorious a personage as the only begotten Son of God lived here by faith in God, how are you and I to live except by trust in God? If we live unto God, this is the absolute necessity of our spiritual life: 'the just shall live by faith.' Shall we be ashamed of that which brings life to us? The cruel ones who saw Jesus die did not say, 'He now and then trusted in God;' nor 'he trusted in the Lord years ago;' but they admitted that faith in God was the constant tenor of his life: they could not deny it. Even though, with malicious cruelty, they turned it into a taunt, yet they did not cast a question upon the fact that 'he trusted in God.' Oh, I want you so to live that those who dislike you most may, nevertheless, know that you do trust in God! When you come to die, may your dear children say of you, 'Our dear mother did trust in the Lord'! May that boy, who has gone furthest away from Christ, and grieved your heart the most, nevertheless say in his heart, 'There may be hypocrites in the world, but my dear father does truly trust in God'! Oh, that our faith may be known unmistakably! We do not wish it to be advertised to our own honour. That be far from our minds. But yet we would have it known that others may be encouraged, and that God may be glorified. If nobody else trusts in God, let us do so; and thus may we uplift a testimony to the honour of his faithfulness. When we die, may this be our epitaph – 'He trusted in God.'

David, in the twenty-second Psalm, represents the enemies as saying of our Lord – 'He trusted on the Lord that he would deliver him.' This *practical faith* is sure to be known wherever it is in operation, because it is exceedingly rare. Multitudes of people have a kind of faith in God, but it does not come to the practical point of trusting that God will deliver them. I see upon the newspaper placards, *'Startling News! People in the Planets!'* Not a very practical discovery. For many a day there has been a tendency to refer God's promises and our faith to the planets, or somewhere beyond this present everyday life. We say to ourselves, 'Oh yes, God delivers his people.' We mean that he did so in the days of Moses, and possibly he may be doing so now in some obscure island of the sea. Ah me! The glory of faith lies in its being fit for everyday wear. Can it be said of you, 'He trusted in God, that he would deliver him'? Have you faith of the kind which will make you lean upon the Lord in poverty, in sickness, in bereavement, in persecution, in slander, in contempt? Have you a trust in God to bear you up in holy living at all costs, and in active service even beyond your strength? Can you trust in God definitely about this and that? Can you trust about food, and raiment, and home? Can you trust God even about your shoes, that they shall be iron and brass, and about the hairs of your head that they are all numbered? What we need is less theory and more actual trust in God.

The faith of the text was personal: 'that he would *deliver him.*' Blessed is that faith which can reach its arm of compassion around the world, but that faith must begin at home. Of what use were the longest arm if it were not fixed to the man himself at the shoulder? If you have no faith about yourself, what faith can you have about others? 'He trusted on the Lord that he would deliver him.' Come, beloved, have you such a faith in the living God? Do you trust in God through Christ Jesus that he will save you? Yes, you poor, unworthy one, the Lord will deliver you if you trust him. Yes, poor woman, or unknown man, the Lord can help you in your present trouble, and in every other, and he will do so if you trust him to that end. May the Holy Spirit lead you to first trust the Lord Jesus for the pardon of sin, and then to trust in God for all things.

Let us pause a minute. Let a man trust in God; not in fiction but in fact, and he will find that he has solid rock under his feet. Let him trust about his own daily needs and trials, and rest assured that the Lord will actually appear for him, and he will not be disappointed. Such a trust in God is a very *reasonable* thing; its absence is most unreasonable. If there be a God, he knows all about my case. If he made my ear he can hear me; if he made my eye he can see me; and therefore he perceives my condition. If he be my Father, as he says he is, he will certainly care for me, and will help me in my hour of need if he can. We are sure that he can, for he is omnipotent. Is there anything unreasonable, then, in trusting in God that he will deliver us? I venture to say that if all the forces in the universe were put together, and all the kindly intents of all who are our friends were put together, and we were then to rely upon those united forces and intents, we should not have a thousandth part so much justification for our confidence as when we depend upon God, whose intents and forces are infinitely greater than those of all the world beside. 'It is better to trust in the Lord than to put confidence in man; it is better to trust in the Lord than to put confidence in princes.' If you view things in the white light of pure reason, it is infinitely more reasonable to trust in the living God than in all his creatures put together.

Certainly, dear friends, it is extremely *comfortable* to trust in God. I find it so, and therefore speak. To roll your burden upon the Lord, since he will sustain you, is a blessed way of being quit of care. We know him to be faithful, and as powerful as he is faithful; and our dependence upon him is the solid foundation of a profound peace.

While it is comfortable, it is also *uplifting*. If you trust in men, the best of men, you are likely to be lowered by your trust. We are apt to cringe before those who patronize us. If your prosperity depends upon a person's smile, you are tempted to pay homage even when it is undeserved. The old saying mentions a certain person as 'knowing on which side his bread is buttered.' Thousands are practically degraded by their trusting in men. But when our reliance is upon the living God we are raised by it, and elevated both morally and spiritually. You may bow in deepest reverence before God, and yet there will be no fawning. You may lie in the dust before the Majesty of heaven, and yet not be dishonoured by your humility; in fact, it is our greatness to be nothing in the presence of the Most High.

This confidence in God makes men *strong*. I should advise the enemy not to oppose the man who trusts in God. In the long run he will be beaten, as Haman found it with Mordecai. He had been warned of this by Zeresh, his wife, and his wise men, who said, 'If Mordecai be of the seed of the Jews, before whom thou hast begun to fall, thou shalt not prevail against him, but shalt surely fall before him.' Contend not with a man who has God at his back. Years ago the Mentonese desired to break away from the dominion of the Prince of Monaco. They therefore drove out his agent. The prince came with his army, not a very great one, it is true, but still formidable to the Mentonese. I know not what the high and mighty princeling was not going to do; but the news came that the King of Sardinia was coming up in the rear to help the Mentonese, and therefore his lordship of Monaco very prudently retired to his own rock. When a believer stands out against evil he may be sure that the Lord of hosts will not be far away. The enemy shall hear the dash of his horse-hoof and the blast of his trumpet, and shall flee before him. Wherefore be of good courage, and compel the world to say of you, 'He trusted in the Lord that he would deliver him.'

II. Secondly, I want you to follow me briefly in considering THE TEST WHICH IS THE ESSENCE OF THE TAUNT which was hurled by the mockers against our Lord – 'Let him deliver him now, if he will have him.'

Such a test will come to all believers. It may come as a taunt from enemies; it will certainly come as a trial of your faith. The arch-enemy will assuredly hiss out, 'Let him deliver him, seeing he delighted in him.'

This taunt has about it *the appearance of being very logical*, and indeed in a measure so it is. If God has promised to deliver us, and we have openly professed to believe the promise, it is only natural that others should say, 'Let us see whether he does deliver him. This man believes that the Lord will help him; and he must help him, or else the man's faith is a delusion.' This is the sort of test to which we ourselves would have put others before our conversion, and we cannot object to be proved in the same manner ourselves. Perhaps we incline to run away from the ordeal, but this very shrinking should be a solemn call to us to question the genuineness of that faith which we are afraid to test. 'He trusted on the Lord,' says the enemy, 'that he would deliver him: let him deliver him;' and surely, however malicious the design, there is no escaping from the logic of the challenge.

It is peculiarly painful to have this stern inference driven home to you in the hour of sorrow. Because one cannot deny the fairness of the appeal, it is all the more trying. In the time of depression of spirit it is hard to have one's faith questioned, or the ground on which it stands made a matter of dispute. Either to be mistaken in one's belief, or to have no real faith, or to find the ground of one's faith fail is an exceedingly grievous thing. Yet as our Lord was not spared this painful ordeal, we must not expect to be kept clear of it, and Satan knows well how to work these questions, till the poison of them sets the blood on fire. 'He trusted on the Lord that he would deliver him; let him deliver him;' he hurls this fiery dart into the soul, till the man is sorely wounded, and can scarcely hold his ground.

The taunt is specially *pointed and personal*. It is put thus: 'He trusted on the Lord that he would deliver him: let him deliver *him*.' 'Do not come to us with your fiddle-faddle about God's helping all his chosen. Here is a man who is one of his people, will he help *him*? Do not talk to us big things about Jehovah at the Red Sea, or in the Desert of Sinai, or God helping his people in ages past. Here is a living man before us who trusted in God that he would deliver him: let him deliver *him* now.' You know how Satan will pick out one of the most afflicted, and pointing his fingers at him will cry, 'Let him deliver HIM.' Brethren, the test is fair. God will be true to every believer. If any one child of God could be lost, it would be quite enough to enable the devil to spoil all the glory of God for ever. If one promise of God to one of his people should fail, that one failure would suffice to mar the veracity of the Lord to all eternity; they would publish it in the 'Diabolical Gazette', and in every street of Tophet they would howl it out, 'God has failed. God has broken his promise. God has ceased to be faithful to his people.' It would then be a horrible reproach – 'He trusted in God to deliver him, but he did not deliver him.'

Much emphasis lies in its being *in the present tense:* 'He trusted in God that he would deliver him: let him deliver him *now*.' I see Thee, O Lord Jesus, thou art not now in the wilderness, where the fiend is saying, 'If thou be the Son of God, command that these stones be made bread.' No. Thou art nailed to the tree; thine enemies have hemmed thee in. The legionaries of Rome are at the foot of the cross, the scribes and Pharisees and raging Jews compass thee about. There is no escape from death for thee! Hence their cry – 'Let him deliver him *now*.' Ah, brothers and sisters! this is how Satan assails us, using our present and pressing tribulations as the barbs of his arrows. Yet here also there is reason and logic in the challenge.

If God does not deliver his servants at one time as well as another, he has not kept his promise. For a man of truth is always true, and a promise once given always stands. A promise cannot be broken now and then, and yet the honour of the person giving it be maintained by his keeping it at other times. The word of a true man stands always good: it is good *now*. This is logic, bitter logic, cold-steel logic, logic which seems to cut right down your backbone and cleave your spine. 'He trusted on the Lord that he would deliver him: let him deliver him now.' Yet this hard logic can be turned to comfort. I told you a story the other day of the brother in Guy's Hospital to whom the doctors said that he must undergo an operation which was extremely dangerous. They gave him a week to consider whether he would submit to it. He was troubled for his young wife and children, and for his work for the Lord. A friend left a bunch of flowers for him, with this verse as its motto, 'He trusted in God; let him deliver him now.' 'Yes,' he thought, '*now*.' In prayer he cast himself upon the Lord, and felt in his heart, 'Come on, doctors, I am ready for you.' When the next morning came, he refused to take chloroform, for he desired to go to heaven in his senses. He bore the operation manfully, and he is yet alive. 'He trusted on the Lord that he would deliver him' then and there, and the Lord did so. In this lies the brunt of the battle.

A Christian man may be beaten in business, he may fail to meet all demands, and then Satan yells, 'Let him deliver him *now*.' The poor man has been out of work for two or three months, tramping the streets of London until he has worn out his boots; he has been brought to his last penny. I think I hear the laugh of the Prince of Darkness as he cries, 'Let him deliver him *now*.' Or else the believer is very ill in body, and low in spirit, and then Satan howls, 'Let him deliver him *now*.' Some of us have been in very trying positions. We were moved with indignation because of deadly error, and we spoke plainly, but men refused to hear. Those we relied upon deserted us; good men sought their own ease and would not march with us, and we had to bear testimony for despised truth alone, until we were ourselves despised. Then the adversary shouted, 'Let him deliver him *now*.' Be it so! We do not refuse the test. Our God whom we serve will deliver us. We will not bow down to modern thought nor worship the image which human wisdom has set up. Our God is God both of hills and of valleys. He will not fail his servants, albeit that for a while he forbears that he may try their faith. We dare accept the test, and say, 'Let him deliver us *now*.'

Beloved friends, we need not be afraid of this taunt if it is brought by adversaries; for, after all, the test will come to us apart from any malice, for *it is inevitable*. All the faith you have will be tried. I can see you heaping it up. How rich you are! What a pile of faith! Friend, you are almost perfect! Open the furnace door and put the heap in. Do you shrink? See how it shrivels! Is there anything left? Bring hither a magnifying glass. Is this all that is left? Yes, this is all that remains of the heap. You say, 'I trusted in God.' Yes, but you had reason to cry, 'Lord, help my unbelief.' Brethren, we have not a tithe of the faith we think we have. But whether or not, all our faith must be tested. God builds no ships but what he sends to sea. In living, in losing, in working, in weeping, in suffering, or in striving, God will find a fitting crucible for every single grain of the precious faith which he has given us. Then he will come to us and say – You trusted in God that he would deliver you, and you shall be delivered now. How you will open your eyes as you see the Lord's hand of deliverance! What a man of wonders you will be when you tell in your riper years to the younger people how the Lord delivered you! Why, there are some Christians I know of who, like the ancient mariner, could detain even a wedding guest with their stories of God's wonders on the deep.

Yes, the test will come again and again. May the gibes of adversaries only make us ready for the sterner ordeals of the judgment to come. O my dear friends, examine your religion. You have a great deal of it, some of you; but what of its quality? Can your religion stand the test of poverty, and scandal, and scorn? Can it stand the test of scientific sarcasm and learned contempt? Will your religion stand the test of long sickness of body and depression of spirit caused by weakness? What are you doing amid the common trials of life? What will you do in the swellings of Jordan? Examine well your faith, since all hangs there. Some of us who have lain for weeks together, peering through the thin veil which parts us from the unseen, have been made to feel that nothing will suffice us but a promise which will answer the taunt, 'Let him deliver us *now*.'

III. I shall finish, in the third place, dear friends, by noticing THE ANSWER to the test. God does deliver those who trust in him. God's interposition for the faithful is not a dream, but a substantial reality. 'Many are the afflictions of the righteous: but the Lord delivereth him out of them all.' All history proves the faithfulness of God. Those who trust God have been in all sorts of troubles; but they have always been delivered. They have been bereaved. What a horrible bereavement was that which fell to the lot of Aaron, when his two sons were struck dead for their profanity in the presence of God! 'And Aaron held his peace'! What grace was there! Thus will the Lord sustain you also should he take away the desire of your eyes with a stroke. Grave after grave has the good man visited till it seemed that his whole race was buried, and yet his heart has not been broken; but he has bowed his soul before the will of the ever-blessed One. Thus has the Lord delivered his afflicted one by sustaining him. In other ways the bush has burned, and yet has not been consumed. Remember the multiplied and multiform trials of Job. Yet God sustained him to the end so that he did not charge God foolishly, but held fast his faith in the Most High. If ever you are called to the afflictions of Job you will also be called to the sustaining grace of Job. Some of God's servants have been defeated in their testimony. They have borne faithful witness for God, but they have been rejected of men. It has been their lot, like Cassandra, to prophesy the truth, but not to be believed. Such was Jeremiah, who was born to a heritage of scorn from those whose benefit he sought. Yet he was delivered. He shrank not from being faithful. His courage could not be silenced. By integrity he was delivered. Godly men have been despised and misrepresented, and yet have been delivered. Remember David and his envious brethren, David and the malignant Saul, David when his men spake of stoning him. Yet he took off the giant's head; yet he came to the throne; yet the Lord built him a house.

Some of God's servants have been bitterly persecuted, but God has delivered them. Daniel came forth from the lions' den, and the three holy children from the midst of the burning fiery furnace. These are only one or two out of millions who trusted God and he delivered them. Out of all manner of ill the Lord delivered them. God brought this crowd of witnesses through all their trials unto his throne, where they rest with Jesus, and share the triumph of their Master at this very day. O my timid brother, nothing has happened to you but what is common to men. Your battle is not different from the warfare of the rest of the saints; and as God has delivered them he will deliver you also, seeing you put your trust in him.

But *God's ways of deliverance are his own*. He does not deliver according to the translation put upon 'deliverance' by the ribald throng. He does not deliver according to the interpretation put upon 'deliverance' by our shrinking flesh and blood. He delivers, but it is in his own way. Let me remark that, *if God delivers you and me in the same way as he delivered his own Son, we can have no cause of complaint*. If the deliverance which he guaranteed to us is of the same kind as that which he guaranteed to the Only Begotten, we may well be content. Well, what kind of a deliverance was that? Did the Father tear up the cross from the earth? Did he proceed to draw out the nails from the sacred hands and feet of his dear Son? Did he set him down upon that 'green hill far away, beyond the city wall,' and place in his hand a sword of fire with which to smite his adversaries? Did he bid the earth open and swallow up all his foes?

No; nothing of the kind. Jehovah did not interpose to spare his Son a single pang; but he let him die. He let him be taken as a dead man down from the cross and laid in a tomb. Jesus went through with his suffering to the bitter end. O brothers and sisters, this may be God's way of delivering us. We have trusted in God that he would deliver us; and his rendering of his promise is, that he will enable us to go through with it; we shall suffer to the last, and triumph in so doing.

Yet God's way of delivering those who trust in him is *always the best way*. If the Father had taken his Son down from the cross, what would have been the result? Redemption unaccomplished, salvation work undone, and Jesus returning with his life-work unfinished. This would not have been deliverance, but defeat. It was much better for our Lord Jesus to die. Now he has paid the ransom for his elect, and having accomplished the great purpose of atonement, he has slept a while in the heart of the earth, and now has ascended to his throne in the endless glories of heaven. It was deliverance of the fullest kind; for from the pangs of his death has come the joy of life to his redeemed. It is not God's will that every mountain should be levelled, but that we should be the stronger for climbing the Hill Difficulty. God will deliver; he must deliver, but he will do it in our cases, as in the case of our Lord, in the best possible manner.

Anyhow, he will deliver his chosen: the taunt of the adversary shall not cause our God to forget or forego his people. I know that the Lord will no more fail me than any other of his servants. He will not leave a faithful witness to his adversaries. 'I know that my Avenger liveth, and that he shall stand at the latter day upon the earth: and though after my skin worms destroy this body, yet in my flesh shall I see God: whom I shall see for myself, and mine eyes shall behold, and not another; though my reins be consumed within me.' Is this also your confidence? Then do not sit down in sorrow, and act as though you despaired. Quit yourselves like men. Be strong, fear not. Cast yourselves on the love that never changeth and never fainteth, and the Lord will answer all the revilings of Rabshakeh, and the blusterings of Sennacherib.

There are times when we may use this text to our comfort. 'Let him deliver him now,' saith the text, 'if he will have him.' You, dear friends, who have never believed in the Lord Jesus Christ before, how I wish you could try him now! You feel this morning full of sin, and full of need. Come, then, and trust the Saviour *now*. See whether he will not save you *now*. Is there one day in the year in which Jesus cannot save a sinner? Come and see whether the 17th of June is that day. Try whether he will not deliver you *now* from the guilt, the penalty, the power of sin. Why not come? You have never, perhaps, been in the Tabernacle before, and when coming here this morning you did not think of finding the Saviour. Oh, that the Saviour may find you! Jesus Christ is a Saviour every day, all the year round. Whoever cometh to him shall find eternal life *now*. 'Oh,' you say, 'I am in such an unfit state; I am in all the *deshabille* of my carelessness and godlessness.' Come along, man, come along, just as you are. Tarry not for improvement or arrangement, for both of these Jesus will give you; come and put your trust in the great Sacrifice for sin, and he will deliver you – deliver you now. Lord, save the sinner, *now!*

Others of you are the children of God, but you are in peculiar trouble. Well, what are you going to do? You have always trusted in God before; are you going to doubt him now? 'O my dear sir, you do not know my distress; I am the most afflicted person in the Tabernacle.' Be it so; but you trusted in the Lord the past twenty years, and I do not believe that you have seen any just cause for denying him your confidence now. Did you say that you have known him from your youth up? What! you seventy years of age? Then you are too near home to begin distrusting your heavenly Father. That will never do. You have been to sea, and have weathered many a storm in mid-ocean, and are you now going to be drowned in a ditch? Think not so. The Lord will deliver you even now. Do not let us suppose that we have come where boundless love and infinite wisdom cannot reach us. Do not fancy that you have leaped upon a ledge of rock so high as to be out of reach of the everlasting arm. If you had done so I would still cry – Throw yourself down into the arms of God, and trust that he will not let you be destroyed.

It may be that some of us are in trouble about the church and the faith. We have defended God's truth as well as we could, and spoken out against deadly error; but craft and numbers have been against us, and at present things seem to have gone wrong. The good are timid, and the evil are false. They say, 'He trusted in God: let him deliver him now.' Sirs, he will deliver us now. We will throw our soul once more into this battle, and see if the Lord does not vindicate his truth. If we have not spoken in God's name we are content to go back to the dust from whence we sprang; but if we have spoken God's truth we defy the whole confederacy to prevail against it.

Perhaps, I speak to some missionary, who is mourning over a time of great trial in a mission which is dear to his heart. Ah, dear friend! Christ intended that the gospel should repeat his own experience, and then should triumph like himself. The gospel lives by being killed, and conquers by defeat. Cast it where you will, it always falls upon its feet. You need not be afraid of it under any trial. Just now, the wisdom of man is its worst foe, but the Lord will deliver it *now*. The gospel lives and reigns. Tell it out among the heathen, that the Lord reigneth from the tree, and from that tree of the curse he issues his supreme commands. The selfsame day in which Jesus died, he took with him into his kingdom and his inmost paradise a thief who had hung at his side. He liveth and reigneth for ever and ever, and calleth to himself whomsoever he hath chosen. Let us drown the taunts of the adversary with our shouts of Hallelujah! The Lord shall reign for ever and ever. Hallelujah. Amen!

10

THE THREE HOURS' DARKNESS[1]

Now from the sixth hour there was darkness over all
the land unto the ninth hour.
MATTHEW 27:45

FROM NINE TILL NOON the usual degree of light was present; so that there was time enough for our Lord's adversaries to behold and insult his sufferings. There could be no mistake about the fact that he was really nailed to the cross; for he was crucified in broad daylight. We are fully assured that it was Jesus of Nazareth, for both friends and foes were eyewitnesses of his agonies: for three long hours the Jews sat down and watched him on the cross, making jests of his miseries. I feel thankful for those three hours of light; for else the enemies of our faith would have questioned whether in very deed the blessed body of our Master was nailed to the tree, and would have started fancies as many as the bats and owls which haunt the darkness. Where would have been the witnesses of this solemn scene if the sun had been hidden from morn till night? As three hours of light gave opportunity for inspection and witness-bearing, we see the wisdom which did not allow it to close too soon.

Never forget that this miracle of the closing of the eye of day at high noon was performed by our Lord in his weakness. He had walked the sea, and raised the dead, and healed the sick, in the

---

[1] Sermon No. 1,896. Preached at the Metropolitan Tabernacle on Sunday morning, 18 April 1886.

days of his strength; but now he has come to his lowest, the fever is on him, he is faint and thirsty. He hangs on the borders of dissolution; yet has he power to darken the sun at noon. He is still very God of very God:

> Behold, a purple torrent run
>   Down from his hands and head,
> The crimson tide puts out the sun;
>   His groans awake the dead.

If he can do this in his weakness, what is he not able to do in his strength? Fail not to remember that this power was displayed in a sphere in which he did not usually put forth his might. The sphere of Christ is that of goodness and benevolence, and consequently of light. When he enters the sphere of darkness-making, and of working judgment, he engages in what he calls his strange work. Wonders of terror are his left-handed deeds. It is but now and then that he causes the sun to go down at noon, and darkens the earth in the clear day (*Amos* 8:9). If our Lord can make darkness at will as he dies, what glory may we not expect now that he lives to be the light of the city of God for ever? The Lamb is the light; and what a light! The heavens bear the impress of his dying power, and lose their brightness; shall not the new heavens and the new earth attest the power of the risen Lord? The thick darkness around the dying Christ is the robe of the Omnipotent: he liveth again, all power is in his hands, and all that power he will put forth to bless his chosen.

What a call must that midday midnight have been to the careless sons of men! They know not that the Son of God was among them; nor that he was working out human redemption. The grandest hour in all history seemed likely to pass by unheeded, when, suddenly, night hastened from her chambers and usurped the day. Every one asked his fellow, 'What means this darkness?' Business stood still: the plough stayed in mid-furrow, and the axe paused uplifted. It was the middle of the day, when men are busiest; but they made a general pause. Not only on Calvary, but on every hill, and in every valley, the gloom settled down. There was a halt in the caravan of life. None could move unless they groped their way like the blind. The master of the house called for a light at noon, and his servant tremblingly obeyed the unusual summons. Other lights were twinkling, and Jerusalem was as a city by night, only men were not in their beds. How startled were mankind! Around the great deathbed an appropriate quiet was secured. I doubt not that a shuddering awe came over the masses of the people, and the thoughtful foresaw terrible things. Those who had stood about the cross, and had dared to insult the majesty of Jesus, were paralysed with fear. They ceased their ribaldry, and with it their cruel exultation. They were cowed though not convinced, even the basest of them; while the better sort 'smote their breasts and returned.' As many as could do so, no doubt, stumbled to their chambers, and endeavoured to hide themselves, for fear of awful judgments which they feared were near. I do not wonder that there should be traditions of strange things that were said during the hush of that darkness. Those whispers of the past may or may not be true: they have been the subject of learned controversy, but the labour of the dispute was energy ill spent. Yet we could not have wondered if one did say as he is reported to have done, 'God is suffering, or the world is perishing.' Nor should I drive from my beliefs the poetic legend that an Egyptian pilot passing down the river heard among the reedy banks a voice out of the rustling rushes, whispering, 'The great Pan is dead.' Truly, the God of nature was expiring, and things less tender than the reeds by the river might well tremble at the sound thereof.

We are told that this darkness was over all the land; and Luke puts it, 'over all the earth.' That portion of our globe which was then veiled in natural night was not affected thereby; but to all men awake, and at their employment, it was the advertisement of a great and solemn event. It was strange beyond all experience, and all men marvelled; for when the light should have been brightest, all things were obscured for the space of three hours.

There must be great teaching in this darkness; for when we come so near the cross, which is the centre of history, every event is full of meaning. Light will come out of this darkness. I love to feel the solemnity of the three hours of deathshade, and to sit down therein and meditate, with no companion but the august sufferer, around whom that darkness lowered. I am going to speak of it in four ways, as the Holy Spirit may help me. First, let us bow our spirits in the presence of *a miracle which amazes us;* secondly, let us regard this darkness as *a veil which conceals;* thirdly, as *a symbol which instructs;* and fourthly, as *a display of sympathy,* which forewarns us by the prophecies which it implies.

I. First, let us view this darkness as A MIRACLE WHICH AMAZES US.

It may seem a trite observation that this darkness was altogether out of the natural course of things. Since the world began was it not heard that at high noon there should be darkness over all the land. It was out of the order of nature altogether. Some deny miracles; and if they also deny God, I will not at this time deal with them. But it is very strange that any one who believes in God should doubt the possibility of miracles. It seems to me that, granted the being of a God, miracle is to be expected as an occasional declaration of his independent and active will. He may make certain rules for his actions, and it may be his wisdom to keep to them; but surely he must reserve to himself the liberty to depart from his own laws, or else he has in a measure laid aside his personal Godhead, deified law, and set it up above himself. It would not increase our idea of the glory of his Godhead if we could be assured that he had made himself subject to rule, and tied his own hands from ever acting except in a certain manner. From the self-existence and freedom of will which enter into our very conception of God, we are led to expect that sometimes he should not keep to the methods which he follows as his general rule. This has led to the universal conviction that miracle is a proof of Godhead. The general works of creation and providence are to my mind the best proofs; but the common heart of our race, for some reason or other, looks to miracle as surer evidence; thus proving that miracle is expected of God. Although the Lord makes it his order that there shall be day and night, he in this case with abundant reason interposes three hours of night in the centre of a day. Behold the reason. The unusual in lower nature is made to consort with the unusual in the dealings of nature's Lord. Certainly this miracle was most congruous with that greater miracle which was happening in the death of Christ. Was not the Lord himself departing from all common ways? Was he not doing that which had never been done from the beginning, and would never be done again? That man should die is so common a thing as to be deemed inevitable. We are not startled now at the sound of a funeral knell: we have become familiar with the grave. As the companions of our youth die at our side we are not seized with amazement; for death is everywhere about us and within us. But that the Son of God should die, this is beyond all expectation, and not only above nature, but contrary thereto. He who is equal with God deigns to hang upon the cross, and die. I know of nothing that seems more out of rule and beyond expectation than this. The sun darkened at noon is a fit accompaniment of the death of Jesus. Is it not so?

Further, this miracle was not only out of the order of nature, but it was one which *would have been pronounced impossible*. It is not possible that there should be an eclipse of the sun at the time of the full moon. The moon at the time when she is in her full is not in a position in which she could possibly cast her shadow upon the earth. The Passover was at the time of the full moon, and therefore it was not possible that the sun should then undergo an eclipse. This darkening of the sun was not strictly an astronomical eclipse; the darkness was doubtless produced in some other way: yet to those who were present it did seem to be a total eclipse of the sun – a thing impossible. Ah, brothers! when we come to deal with man, and the fall, and sin, and God, and Christ, and the atonement, we are at home with impossibilities. We have now reached a region where prodigies, and marvels, and surprises, are the order of the day: sublimities become commonplaces when we come within the circle of eternal love. Yea, more; we have now quitted the solid land of the possible, and have put out to sea, where we see the works of the Lord, and his wonders in the deep. When we think of impossibilities in other spheres we start back; but the way of the cross is ablaze with the divine, and we soon perceive that 'with God all things are possible.' See, then, in the death of Jesus, the possibility of the impossible; Behold here how the Son of God can die. We sometimes pause when we meet with an expression in a hymn which implies that God can suffer or die; we think that the poet has used too great a license: yet it behoves us to refrain from hypercriticism, since in Holy Writ there are words like it. We even read (*Acts* 20:28) of 'the church of God which he hath purchased with his own blood' – the blood of God! Ah well! I am not careful to defend the language of the Holy Ghost; but in its presence I take liberty to justify the words which we sang just now:

> Well might the sun in darkness hide,
>   And shut his glories in,
> When God, the mighty Maker, died
>   For man, the creature's sin.

I will not venture to explain the death of the incarnate God. I am content to believe it, and to rest my hope upon it.

How should the Holy One have sin laid upon him? That also I do not know. A wise man has told us, as if it were an axiom, that the imputation or the non-imputation of sin is an impossibility. Be it so: we have become familiar with such things since we have beheld the cross. Things which men call absurdities have become foundation truths to us. The doctrine of the cross is to them that perish foolishness. We do know that in our Lord was no sin, and yet he his own self bare our sins in his own body on the tree. We do not know how the innocent Son of God could be permitted to suffer for sins that were not his own; it amazes us that justice should permit one so perfectly holy to be forsaken of his God, and to cry out, 'Eloi, Eloi, lama sabachthani?' But it was so; and it was so by the decree of the highest justice; and we rejoice therein. As it was so, that the sun was eclipsed when it was impossible that he should be eclipsed, so has Jesus performed on our behalf; in the agonies of his death, things which, in the ordinary judgment of men, must be set down as utterly impossible. Our faith is at home in wonderland, where the Lord's thoughts are seen to be as high above our thoughts as the heavens are above the earth.

Concerning this miracle, I have also further to remark that *this darkening of the sun surpassed all ordinary and natural eclipses.* It lasted longer than an ordinary eclipse, and it came in a different manner. According to Luke, the darkness all over the land came first, and the sun was darkened afterwards: the darkness did not begin with the sun, but mastered the sun. It was unique and supernatural. Now, among all griefs no grief is comparable to the grief of Jesus: of all woes none can parallel the woes of our great Substitute. As strongest light casts deepest shade, so has the surprising love of Jesus cost him a death such as falls not to the common lot of men. Others die, but this man is 'obedient unto death'. Others drink the fatal draught, yet reek not of its wormwood and gall; but he 'tasted death'. 'He poured out his soul unto death.' Every part of his being was darkened with that extraordinary deathshade; and the natural darkness outside of him did but shroud a special death which was entirely by itself.

And now, when I come to think of it, *this darkness appears to have been most natural and fitting*. If we had to write out the story of our Lord's death we could not omit the darkness without neglecting a most important item. The darkness seems a part of the natural furniture of that great transaction. Read the story through and you are not at all startled with the darkness; after once familiarizing your mind with the thought that this is the Son of God, and that he stretches his hands to the cruel death of the cross, you do not wonder at the rending of the veil of the temple; you are not astonished at the earthquake or at the rising of certain of the dead. These are proper attendants of our Lord's passion; and so is the darkness. It drops into its place, it seems as if it could not have been otherwise.

> That sacrifice! – the death of him –
>   The high and ever Holy One!
> Well may the conscious heaven grow dim,
>   And blacken the beholding sun.

For a moment think again. Has not it appeared as if the death which that darkness shrouded was also a natural part of the great whole? We have grown at last to feel as if the death of the Christ of God were an integral part of human history. You cannot take it out of man's chronicle; can you? Introduce the Fall, and see Paradise Lost, and you cannot make the poem complete till you have introduced that greater Man who did redeem us, and by his death gave us our Paradise Regained. It is a singular characteristic of all true miracles, that though your wonder never ceases they never appear to he unnatural: they are marvellous, but never monstrous. The miracles of Christ dovetail into the general run of human history: we cannot see how the Lord could be on earth and Lazarus not be raised from the dead when the grief of Martha and Mary had told its tale. We cannot see how the disciples could have been tempest tossed on the Lake of Galilee and the Christ not walk on the water to deliver them. Wonders of power are expected parts of the narrative where Jesus is. Everything fits into its place with surrounding facts. A Romish miracle is always monstrous and devoid of harmony with all beside it. What if St Winifred's head did come up from the well and speak from the coping to the astonished peasant who was about to draw water! I do not care whether it did or did not; it does not alter history a bit, nor even colour it; it is tagged on to the record, and is no part of it. But the miracles of Jesus, this of the darkness among them, are essential to human history; and especially is this so in the case of his death and this great darkness which shrouded it. All things in human history converge to the cross, which seems not to be an afterthought nor an expedient, but the fit and foreordained channel through which love should run to guilty men.

I cannot say more from want of voice, though I had many more things to say. Sit down, and let the thick darkness cover you till you cannot even see the cross, and only know that out of reach of mortal eye your Lord wrought out the redemption of his people. He wrought in silence a miracle of patience and of love, by which light has come to those who sit in darkness and in the valley of the shadow of death.

II. Secondly, I desire you to regard this darkness as A VEIL WHICH CONCEALS. The Christ is hanging on yonder tree. I see the dreadful cross. I can see the thieves on either side. I look around, and I sorrowfully mark that motley group of citizens from Jerusalem, and scribes, and priests, and strangers from different countries, mingled with Roman soldiers. They turn their eyes on him, and for the most part gaze with cruel scorn upon the Holy One who is in the centre. In truth it is an awful sight. Mark those dogs of the common sort and those bulls of Bashan of more notable rank, who all unite to dishonour the meek and lowly One.

I must confess I never read the story of the Master's death, knowing what I do of the pain of crucifixion, without deep anguish: crucifixion was a death worthy to have been invented by devils. The pain which it involved was immeasurable; I will not torture you by describing it. I know dear hearts that cannot read of it without tears, and without lying awake for nights afterwards.

But there was more than anguish upon Calvary: ridicule and contempt embittered all. Those jests, those cruel gibes, those mockeries, those thrustings out of the tongue, what shall we say of these? At times I have felt some little sympathy with the French Prince who cried, 'If I had been there with my guards, I would soon have swept those wretches away.' It was too terrible a sight: the pain of the victim was grievous enough, but the abominable wickedness of the mockers who could bear? Let us thank God that in the middle of the crime there came down a darkness which rendered it impossible for them to go further with it. Jesus must die; for his pains there must be no alleviation, and from death there must be for him no deliverance; but the scoffers must be silenced. Most effectually their mouths were closed by the dense darkness which shut them in.

What I see in that veil is, first of all, that it was *a concealment for those guilty enemies*. Did you ever think of that? It is as if God himself said, 'I cannot bear it. I will not see this infamy! Descend, O veil!' Down fell the heavy shades.

> I asked the heavens, 'What foe to God hath done
> This unexampled deed?' The heavens exclaim,
> 'Twas man; and we in horror snatched the sun
> From such a spectacle of guilt and shame.

Thank God, the cross is a hiding place. It furnishes for guilty men a shelter from the all-seeing eye, so that justice need not see and strike. When God lifts up his Son, and makes him visible, he hides the sin of men. He says that 'the times of their ignorance he winks at.' Even the greatness of their sin he casts behind his back, so that he need not see it, but may indulge his long-suffering, and permit his pity to endure their provocations. It must have grieved the heart of the eternal God to see such wanton cruelty of men towards him who went about doing good, and healing all manner of diseases. It was horrible to see the teachers of the people rejecting him with scorn, the seed of Israel, who ought to have accepted him as their Messiah, casting him out as a thing despised and abhorred. I therefore feel gratitude to God for bidding that darkness cover all the land, and end that shameful scene. I would say to any guilty ones here: Thank God that the Lord Jesus has made it possible for your sins to be hidden more completely than by thick darkness. Thank God that in Christ he does not see you with that stern eye of justice which would involve your destruction. Had not Jesus interposed, whose death you have despised, you had wrought out in your own death the result of your own sin long ago; but for your Lord's sake you are allowed to live as if God did not see you. This long-suffering is meant to bring you to repentance. Will you not come?

But, further, that darkness was *a sacred concealment for the blessed Person of our divine Lord*. So to speak, the angels found for their King a pavilion of thick clouds, in the which his Majesty might be sheltered in its hour of misery. It was too much for wicked eyes to gaze so rudely on that immaculate Person. Had not his enemies stripped him naked, and cast lots upon his vesture? Therefore it was meet that the holy manhood should at length find suitable concealment. It was not fit that brutal eyes should see the lines made upon that blessed form by the graving tool of sorrow. It was not meet that revellers should see the contortions of that sacred frame, indwelt with Deity, while he was being broken beneath the iron rod of divine wrath on our behalf. It was meet that God should cover him, so that none should see all he did and all he bare when he was made sin for us. I bless God devoutly for thus hiding my Lord away: thus was he screened from eyes which were not fit to see the sun much less to look upon the Sun of Righteousness.

This darkness also warns us, even us who are most reverent. This darkness tells us all that *the Passion is a great mystery, into which we cannot pry*. I try to explain it as substitution, and I feel that where the language of Scripture is explicit, I may and must be explicit too. But yet I feel that the idea of substitution does not cover the whole of the matter, and that no human conception can completely grasp the whole of the dread mystery. It was wrought in darkness, because the full, far-reaching meaning and result cannot be beheld of finite mind. Tell me the death of the Lord Jesus was a grand example of self-sacrifice – I can see *that* and much more. Tell me it was a wondrous obedience to the will of God – I can see *that* and much more. Tell me it was the bearing of what ought to have been borne by myriads of sinners of the human race, as the chastisement of their sin – I can see *that,* and found my best hope upon it. But do not tell me that this is all that is in the cross. No, great as this would be, there is much more in our Redeemer's death. God only knows the love of God: Christ only knows all that he accomplished when he bowed his head and gave up the ghost. There are common mysteries of nature into which it were irreverence to pry; but this is a divine mystery, before which we put our shoes from off our feet, for the place called Calvary is holy ground. God veiled the cross in darkness, and in darkness much of its deeper meaning lies; not because God would not reveal it, but because we have not capacity enough to discern it all. God was manifest in the flesh, and in that human flesh he put away sin by his own sacrifice: this we all know; But 'without controversy great is the mystery of godliness.'

Once again, this veil of darkness also pictures to me the way in which *the powers of darkness will always endeavour to conceal the cross of Christ.* We fight with darkness when we try to preach the cross. 'This is your hour, and the power of darkness,' said Christ; and I doubt not that the infernal hosts made in that hour a fierce assault upon the spirit of our Lord. Thus much also we know, that if the prince of darkness be anywhere in force, it is sure to be where Christ is lifted up. To becloud the cross is the grand object of the enemy of souls. Did you ever notice it? These fellows who hate the gospel will let every other doctrine pass muster; but if the atonement be preached, and the truths which grow out of it, straightaway they are aroused. Nothing provokes the devil like the cross. Modern theology has for its main object the obscuration of the doctrine of atonement. These modern cuttlefishes make the water of life black with their ink. They make out sin to be a trifle, and the punishment of it to be a temporary business; and thus they degrade the remedy by underrating the disease. We are not ignorant of their devices. Expect, my brethren, that the clouds of darkness will gather as to a centre around the cross, that they may hide it from the sinner's view. But expect this also, that there darkness shall meet its end. Light springeth out of that darkness – the light eternal of the undying Son of God, who having risen from the dead, liveth for ever to scatter the darkness of evil.

III. Now we pass on to speak of this darkness as A SYMBOL WHICH INSTRUCTS.

The veil falls down and conceals; but at the same time, as an emblem, it reveals. It seems to say, 'Attempt not to search within, but learn from the veil itself: it hath cherub work upon it.' This darkness teaches us what Jesus suffered: it aids us to guess at the griefs which we may not actually see.

The darkness is the symbol of *the wrath of God which fell on those who slew his only begotten Son*. God was angry, and his frown removed the light of day. Well might he be angry, when sin was murdering his only Son; when the Jewish husbandmen were saying, 'This is the heir; come, let us kill him, and let us seize on his inheritance.' This is God's wrath towards all mankind, for practically all men concurred in the death of Jesus. That wrath has brought men into darkness; they are ignorant, blinded, bewildered. They have come to love darkness better than light because their deeds are evil. In that darkness they do not repent, but go on to reject the Christ of God. Into this darkness God cannot look upon them in complacency; but he views them as children of darkness, and heirs of wrath, for whom is reserved the blackness of darkness for ever.

The symbol also tells us *what our Lord Jesus Christ endured*. The darkness outside of him was the figure of the darkness that was within him. In Gethsemane a thick darkness fell upon our Lord's spirit. He was 'exceeding sorrowful, even unto death.' His joy was communion with God – that joy was gone, and he was in the dark. His day was the light of his Father's face: that face was hidden and a terrible night gathered around him. Brothers, I should sin against that veil if I were to pretend that I could tell you what the sorrow was which oppressed the Saviour's soul: only so far can I speak as it has been given me to have fellowship with him in his sufferings. Have you ever felt a deep and overwhelming horror of sin – your own sin and the sins of others? Have you ever seen sin in the light of God's love? Has it ever darkly hovered over your sensitive conscience? Has an unknown sense of wrath crept over you like midnight gloom; and has it been about you, around you, above you, and within you? Have you felt shut up in your feebleness, and yet shut out from God? Have you looked around and found no help, no comfort even in God – no hope, no peace? In all this you have sipped a little of that salt sea into which our Lord was cast. If, like Abraham, you have felt a horror of great darkness creep over you, then have you had a taste of what your divine Lord suffered when it pleased the Father to bruise him and to put him to grief. This it was that made him sweat great drops of blood falling to the ground; and this it was which on the cross made him utter that appalling cry, 'My God, my God, why hast thou forsaken me?' It was not the crown of thorns, or the scourge, or the cross which made him cry, but the darkness, the awful darkness of desertion which oppressed his mind and made him feel like one distraught. All that could comfort him was withdrawn, and all that could distress him was piled upon him. 'The spirit of a man will sustain his infirmity; but a wounded spirit who can bear?' Our Saviour's spirit was wounded, and he cried, 'My heart is like wax, it is melted in the midst of my bowels.' Of all natural and spiritual comfort he was bereft, and his distress was utter and entire. The darkness of Calvary did not, like an ordinary night, reveal the stars; but it darkened every lamp of heaven. His strong crying and tears denoted the deep sorrow of his soul. He bore all it was possible for his capacious mind to bear, though enlarged and invigorated by union with the Godhead. He bore the equivalent of hell; nay, not that only, but he bore that which stood instead of ten thousand hells so far as the vindication of the law is concerned. Our Lord rendered in his death agony a homage to justice far greater than if a world had been doomed to destruction. When I have said that, what more can I say? Well may I tell you that this unutterable darkness, this hiding of the Divine face, expresses more of the woes of Jesus than words can ever tell.

Again, I think I see in that darkness, also *what it was that Jesus was battling with*, for we must never forget that the cross was a battlefield to him, wherein he triumphed gloriously. He was fighting then with darkness; with the powers of darkness of which Satan is the head; with the darkness of human ignorance, depravity, and falsehood. The battle thus apparent at Golgotha has been raging ever since. Then was the conflict at its height; for the chiefs of the two great armies met in personal conflict. The present battle in which you and I take our little share is as nothing compared with that wherein all the powers of darkness in their dense battalions hurled themselves against the Almighty Son of God. He bore their onset, endured the tremendous shock of their assault, and in the end, with shout of victory, he led captivity captive. He by his power and Godhead turned midnight into day again, and brought back to this world a reign of light which, blessed be God, shall never come to a close. Come to battle again, ye hosts of darkness, if ye dare! The cross has defeated you: the cross shall defeat you. Hallelujah! The cross is the ensign of victory; its light is the death of darkness. The cross is the light-house which guides poor weather-beaten humanity into the harbour of peace: this is the lamp which shines over the door of the great Father's house to lead his prodigals home.

Let us not be afraid of all the darkness which besets us on our way home, since Jesus is the light which conquers it all.

The darkness never came to an end till the Lord Jesus broke the silence. All had been still, and the darkness had grown terrible. At last he spoke, and his voice uttered a psalm. It was the twenty-second Psalm. 'My God,' saith he, 'my God, why hast thou forsaken me?' Each repeated 'Eloi' flashed morning upon the scene. By the time he had uttered the cry 'Why hast thou forsaken me?' men had begun to see again, and some even ventured to misinterpret his words, more in terror than in ignorance. They said, 'He calleth Elijah:' they may have meant a mock, but I think not. At any rate there was no heart in what they said, nor in the reply of their fellows. Yet the light had come by which they could see to dip the sponge in vinegar. Brethren, no light will ever come to dark hearts unless Jesus shall speak; and the light will not be clear until we hear the voice of his sorrows on our behalf, as he cries, 'Why hast thou forsaken me?' His voice of grief must be the end of our griefs: his cry out of the darkness must cheer away our gloom, and bring the heavenly morning to our minds.

You see how much there is in my text. It is a joy to speak on such a theme when one is in good health, and full of vigour; then are we as Naphtali, a hind let loose; then give we goodly words: but this day I am in pain as to my body, and my mind seems frozen. Nevertheless, the Lord can bless my feeble words, and make you see that in this darkness there is meaning deep and wide which none of us should neglect. If God shall help your meditations this darkness will be light about you.

IV. I come to my fourth point, and my closing words will deal with THE SYMPATHY WHICH PROPHESIES. Do you see the sympathy of nature with her Lord – the sympathy of the sun in the heavens with the Sun of Righteousness? It was not possible for him by whom all things were made to be in darkness, and for nature to remain in the light.

The first sympathetic fact I see is this: *all lights are dim when Christ shines not.* All is dark when he does not shine. In the church, if Jesus be not there, what is there? The sun itself could not yield us light if Jesus were withdrawn. The seven golden lamps are ready to go out unless he walks among them, and trims them with the holy oil. Brethren, you soon grow heavy, and your spirits faint, and your hands are weary, if the Christ be not with you. If Jesus Christ be not fully preached, if he be not with us by his Spirit, then everything is in darkness. Obscure the cross, and you have obscured all spiritual teaching. You cannot say, 'We will be perspicuous in every other point, and clear upon every other doctrine, but we will shun the atonement, since so many cavil at it.' No, sirs, if that candle be put under a bushel the whole house is dark. All theology sympathizes with the cross, and is coloured and tinctured by it. Your pious service, your books, your public worship, will all be in sympathy with the cross one way or another. If the cross is in the dark, so will all your work be.

> What think ye of Christ? is the test
> To try both your work and your scheme;
> You cannot be right in the rest
> Unless you think rightly of him.

Conjure up your doubts; fabricate your philosophies; and compose your theories: there will be no light in them if the cross be left out. Vain are the sparks of your own making, you shall lie down in sorrow. All our work and travail shall end in vanity unless the work and travail of Christ be our first and sole hope. If you are dark upon that point, which alone is light, how great is your darkness!

Next, *see the dependence of all creation upon Christ,* as evidenced by its darkness when he withdraws. It was not meet that he who made all worlds should die, and yet all worlds should go on just as they had done. If he suffers eclipse, they must suffer eclipse too; if the Sun of Righteousness be made to set in blood, the natural sun must keep in touch with him. I believe, my friends, that there is a much more wonderful sympathy between Christ and the world of nature than any of us have ever dreamed. The whole creation groaneth and travaileth in pain together until now, because Christ in the Church is in his travail pangs. Christ in his mystical body is in travail, and so the whole creation must wait for the manifestation of the Son of God. We are waiting for the coming of the Lord from heaven, and there is no hill or dale, there is no mountain or sea, but what is in perfect harmony with the waiting church. Wonder not that there should be earthquakes in divers places, blazing volcanoes, terrible tempests, and sore spreadings of deadly disease. Marvel not when you hear of dire portents, and things that make one's heart to quail, for such things must be till the end shall come. Until the great Shepherd shall make his crook into a sceptre, and shall begin his unsuffering reign, this poor earth must bleed at every vein. There must be darkness till these days of delay are ended. You that expect placid history till Christ shall come expect you know not what. You that think that generous politics shall create order and content, and that the extension of free trade shall breathe universal peace over the nations, look for the living among the dead. Till the Lord shall come, the word has gone out, 'Overturn, overturn, overturn,' and overturned all things must be, not only in other kingdoms, but in this also, till Jesus comes. All that can be shaken shall be shaken, and only his immovable throne and truth shall abide. Now is the time of the Lord's battle with darkness, and we may not hope as yet for unbroken light.

Dear friends, the sin which darkened Christ and made him die in the dark darkens the whole world. The sin that darkened Christ and made him hang upon the cross in the dark is darkening you who do not believe in him, and you will live in the dark and die in the dark unless you get to him who only is the light of the world, and can give light to you. There is no light for any man except in Christ; and till you believe in him thick darkness shall blind you, and you shall stumble in it and perish. That is the lesson I would have you learn.

Another practical lesson is this: If we are in the dark at this time, if our spirits are sunk in gloom, let us not despair, for the Lord Christ himself was there. If I have fallen into misery on account of sin, let me not give up all hope, for the Father's Well-beloved passed through denser darkness than mine. O believing soul, if thou art in the dark thou art near the King's cellars, and there are wines on the lees well refined lying there. Thou hast gotten into the pavilion of the Lord, and now mayest thou speak with him. You will not find Christ in the gaudy tents of pride, nor in the foul haunts of wickedness: you will not find him where the violin, and the dance, and the flowing bowl inflame the lusts of men, but in the house of mourning you will meet the Man of Sorrows. He is not where Herodias dances, nor where Bernice displays her charms; but he is where the woman of a sorrowful spirit moves her lips in prayer. He is never absent where penitence sits in darkness and bewails her faults.

> Yes, Lord, in hours of gloom,
> When shadows fill my room,
> When pain breathes forth its groans,
> And grief its sighs and moans,
>   Then thou art near.

If you are under a cloud, feel after your Lord, if haply you may find him. Stand still in your black sorrow, and say, 'O Lord, the preacher tells me that thy cross once stood in such darkness as this – O Jesus hear me!' He will respond to you: the Lord will look out of the pillar of cloud, and shed a light upon you. 'I know their sorrows,' saith he. He is no stranger to heartbreak. Christ also once suffered for sin. Trust him, and he will cause his light to shine upon you. Lean upon him, and he will bring you up out of the gloomy wilderness into the land of rest. God help you to do so!

Last Monday I was cheered beyond all I can tell you by a letter from a brother who had been restored to life, light, and liberty by the discourse of last Sabbath morning. I know no greater joy than to be useful to your souls. For this reason, I have tried to preach this morning, though I am quite unfit for it physically. Oh, I do pray I may hear more news from saved ones! Oh that some spirit that has wandered out into the dark moor land may spy the candle in my window, and find its way home! If you have found my Lord, I charge you never let him go, but cleave to him till the day break, and the shadows flee away.

God help you so to do for Jesus' sake! Amen.

11

'LAMA SABACHTHANI?'[1]

And about the ninth hour Jesus cried with a loud voice, saying, Eli, Eli, lama sabachthani? that is to say, My God, my God, why hast thou forsaken me?
MATTHEW 27:46

'THERE WAS DARKNESS over all the land unto the ninth hour': this cry came out of that darkness. Expect not to see through its every word, as though it came from on high as a beam from the unclouded Sun of Righteousness. There is light in it, bright, flashing light; but there is a centre of impenetrable gloom, where the soul is ready to faint because of the terrible darkness.

Our Lord was then in the darkest part of his way. He had trodden the winepress now for hours, and the work was almost finished. He had reached the culminating point of his anguish. This is his dolorous lament from the lowest pit of misery – 'My God, my God, why hast thou forsaken me?' I do not think that the records of time, or even of eternity, contain a sentence more full of anguish. Here the wormwood and the gall, and all the other bitternesses, are outdone. Here you may look as into a vast abyss; and though you strain your eyes, and gaze till sight fails you, yet you perceive no bottom; it is measureless, unfathomable, inconceivable. This anguish of the Saviour on your behalf and mine is no more to be measured and weighed than the sin which needed it, or the love which endured it. We will adore where we cannot comprehend.

I have chosen this subject that it may help the children of God to understand a little of their infinite obligations to their redeeming

---

[1] Sermon No. 2,133. Preached at the Metropolitan Tabernacle on Sunday morning, 2 March 1890.

Lord. You shall measure the height of his love, if it be ever measured, by the depth of his grief, if that can ever be known. See with what a price he hath redeemed us from the curse of the law! As you see this, say to yourselves: What manner of people ought we to be! What measure of love ought we to return to one who bore the utmost penalty, that we might be delivered from the wrath to come? I do not profess that I can dive into this deep: I will only venture to the edge of the precipice, and bid you look down, and pray the Spirit of God to concentrate your mind upon this lamentation of our dying Lord, as it rises up through the thick darkness – 'My God, my God, why hast thou forsaken me?'

Our first subject of thought will be *the fact;* or, what he suffered – God had forsaken him. Secondly, we will note, *the enquiry;* or, why he suffered: this word 'why' is the edge of the text. 'Why hast thou forsaken me?' Then, thirdly, we will consider *the answer;* or, what came of his suffering. The answer flowed softly into the soul of the Lord Jesus without the need of words, for he ceased from his anguish with the triumphant shout of, 'It is finished.' His work was finished, and his bearing of desertion was a chief part of the work he had undertaken for our sake.

I. By the help of the Holy Spirit, let us first dwell upon THE FACT; or, what our Lord suffered. God had forsaken him. Grief of mind is harder to bear than pain of body. You can pluck up courage and endure the pang of sickness and pain, so long as the spirit is hale and brave; but if the soul itself be touched, and the mind becomes diseased with anguish, then every pain is increased in severity, and there is nothing with which to sustain it. Spiritual sorrows are the worst of mental miseries. A man may bear great depression of spirit about worldly matters, if he feels that he has his God to go to. He is cast down, but not in despair. Like David, he dialogues with himself, and he enquires, 'Why art thou cast down, O my soul? and why art thou disquieted in me? Hope thou in God: for I shall yet praise him.' But if the Lord be once withdrawn, if the comfortable light of his presence be shadowed even for an hour, there is a torment within the breast, which I can only liken to the prelude of hell. This is the greatest of all weights that can press upon the heart. This made the Psalmist plead, 'Hide not thy face from me; put not thy servant away in anger.' We can bear a bleeding body, and even a wounded spirit; but a soul conscious of desertion by God is beyond conception unendurable. When he holdeth back the face of his throne, and spreadeth his cloud upon it, who can endure the darkness?

This voice out of 'the belly of hell' marks the lowest depth of the Saviour's grief. *The desertion was real.* Though under some aspects our Lord could say, 'The Father is with me'; yet was it solemnly true that God did forsake him. It was not a failure of faith on his part which led him to imagine what was not actual fact. Our faith fails us, and then we think that God has forsaken us; but our Lord's faith did not for a moment falter, for he says twice, '*My* God, *my* God.' Oh, the mighty double grip of his unhesitating faith! He seems to say, 'Even if thou hast forsaken me, I have not forsaken thee.' Faith triumphs, and there is no sign of any faintness of heart towards the living God. Yet, strong as is his faith, he feels that God has withdrawn his comfortable fellowship, and he shivers under the terrible deprivation.

It was no fancy, or delirium of mind, caused by his weakness of body, the heat of the fever, the depression of his spirit, or the near approach of death. He was clear of mind even to this last. He bore up under pain, loss of blood, scorn, thirst, and desolation; making no complaint of the cross, the nails, and the scoffing. We read not in the Gospels of anything more than the natural cry of weakness, 'I thirst.' All the tortures of his body he endured in silence; but when it came to being forsaken of God, then his great heart burst out into its 'Lama sabachthani?' His one moan is concerning his God. It is not, 'Why has Peter forsaken me? Why has Judas betrayed me?' These were sharp griefs, but this is the sharpest. This stroke has cut him to the quick: 'My God, my God, why hast *thou* forsaken me?' It was no phantom of the gloom; it was a real absence which he mourned.

This was *a very remarkable desertion.* It is not the way of God to leave either his sons or his servants. His saints, when they come to die, in their great weakness and pain, find him near. They are made to sing because of the presence of God: 'Yea, though I walk through the valley of the shadow of death, I will fear no evil: for thou art with me.' Dying saints have clear visions of the living God.

Our observation has taught us that if the Lord be away at other times, he is never absent from his people in the article of death, or in the furnace of affliction. Concerning the three holy children, we do not read that the Lord was ever visibly with them till they walked the fires of Nebuchadnezzar's furnace; but there and then the Lord met with them. Yes, beloved, it is God's use and wont to keep company with his afflicted people; and yet he forsook his Son in the hour of his tribulation! How usual it is to see the Lord with his faithful witnesses when resisting even unto blood! Read the Book of Martyrs, and I care not whether you study the former or the later persecutions, you will find them all lit up with the evident presence of the Lord with his witnesses. Did the Lord ever fail to support a martyr at the stake? Did he ever forsake one of his testifiers upon the scaffold? The testimony of the church has always been, that while the Lord has permitted his saints to suffer in body he has so divinely sustained their spirits that they have been more than conquerors, and have treated their sufferings as light afflictions. The fire has not been a 'bed of roses', but it has been a chariot of victory. The sword is sharp, and death is bitter; but the love of Christ is sweet, and to die for him has been turned into glory. No, it is not God's way to forsake his champions, nor to leave even the least of his children in the trial hour.

As to our Lord, this forsaking was *singular*. Did his Father ever leave him before? Will you read the four Evangelists through and find any previous instance in which he complains of his Father for having forsaken him? No. He said, 'I know that thou hearest me always.' He lived in constant touch with God. His fellowship with the Father was always near and dear and clear; but now, for the first time, he cries, 'why hast thou forsaken me?' It was very remarkable. It was a riddle only to be solved by the fact that he loved us and gave himself for us, and in the execution of his loving purpose came even unto this sorrow, of mourning the absence of his God.

This forsaking was *very terrible*. Who can fully tell what it is to be forsaken of God? We can only form a guess by what we have ourselves felt under temporary and partial desertion. God has never left us altogether; for he has expressly said, 'I will never leave thee, nor forsake thee;' yet we have sometimes felt as if he had cast us off. We have cried, 'Oh, that I knew where I might find him!' The clear shinings of his love have been withdrawn. Thus we are able to form some little idea of how the Saviour felt when his God had forsaken him. The mind of Jesus was left to dwell upon one dark subject, and no cheering theme consoled him. It was the hour in which he was made to stand before God as consciously the sin-bearer, according to that ancient prophecy, 'He shall bear their iniquities.' Then was it true, 'He hath made him to be sin for us.' Peter puts it, 'He his own self bare our sins in his own body on the tree.' Sin, sin, sin was everywhere around and about Christ. He had no sin of his own; but the Lord had 'laid on him the iniquity of us all.' He had no strength given him from on high, no secret oil and wine poured into his wounds; but he was made to appear in the lone character of the Lamb of God, which taketh away the sin of the world; and therefore he must feel the weight of sin, and the turning away of that sacred face which cannot look thereon.

His Father, at that time, gave him no open acknowledgment. On certain other occasions a voice had been heard, saying, 'This is my beloved Son, in whom I am well pleased;' but now, when such a testimony seemed most of all required, the oracle was dumb. He was hung up as an accursed thing upon the cross; for he was 'made a curse for us, as it is written, Cursed is every one that hangeth on a tree;' and the Lord his God did not own him before men. If it had pleased the Father, he might have sent him twelve legions of angels; but not an angel came after the Christ had quitted Gethsemane. His despisers might spit in his face, but no swift seraph came to avenge the indignity. They might bind him, and scourge him, but none of all the heavenly host would interpose to screen his shoulders from the lash. They might fasten him to the tree with nails, and lift him up, and scoff at him; but no cohort of ministering spirits hastened to drive back the rabble, and release the Prince of life. No, he appeared to be forsaken, 'smitten of God, and afflicted,' delivered into the hands of cruel men, whose wicked hands worked him misery without stint. Well might he ask, 'My God, my God, why hast thou forsaken me?'

But this was not all. His Father now dried up that sacred stream of peaceful communion and loving fellowship which had flowed hitherto throughout his whole earthly life. He said himself, as you remember, 'Ye shall be scattered, every man to his own, and shall leave me alone: and yet I am not alone, because the Father is with me.' Here was his constant comfort: but all comfort from this source was to be withdrawn. The divine Spirit did not minister to his human spirit. No communications with his Father's love poured into his heart. It was not possible that the Judge should smile upon one who represented the prisoner at the bar. Our Lord's faith did not fail him, as I have already shown you, for he said, 'My God, my God': yet no sensible supports were given to his heart, and no comforts were poured into his mind. One writer declares that Jesus did not taste of divine wrath, but only suffered a withdrawal of divine fellowship. What is the difference? Whether God withdraw heat or create cold is all one. He was not smiled upon, nor allowed to feel that he was near to God; and this, to his tender spirit, was grief of the keenest order. A certain saint once said that in his sorrow he had from God 'necessaries, but not suavities'; that which was meet, but not that which was sweet. Our Lord suffered to the extreme point of deprivation. He had not the light which makes existence to be life, and life to be a boon. You that know, in your degree, what it is to lose the conscious presence and love of God, you can faintly guess what the sorrow of the Saviour was, now that he felt he had been forsaken of his God. 'If the foundations be removed, what can the righteous do?' To our Lord, the Father's love was the foundation of everything; and when that was gone, all was gone. Nothing remained, within, without, above, when his own God, the God of his entire confidence, turned from him. Yes, God in very deed forsook our Saviour.

To be forsaken of God was *much more a source of anguish to Jesus than it would be to us.* 'Oh,' say you, 'how is that?' I answer, because he was perfectly holy. A rupture between a perfectly holy being and the thrice holy God must be in the highest degree strange, abnormal, perplexing, and painful. If any man here, who is not at peace with God, could only know his true condition, he would swoon with fright. If you unforgiven ones only knew where you are, and what you are at this moment in the sight of God, you would never smile again till you were reconciled to him. Alas! we are insensible, hardened by the deceitfulness of sin, and therefore we do not feel our true condition. His perfect holiness made it to our Lord a dreadful calamity to be forsaken of the thrice holy God.

I remember, also, that our blessed Lord had lived in unbroken fellowship with God, and to be forsaken was a new grief to him. He had never known what the dark was till then: his life had been lived in the light of God. Think, dear child of God, if you had always dwelt in full communion with God, your days would have been as the days of heaven upon earth; and how cold it would strike to your heart to find yourself in the darkness of desertion. If you can conceive such a thing as happening to a perfect man, you can see why to our Well-beloved it was a special trial. Remember, he had enjoyed fellowship with God more richly, as well as more constantly, than any of us. His fellowship with the Father was of the highest, deepest, fullest order; and what must the loss of it have been? We lose but drops when we lose our joyful experience of heavenly fellowship; and yet the loss is killing: but to our Lord Jesus Christ the sea was dried up – I mean his sea of fellowship with the infinite God.

Do not forget that he was such a One that to him to be without God must have been an overwhelming calamity. In every part he was perfect, and in every part fitted for communion with God to a supreme degree. A sinful man has an awful need of God, but he does not know it; and therefore he does not feel that hunger and thirst after God which would come upon a perfect man could he be deprived of God. The very perfection of his nature renders it inevitable that the holy man must either be in communion with God, or be desolate. Imagine a stray angel! a seraph who has lost his God! Conceive him to be perfect in holiness, and yet to have fallen into a condition in which he cannot find his God! I cannot picture him; perhaps Milton might have done so. He is sinless and trustful, and yet he has an overpowering feeling that God is absent from him. He has drifted into the nowhere – the unimaginable region behind the back of God. I think I hear the wailing of the cherub: 'My God, my God, my God, where art thou?' What a sorrow for one of the sons of the morning! But here we have the lament of a Being far more capable of fellowship with the Godhead. In proportion as he is more fitted to receive the love of the great Father, in that proportion is his pining after it the more intense. As a Son, he is more able to commune with God than ever a servant-angel could be; and now that he is forsaken of God, the void within is the greater, and the anguish more bitter.

Our Lord's heart, and all his nature were, morally and spiritually, so delicately formed, so sensitive, so tender, that to be without God, was to him a grief which could not be weighed. I see him in the text bearing desertion, and yet I perceive that he cannot bear it. I know not how to express my meaning except by such a paradox. He cannot endure to be without God. He had surrendered himself to be left of God, as the representative of sinners must be, but his pure and holy nature, after three hours of silence, finds the position unendurable to love and purity; and breaking forth from it, now that the hour was over, he exclaims, 'Why hast thou forsaken me?' He quarrels not with the suffering, but he cannot abide in the position which caused it. He seems as if he must end the ordeal, not because of the pain, but because of the moral shock. We have here the repetition after his passion of that loathing which he felt before it, when he cried, 'If it be possible let this cup pass from me: nevertheless not as I will, but as thou wilt.' 'My God, my God, why hast thou forsaken me?' is the holiness of Christ amazed at the position of substitute for guilty men.

There, friends; I have done my best, but I seem to myself to have been prattling like a little child, talking about something infinitely above me. So I leave the solemn fact, that our Lord Jesus was on the tree forsaken of his God.

II. This brings us to consider THE ENQUIRY, or, why he suffered.

Note carefully this cry – 'My God, my God, why hast thou forsaken me?' It is pure anguish, undiluted agony, which crieth like this; but it is the agony of a godly soul; for only a man of that order would have used such an expression. Let us learn from it useful lessons. This cry is taken from 'the Book'. Does it not show our Lord's love of the sacred volume, that when he felt his sharpest grief, he turned to the Scripture to find a fit utterance for it? Here we have the opening sentence of the twenty-second Psalm. Oh, that we may so love the inspired Word that we may not only sing to its score, but even weep to its music!

Note, again, that our Lord's lament is an address to God. The godly, in their anguish, turn to the hand which smites them. The Saviour's outcry is not *against* God, but *to* God. 'My God, my God': he makes a double effort to draw near. True Sonship is here. The child in the dark is crying after his Father – 'My God, my God'. Both the Bible and prayer were dear to Jesus in his agony.

Still, observe, it is a faith-cry; for though it asks, 'Why hast thou forsaken me?' yet it first says, twice over, 'My God, my God'. The grip of appropriation is in the word 'my'; but the reverence of humility is in the word 'God'. It is '"My *God*, my *God*," thou art ever God to me, and I a poor creature. I do not quarrel with thee. Thy rights are unquestioned, for thou art my *God*. Thou canst do as thou wilt, and I yield to thy sacred sovereignty. I kiss the hand that smites me, and with all my heart I cry, "My God, my God."' When you are delirious with pain, think of your Bible still: when your mind wanders, let it roam towards the mercy seat; and when your heart and your flesh fail, still live by faith, and still cry, 'My God, my God'.

Let us come close to the enquiry. It looked to me, at first sight, like *a question as of one distraught,* driven from the balance of his mind – not unreasonable, but too much reasoning, and therefore tossed about. 'Why hast thou forsaken me?' Did not Jesus know? Did he not know why he was forsaken? He knew it most distinctly, and yet his manhood, while it was being crushed, pounded, dissolved, seemed as though it could not understand the reason for so great a grief. He must be forsaken; but could there be a sufficient cause for so sickening a sorrow? The cup must be bitter; but why this most nauseous of ingredients? I tremble lest I say what I ought not to say. I have said it, and I think there is truth – the Man of Sorrows was overborne with horror. At that moment the finite soul of the man Christ Jesus came into awful contact with the infinite justice of God. The one Mediator between God and man, the man Christ Jesus, beheld the holiness of God in arms against the sin of man, whose nature he had espoused. God was for him and with him in a certain unquestionable sense; but for the time, so far as his feeling went, God was against him, and necessarily withdrawn from him. It is not surprising that the holy soul of Christ should shudder at finding itself brought into painful contact with the infinite justice of God, even though its design was only to vindicate that justice, and glorify the Lawgiver. Our Lord could now say, 'All thy waves and thy billows are gone over me;' and therefore he uses language which is all too hot with anguish to be dissected by the cold hand of a logical criticism. Grief has small regard for the laws of the grammarian. Even the holiest, when in extreme agony, though they cannot speak otherwise than according to purity and truth, yet use a language of their own, which only the ear of sympathy can fully receive. I see not all that is here, but what I can see I am not able to put in words for you.

I think I see, in the expression, submission and resolve. Our Lord does not draw back. There is a forward movement in the question: they who quit a business ask no more questions about it. He does not ask that the forsaking may end prematurely, he would only understand anew its meaning. He does not shrink, but the rather dedicates himself anew to God by the words, 'My God, my God', and by seeking to review the ground and reason of that anguish which he is resolute to bear even to the bitter end. He would fain feel anew the motive which has sustained him, and must sustain him to the end. The cry sounds to me like deep submission and strong resolve, pleading with God.

Do you not think that *the amazement of our Lord, when he was 'made sin for us'* (2 Cor. 5:21), led him thus to cry out? For such a sacred and pure being to be made a sin-offering was an amazing experience. Sin was laid on him, and he was treated as if he had been guilty, though he had personally never sinned; and now the infinite horror of rebellion against the most holy God fills his holy soul, the unrighteousness of sin breaks his heart, and he starts back from it, crying, 'My God, my God, why hast thou forsaken *me*?' Why must I bear the dread result of conduct I so much abhor?

Do you not see, moreover, *there was here a glance at his eternal purpose, and at his secret source of joy?* That 'why' is the silver lining of the dark cloud, and our Lord looked wishfully at it. He knew that the desertion was needful in order that he might save the guilty, and he had an eye to that salvation as his comfort. He is not forsaken needlessly, nor without a worthy design. The design is in itself so dear to his heart that he yields to the passing evil, even though that evil be like death to him. He looks at that 'why', and through that narrow window the light of heaven comes streaming into his darkened life.

'My God, my God, why hast thou forsaken me?' Surely our Lord dwelt on that 'why', *that we might also turn our eyes that way*. He would have us see the why and the wherefore of his grief. He would have us mark the gracious motive for its endurance. Think much of all your Lord suffered, but do not overlook the reason of it. If you cannot always understand how this or that grief worked toward the great end of the whole passion, yet believe that it has its share in the grand 'why'. Make a life-study of that bitter but blessed question, 'Why hast thou forsaken me?' Thus the Saviour raises an inquiry not so much for himself as for us; and not so much because of any despair within his heart as because of a hope and a joy set before him, which were wells of comfort to him in his wilderness of woe.

Call to mind, for a moment, that the Lord God, in the broadest and most unreserved sense, could never, in very deed, have forsaken his most obedient Son. He was ever with him in the grand design of salvation. Towards the Lord Jesus, personally, God himself, personally, must ever have stood on terms of infinite love. Truly the Only Begotten was never more lovely to the Father than when he was obedient unto death, even the death of the cross! But we must look upon God here as the Judge of all the earth, and we must look upon the Lord Jesus also in his official capacity, as the Surety of the covenant, and the Sacrifice for sin. The great Judge of all cannot smile upon him who has become the substitute for the guilty. Sin is loathed of God; and if, in order to its removal, his own Son is made to bear it, yet, as sin, it is still loathsome, and he who bears it cannot be in happy communion with God. This was the dread necessity of expiation; but in the essence of things the love of the great Father to his Son never ceased, nor ever knew a diminution. Restrained in its flow it must be, but lessened at its fountain head it could not be. Therefore, wonder not at the question, 'Why hast thou forsaken me?'

III. Hoping to be guided by the Holy Spirit, I am coming to THE ANSWER, concerning which I can only use the few minutes which remain to me. 'My God, my God, why hast thou forsaken me?' What is the outcome of this suffering? What was the reason for it? Our Saviour could answer his own question. If for a moment his manhood was perplexed, yet his mind soon came to clear apprehension; for he said, 'It is finished;' and, as I have already said, he then referred to the work which in his lonely agony he had been performing. Why, then, did God forsake his Son? I cannot conceive any other answer than this – *he stood in our stead*. There was no reason in Christ why the Father should forsake him: he was perfect, and his life was without spot. God never acts without reason; and since there were no reasons in the character and person of the Lord Jesus why his Father should forsake him, we must look elsewhere. I do not know how others answer the question. I can only answer it in this one way.

> Yet all the griefs he felt were ours,
>   Ours were the woes he bore;
> Pangs, not his own, his spotless soul
>   With bitter anguish tore.

> We held him as condemn'd of heaven,
>   An outcast from his God;
> While for our sins he groaned, he bled,
>   Beneath his Father's rod.

He bore the sinner's sin, and he had to be treated, therefore, as though he were a sinner, though sinner he could never be. With his own full consent he suffered as though he had committed the transgressions which were laid on him. Our sin, and his taking it upon himself, is the answer to the question, 'Why hast thou forsaken me?'

In this case we now see that *his obedience was perfect*. He came into the world to obey the Father, and he rendered that obedience to the very uttermost. The spirit of obedience could go no farther than for one who feels forsaken of God still to cling to him in solemn, avowed allegiance, still declaring before a mocking multitude his confidence in the afflicting God. It is noble to cry, 'My God, my God', when one is asking, 'Why hast thou forsaken me?' How much farther can obedience go? I see nothing beyond it. The soldier at the gate of Pompeii remaining at his post as sentry when the shower of burning ashes is falling, was not more true to his trust than he who adheres to a forsaking God with loyalty of hope.

Our Lord's suffering in this particular form was appropriate and necessary. It would not have sufficed for our Lord merely to have been pained in body, nor even to have been grieved in mind in other ways: he must suffer in this particular way. He must feel forsaken of God, because this is the necessary consequence of sin. For a man to be forsaken of God is the penalty which naturally and inevitably follows upon his breaking his relation with God. What is death? What was the death that was threatened to Adam? 'In the day that thou eatest thereof thou shalt surely die.' Is death annihilation? Was Adam annihilated that day? Assuredly not: he lived many a year afterwards. But in the day in which he ate of the forbidden fruit he died, by being separated from God. The separation of the soul from God is spiritual death; just as the separation of the soul from the body is natural death. The sacrifice for sin must be put in the place of separation, and must bow to the penalty of death. By this placing of the Great Sacrifice under forsaking and death, it would be seen by all creatures throughout the universe that God could not have fellowship with sin. If even the Holy One, who stood the Just for the unjust, found God forsaking him, what must the doom of the actual sinner be! Sin is evidently always, in every case, a dividing influence, putting even the Christ himself, as a sin-bearer, in the place of distance.

This was necessary for another reason: there could have been no laying on of suffering for sin without the forsaking of the vicarious Sacrifice by the Lord God. So long as the smile of God rests on the man the law is not afflicting him. The approving look of the great Judge cannot fall upon a man who is viewed as standing in the place of the guilty. Christ not only suffered *from* sin, but *for* sin. If God will cheer and sustain him, he is not suffering for sin. The Judge is not inflicting suffering for sin if he is manifestly succouring the smitten one. There could have been no vicarious suffering on the part of Christ for human guilt, if he had continued consciously to enjoy the full sunshine of the Father's presence. It was essential to being a victim in our place that he should cry, 'My God, my God, why hast thou forsaken me?'

Beloved, see how marvellously, in the person of Christ, the Lord our God has vindicated his law! If to make his law glorious, he had said, 'These multitudes of men have broken my law, and therefore they shall perish,' the law would have been terribly magnified. But, instead thereof, he says, 'Here is my Only Begotten Son, my other self; he takes on himself the nature of these rebellious creatures, and he consents that I should lay on him the load of their iniquity, and visit in his person the offences which might have been punished in the persons of all these multitudes of men: and I will have it so.' When Jesus bows his head to the stroke of the law, when he submissively consents that his Father shall turn away his face from him, then myriads of worlds are astonished at the perfect holiness and stern justice of the Lawgiver.

There are, probably, worlds innumerable throughout the boundless creation of God, and all these will see, in the death of God's dear Son, a declaration of his determination never to allow sin to be trifled with. If his own Son is brought before him, bearing the sin of others upon him, he will hide his face from him, as well as from the actually guilty. In God infinite love shines over all, but it does not eclipse his absolute justice any more than his justice is permitted to destroy his love. God hath all perfections in perfection, and in Christ Jesus we see the reflection of them. Beloved, this is a wonderful theme! Oh, that I had a tongue worthy of this subject! but who could ever reach the height of this great argument?

Once more, when enquiring, Why did Jesus suffer to be forsaken of the Father? we see the fact that *the Captain of our salvation was thus made perfect through suffering.* Every part of the road has been traversed by our Lord's own feet. Suppose, beloved, the Lord Jesus had never been thus forsaken, then one of his disciples might have been called to that sharp endurance, and the Lord Jesus could not have sympathized with him in it. He would turn to his Leader and Captain, and say to him, 'Didst thou, my Lord, ever feel this darkness?' Then the Lord Jesus would answer, 'No. This is a descent such as I never made.' What a dreadful lack would the tried one have felt! For the Servant to bear a grief his Master never knew would be sad indeed.

There would have been a wound for which there was no ointment, a pain for which there was no balm. But it is not so now. 'In all their affliction he was afflicted.' 'He was in all points tempted like as we are, yet without sin.' Wherein we greatly rejoice at this time, and so often as we are cast down. Underneath us is the deep experience of our forsaken Lord.

I have done when I have said three things. The first is, you and I that are believers in the Lord Jesus Christ, and are resting in him alone for salvation, *let us lean hard,* let us bear with all our weight on our Lord. He will bear the full weight of all our sin and care. As to my sin, I hear its harsh accusings no more when I hear Jesus cry, 'Why hast thou forsaken me?' I know that I deserve the deepest hell at the hand of God's vengeance; but I am not afraid. He will never forsake me, for he forsook his Son on my behalf. I shall not suffer for my sin, for Jesus has suffered to the full in my stead; yea, suffered so far as to cry, 'My God, my God, why hast thou forsaken me?' Behind this brazen wall of substitution a sinner is safe. These 'munitions of rock' guard all believers, and they may rest secure. The rock is cleft for me; I hide in its rifts, and no harm can reach me. You have a full atonement, a great sacrifice, a glorious vindication of the law; wherefore rest at peace, all you that put your trust in Jesus.

Next, if ever in our lives henceforth we should think that God hath deserted us, *let us learn from our Lord's example how to behave ourselves.* If God hath left thee, do not shut up thy Bible; nay, open it, as thy Lord did, and find a text that will suit thee. If God hath left thee, or thou thinkest so, do not give up prayer; nay, pray as thy Lord did, and be more earnest than ever. If thou thinkest God has forsaken thee, do not give up thy faith in him; but, like thy Lord, cry thou, 'My God, my God, again and again. If thou hast had one anchor before, cast out two anchors now, and double the hold of thy faith. If thou canst not call Jehovah 'Father', as was Christ's wont, yet call him thy 'God'. Let the personal pronouns take their hold – 'My God, my God'. Let nothing drive thee from thy faith. Still hold on Jesus, sink or swim. As for me, if ever I am lost, it shall be at the foot of the cross. To this pass have I come, that if I never see the face of God with acceptance, yet I will believe that he will be faithful to his Son, and true to the covenant sealed by oaths and blood. He that believeth in Jesus hath everlasting life: there I cling, like the limpet to the rock. There is but one gate of heaven; and even if I may not enter it, I will cling to the posts of its door. What am I saying? I shall enter in; for that gate was never shut against a soul that accepted Jesus; and Jesus saith, 'Him that cometh to me I will in no wise cast out.'

The last of the three points is this, *let us abhor the sin which brought such agony upon our beloved Lord*. What an accursed thing is sin, which crucified the Lord Jesus! Do you laugh at it? Will you go and spend an evening to see a mimic performance of it? Do you roll sin under your tongue as a sweet morsel, and then come to God's house, on the Lord's Day morning, and think to worship him? Worship him! Worship him, with sin indulged in your breast! Worship him, with sin loved and pampered in your life! O sirs, if I had a dear brother who had been murdered, what would you think of me if I valued the knife which had been crimsoned with his blood? – if I made a friend of the murderer, and daily consorted with the assassin, who drove the dagger into my brother's heart? Surely I, too, must be an accomplice in the crime! Sin murdered Christ; will you be a friend to it? Sin pierced the heart of the Incarnate God; can you love it? Oh, that there was an abyss as deep as Christ's misery, that I might at once hurl this dagger of sin into its depths, whence it might never be brought to light again! Begone, O sin! Thou art banished from the heart where Jesus reigns! Begone, for thou hast crucified my Lord, and made him cry, 'Why hast thou forsaken me?' O my hearers, if you did but know yourselves, and know the love of Christ, you would each one vow that you would harbour sin no longer. You would be indignant at sin, and cry,

> The dearest idol I have known,
> Whate'er that idol be,
> Lord, I will tear it from its throne,
> And worship only thee.

May that be the issue of my morning's discourse, and then I shall be well content. The Lord bless you! May the Christ who suffered for you, bless you, and out of his darkness may your light arise! Amen.

12

THE SADDEST CRY FROM THE CROSS[1]

And about the ninth hour Jesus cried with a loud voice,
saying, Eli, Eli, lama sabachthani? that is to say,
My God, my God, why hast thou forsaken me
MATTHEW 27:46.

DURING THE TIME that 'Moses kept the flock of Jethro, his father-in-law,' he 'came to the mountain of God, even to Horeb,' and there he saw a strange sight' – a bush that burned with fire, and yet was not consumed. Then Moses, apparently constrained by curiosity, was drawing near, in order to examine this phenomenon, when he heard God's voice say to him, 'Draw not nigh hither: put off thy shoes from off thy feet, for the place whereon thou standest is holy ground.' We also may well feel, as we think of our Lord Jesus in his agony, that the voice of God speaks to us from the cross, and says, 'Curiosity – bold, daring, prying intellect – draw not nigh hither; put off thy shoes from off thy feet, for the place whereon thou standest is the very Holy of Holies, unto which no man may come except as the Spirit of God shall conduct him thither.'

I think I can understand the words, 'My God, my God, why hast thou forsaken me?' as they are written by David in the 22nd Psalm; but the same words, 'My God, my God, why hast thou forsaken me?' when uttered by Jesus on the cross, I cannot comprehend, so I shall not pretend to be able to explain them. There is no plummet

[1] Sermon No. 2,803. Preached at the Metropolitan Tabernacle on Sunday evening, 7 January 1877.

that can fathom this deep; there is no eagle's eye that can penetrate the mystery that surrounds this strange question. I have read that, once upon a time, Martin Luther sat him down in his study to consider this text. Hour after hour, that mighty man of God sat still; and those who waited on him came into the room, again and again, and he was so absorbed in his meditation that they almost thought he was a corpse. He moved neither hand nor foot, and neither ate nor drank; but sat with his eyes wide open, like one in a trance, thinking over these wondrous words, 'My God, my God, why hast thou forsaken me?' And when, after many long hours, in which he seemed to be utterly lost to everything that went on around him, he rose from his chair, someone heard him say, 'God forsaking God! No man can understand that'; and so he went his way. Though that is hardly the correct expression to use – I should hesitate to endorse it – yet I do not marvel that our text presented itself to the mind of Luther in that light. It is said that he looked like a man who had been down a deep mine, and who had come up again to the light. I feel more like one who has not been down the mine, but who has looked into it – or like one who has been part of the way down, and shuddered as he passed through the murky darkness but who would not dare to go much lower, for this cry, 'Eli, Eli, lama sabachthani?' 'is a tremendous deep; no man will ever be able to fathom it'.

So I am not going to try to explain it; but, first, to utter *some thoughts about it* and then, secondly, to draw *some lessons from it*. We may find many practical uses for things which are beyond the grasp of our minds, and this saying of our Lord may be of great service to us even though we cannot comprehend it.

I. First, then, let me utter SOME THOUGHTS ABOUT THIS STRANGE QUESTION: 'My God, my God, why hast thou forsaken me?'

Jesus was accustomed to address God as his Father. If you turn to his many prayers, you will find him almost invariably – if not invariably – speaking to God as his Father. And, truly, he stands in that relationship both as God and as man. Yet, in this instance, he does not say, 'Father'; but 'My God, my God.' Was it that he had any doubt about his Sonship? Assuredly not; Satan had assailed him in the wilderness with the insinuation, 'If thou be the Son of God', but Christ had put him to the rout; and I feel persuaded that Satan had not gained any advantage over him, even on the cross, which could have made him doubt whether he was the Son of God or not.

I think that *our Saviour was speaking then as man,* and that this is the reason why he cried, 'My God, my God,' rather than 'My Father'. I think he must have been speaking as man; as I can scarcely bring my mind to the point of conceiving that God the Son could say to God the Father, 'My God, my God.' There is such a wonderful blending of the human and the Divine in the person of the Lord Jesus Christ that, though it may not be absolutely accurate to ascribe to the Deity some things in the life of Christ, yet is he so completely God and man that, often, Scripture does speak of things that must belong to the humanity only as if they belonged to the Godhead. For instance, in his charge to the Ephesian elders, the apostle Paul said, 'Feed the church of God, which he hath purchased with his own blood' – an incorrect expression, if judged according to the rule of the logician; but accurate enough according to the Scriptural method of using words in their proper sense. Yet I do think that we must draw a distinction between the Divinity and the humanity here. As the Lord Jesus said, 'My God, my God,' it was because it was his humanity that was mainly to be considered just then.

And O my brethren, does it not show us *what a real man, the Christ of God was, that he could be forsaken of his God?* We might have supposed that, Christ being Emmanuel – God with us – the Godhead and the manhood being indissolubly united in one person, it would have been impossible for him to be forsaken of God. We might also have inferred, for the same reason, that it would have been impossible for him to have been scourged, and spit upon, and especially that it would not have been possible for him to die. Yet all these things were made, not only possible, but also sacredly certain. In order to complete the redemption of his chosen people, it was necessary for him to be both God's well-beloved Son, and to be forsaken of his Father; he could truly say, as his saints also have sometimes had to say, 'My God, my God, why hast thou forsaken me?' Persecuted and forsaken believer, behold your Brother in adversity! Behold the One who has gone wherever you may have to go, who has suffered more than you can ever suffer, and who has taken his part in the direst calamity that ever happened to human nature, so that he had to cry out, in the agony of his soul, 'My God, my God, why hast thou forsaken me?'

What was this forsaking? We are trying to come a little closer to this burning yet unconsumed bush – with our shoes off our feet, I hope, all the while – and in this spirit we ask, 'What was this forsaking?' A devout writer says that it was *horror at the sight of human misery.* He affirms, what is quite true, that our Lord Jesus Christ saw all that man had to suffer because of sin; that he perceived the total sum of the miseries brought by sin upon all the past, present, and future generations of the human race – and that he must have had a holy horror as he thought of all the woes of man, caused by sin, in this life, and in that which is to come – and being completely one with man, he spoke in the name of man, and said, 'My God, my God, why hast thou forsaken me?' That is all true, yet that explanation will not suffice, my brethren; because our Saviour did not say, 'My God, my God, why hast thou forsaken *man?*' but, 'Why hast thou forsaken *me?*' This forsaking was something personal to himself.

Others have said that *it was a dreadful shrinking in his soul on account of human sin.* I have read of a child, who had done wrong, and whose father had faithfully rebuked and punished him; but the boy remained callous and sullen. He sat in the same room with his father, yet he refused to confess that he had done wrong. At last, the father, under a sense of his child's great wickedness, burst into tears, and sobbed and sighed. Then the boy came to his father, and asked him why he sorrowed so, and he answered, 'Because of my child's hardness of heart.' It is true that our Lord Jesus Christ did feel as that father felt; only far more acutely; but our text cannot be fully explained by any such illustration as that; that would be only explaining it away, for Christ did not say, 'My God, my God, why has man forsaken thee, and why hast thou so completely left men in their sin?' No; his cry was, 'Why hast thou forsaken *me?*' It was not so much the God of man to whom he appealed, but 'My God, *my* God.' It was a personal grief that wrung from him the personal cry, 'My God, my God, why hast thou forsaken me?' for this forsaking, by his Father in whom he trusted, related peculiarly to himself.

What was this forsaking? *Was it physical weakness?* Some of you may know that, when the body is in a low condition, the soul also sinks. Quite involuntarily, unhappiness of mind, depression of spirit, and sorrow of heart will come upon you. You may he without any real reason for grief, and yet may be among the most unhappy of men because, for the time, your body has conquered your soul. But, my brethren and sisters, this explanation is not supposable in the case of Christ, for it was not many moments after this that he shouted, 'with a loud voice', his conquering cry, 'It is finished', and so passed from the conflict to his coronation. His brave spirit overcame his physical weakness; and though he was 'brought into the dust of death', and plunged into the deepest depths of depression of spirit, yet, still, the cry, 'My God, my God,' which also was uttered 'with a loud voice,' proves that there was still a considerable amount of mental strength, notwithstanding his physical weakness, so that mere depression of spirit, caused by physical reasons, would not account for this agonizing cry.

And, certainly, my brethren, *this cry was not occasioned by unbelief.* You know that, sometimes, a child of God, in sore trial, and with many inward struggles, cries out, 'My God, my God, why hast thou forsaken me?' when, all the while, the Lord has been remembering the tried soul, and dealing graciously with it. As long ago as Isaiah's day, 'Zion said, The Lord hath forsaken me, and my Lord hath forgotten me.' But the Lord's reply was, 'Can a woman forget her sucking child, that she should not have compassion on the son of her womb? yea, they may forget, yet will I not forget thee. Behold, I have graven thee upon the palms of my hand.' Unbelief often makes us talk about God forgetting us when he does nothing of the kind, but our Lord Jesus Christ was a stranger to unbelief. It was impossible for him to cherish any doubt about the faithfulness and lovingkindness of his Father; so his cry did not arise from that cause.

And, another thing, *it did not arise from a mistake.* I have known believers, in sore trouble, make great blunders concerning what God was doing with them. They have thought that he had forsaken them, for they misinterpreted certain signs, and dealings of God, and they said, 'All these things are against us; the hand of God has gone out against us to destroy us.' But Christ made no mistake about this matter, for God had forsaken him. It was really so. When he said, 'Why hast thou forsaken me?' he spoke infallible truth, and his mind was under no cloud whatsoever. He knew what he was saying, and he was right in what he said, for his Father had forsaken him for the time.

What, then, can this expression mean? *Does it mean that God did not love his Son?* O beloved, let us, with the utmost detestation, fling away any suspicion of the kind that we may have harboured! God did forsake his Son but he loved him as much when he forsook him as at any other period. I even venture to say that, if it had been possible for God's love towards his Son to be increased, he would have delighted in him more when he was standing as the suffering Representative of his chosen people than ever he had delighted in him before. We do not indulge, for a single moment, the thought that God was angry with him personally, or looked upon him as unworthy of his love, or regarded him as one upon whom he could not smile, because of anything displeasing in himself; yet the fact remains that God had forsaken him, for Christ was under no mistake about that matter. He rightly felt that his Father had withdrawn the comfortable light of his countenance, that he had, for the time being, lost the sense of his Father's favour – not the favour itself, but the consciousness of that divine aid and succour which he had formerly enjoyed – so he felt himself like a man left all alone; and he was not only left all alone by his friends, but also by his God.

Can we at all imagine the state of mind in which our Lord was when he cried, 'My God, my God, why hast thou forsaken me?' No; that is not possible, yet I will try to help you to understand it. Can you imagine the misery of a lost soul in hell – one who is forsaken of God, and who cries, in bitterest agony, 'God will never look upon me in mercy, or delight, or favour,' – can you picture that sad state? Well, if you can, you will not, even then, have got anywhere near the position of Christ, because that soul in hell does not want God's favour, and does not seek it, or ask for it. That lost soul is so hardened in sin that it never troubles about whether God would receive it if it repented; the truth is, that it does not want to repent. The misery, that men will suffer in the world to come, will be self-created misery arising out of the fact that they loved sin so much that they brought eternal sorrow upon themselves. It must be an awful thing for a soul, in the next world, to be without God; but, as far as its own consciousness is concerned, it will be so hardened that it will abide without God, yet not realizing all that it has lost because it is itself incapable of knowing the beauty of holiness, and the perfection of the God from whom it is separated for ever. Yet how different was the case of our Lord Jesus Christ when upon the cross! He knew, as no mere man could ever know, what separation from God meant.

Think of a case of another kind. King Saul, when the witch of Endor brought up the spirit of Samuel, said to him, 'God is departed from me, and answereth me no more.' You recollect the state of mind that he was in when the evil spirit was upon him, and he needed David's harp to charm it away; but at last, even that failed, and I know of no more unhappy character than Saul when God had departed from him. But, somehow, there was not the anguish in the soul of Saul that there would have been if he had ever really known the Lord. I do not think that he ever did really, in his inmost soul, know the Lord. After Samuel anointed him, he was 'turned into another man', but he never became a new man; and the sense of God's presence that he had was not, for a moment, comparable to that presence of God which a true saint enjoys, and which Christ ever enjoyed, except when he was on the cross. So, when Saul lost the consciousness of that presence, he did not suffer so great a loss, and, consequently, so great an anguish, as afterwards happened to our Lord.

Coming nearer to our own circumstances, I remind you that there are some of God's people, who do really love him, and who have walked in the light of his countenance, yet, for some reason or other, they have lost the comfortable enjoyment of God's love. If any of you, dear friends, know what that sad experience is, you are getting a faint impression of the meaning of this cry, 'My God, my God, why hast thou forsaken me?' Oh, what an anguish it is – what heartbreak – even to think that one is forsaken of God! I have heard of people dying of broken hearts; but I do believe that the man, who has been made to utter this cry, has gone as near to dying of a broken heart as anyone might well do without actually dying. To be without God, is to be without life; and we, who love him, can say, with Dr Watts –

> My God, my life, my love,
> To thee, to thee I call:
> I cannot live, if thou remove,
> For thou art All-in-all.

But, my dear brethren, you have not got the whole truth yet, for *no saint knows the presence of God as Christ knew it*. No saint has, to the full, enjoyed the love of God as Christ enjoyed it; and, consequently, if he does lose it, he only seems to lose the moonlight whereas Christ lost the sunlight when, for a time, the face of his Father was withdrawn from him. Only think what must have been the anguish of the Saviour, especially as contrasted with his former enjoyment. Never did any mere human being know so much and enjoy so much of the love of God as Christ had done. He had lived in it, basked in it; there had never been any interruption to it. 'I do always those things that please him,' said he, concerning his Father; and his Father twice said, concerning him, 'This is my beloved Son, in whom I am well pleased.' Now, as our Lord Jesus Christ had enjoyed the love of God to the very full, think what it must have been for him to lose the conscious enjoyment of it. You know that you may go into a room, and blow out the candle, but the blind people will not miss it. They miss the light most who have enjoyed it most; and Christ missed the light of God's countenance most because he had enjoyed it most. Then, reflect upon his intense love to God. Jesus Christ – the man Christ Jesus – loved God with all his heart, and mind, and soul and strength, as you and I have never yet been able to do. The love of Christ towards his Father was boundless. Well, then, for a frown to be upon his Father's face, or for the light of that Father's face to be taken away from him, must have made it correspondingly dark and terrible to him.

Remember, too, the absolute purity of Christ's nature. In him there was no taint of sin, nor anything approaching to it. Now, holiness delights in God. God is the very sea in which holiness swims – the air which holiness breathes. Only think, then, of the perfectly Holy One, fully agreed with his Father in everything, finding out that the Father had, for good and sufficient reasons, turned away his face from him. O brother, in proportion as you are holy, the absence of the light of God's countenance will be grief to you; and as Jesus was perfectly holy, it was the utmost anguish to him to have to cry to his Father, 'Why hast thou forsaken me?'

After all, beloved, the only solution of the mystery is this, *Jesus Christ was forsaken of God because we deserved to be forsaken of God.* He was there, on the cross, in our room, and place, and stead; and as the sinner, by reason of his sin, deserves not to enjoy the favour of God, so Jesus Christ, standing in the place of the sinner, and enduring that which would vindicate the justice of God, had to come under the cloud, as the sinner must have come, if Christ had not taken his place. But, then, since he has come under it, let us recollect that he was thus left of God that you and I, who believe in him, might never be left of God. Since he, for a little while, was separated from his Father, we may boldly cry, 'Who shall separate us from the love of Christ?' and, with the apostle Paul, we may confidently affirm that nothing in the whole universe shall be able to separate us from the love of God, which is in Christ Jesus our Lord.'

Before I leave this point, let me say that *the doctrine of substitution is the key to all the sufferings of Christ.* I do not know how many theories have been invented to explain away the death of Christ. The modern doctrine of the apostles of 'culture' is that Jesus Christ did something or other, which, in some way or other, was, in some degree or other, connected with our salvation; but it is my firm belief that every theory, concerning the death of Christ, which can only be understood by the highly-cultured, must be false. 'That is strong language,' says someone. Perhaps it is, but it is true.

I am quite sure that the religion of Jesus Christ was never intended for the highly-cultured only, or even for them in particular. Christ's testimony concerning his own ministry was, 'The poor have the gospel preached to them'; so if you bring me a gospel which can only be understood by gentlemen who have passed through Oxford or Cambridge University, I know that it cannot be the gospel of Christ. He meant the good news of salvation to be proclaimed to the poorest of the poor; in fact, the gospel is intended for humanity in general; so, if you cannot make me understand it, or if, when I do understand it, it does not tell me how to deliver its message in such plain language that the poorest man can comprehend it, I tell you, sirs, that your newfangled gospel is a lie, and I will stick to the old one, which a man, only a little above an idiot in intellect, can understand. I cling to the old gospel for this, among many other reasons, that all the modern gospels, that leave out the great central truth of substitution, prevent the message from being of any use to the great mass of mankind. If those other gospels, which are not really gospels, please your taste and fancy, and suit the readers of *Quarterly Reviews*, and eloquent orators and lecturers, there are the poor people in our streets, and the millions of working men, the vast multitudes who cannot comprehend anything that is highly metaphysical; and you cannot convince me that our Lord Jesus Christ sent, as his message to the whole world, a metaphysical mystery that would need volume upon volume before it could even be stated. I am persuaded that he gave us a rough and ready gospel like this, 'The Son of man is come to seek and to save that which was lost;' or this, 'With his stripes we are healed;' or this, 'The chastisement of our peace was upon him;' or this, 'He died the Just for the unjust to bring us to God.' Do not try to go beyond this gospel, brethren; you will get into the mud if you do. But it is safe standing here; and standing here, I can comprehend how our Lord Jesus took the sinner's place, and passing under the sentence which the sinner deserved, or under a sentence which was tantamount thereto, could cry, 'My God, my God, why hast thou forsaken me?'

II. Now, in closing, I am going to draw A FEW LESSONS FROM THIS UTTERANCE OF CHRIST.

The first lesson is, *Behold how he loved us!* When Christ stood and wept at the grave of Lazarus, the Jews said, 'Behold how he loved him!' But on the cross he did not weep, he bled; and he not merely bled, he died; and, before he died, his spirit sank within him, for he was forsaken of his God. Was there ever any other love like this – that the Prince of life and glory should condescend to this shame and death?

Then, next, brothers and sisters, as he suffered so much for us, *let us be ready to suffer anything for his sake.* Let us be willing even to lose all the joy of religion, if that would glorify God. I do not know that it would; but I think the spirit of Christ ought to carry us even as far as Moses went, when he pleaded for the guilty nation of Israel, and was willing to have his own name blotted out of the book of life rather than that God's name should be dishonoured. We have never had to go so far as that, and we never shall; yet let us be willing to part with our last penny, for Christ's name's sake, if he requires it. Let us be willing to lose our reputation. And, it is a difficult thing to give that up! Some of us, when we first came into public notice, and found our words picked to pieces, and our character slandered, felt it rather hard. We have got used to it now; but it was very trying at first. But, oh! if one had to be called a devil – if one had to go through this world, and to be spat upon by every passer-by – still, if it were endured for Christ's sake, remembering how he was forsaken of God for us, we ought to take up even that cross with thankfulness that we were permitted to bear it.

Another lesson is that, if ever you and I should feel that we are forsaken of God – *if we should get into this state in any way, remember that we are only where Christ has been before us.* If ever, in our direst extremity, we should be compelled to cry, 'My God, my God, why hast thou forsaken me?' we shall have gone down no deeper than Christ himself went. He knows that feeling, and that state of heart, for he has felt the same. This fact should tend greatly to cheer you. Your deep depression is not a proof of reprobation; that is evident, for Christ himself endured even more. A man may say, 'I cannot be a child of God, or else I should not feel as I do.' Ah! you do not know what true children of God may feel; strange thoughts pass through their minds in times of storm and doubt. A Puritan preacher was standing by the deathbed of one of his members who had been for thirty years in gloom of soul. The good old minister expected that the man would get peace at last, for he had been an eminent Christian and had greatly rejoiced in his Saviour; but, for thirty years or more, he had fallen into deep gloom. The minister was trying to speak a word of comfort to him, but the man said, 'Ah, sir! but what can you say to a man who is dying, and yet who feels that God has forsaken him?' The pastor replied, 'But what became of that Man who died, whom God did really forsake? Where is HE now?' The dying man caught at that, and said, 'He is in glory, and I shall be with him; I shall be with him where he is.' And so the light came to the dying man who had been so long in the dark; he saw that Christ had been just where he was, and that he should be where Christ was, even at the right hand of the Father. I hope, brothers and sisters, that you will never get down so low as that; but I beseech you, if you ever meet with any others who are there, do not be rough with them. Some strong-minded people are very apt to be hard upon nervous folk, and to say, 'They should not get into that state.' And we are liable to speak harshly to people who are very depressed in spirit, and to say to them, 'Really, you ought to rouse yourself out of such a state.' I hope none of you will ever have such an experience of this depression of spirit as I have had; yet I have learnt from it to be very tender with all fellow-sufferers. The Lord have mercy on them, and help them out of the Slough of Despond; for, if he does not, they will sink in deep mire, where there is no standing.

I pray God specially to bless this inference from our text. *There is hope for you, brother, or sister, if you are in this condition.* Christ came through it, and he will be with you in it; and, after all, you are not forsaken as he was, be you sure of that. With you, the forsaking is only in the apprehension; that is bad enough, but it is not a matter of fact, for 'the Lord will not forsake his people,' nor cast away even one of those whom he has chosen.

I will tell you what is a much more awful thing even than crying out, 'My God, my God, why hast thou forsaken me?' If you are afraid that God has left you, and the sweat stands on your brow in very terror, and if your soul seems to long for death rather than life, in such a state as that, you are not in the worst possible condition. 'Why!' you ask, 'is there anything worse than that?' Yes, I will tell you what is much worse than that; that is, to be without God, and not to care about it – to be living, like some whom I am now addressing, without God, and without hope, yet that never concerns them at all. I can pity the agony of the man who cannot bear to be without his God; but, at the same time, I can bless the

Lord that he feels such agony as that, for that proves to me that his soul will never perish. But those whom I look upon with fear and trembling are the men who make a profession of religion, yet who never have any communion with God, and, all the while are quite happy about it – or backsliders, who have gone away from God, and yet seem perfectly at ease. You, worldlings, who are quite satisfied with the things of this world, and have no longings for the world that is to come, I wish you had got as far as to be unhappy; I wish you had got as far as to be in an agony for that is the road to heavenly joy. It was thus that Christ won it for us and it is by such a path as this, that many a soul is first led into the experience of his saving power. Brethren, weep not for those of us who sometimes have to cry out in anguish of soul; mourn not for us who are cast down because we cannot live without Christ. You see that our Lord has made us covet the highest blessings; our heads have been so often on his bosom that, if they are not always there, we keep on crying till we get back to that blessed position again.

This is a sweet sorrow; may we have more and more of it! But, oh! I pray you, pity those who never ate the bread of heaven – never drank of the water of life – never knew the sweetness of the kisses of Christ's mouth – and never knew what it was to have a heaven begun below in the enjoyment of fellowship with him. In such cases, your pity is indeed required.

I have finished when I have just said this – as you come to the table of your Lord, come, brothers and sisters, with this cry of Christ ringing in your ears, to make you love him more than ever; and, as you eat the bread, and drink the wine, do it all out of fervent love to him; and the Lord bless you, for his name's sake! Amen.

13

THE SHORTEST OF THE SEVEN CRIES[1]

After this, Jesus knowing that all things were
now accomplished, that the scripture might
be fulfilled, saith, I thirst.
JOHN 19:28

IT WAS MOST FITTING that every word of our Lord upon the cross should be gathered up and preserved. As not a bone of him shall be broken, so not a word shall be lost. The Holy Spirit took special care that each of the sacred utterances should be fittingly recorded. There were, as you know, seven of those last words, and seven is the number of perfection and fullness; the number which blends the three of the infinite God with the four of complete creation. Our Lord in his death-cries, as in all else, was perfection itself. There is a fullness of meaning in each utterance which no man shall be able fully to bring forth, and when combined they make up a vast deep of thought, which no human line can fathom. Here, as everywhere else, we are constrained to say of our Lord, 'Never man spake like this man.' Amid all the anguish of his spirit his last words prove him to have remained fully self-possessed, true to his forgiving nature, true to his kingly office, true to his filial relationship, true to his God, true to his love of the written Word, true to his glorious work, and true to his faith in his Father.

As these seven sayings were so faithfully recorded, we do not wonder that they have frequently been the subject of devout

---

[1] Sermon No. 1,409. Preached at the Metropolitan Tabernacle on Sunday morning, 14 April 1878.

meditation. Fathers and confessors, preachers and divines have delighted to dwell upon every syllable of these matchless cries. These solemn sentences have shone like the seven golden candlesticks or the seven stars of the Apocalypse, and have lighted multitudes of men to him who spake them. Thoughtful men have drawn a wealth of meaning from them, and in so doing have arranged them into different groups, and placed them under several heads. I cannot give you more than a mere taste of this rich subject, but I have been most struck with two ways of regarding our Lord's last words. First, they teach and confirm many of the doctrines of our holy faith. *'Father, forgive them; for they know not what they do'* is the first. Here is the forgiveness of sin – free forgiveness in answer to the Saviour's plea. *'Today shalt thou be with me in paradise.'* Here is the safety of the believer in the hour of his departure, and his instant admission into the presence of his Lord. It is a blow at the fable of purgatory which strikes it to the heart. *'Woman, behold thy son!'* This very plainly sets forth the true and proper humanity of Christ, who to the end recognised his human relationship to Mary, of whom he was born.

Yet his language teaches us not to worship *her*, for he calls her 'woman', but to honour him who in his direst agony thought of her needs and griefs, as he also thinks of all his people, for these are his mother and sister and brother. *'Eloi, Eloi, lama sabachthani?'* is the fourth cry, and it illustrates the penalty endured by our Substitute when he bore our sins, and so was forsaken of his God. The sharpness of that sentence no exposition can fully disclose to us: it is keen as the very edge and point of the sword which pierced his heart. *'I thirst'* is the fifth cry, and its utterance teaches us the truth of Scripture, for all things were accomplished, that the Scripture might be fulfilled, and therefore our Lord said, 'I thirst.' Holy Scripture remains the basis of our faith, established by every word and act of our Redeemer. The last word but one is, *'It is finished.'* There is the complete justification of the believer, since the work by which he is accepted is fully accomplished. The last of his last words is also taken from the Scriptures, and shows where his mind was feeding. He cried, ere he bowed the head which he had held erect amid all his conflict, as one who never yielded, *'Father, into thy hands I commend my spirit.'* In that cry there is reconciliation to God. He who stood in our stead has finished all his work, and now his spirit comes back to the Father, and he brings us with him. Every word, therefore, you see teaches us some grand fundamental doctrine of our blessed faith. 'He that hath ears to hear, let him hear.'

A second mode of treating these seven cries is to view them as setting forth the person and offices of our Lord who uttered them. *'Father, forgive them; for they know not what they do'* – here we see the Mediator interceding: Jesus standing before the Father pleading for the guilty. *'Verily I say unto thee, today shalt thou be with me in paradise'* – this is the Lord Jesus in kingly power, opening with the key of David a door which none can shut, admitting into the gates of heaven the poor soul who had confessed him on the tree. Hail, everlasting King in heaven, thou dost admit to thy paradise whomsoever thou wilt! Nor dost thou set a time for waiting, but instantly thou dost set wide the gate of pearl; thou hast all power in heaven as well as upon earth. Then came, *'Woman, behold thy son!'* wherein we see the Son of man in the gentleness of a son caring for his bereaved mother. In the former cry, as he opened Paradise, you saw the Son of God; now you see him who was verily and truly born of a woman, made under the law; and under the law you see him still, for he honours his mother and cares for her in the last article of death. Then comes the *'My God, my God, why hast thou forsaken me?'* Here we behold his human soul in anguish, his inmost heart overwhelmed by the withdrawing of Jehovah's face, and made to cry out as if in perplexity and amazement. *'I thirst,'* is his human *body* tormented by grievous pain. Here you see how the mortal flesh had to share in the agony of the inward spirit. *'It is finished'* is the last word but one, and there you see the perfected Saviour, the Captain of our salvation, who has completed the undertaking upon which he had entered, finished transgression, made an end of sin, and brought in everlasting righteousness.

The last expiring word in which he *commended his spirit to his Father,* is the note of acceptance for himself and for us all. As he commends his spirit into the Father's hand, so does he bring all believers nigh to God, and henceforth we are in the hand of the Father, who is greater than all, and none shall pluck us thence. Is not this a fertile field of thought? May the Holy Spirit often lead us to glean therein.

There are many other ways in which these words might be read, and they would be found to be all full of instruction. Like the steps of a ladder or the links of a golden chain, there is a mutual dependence and interlinking of each of the cries, so that one leads to another and that to a third. Separately or in connection our Master's words overflow with instruction to thoughtful minds: but of all save one I must say, 'Of which we cannot now speak particularly.'

Our text is the shortest of all the words of Calvary; it stands as two words in our language – 'I thirst,' but in the Greek it is only one. I cannot say that it is short and sweet, for, alas, it was bitterness itself to our Lord Jesus; and yet out of its bitterness I trust there will come great sweetness to us. Though bitter to him in the speaking it will be sweet to us in the hearing – so sweet that all the bitterness of our trials shall be forgotten as we remember the vinegar and gall of which he drank.

We shall by the assistance of the Holy Spirit try to regard these words of our Saviour in a fivefold light. First, we shall look upon them as THE ENSIGN OF HIS TRUE HUMANITY. Jesus said, 'I thirst,' and this is the complaint of a man. Our Lord is the Maker of the ocean and the waters that are above the firmament: it is his hand that stays or opens the bottles of heaven, and sendeth rain upon the evil and upon the good. 'The sea is his, and he made it,' and all fountains and springs are of his digging. He poureth out the streams that run among the hills, the torrents which rush adown the mountains, and the flowing rivers which enrich the plains. One would have said, If he were thirsty he would not tell us, for all the clouds and rains would be glad to refresh his brow, and the brooks and streams would joyously flow at his feet. And yet, though he was Lord of all he had so fully taken upon himself the form of a servant and was so perfectly made in the likeness of sinful flesh, that he cried with fainting voice, 'I thirst.' How truly man he is; he is, indeed, 'bone of our bone and flesh of our flesh,' for he bears our infirmities. I invite you to meditate upon the true humanity of our Lord very reverently, and very lovingly. Jesus was proved to be really man, because he suffered the pains which belong to manhood. Angels cannot suffer thirst. A phantom, as some have called him, could not suffer in this fashion: but Jesus really suffered, not only the more refined pains of delicate and sensitive minds, but the rougher and commoner pangs of flesh and blood. Thirst is a commonplace misery, such as may happen to peasants or beggars; it is a real pain, and not a thing of a fancy or a nightmare of dreamland. Thirst is no royal grief, but an evil of universal manhood; Jesus is brother to the poorest and most humble of our race. Our Lord, however, endured thirst to an extreme degree, for it was the thirst of death which was upon him, and more, it was the thirst of one whose death was not a common one, for 'he tasted death for every man.' That thirst was caused, perhaps, in part by the loss of blood, and by the fever created by the irritation caused by his four grievous wounds. The nails were fastened in the most sensitive parts of the body, and the wounds were widened as the weight of his body dragged the nails through his blessed flesh, and tore his tender nerves. The extreme tension produced a burning feverishness. It was pain that dried his mouth and made it like an oven, till he declared, in the language of the twenty-second psalm, 'My tongue cleaveth to my jaws.' It was a thirst such as none of us have ever known, for not yet has the death dew condensed upon our brows. We shall perhaps know it in a measure in our dying hour, but not yet, nor ever so terribly as he did. Our Lord felt that grievous drought of dissolution by which all moisture seems dried up, and the flesh returns to the dust of death: this those know who have commenced to tread the valley of the shadow of death. Jesus, being a man, escaped none of the ills which are allotted to man in death. He is indeed 'Immanuel, God with us' everywhere.

Believing this, let us tenderly feel how very near akin to us our Lord Jesus has become. You have been ill, and you have been parched with fever as he was, and then you too have gasped out 'I thirst.' Your path runs hard by that of your Master. He said, 'I thirst,' in order that some one might bring him drink, even as you have wished to have a cooling draught handed to you when you could not help yourself. Can you help feeling how very near Jesus is to us when his lips must be moistened with a sponge, and he must be so dependent upon others as to ask a drink from their hand? Next time your fevered lips murmur 'I am very thirsty,' you may say to yourself 'Those are sacred words, for my Lord spake in that fashion' The words, 'I thirst,' are a common voice in death chambers. We can never forget the painful scenes of which we have been witness, when we have watched the dissolving of the human frame. Some of those whom we loved very dearly we have seen quite unable to help themselves; the death sweat has been upon them, and this has been one of the marks of their approaching dissolution, that they have been parched with thirst, and could only mutter between their half-closed lips, 'Give me to drink.' Ah, beloved, our Lord was so truly man that all our griefs remind us of him: the next time we are thirsty we may gaze upon him; and whenever we see a friend faint and thirsting while dying we may behold our Lord dimly, but truly, mirrored in his members. How near akin the thirsty Saviour is to us; let us love him more and more.

How great the love which led him to such a condescension as this! Do not let us forget the infinite distance between the Lord of glory on his throne and the Crucified dried up with thirst. A river of the water of life, pure as crystal, proceedeth today out of the throne of God and of the Lamb, and yet once he condescended to say, 'I thirst.' He is Lord of fountains and all deeps, but not a cup of cold water was placed to his lips. Oh, if he had at any time said, 'I thirst,' before his angelic guards, they would surely have emulated the courage of the men of David when they cut their way to the well of Bethlehem that was within the gate, and drew water in jeopardy of their lives. Who among us would not willingly pour out his soul unto death if he might but give refreshment to the Lord? And yet he placed himself for our sakes into a position of shame and suffering where none would wait upon him, but when he cried, 'I thirst,' they gave him vinegar to drink. Glorious stoop of our exalted Head! O Lord Jesus, we love thee and we worship thee! We would gladly lift thy name on high in grateful remembrance of the depths to which thou didst descend!

While thus we admire his condescension let our thoughts also turn with delight to his sure sympathy for if Jesus said, 'I thirst,' then he knows all our frailties and woes. The next time we are in pain or are suffering depression of spirit we will remember that our Lord understands it all, for he has had practical, personal experience of it. Neither in torture of body nor in sadness of heart are we deserted by our Lord; his line is parallel with ours. The arrow which has lately pierced thee, my brother, was first stained with his blood. The cup of which thou art made to drink, though it be very bitter, bears the mark of his lips about its brim. He hath traversed the mournful way before thee, and every footprint thou leavest in the sodden soil is stamped side by side with his foot-marks. Let the sympathy of Christ, then, be fully believed in and deeply appreciated, since he said, 'I thirst.'

Henceforth, also, let us cultivate the spirit of resignation, for we may well rejoice to carry a cross which his shoulders have borne before us. Beloved, if our Master said, 'I thirst,' do we expect every day to drink of streams from Lebanon? He was innocent, and yet he thirsted; shall we marvel if guilty ones are now and then chastened? If he was so poor that his garments were stripped from him, and he was hung up upon the tree, penniless and friendless, hungering and thirsting, will you henceforth groan and murmur because you bear the yoke of poverty and want? There is bread upon your table today, and there will be at least a cup of cold water to refresh you. You are not, therefore, so poor as he. Complain not, then. Shall the servant be above his Master, or the disciple above his Lord? Let patience have her perfect work. You do suffer. Perhaps, dear sister, you carry about with you a gnawing disease which eats at your heart, but Jesus took our sicknesses, and his cup was more bitter than yours. In your chamber let the gasp of your Lord as he said, 'I thirst,' go through your ears, and as you hear it let it touch your heart and cause you to gird up yourself and say, 'Doth he say, "I thirst"? Then I will thirst with him and not complain, I will suffer with him and not murmur.' The Redeemer's cry of 'I thirst' is a solemn lesson of patience to his afflicted.

Once again, as we think of this 'I thirst,' which proves our Lord's humanity, let us resolve to shun no denials, but rather court them that we may be conformed to his image. May we not be half ashamed of our pleasures when *he* says, 'I thirst'? May we not despise our loaded table while *he* is so neglected? Shall it ever be a hardship to be denied the satisfying draught when *he* said, 'I thirst.'

Shall carnal appetites be indulged and bodies pampered when Jesus cried 'I thirst'? What if the bread be dry, what if the medicine be nauseous; yet for his thirst there was no relief but gall and vinegar, and dare we complain? For his sake we may rejoice in self-denials, and accept Christ and a crust as all we desire between here and heaven. A Christian living to indulge the base appetites of a brute beast, to eat and to drink almost to gluttony and drunkenness, is utterly unworthy of the name. The conquest of the appetites, the entire subjugation of the flesh, must be achieved, for before our great Exemplar said, 'It is finished,' wherein I think he reached the greatest height of all, he stood as only upon the next lower step to that elevation, and said, 'I thirst.' The power to suffer for another, the capacity to be self-denying even to an extreme to accomplish some great work for God – this is a thing to be sought after, and must be gained before our work is done, and in this Jesus is before us, our example and our strength.

Thus have I tried to spy out a measure of teaching, by using that one glass for the soul's eye, through which we look upon 'I thirst' as the ensign of his true humanity.

II. Secondly, we shall regard these words, 'I thirst,' as THE TOKEN OF HIS SUFFERING SUBSTITUTION. The great Surety says, 'I thirst,' because he is placed in the sinner's stead, and he must therefore undergo the penalty of sin for the ungodly. 'My God, my God, why hast thou forsaken me?' points to the anguish of his soul; 'I thirst' expresses in part the torture of his body; and they were both needful, because it is written of the God of justice that he is 'able to destroy both soul and body in hell,' and the pangs that are due to law are of both kinds, touching both heart and flesh. See, brethren, where sin begins, and mark that there it ends. It began with the mouth of appetite, when it was sinfully gratified, and it ends when a kindred appetite is graciously denied. Our first parents plucked forbidden fruit, and by eating slew the race. Appetite was the door of sin, and therefore in that point our Lord was put to pain. With 'I thirst' the evil is destroyed and receives its expiation. I saw the other day the emblem of a serpent with its tail in its mouth, and if I carry it a little beyond the artist's intention the symbol may set forth appetite swallowing up itself.

A carnal appetite of the body, the satisfaction of the desire for food, first brought us down under the first Adam, and now the pang of thirst, the denial of what the body craved for, restores us to our place.

Nor is this all. We know from experience that the present effect of sin in every man who indulges in it is thirst of soul. The mind of man is like the daughters of the horseleech, which cry for ever 'Give, give.' Metaphorically understood, thirst is dissatisfaction, the craving of the mind for something which it has not, but which it pines for. Our Lord says, 'If any man thirst, let him come unto me and drink,' that thirst being the result of sin in every ungodly man at this moment. Now Christ standing in the stead of the ungodly suffers thirst as a type of his enduring the result of sin. More solemn still is the reflection that according to our Lord's own teaching, thirst will also be the eternal result of sin, for he says concerning the rich glutton, 'In hell he lift up his eyes, being in torment,' and his prayer, which was denied him, was, 'Father Abraham, send Lazarus, that he may dip the tip of his finger in water and cool my tongue, for I am tormented in this flame.' Now recollect, if Jesus had not thirsted, every one of us would have thirsted for ever afar off from God, with an impassable gulf between us and heaven. Our sinful tongues, blistered by the fever of passion, must have burned for ever had not his tongue been tormented with thirst in our stead. I suppose that the 'I thirst' was uttered softly, so that perhaps only one and another who stood near the cross heard it at all; in contrast with the louder cry of '*Lama sabachthani*' and the triumphant shout of 'It is finished': but that soft, expiring sigh, 'I thirst,' has ended for us the thirst which else, insatiably fierce, had preyed upon us throughout eternity. Oh, wondrous substitution of the just for the unjust, of God for man, of the perfect Christ for us guilty, hell-deserving rebels. Let us magnify and bless our Redeemer's name.

It seems to me very wonderful that this 'I thirst' should be, as it were, the clearance of it all. He had no sooner said 'I thirst,' and sipped the vinegar, than he shouted, 'It is finished'; and all was over: the battle was fought and the victory won for ever, and our great Deliverer's thirst was the sign of his having smitten the last foe. The flood of his grief had passed the high water mark, and began to be assuaged. The 'I thirst' was the bearing of the last pang; what if I say it was the expression of the fact that his pangs had at last begun to cease, and their fury had spent itself, and left him able to note his lesser pains? The excitement of a great struggle makes men forget thirst and faintness; it is only when all is over that they come back to themselves and note the spending of their strength. The great agony of being forsaken by God was over, and he felt faint when the strain was withdrawn. I like to think of our Lord's saying, 'It is finished,' directly after he had exclaimed, 'I thirst'; for these two voices come so naturally together. Our glorious Samson had been fighting our foes; heaps upon heaps he had slain his thousands, and now like Samson he was sore athirst. He sipped of the vinegar, and he was refreshed, and no sooner has he thrown off the thirst than he shouted like a conqueror, 'It is finished,' and quitted the field, covered with renown. Let us exult as we see our Substitute going through with his work even to the bitter end, and then with a *'Consummatum est'* returning to his Father, God. O souls, burdened with sin, rest ye here, and resting live.

III. We will now take the text in a third way, and may the Spirit of God instruct us once again. The utterance of 'I thirst' brought out A TYPE OF MAN'S TREATMENT OF HIS LORD. It was a confirmation of the Scripture testimony with regard to man's natural enmity to God. According to modern thought man is a very fine and noble creature, struggling to become better. He is greatly to be commended and admired, for his sin is said to be a seeking after God, and his superstition is a struggling after light. Great and worshipful being that he is, truth is to be altered for him, the gospel is to be modulated to suit the tone of his various generations, and all the arrangements of the universe are to be rendered subservient to his interests. Justice must fly the field lest it be severe to so deserving a being; as for punishment, it must not be whispered to his ears polite. In fact, the tendency is to exalt man above God and give him the highest place. But such is not the truthful estimate of man according to the Scriptures: there man is a fallen creature, with a carnal mind which cannot be reconciled to God; a worse than brutish creature, rendering evil for good, and treating his God with vile ingratitude.

Alas, man is the slave and the dupe of Satan, and a black-hearted traitor to his God. Did not the prophecies say that man would give to his incarnate God gall to eat and vinegar to drink? It is done, he came to save, and man denied him hospitality: at the first there was no room for him at the inn, and at the last there was not one cool cup of water for him to drink; but when he thirsted they gave him vinegar to drink. This is man's treatment of his Saviour. Universal manhood, left to itself, rejects, crucifies, and mocks the Christ of God. This was the act too of man at his best, when he is moved to pity; for it seems clear that he who lifted up the wet sponge to the Redeemer's lips, did it in compassion. I think that Roman soldier meant well, at least well for a rough warrior with his little light and knowledge.

He ran and filled a sponge with vinegar: it was the best way he knew of putting a few drops of moisture to the lips of one who was suffering so much; but though he felt a degree of pity, it was such as one might show to a dog; he felt no reverence, but mocked as he relieved. We read, 'The soldiers also mocked him, offering him vinegar.' When our Lord cried, 'Eloi, Eloi,' and afterwards said, 'I thirst,' the persons around the cross said, 'Let be, let us see whether Elias will come to save him,' mocking him; and, according to Mark, he who gave the vinegar uttered much the same words. He pitied the sufferer, but he thought so little of him that he joined in the voice of scorn. Even when man compassionates the sufferings of Christ, and man would have ceased to be human if he did not, still he scorns him; the very cup which man gives to Jesus is at once scorn and pity, for 'the tender mercies of the wicked are cruel.' See how man at his best mingles admiration of the Saviour's person with scorn of his claims; writing books to hold him up as an example and at the same moment rejecting his deity; admitting that he was a wonderful man, but denying his most sacred mission; extolling his ethical teaching and then trampling on his blood: thus giving him drink, but that drink vinegar. O my hearers, beware of praising Jesus and denying his atoning sacrifice. Beware of rendering him homage and dishonouring his name at the same time.

Alas, my brethren, I cannot say much on the score of man's cruelty to our Lord without touching myself and you. Have *we* not often given him vinegar to drink? Did we not do so years ago before we knew him? We used to melt when we heard about his sufferings, but we did not turn from our sins. We gave him our tears and then grieved him with our sins. We thought sometimes that we loved him as we heard the story of his death, but we did not change our lives for his sake, nor put our trust in him, and so we gave him vinegar to drink. Nor does the grief end here, for have not the best works we have ever done, and the best feelings we have ever felt, and the best prayers we have ever offered, been tart and sour with sin? Can they be compared to generous wine? Are they not more like sharp vinegar?

I wonder he has ever received them, as one marvels why he received this vinegar; and yet he has received them, and smiled upon us for presenting them. He knew once how to turn water into wine, and in matchless love he has often turned our sour drink-offerings into something sweet to himself, though in themselves, methinks, they have been the juice of sour grapes, sharp enough to set his teeth on edge. We may therefore come before him, with all the rest of our race, when God subdues them to repentance by his love, and look on him whom we have pierced, and mourn for him as one that is in bitterness for his firstborn. We may well remember our faults this day,

> We, whose proneness to forget
> Thy dear love, on Olivet
> Bathed thy brow with bloody sweat;
>
> We, whose sins, with awful power,
> Like a cloud did o'er thee lour,
> In that God-excluding hour;
>
> We, who still, in thought and deed,
> Often hold the bitter reed
> To thee, in thy time of need.

I have touched that point very lightly because I want a little more time to dwell upon a fourth view of this scene. May the Holy Ghost help us to hear a fourth tuning of the dolorous music, 'I thirst.'

IV. I think, beloved friends, that the cry of 'I thirst' was THE MYSTICAL EXPRESSION OF THE DESIRE OF HIS HEART – 'I thirst.' I cannot think that natural thirst was all he felt. He thirsted for water doubtless, but his soul was thirsty in a higher sense; indeed, he seems only to have spoken that the Scriptures might be fulfilled as to the offering him vinegar. Always was he in harmony with himself, and his body was always expressive of his soul's cravings as well as of its own longings. 'I thirst' meant that his heart was thirsting to save men. This thirst had been on him from the earliest of his earthly days. 'Wist ye not,' said he, while yet a boy, 'that I must be about my Father's business?' Did he not tell his disciples, 'I have a baptism to be baptized with and how am I straitened till it be accomplished?'

He thirsted to pluck us from between the jaws of hell, to pay our redemption price, and set us free from the eternal condemnation which hung over us; and when on the cross the work was almost done his thirst was not assuaged, and could not be till he could say, 'It is finished.' It is almost done, thou Christ of God; thou hast almost saved thy people; there remaineth but one thing more, that thou shouldst actually die, and hence thy strong desire to come to the end and complete thy labour. Thou wast still straitened till the last pang was felt and the last word spoken to complete the full redemption, and hence thy cry, 'I thirst.'

Beloved, there is now upon our Master, and there always has been, a thirst after the love of his people. Do you not remember how that thirst of his was strong in the old days of the prophet? Call to mind his complaint in the fifth chapter of Isaiah, 'Now will I sing to my well beloved a song of my beloved touching his vineyard. My well beloved hath a vineyard in a very fruitful hill: and he fenced it, and gathered out the stones thereof, and planted it with the choicest vine, and built a tower in the midst of it, and also made a winepress therein.' What was he looking for from his vineyard and its winepress? What but for the juice of the vine that he might be refreshed? 'And he looked that it should bring forth grapes, and it brought forth wild grapes' – vinegar, and not wine; sourness, and not sweetness. So he was thirsting then. According to the sacred canticle of love, in the fifth chapter of the Song of Songs, we learn that when he drank in those olden times it was in the garden of his church that he was refreshed. What doth he say? 'I am come into my garden, my sister, my spouse: I have gathered my myrrh with my spice; I have eaten my honeycomb with my honey; I have drunk my wine with my milk; eat, O friends; drink, yea, drink abundantly, O beloved.' In the same song he speaks of his church, and says, 'The roof of thy mouth is as the best wine for my beloved, that goeth down sweetly, causing the lips of those that are asleep to speak.' And yet again in the eighth chapter the bride saith, 'I would cause thee to drink of spiced wine of the juice of my pomegranate.' Yes, he loves to be with his people; they are the garden where he walks for refreshment, and their love, their graces, are the milk and wine of which he delights to drink. Christ was always thirsty to save men, and to be loved of men; and we see a type of his lifelong desire when, being weary, he sat thus on the well and said to the woman of Samaria, 'Give me to drink.' There was a deeper meaning in his words than she dreamed of, as a verse further down fully proves, when he said to his disciples, 'I have meat to eat that ye know not of.' He derived spiritual refreshment from the winning of that woman's heart to himself.

And now, brethren, our blessed Lord has at this time a thirst for communion with each one of you who are his people, not because you can do him good, but because he can do you good. He thirsts to bless you and to receive your grateful love in return; he thirsts to see you looking with believing eye to his fullness, and holding out your emptiness that he may supply it. He saith, 'Behold, I stand at the door and knock.' What knocks he for? It is that he may eat and drink with you, for he promises that if we open to him he will enter in and sup with us and we with him. He is thirsty still, you see, for our poor love, and surely we cannot deny it to him. Come let us pour out full flagons, until his joy is fulfilled in us. And what makes him love us so? Ah, that I cannot tell, except his own great love. He *must* love; it is his nature. He must love his chosen whom he has once begun to love, for he is the same yesterday, today, and for ever. His great love makes him thirst to have us much nearer than we are; he will never be satisfied till all his redeemed are beyond gunshot of the enemy. I will give you one of his thirsty prayers – 'Father, I will that they also whom thou hast given me be with me where I am, that they may behold my glory.' He wants you brother, he wants you, dear sister, he longs to have you wholly to himself. Come to him in prayer, come to him in fellowship, come to him by perfect consecration, come to him by surrendering your whole being to the sweet mysterious influences of his Spirit. Sit at his feet with Mary, lean on his breast with John; yea, come with the spouse in the song and say, 'Let him kiss me with the kisses of his mouth, for his love is better than wine.' He calls for that: will you not give it to him? Are you so frozen at heart that not a cup of cold water can be melted for Jesus? Are you lukewarm? O brother, if he says, 'I thirst' and you bring him a lukewarm heart, that is worse than vinegar, for he has said, 'I will spue thee out of my mouth.' He can receive vinegar, but not lukewarm love. Come, bring him your warm heart, and let him drink from that purified chalice as much as he wills. Let all your love be his. I know he loves to receive from you, because he delights even in a cup of cold water that you give to one of his disciples; how much more will he delight in the giving of your whole self to him? Therefore while he thirsts give him to drink this day.

V. Lastly, the cry of 'I thirst' is to us THE PATTERN OF OUR DEATH WITH HIM. Know ye not, beloved – for I speak to those who know the Lord – that ye are crucified together with Christ? Well, then, what means this cry, 'I thirst,' but this, that we should thirst too? We do not thirst after the old manner wherein we were bitterly afflicted, for he hath said, 'He that drinketh of this water shall never thirst': but now we covet a new thirst, a refined and heavenly appetite, a craving for our Lord. O thou blessed Master, if we are indeed nailed up to the tree with thee, give us to thirst after thee with a thirst which only the cup of 'the new covenant in thy blood' can ever satisfy. Certain philosophers have said that they love the pursuit of truth even better than the knowledge of truth. I differ from them greatly, but I will say this, that next to the actual enjoyment of my Lord's presence I love to hunger and to thirst after him. Rutherford used words somewhat to this effect, 'I thirst for my Lord and this is joy; a joy which no man taketh from me. Even if I may not come at him, yet shall I be full of consolation, for it is heaven to thirst after him, and surely he will never deny a poor soul liberty to admire him, and adore him, and thirst after him.' As for myself, I would grow more and more insatiable after my divine Lord, and when I have much of him I would still cry for more; and then for more, and still for more. My heart shall not be content till he is all in all to me, and I am altogether lost in him. O to be enlarged in soul so as to take deeper draughts of his sweet love, for our heart cannot have enough. One would wish to be as the spouse, who, when she had already been feasting in the banqueting-house, and had found his fruit sweet to her taste, so that she was overjoyed, yet cried out, 'Stay me with flagons, comfort me with apples, for I am sick of love.' She craved full flagons of love though she was already overpowered by it. This is a kind of sweet whereof if a man hath much he must have more, and when he hath more he is under a still greater necessity to receive more, and so on, his appetite for ever growing by that which it feeds upon, till he is filled with all the fullness of God. 'I thirst' – ay, this is my soul's word with her Lord. Borrowed from his lips it well suiteth my mouth.

> I thirst, but not as once I did,
> The vain delights of earth to share;
> Thy wounds, Emmanuel, all forbid
> That I should seek my pleasures there.
>
> Dear fountain of delight unknown!
> No longer sink below the brim;
> But overflow, and pour me down
> A living and life-giving stream.

Jesus thirsted, then let us thirst in this dry and thirsty land where no water is. Even as the hart panteth after the water brooks, our souls would thirst after thee, O God.

Beloved, let us thirst for the souls of our fellow men. I have already told you that such was our Lord's mystical desire; let it be ours also. Brother, thirst to have your children saved. Brother, thirst I pray you to have your work-people saved. Sister, thirst for the salvation of your class, thirst for the redemption of your family, thirst for the conversion of your husband. We ought all to have a longing for conversions. Is it so with each one of you? If not, bestir yourselves at once. Fix your hearts upon some unsaved one, and thirst until he is saved. It is the way whereby many shall be brought to Christ, when this blessed soul-thirst of true Christian charity shall be upon those who are themselves saved. Remember how Paul said, 'I say the truth in Christ, I lie not, my conscience also bearing me witness in the Holy Ghost, that I have great heaviness and continual sorrow in my heart. For I could wish that myself were accursed from Christ for my brethren, my kinsmen according to the flesh.' He would have sacrificed himself to save his countrymen, so heartily did he desire their eternal welfare. Let this mind be in you also.

As for yourselves, thirst after perfection. Hunger and thirst after righteousness, for you shall be filled. Hate sin, and heartily loathe it; but thirst to be holy as God is holy, thirst to be like Christ, thirst to bring glory to his sacred name by complete conformity to his will.

May the Holy Ghost work in you the complete pattern of Christ crucified, and to him shall be praise for ever and ever. Amen.

14

CHRIST'S DYING WORD FOR HIS CHURCH[1]

It is finished.
JOHN 19:30

IN THE ORIGINAL GREEK of John's Gospel, there is only one word for this utterance of our Lord. To translate it into English, we have to use three words; but when it was spoken, it was only one – an ocean of meaning in a drop of language, a mere drop, for that is all that we can call one word. 'It is finished.' Yet it would need all the other words that ever were spoken, or ever can be spoken, to explain this one word. It is altogether immeasurable. It is high; I cannot attain to it. It is deep; I cannot fathom it. 'Finished.' I can half imagine the tone in which our Lord uttered this word, with a holy glorying, a sense of relief, the bursting out of a heart that had long been shut up within walls of anguish. 'Finished.' It was a Conqueror's cry; it was uttered with a loud voice. There is nothing of anguish about it, there is no wailing in it. It is the cry of One who has completed a tremendous labour, and is about to die; and ere he utters his death-prayer, 'Father, into thy hands I commend my spirit,' he shouts his life's last hymn in that one word, 'Finished.'

May God the Holy Spirit help me to handle aright this text that is at once so small and yet so great! There are four ways in which I wish to look at it with you. First, I will speak of this dying saying

[1] Sermon No. 2,344. Preached at the Metropolitan Tabernacle on Sunday evening, 3 November 1889.

of our Lord *to his glory;* secondly, I will use the text *to the church's comfort;* thirdly, I will try to handle the subject *to every believer's joy;* and fourthly, I will seek to show how our Lord's words ought *to lead to our own arousement.*

I. First, then, I will endeavour to speak of this dying saying of Christ TO HIS GLORY. Let us begin with that.

Jesus said, 'It is finished.' Let us glory in him that it is finished. You and I may well do this when we recollect how very few things we have finished. We begin many things; and, sometimes, we begin well. We commence running like champions who must win the race; but soon we slacken our pace, and we fall exhausted on the course. The race commenced is never completed. In fact, I am afraid that we have never finished anything perfectly. You know what we say of some pieces of work, 'Well, the man has done it; but there is no "finish" about it.' No, and you must begin with 'finish', and go on with 'finish', if you are at last able to say broadly as the Saviour said without any qualification, 'It is finished.'

What was it that was finished? His life-work and his atoning sacrifice on our behalf. He had interposed between our souls and divine justice, and he had stood in our stead, to obey and suffer on our behalf. He began this work early in life, even while he was a child. He persevered in holy obedience three and thirty years. That obedience cost him many a pang and groan. Now it is about to cost him his life; and as he gives away his life to finish the work of obedience to the Father, and of redemption for us, he says, 'It is finished.' It was a wonderful work even to contemplate; only infinite love would have thought of devising such a plan. It was a wonderful work to carry on for so long; only boundless patience would have continued at it; and now that it requires the offering of himself, and the yielding up of his earthly life, only a Divine Saviour, very God of very God, would or could have consummated it by the surrender of his breath. What a work it was! Yet it was finished; while you and I have lots of little things lying about that we have never finished. We have begun to do something for Jesus that would bring him a little honour and glory; but we have never finished it. We did mean to glorify Christ; have not some of you intended, oh! so much? Yet it has never come to anything; but

Christ's work, which cost him heart and soul, body and spirit, cost him everything, even to his death on the cross, he pushed through all that till it was accomplished, and he could say, 'It is finished.'

To whom did our Saviour say, 'It is finished'? He said it to all whom it might concern; but it seems to me that he chiefly said it to his Father, for, immediately after, apparently in a lower tone of voice, he said, 'Father, into thy hands I commend my spirit.' Beloved, it is one thing for me to say to you, 'I have finished my work' – possibly, if I were dying, you might say that I had finished my work; but for the Saviour to say that to God, to hang in the presence of him whose eyes are as a flame of fire, the great Reader and Searcher of all hearts, for Jesus to look the dread Father in the face, and say, as he bowed his head, 'Father, it is finished; I have finished the work which thou gavest me to do' – oh, who but he could venture to make such a declaration as that? We can find a thousand flaws in our best works; and when we lie dying, we shall still have to lament our shortcomings and excesses; but there is nothing of imperfection about him who stood as Substitute for us; and unto the Father himself he can say, concerning all his work, 'It is finished.' Wherefore, glorify him tonight. Oh, glorify him in your hearts tonight that, even in the presence of the Great Judge of all, your Surety and your Substitute is able to claim perfection for all his service!

Just think also, for a minute or two, now that you have remembered what Jesus finished, and to whom he said that he had finished it, *how truly he had finished it.* From the beginning to the end of Christ's life there is nothing omitted, no single act of service ever left undone; neither is there any action of his slurred over, or performed in a careless manner. 'It is finished,' refers as much to his childhood as to his death. The whole of the service that he was to render to God, when he came here in human form, was finished in every single part and portion of it. I take up a piece of a cabinet maker's work; and it bears a good appearance. I open the lid, and am satisfied with the workmanship; but there is something about the hinge that is not properly finished. Or, perhaps, if I turn it over, and look at the bottom of the box, I shall see that there is a piece that has been scamped, or that one part has not been well planed or properly polished. But if you examine the Master's work right through, if you begin at Bethlehem and go on to Golgotha, and look minutely at every portion of it, the private as well as the public, the silent as well as the spoken part, you will find that it is finished, completed, perfected. We may say of it that, among all works, there is none like it; a multitude of perfections joined together to make up one absolute perfection. Wherefore, let us glorify the name of our blessed Lord. Crown him; crown him; for he hath done his work well. Come, ye saints, speak much to his honour, and in your hearts keep on singing to the praise of him who did so thoroughly, so perfectly, all the work which his Father gave him to do.

In the first place, then, we use our Lord's words to his glory. Much might be said upon such a theme; but time will not permit it now.

II. Secondly, we will use the text TO THE CHURCH'S COMFORT. I am persuaded that it was so intended to be used, for none of the words of our Lord on the cross are addressed to his church but this one. I cannot believe that, when he was dying, he left his people, for whom he died, without a word. 'Father, forgive them; for they know not what they do,' is for sinners, not for saints. 'I thirst,' is for himself; and so is that bitter cry, 'My God, my God, why hast thou forsaken me?' 'Woman, behold thy son!' is for Mary. 'Today shalt thou be with me in paradise,' is for the penitent thief. 'Into thy hands I commend my spirit,' is for the Father. Jesus must have had something to say, in the hour of death, for his church; and, surely, this is his dying word for her. He tells her, shouting it in her ear that has become dull and heavy with despair, 'It is finished.' 'It is finished, O my redeemed one, my bride, my well-beloved, for whom I came to lay down my life; it is finished, the work is done!'

> Love's redeeming work is done;
> Fought the fight, the battle won.

'Christ loved the church, and gave himself for it.' John, in the Revelation, speaks of the Redeemer's work as already accomplished, and therefore he sings, 'Unto him that loved us, and washed us from our sins in his own blood, and hath made us kings and priests unto God and his Father; to him be glory and dominion for ever and ever. Amen.' This truth is full of comfort to the people of God.

And, first, as it concerns Christ, do you not feel greatly comforted to think that he is to be humiliated no longer? *His suffering and shame are finished.* I often sing, with sacred exultation and pleasure, those lines of Dr Watts –

> No more the bloody spear,
> The cross and nails no more,
> For hell itself shakes at his name,
> And all the heavens adore.
>
> There his full glories shine
> With uncreated rays,
> And bless his saints' and angels' eyes
> To everlasting days.

I like also that expression in another of our hymns –

> Now both the Surety and sinner are free.

Not only are they free for whom Christ became a Surety, but he himself is for ever free from all the obligations and consequences of his suretyship. Men will never spit in his face again; the Roman soldiers will never scourge him again. Judas, where art thou? Behold the Christ sitting upon his great white throne, the glorious King who was once the Man of sorrows! Now, Judas, come, and betray him with a kiss! What, man, dare you not do it? Come Pilate, and wash your hands in pretended innocency, and say now that you are guiltless of his blood! Come, ye Scribes and Pharisees, and accuse him; and oh, ye Jewish mob and Gentile rabble, newly risen from the grave, shout now, 'Away with him! Crucify him!' But see! they flee from him; they cry to the mountains and rocks, 'Fall on us, and hide us from the face of him that sitteth on the throne!' Yet that is the face that was more marred than any man's, the face of him whom they once despised and rejected. Are you not glad to think that they cannot despise him now, that they cannot ill-treat him now?

> 'Tis past – that agonizing hour
> Of torture and of shame;

and Jesus says of it, 'It is finished.'

We derive further comfort and joy as we think that, not only are Christ's pangs and sufferings finished, but *his Father's will and sword have had a perfect completion.* Certain things were written that were to be done; and these are done. Whatsoever the Father required has been rendered. 'It is finished.' My Father will never say to me, 'I cannot save thee by the death of my Son, for I am dissatisfied with his work.' Oh, no, beloved; God is well pleased with Christ, and with us in him! There is nothing which was arranged in the eternal mind to be done, yea, not a jot or tittle, but what Christ has done it all. As his eye, that eye that often wept for us, reads down the ancient writing, Christ is able to say, 'I have finished the work which my Father gave me to do. Wherefore, be comforted, O my people, for my Father is well pleased with me, and well pleased with you in me!' I like, when I am in prayer, some-times to say to the great Father, 'Father; look on thy Son. Is he not all loveliness? Are there not in him unutterable beauties? Dost thou not delight in him? If thou hast looked on me, and grown sick of me, as well thou mayest, now refresh thyself by looking on thy Well-beloved, delight thyself in him –

> Him, and then the sinner see,
> Look through Jesus' wounds on me.

The perfect satisfaction of the Father with Christ's work for his people, so that Christ could say, 'It is finished,' is a ground of solid comfort to his church evermore.

Dear friends, once more, take comfort from this 'It is finished,' for *the redemption of Christ's church is perfected!* There is not another penny to be paid for her full release. There is no mortgage upon Christ's inheritance. Those whom he bought with blood are for ever clear of all charges, paid for to the utmost. There was a handwriting of ordinances against us; but Christ hath taken it away, he hath nailed it to his cross. 'It is finished,' finished for ever. All those overwhelming debts, which would have sunk us to the lowest hell, have been discharged; and they who believe in Christ may appear with boldness even before the throne of God itself. 'It is finished.' What comfort there is in this glorious truth!

> Lamb of God! thy death hath given
> Pardon, peace, and hope of heaven:
> 'It is finished,' let us raise
> Songs of thankfulness and praise!

And I think that we may say to the church of God that, when Jesus said, 'It is finished,' *her ultimate triumph was secured*. 'Finished!' By that one word he declared that he had broken the head of the old dragon. By his death, Jesus has routed the hosts of darkness, and crushed the rising hopes of hell. We have a stern battle yet to fight; nobody can tell what may await the church of God in years to come, it would be idle for us to attempt to prophesy; but it looks as if there were to be sterner times and darker days than we have ever yet known; but what of that? Our Lord has defeated the foe; and we have to fight with one who is already vanquished. The old serpent has been crushed, his head is bruised, and we have now to trample on him. We have this sure word of promise to encourage us, 'The God of peace shall bruise Satan under your feet shortly.' Surely, 'It is finished,' sounds like the trumpet of victory; let us have faith to claim that victory through the blood of the Lamb, and let every Christian here, let the whole church of God, as one mighty army, take comfort from this dying word of the now risen and ever-living Saviour, 'It is finished.' His church may rest perfectly satisfied that his work for her is fully accomplished.

III. Now, thirdly, I want to use this expression, 'It is finished,' TO EVERY BELIEVER'S JOY.

When our Lord said, 'It is finished,' there was something to make every believer in him glad. What did that utterance mean? You and I have believed in Jesus of Nazareth; we believe him to be the Messiah, sent of God. Now, if you will turn to the Old Testament, you will find that the marks of the Messiah are very many, and very complicated; and if you will then turn to the life and death of Christ, you will see in him *every mark of the Messiah plainly exhibited*. Until he had said, 'It is finished,' and until he had actually died, there was some doubt that there might be some one prophecy unfulfilled; but now that he hangs upon the cross, every mark, and every sign, and every token of his Messiahship have been fulfilled, and he says, 'It is finished.' The life and death of Christ and the types of the Old Testament fit each other like hand and glove. It would be quite impossible for any person to write the life of a man, by way of fiction, and then in another book to write out a series of types, personal and sacrificial, and to make the character of the man fit all the types; even if he had permission to make both books, he could not do it. If he were allowed to make both the lock and the key, he could not do it; but here we have the lock made beforehand. In all the Books of the Old Testament, from the prophecy in the Garden of Eden right away down to Malachi, the last of the prophets, there were certain marks and tokens of the Christ. All these were so very singular that it did not appear as if they could all meet in one person; but they did all meet in One, every one of them, whether it concerned some minute point or some prominent characteristic. When the Lord Jesus Christ had ended his life, he could say, 'It is finished; my life has tallied with all that was said of it from the first word of prophecy even to the last.' Now, that ought greatly to encourage your faith. You are not following cunningly devised fables; but you are following One who must be the Messiah of God, since he so exactly fits all the prophecies and all the types that were given before concerning him.

'It is finished.' Let every believer be comforted in another respect, that *every honour which the law of God could require has been rendered to it*. You and I have broken that law, and all the race of mankind has broken it, too. We have tried to thrust God from his throne; we have dishonoured his law; we have broken his commandments wilfully and wickedly; but there has come One who is himself God, the Lawgiver; and he has taken human nature, and in that nature he has kept the law perfectly; and inasmuch as the law had been broken by man, he has in the nature of man borne the sentence due for all man's transgressions. The Godhead, being linked with the manhood, gave supreme virtue to all that the manhood suffered; and Christ, in life and in death, has magnified the law, and made it honourable; and God's law at this day is raised to even greater honour than it had before man broke it. The death of the Son of God, the sacrifice of the Lord Jesus Christ, has vindicated the great moral principle of God's government, and made his throne to stand out gloriously before the eyes of men and angels for ever and ever. If hell were filled with men, it would not be such a vindication of divine justice as when God spared not his own Son, but delivered him up for us all, and made him to die, the Just for the unjust, to bring us to God. Now let every believer rejoice in the great fact that, by the death of Christ, the law of God is abundantly honoured. You can be saved without impugning the holiness of God; you are saved without putting any stain upon the divine statute book. The law is kept, and mercy triumphs, too.

And, beloved, here is included, of necessity, another comforting truth. Christ might well say, 'It is finished,' for *every solace conscience can need is now given*. When your conscience is disturbed and troubled, if it knows that God is perfectly honoured, and his law vindicated, then it becomes easy. Men are always starting some new theory of the atonement; and one has said lately that the atonement was simply meant as an easement to the conscience of men. It is not so, my brethren; there would be no easing of the conscience by anything that was meant for that alone. Conscience can only be satisfied if God is satisfied. Until I see how the law is vindicated, my troubled conscience can never find rest. Dear heart, are thine eyes red with weeping? Yet look thou to him who hangs upon the tree. Is thy heart heavy even to despair? Look to him who hangs upon the tree, and believe in him. Take him to be thy soul's atoning Lamb, suffering in thy stead. Accept of him as thy Representative, dying thy death that thou mayest live his life, bearing thy sin that thou mayest be made the righteousness of God in him. This is the best *quietus* in the world for every fear that conscience can raise; let every believer know that it is so.

Once more, there is joy to every believer when he remembers that, as Christ said, 'It is finished,' *every guarantee was given of the eternal salvation of all the redeemed*. It appears to me that, if Christ finished the work for us, he will finish the work in us. If he has undertaken so supreme a labour as the redemption of our souls by blood, and that is finished, then the great but yet minor labour of renewing our natures, and transforming us even unto perfection, shall be finished, too. If, when we were sinners, Christ loved us so as to die for us, now that he has redeemed us, and has already reconciled us to himself, and made us his friends and his disciples, will he not finish the work that is necessary to make us fit to stand among the golden lamps of heaven, and to sing his praises in the country where nothing that defileth can ever enter?

> The work which his goodness began,
>   The arm of his strength will complete;
> His promise is yea and Amen,
>   And never was forfeited yet:
> Things future, nor things that are now,
>   Not all things below nor above,
> Can make him his purpose forgo,
>   Or sever my soul from his love.

I believe it, my brethren. He who has said, 'It is finished,' will never leave anything undone. It shall never be said of him, 'This Man began, but was not able to finish.' If he has bought me with his blood, and called me by his grace, and I am resting on his promise and power, I shall be with him where he is, and I shall behold his glory, as surely as he is Christ the Lord, and I am a believer in him. What comfort this truth brings to every child of God!

Are there any of you here who are trying to do something to make a righteousness of your own? How dare you attempt such a work when Jesus says, 'It is finished'? Are you trying to put a few of your own merits together, a few odds and ends, fig leaves and filthy rags of your own righteousness? Jesus says, 'It is finished.' Why do you want to add anything of your own to what he has completed? Do you say that you are not fit to be saved? What! have you to bring some of your fitness to eke out Christ's work? 'Oh!' say you, 'I hope to come to Christ one of these days when I get better.' What! What! What! What! Are you to make yourself better, and then is Christ to do the rest of the work? You remind me of the railways to our country towns; you know that, often, the station is half a mile or a mile out of the town, so that you cannot get to the station without having an omnibus to take you there. But my Lord Jesus Christ comes right to the town of Mansoul. His railway runs close to your feet, and there is the carriage-door wide open; step in. You have not even to go over a bridge, or under a subway; there stands the carriage just before you. This royal railroad carries souls all the way from hell's dark door, where they lie in sin, up to heaven's great gate of pearl, where they dwell in perfect righteousness for ever. Cast yourself on Christ; take him to be everything you need, for he says of the whole work of salvation, 'It is finished.'

I recollect the saying of a Scottish woman, who had applied to be admitted to the communion of the Kirk. Being thought to be very ignorant, and little instructed in the things of God, she was put back by the elders. The minister also had seen her, and thought that, at least for a while, she should wait. I wish I could speak Scotch, so as to give you her answer, but I am afraid that I should make a mistake if I tried it. It is a fine language, doubtless, for those who can speak it. She said something like this, "Aweel, sir; aweel, sir, but I ken ae thing. As the lintbell opens to the sun, so my heart opens to the name of Jesus.' You have, perhaps, seen the flax-flower shut itself up when the sun has gone; and, if so, you know that, whenever the sun has come back, the flower opens itself at once. 'So,' said the poor woman, 'I ken one thing, that as the flower opens to the sun, so my heart opens to the name of Jesus.' Do you know that, friends? Do you ken that one thing? Then I do not care if you do not ken much else; if that one thing is known by you, and if it be really so, you may be far from perfect in your own estimation, but you are a saved soul.

One said to me, when she came to join the church, and I asked her whether she was perfect, 'Perfect? Oh, dear no, sir! I wish that I could be.' 'Ah, yes!' I replied, 'that would just please you, would it not?' 'Yes; it would indeed,' she answered. 'Well, then,' I said, 'that shows that your heart is perfect, and that you love perfect things; you are pining after perfection; there is a something in you, an "I" in you, that sinneth not, but that seeketh after that which is holy; and yet you do that which you would not, and you groan because you do, and the apostle is like you when he says, "It is no more I, the real I, that do it, but sin that dwelleth in me.'" May the Lord put that 'I' into many of you tonight, that 'I' which will hate sin, that 'I' which will find its heaven in being perfectly free from sin, that 'I' which will delight itself in the Almighty, that 'I' which will sun itself in the smile of Christ, that 'I' which will strike down every evil within as soon as ever it shows its head! So will you sing that familiar prayer of Toplady's that we have often sung –

> Let the water and the blood,
> From thy riven side which flow'd,
> Be of sin the double cure,
> Cleanse me from its guilt and power!

IV. I close by saying, in the fourth place, that we shall use this text, 'It is finished,' TO OUR OWN AROUSEMENT.

Somebody once wickedly said, 'Well, if Christ has finished it, there is nothing for me to do now but to fold my hands, and go to sleep.' That is the speech of a devil, not of a Christian! There is no grace in the heart when the mouth can talk like that. On the contrary, the true child of God says, 'Has Christ finished his work for me? Then tell me what work I can do for him.' You remember the two questions of Saul of Tarsus. The first enquiry, after he had been struck down, was, 'Who art thou, Lord?' And the next was, 'Lord, what wilt thou have me to do?' If Christ has finished the work for you which you could not do, now go and finish the work for him which you are privileged and permitted to do. Seek to –

> Rescue the perishing, care for the dying,
> Snatch them in pity from sin and the grave;
> Weep o'er the erring one, lift up the fallen,
> Tell them of Jesus, the Mighty to save.

My inference from this saying of Christ, 'It is finished,' is this – Has he finished his work for me? Then I must get to work for him, and *I must persevere until I finish my work, too*; not to save myself, for that is all done, but because I am saved. Now I must work for him with all my might; and if there come discouragements, if there come sufferings, if there comes a sense of weakness and exhaustion, yet let me not give way to it; but, inasmuch as he pressed on till he could say, 'It is finished,' let me press on till I, too, shall be able to say, 'I have finished the work which thou gavest me to do.' You know how men who go fishing look out for the fish. I have heard of a man going to Keston Ponds on Saturday fishing, and stopping all day Sunday, Monday, Tuesday, Wednesday. There was another man fishing there, and the other man had only been there two days. He said, 'I have been here two days, and I have only had one bite.' 'Why!' replied the other, 'I have been here ever since last Saturday, and I have not had a bite yet; but I mean to keep on.' 'Well,' answered the other, 'I cannot keep on without catching anything.' 'Oh!' said number one, 'but I have such a longing to catch some fish that I shall stop here till I do.' I believe that fellow would catch some fish ultimately, if there were any to be caught; he is the kind of fisherman to do it, and we want to have men who feel that they must win souls for Christ, and that they will persevere till they do. It must be so with us, brethren and sisters; we cannot let men go down to hell if there is any way of saving them.

The next inference is, that *we can finish our work, for Christ finished his.* You can put a lot of 'finish' into your work, and you can hold on to the end, and complete the work by divine grace; and that grace is waiting for you, that grace is promised to you. Seek it, find it, get it. Do not act as some do, ah, even some who are before me now! They served God once, and then they ran away from him. They have come back again; God bless them, and help them to be more useful! But future earnest service will never make up for that sad gap in their earlier career. It is best to keep on, and on, and on, from the commencement to the close; the Lord help us to persevere to the end, till we can truly say of our life-work, 'It is finished'!

One word of caution I must give you. *Let us not think that our work is finished till we die.* 'Well,' says one, 'I was just going to say of my work, "It is finished."' Were you? Were you? I remember that, when John Newton wrote a book about grace in the blade, and grace in the ear, and grace in the full corn in the ear, a very talkative body said to him, 'I have been reading your valuable book, Mr Newton; it is a splendid work; and when I came to that part, "The full corn in the ear," I thought how wonderfully you had described me.' 'Oh!' replied Mr Newton, 'but you could not have read the book rightly, for it is one of the marks of the full corn in the ear that it hangs its head very low.' So it is; and when a man, in a careless, boastful spirit, says of his work, 'It is finished,' I am inclined to ask, 'Brother, was it ever begun? If your work for Christ is finished, I should think that you never realized what it ought to be.' As long as there is breath in our bodies, let us serve Christ; as long as we can think, as long as we can speak, as long as we can work, let us serve him, let us even serve him with our last gasp; and, if it be possible, let us try to set some work going that will glorify him when we are dead and gone. Let us scatter some seed that may spring up when we are sleeping beneath the hillock in the cemetery.

Ah, beloved, we shall never have finished our work for Christ until we bow our heads, and give up the ghost! The oldest friend here has a little something to do for the Master. Someone said to me, the other day, 'I cannot think why old Mrs So-and-so is spared; she is quite a burden to her friends.' 'Ah!' I replied, 'she has something yet to do for her Lord, she has another word to speak for him.' Sister, look up your work, and get it done; and you, brother, see what remains of your life-work yet incomplete. Wind off the ends, get all the little corners finished. Who knows how long it may be before you and I may have to give in our account? Some are called away very suddenly; they are apparently in good health one day, and they are gone the next. I should not like to leave a half-finished life behind me. The Lord Jesus Christ said, 'It is finished,' and your heart should say, 'Lord, and I will finish, too; not to mix my work with thine, but because thou hast finished thine, I will finish mine.'

Now may the Lord give us the joy of his presence at his table! May the bread and wine speak to you much better than I can! May every heir of heaven see Christ tonight, and rejoice in his finished work, for his dear name's sake! Amen.

15

'IT IS FINISHED'[1]

When Jesus therefore had received the vinegar,
he said, It is finished: and he bowed his head,
and gave up the ghost.
JOHN 19:30

MY BRETHREN, I would have you attentively observe the singular clearness, power, and quickness of the Saviour's mind in the last agonies of death. When pains and groans attend the last hour, they frequently have the effect of discomposing the mind, so that it is not possible for the dying man to collect his thoughts, or having collected them, to utter them so that they can be understood by others. In no case could we expect a remarkable exercise of memory, or a profound judgment upon deep subjects from an expiring man. But the Redeemer's last acts were full of wisdom and prudence, although his sufferings were beyond all measure excruciating. Consider how clearly he perceived the significance of every type! How plainly he could read with dying eye those divine symbols which the eyes of angels could only desire to look into! He saw the secrets which have bewildered sages and astonished seers, all fulfilled in his own body. Nor must we fail to observe the power and comprehensiveness by which he grasped the chain which binds the shadowy past with the sunlit present. We must not forget the brilliance of that intelligence which threaded all the ceremonies and sacrifices on one string of thought, beheld all the prophecies as one great revelation, and all the

---

[1] Sermon No. 421. Preached at the Metropolitan Tabernacle on Sunday morning, 1 December 1861.

promises as the heralds of one person, and then said of the whole, 'It is finished, finished in me.' What quickness of mind was that which enabled him to traverse all the centuries of prophecy, to penetrate the eternity of the covenant, and then to anticipate the eternal glories! And all this when he is mocked by multitudes of enemies, and when his hands and feet are nailed to the cross. What force of mind must the Saviour have possessed, to soar above those Alps of Agony, which touched the very clouds. In what a singular mental condition must he have been during the period of his crucifixion, to be able to review the whole roll of inspiration!

Now, this remark may not seem to be of any great value, but I think its value lies in certain inferences that may be drawn from it. We have sometimes heard it said, 'How could Christ, in so short a time, bear suffering which should be equivalent to the torments – the eternal torments of hell?' Our reply is, we are not capable of judging what the Son of God might do even in a moment, much less what he might do and what he might suffer in his life and in his death. It has been frequently affirmed by persons who have been rescued from drowning, that the mind of a drowning man is singularly active. One who, after being some time in the water was at last painfully restored, said that the whole of his history seemed to come before his mind while he was sinking, and that if any one had asked him how long he had been in the water, he should have said twenty years, whereas he had only been there for a moment or two. The wild romance of Muhammad's journey upon Alborak is not an unfitting illustration. He affirmed that when the angel came in vision to take him on his celebrated journey to Jerusalem, he went through all the seven heavens, and saw all the wonders thereof, and yet he was gone so short a time, that though the angel's wing had touched a basin of water when they started, they returned soon enough to prevent the water from being spilt. The long dream of the epileptic impostor may really have occupied but a second of time. The intellect of mortal man is such that if God wills it, when it is in certain states, it can think out centuries of thought at once; it can go through in one instant what we should have supposed would have taken years upon years of time for it to know or feel.

We think, therefore, that from the Saviour's singular clearness and quickness of intellect upon the cross, it is very possible that he did in the space of two or three hours endure not only the agony which might have been contained in centuries, but even an equivalent for that which might be comprehended in everlasting punishment. At any rate, it is not for us to say that it could not be so. When the Deity is arrayed in manhood, then manhood becomes omnipotent to suffer; and just as the feet of Christ were once almighty to tread the seas, so now was his whole body become almighty to dive into the great waters, to endure an immersion in 'unknown agonies.' Do not, I pray you, let us attempt to measure Christ's sufferings by the finite line of your own ignorant reason, but let us know and believe that what he endured there was accepted by God as an equivalent for all our pains, and therefore it could not have been a trifle, but must have been all that Hart conceived it to be, when he says he bore –

> All that incarnate God could bear,
> With strength enough, but none to spare.

My discourse will, I have no doubt, more fully illustrate the remark with which I have commenced, let us proceed to it at once. First, *let us hear the text and understand it;* then *let us hear it and wonder at it;* and then, thirdly, *let us hear it and proclaim it.*

I. LET US HEAR THE TEXT AND UNDERSTAND IT.

The Son of God has been made man. He has lived a life of perfect virtue and of total self-denial. He has been all that life long despised and rejected of men, a man of sorrows and acquainted with grief. His enemies have been legion; his friends have been few, and those few faithless. He is at last delivered over into the hands of them that hate him. He is arrested while in the act of prayer; he is arraigned before both the spiritual and temporal courts. He is robed in mockery, and then unrobed in shame. He is set upon his throne in scorn, and then tied to the pillar in cruelty. He is declared innocent, and yet he is delivered up by the judge who ought to have preserved him from his persecutors. He is dragged through the streets of that Jerusalem which had killed the prophets, and would now crimson itself with the blood of the prophets' Master. He is brought to the cross, he is nailed fast to the cruel wood. The sun burns him. His cruel wounds increase the fever. God forsakes him. 'My God, my God, why hast thou forsaken me?' contains the concentrated anguish of the world. While he hangs there in mortal conflict with sin and Satan, his heart is broken, his limbs are dislocated. Heaven fails him, for the sun is veiled in darkness. Earth forsakes him, for 'his disciples forsook him and fled.' He looks everywhere, and there is none to help; he casts his eye around, and there is no man that can share his toil. He treads the winepress alone; and of the people there is none with him. On, on, he goes, steadily determined to drink the last dreg of that cup which must not pass from him if his Father's will be done. At last he cries – 'It is finished', and he gives up the ghost. Hear it, Christians, hear this shout of triumph as it rings today with all the freshness and force which it had eighteen hundred years ago! Hear it from the Sacred Word, and from the Saviour's lips, and may the Spirit of God open your ears that you may hear as the learned, and understand what you hear!

1. What meant the Saviour, then, by this – 'It is finished'? He meant, first of all, *that all the types, promises, and prophecies were now fully accomplished in him.* Those who are acquainted with the original will find that the words – 'It is finished', occur twice within three verses. In the 28th verse, we have the word in the Greek, it is translated in our version 'accomplished', but there it stands – 'After this, Jesus knowing that all things were now *finished*, that the Scripture might be fulfilled, saith, I thirst.' And then he afterwards said, 'It is finished.' This leads us to see his meaning very clearly, that all the Scripture was now fulfilled, that when he said, 'It is finished', the whole book, from the first to the last, in both the law and the prophets, was finished in him. There is not a single jewel of promise, from that first emerald which fell on the threshold of Eden, to that last sapphire stone of Malachi, which was not set in the breast plate of the true High Priest. Nay, there is not a type, from the red heifer downward to the turtle-dove, from the hyssop upwards to Solomon's temple itself, which was not fulfilled in him; and not a prophecy, whether spoken on Chebar's bank, or on the shores of Jordan, not a dream of wise men, whether they had received it in Babylon, or in Samaria, or in

Judea, which was not now fully wrought out in Christ Jesus. And, brethren, what a wonderful thing it is, that a mass of promises, and prophecies, and types, apparently so heterogeneous, should all be accomplished in one person! Take away Christ for one moment, and I will give the Old Testament to any wise man living, and say to him, 'Take this; this is a problem, go home and construct in your imagination an ideal character who shall exactly fit all that which is herein foreshadowed; remember, he must be a prophet like unto Moses, and yet a champion like to Joshua; he must be an Aaron and a Melchisedek; he must be both David and Solomon, Noah and Jonah, Judah and Joseph. Nay, he must not only be the lamb that was slain, and the scapegoat that was not slain, the turtle-dove that was dipped in blood, and the priest who slew the bird, but he must be the altar, the tabernacle, the mercy-seat, and the showbread.' Nay, to puzzle this wise man, further, we remind him of prophecies so apparently contradictory, that one would think they never could meet in one man such as these, 'All kings shall fall down before him, and all nations shall serve him'; and yet, 'He is despised and rejected of men.' He must begin by show-ing a man born of a virgin mother – 'A virgin shall conceive and bear a son.' He must be a man without spot or blemish, but yet one upon whom the Lord doth cause to meet the iniquities of us all. He must be a glorious one, a Son of David, but yet a root out of a dry ground.

Now, I say it boldly, if all the greatest intellects of all the ages could set themselves to work out this problem, to invent another key to the types and prophecies, they could not do it. I see you, ye wise men, ye are poring over these hieroglyphs, one suggests one key, and it opens two or three of the figures, but you cannot proceed, for the next one puts you at a nonplus. Another learned man suggests another clue, but that fails most where it is most needed, and another, and another, and thus these wondrous hieroglyphs traced of old by Moses in the wilderness, must be left unexplained, till one comes forward and proclaims, 'The cross of Christ and the Son of God incarnate', then the whole is clear, so that he that runs may read, and a child may understand. Blessed Saviour! In thee we see everything fulfilled, which God spoke of old by the prophets; in thee we discover everything carried out in substance, which God had set forth to us in the dim mist of sacrificial smoke. Glory be unto thy name! 'It is finished' – everything is summed up in thee.

2. But the words have richer meaning. Not only were all types, and prophecies, and promises thus finished in Christ, *but all the typical sacrifices of the old Jewish law, were now abolished as well as explained.* They were finished – finished in him. Will you imagine for a minute the saints in heaven looking down upon what was done on earth – Abel and his friends who had long ago before the flood been sitting in the glories above. They watch while God lights star after star in heaven. Promise after promise flashes light upon the thick darkness of earth. They see Abraham come, and they look down and wonder while they see God revealing Christ to Abraham in the person of Isaac. They gaze just as the angels do, desiring to look into the mystery. From the times of Noah, Abraham, Isaac, and Jacob, they see altars smoking, recognitions of the fact that man is guilty, and the spirits before the throne say, 'Lord, when will sacrifices finish? – when will blood no more be shed?' The offering of bloody sacrifices soon increases. It is now carried on by men ordained for the purpose. Aaron and the high priests and the Levites, every morning and every evening offer a lamb, while great sacrifices are offered on special occasions. Bullocks groan, rams bleed, the necks of doves are wrung, and all the while the saints are crying, 'O Lord, how long? – when shall the sacrifice cease?'

Year after year the high priest goes within the veil and sprinkles the mercy-seat with blood; the next year sees him do the like, and the next, and again, and again, and again. David offers great public sacrifices, Solomon slaughters tens of thousands, Hezekiah offers rivers of oil, Josiah gives thousands of the fat of fed beasts, and the spirits of the just say, 'Will it never be complete? – will the sacrifice never be finished? – must there always be a remembrance of sin? – will not the last high priest soon come? – will not the order and line of Aaron soon lay aside its labour, because the whole is finished? 'Not yet, not yet, ye spirits of the just, for after the captivity the slaughter of victims still remains. But lo, he comes! Gaze more intently than before – he comes who is to close the line of priests! Lo! there he stands, clothed – not now with linen ephod, not with ringing bells, nor with sparkling jewels on his breastplate – but arrayed in human flesh he stands, his cross his altar, his body and his soul the victim, himself the priest, and lo! before his God he offers up his own soul within the veil of thick darkness which hath covered him from the sight of men. Presenting his own blood, he enters within the veil, sprinkles it there, and coming forth from the midst of the darkness, he looks down on the astonished earth, and upward to expectant heaven, and cries, 'It is finished! It is finished!' – that for which ye looked so long, is fully achieved and perfected for ever.

3. The Saviour meant, we doubt not, that in this moment *his perfect obedience was finished*. It was necessary, in order that man might be saved, that the law of God should be kept, for no man can see God's face except he be perfect in righteousness. Christ undertook to keep God's law for his people, to obey its every man-date and preserve its every statute intact. Throughout the first years of his life he privately obeyed, honouring his father and his mother, during the next three years he publicly obeyed God, spending and being spent in his service, till if you would know what a man would be whose life was wholly conformed to the law of God, you may see him in Christ.

> My dear Redeemer and my Lord,
> I read my duty in thy word,
> But in thy life the law appears
> *Drawn out in living characters.*

It needed nothing to complete the perfect virtue of life but the entire obedience of death. He who would serve God must be will-ing not only to give all his soul and his strength while he lives, but he must stand prepared to resign life when it shall be for God's glory. Our perfect Substitute put the last stroke upon his work by dying, and therefore he claims to be absolved from further debt, for 'It is finished.' Yes, glorious Lamb of God, it is finished! Thou hast been tempted in all points like as we are, yet hast thou sinned in none! It was finished, for the last arrow out of Satan's quiver had been shot at thee; the last blasphemous insinuation, the last wicked temptation had spent its fury on thee, the prince of this world had surveyed thee from head to foot, within and without, but he had found nothing in thee. Now thy trial is over, thou hast finished the work which thy Father gave thee to do, and so finished it that hell itself cannot accuse thee of a flaw. And now, looking upon thine entire obedience thou sayest, 'It is finished', and we thy people believe most joyously that it is even so.

Brothers and sisters, this is more than you or I could have said if Adam had never fallen. If we had been in the Garden of Eden today we could never have boasted a finished righteousness, since a creature can never finish its obedience. As long as a creature lives it is bound to obey, and as long as a free agent exists on earth it would be in danger of violating the vow of its obedience. If Adam had been in Paradise from the first day until now, he might fall tomorrow. Left to himself there would be no reason why that king of nature should not yet be uncrowned. But Christ the Creator, who finished creation, has perfected redemption. God can ask no more. The law has received all it claims, the largest extent of justice cannot demand another hour's obedience. It is done, it is complete; the last throw of the shuttle is over, and the robe is woven from the top throughout. Let us rejoice, then, in this that the Master meant by his dying cry that his perfect righteousness wherewith he covers us was finished.

4. But next, the Saviour meant *that the satisfaction which he rendered to the justice of God was finished*. The debt was now, to the last farthing, all discharged. The atonement and propitiation were made once for all, and for ever, by the one offering made in Jesu's body on the tree. There was the cup, hell was in it, the Saviour drank it – not a sip and then a pause; not a draught and then a ceasing, but he drained it till there is not a dreg left for any of his people. The great ten-thonged whip of the law was worn out upon his back. There is no lash left with which to smite one for whom Jesus died. The great cannonade of God's justice has exhausted all its ammunition, there is nothing left to be hurled against a child of God. Sheathed is thy sword, O Justice! Silenced is thy thunder, O Law! There remaineth nothing now of all the griefs, and pains,

and agonies which chosen sinners ought to have suffered for their sins, for Christ has endured all for his own beloved, and 'It is finished.' Brethren, *it is more than the damned in hell can ever say*. If you and I had been constrained to make satisfaction to God's justice by being sent to hell we never could have said, 'It is finished.' Christ has paid the debt which all the torments of eternity could not have paid. Lost souls, ye suffer today as ye have suffered for ages past, but God's justice is not satisfied, his law is not fully magnified. And when time shall fail, and eternity shall have been flying on, still for ever, for ever, the uttermost never having been paid, the chastisement for sin must fall upon unpardoned sinners. But Christ has done what all the flames of the pit could not do in all eternity; he has magnified the law and made it honourable, and now from the cross he cries – 'It is finished.'

5. Once again: when he said, 'It is finished', *Jesus had totally destroyed the power of Satan, of sin, and of death*. The champion had entered the lists to do battle for our soul's redemption, against all our foes. He met Sin. Horrible, terrible, all but omnipotent Sin nailed him to the cross; but in that deed, Christ nailed Sin also to the tree. There they both did hang together – Sin, and Sin's destroyer. Sin destroyed Christ, and by that destruction Christ destroyed Sin. Next came the second enemy, Satan. He assaulted Christ with all his hosts. Calling up his myrmidons[1] from every corner and quarter of the universe, he said, 'Awake, arise, or be for ever fallen! Here is our great enemy who has sworn to bruise my head; now let us bruise his heel!' They shot their hellish darts into his heart; they poured their boiling cauldrons on his brain, they emptied their venom into his veins; they spat their insinuations into his face; they hissed their devilish fears into his ear. He stood alone, the lion of the tribe of Judah, hounded by all the dogs of hell. Our champion quailed not, but used his holy weapons, striking right and left with all the power of God-supported manhood. On came the hosts, volley after volley was discharged against him. No mimic thunders were these, but such as might

---

[1] Myrmidon: one of a tribe of warriors who accompanied Achilles to Troy; one who carries out another's orders without fear or pity.

shake the very gates of hell. The Conqueror steadily advanced, overturning their ranks, dashing in pieces his enemies, breaking the bow and cutting the spear in sunder, and burning the chariots in the fire, while he cried, 'In the name of God will I destroy ye!' At last, foot to foot, he met the champion of hell, and now our David fought with Goliath. Not long was the struggle; thick was the darkness which gathered round them both; but he who is the Son of God as well as the Son of Mary, knew how to smite the fiend, and he did smite him with divine fury, till, having despoiled him of his armour, having quenched his fiery darts, and broken his head, he cried, 'It is finished', and sent the fiend, bleeding and howling, down to bed. We can imagine him pursued by the eternal Saviour, who exclaims –

> Traitor! This bolt shalt find and pierce thee through,
> Though under hell's profoundest wave
> Thou div'st, to seek a shelt'ring grave.

His thunderbolt o'ertook the fiend, and grasping him with both his hands, the Saviour drew around him the great chain. The angels brought the royal chariot from on high, to whose wheels the captive fiend was bound. Lash the coursers up the everlasting hills! Spirits made perfect come forth to meet him. Hymn the Conqueror who drags death and hell behind him, and leads captivity captive! 'Lift up your heads, O ye gates, and be ye lifted up, ye everlasting doors, that the King of glory may come in.' But stay; ere he enters, let him be rid of this his burden. Lo! he takes the fiend, and hurls him down through illimitable night, broken, bruised, with his power destroyed, bereft of his crown, to lie for ever howling in the pit of hell.

Thus when the Saviour cried, 'It is finished', he had defeated Sin and Satan; nor less had he vanquished Death. Death had come against him, as Christmas Evans puts it, with his fiery dart, which he struck right through the Saviour, till the point fixed in the cross, and when he tried to pull it out again, he left the sting behind. What could he do more? He was disarmed. Then Christ set some of his prisoners free; for many of the saints arose and were seen of many: then he said to him, 'Death, I take from thee thy keys; thou must live for a little while to be the warder of those beds in which my saints shall sleep but give me thy keys.' And lo! the Saviour stands today with the keys of death hanging at his girdle, and he waits until the hour shall come of which no man knoweth, when the trump of the archangel shall ring like the silver trumpets of Jubilee, and then he shall say, 'Let my captives go free.' Then shall the tombs be opened in virtue of Christ's death, and the very bodies of the saints shall live again in an eternity of glory.

'It is finish'd!'
Hear the dying Saviour cry.

II. Secondly, LET US HEAR AND WONDER.

Let us perceive what mighty things were effected and secured by these words, 'It is finished.' Thus he *ratified the covenant.* That covenant was signed and sealed before, and in all things it was ordered well, but when Christ said, 'It is finished', then the covenant was made doubly sure; when the blood of Christ's heart bespattered the divine roll, then it could never be reversed, nor could one of its ordinances be broken, nor one of its stipulations fail. You know the covenant was on this wise. God covenants on his part that he would give Christ to see of the travail of his soul; that all who were given to him should have new hearts and right spirits; that they should be washed from sin, and should enter into life through him. Christ's side of the covenant was this – 'Father, I will do thy will; I will pay the ransom to the last jot and tittle; I will give thee perfect obedience and complete satisfaction.' Now if this second part of the covenant had never been fulfilled, the first part would have been invalid, but when Jesus said, 'It is finished', then there was nothing left to be performed on his part, and now the covenant is all on one side. It is God's 'I will', and 'They shall'. 'A new heart will I give you, and a right spirit will I put within you.' 'I will sprinkle clean water upon you and ye shall be clean.' 'From all your iniquities will I cleanse you.' 'I will lead you by a way that ye know not.' 'I will surely bring them in.' The covenant that day was ratified. When Christ said, 'It is finished', *his Father was honoured, and divine justice was fully displayed.* The Father always did love his people. Do not think that Christ died to make God the Father loving. He always had loved them from before the foundation of the world, but – 'It is finished', took away the barriers which were in the Father's way. He would, as a God of love, and now he could as a God of justice, bless poor sinners. From that day the Father is well pleased to receive sinners to his bosom. When Christ said – 'It is finished', *he himself was glorified*. Then on his head descended the all-glorious crown. Then did the Father give to him honours, which he had not before. He had honour as God, but as man he was despised and rejected; now as God and man Christ was made to sit down for ever on his Father's throne crowned with honour and majesty. Then, too, by 'It is finished', *the Spirit was procured for us.*

'Tis by the merit of his death
Who hung upon the tree,
The Spirit is sent down to breathe
On such dry bones as we.

Then the Spirit which Christ had aforetime promised, perceived a new and living way by which he could come to dwell in the hearts of men, and men might come up to dwell with him above. That day too, when Christ said – 'It is finished', *the words had effect on heaven.* Then the walls of chrysolite stood fast; then the jasper-light of the pearly-gated city shone like the light of seven days. Before, the saints had been saved as it were on credit. They had entered heaven, God having faith in his Son Jesus. Had not Christ finished his work, surely they must have left their shining spheres, and suffered in their own persons for their own sins. I might represent heaven, if my imagination might be allowed a moment, as being ready to totter if Christ had not finished his work; its stones would have been unloosed; massive and stupendous though its bastions are, yet had they fallen as earthly cities reel under the throes of earthquake. But Christ said, 'It is finished', and oath, and covenant, and blood set fast the dwelling place of the redeemed, made their mansions safely and eternally their own, and bade their feet stand immovably upon the rock.

Nay, more, that word 'It is finished' took effect in the gloomy caverns and depths of HELL. Then Satan bit his iron bands in rage, howling, 'I am defeated by the very man whom I thought to overcome, my hopes are blasted; never shall an elect one come into my prison house, never a blood-bought one be found in my abode.' Lost souls mourned that day, for they said – '"It is finished"! and if Christ himself, the substitute, could not be permitted to go free till he had finished all his punishment, then we shall never be free.' It was their double death knell, for they said 'Alas for us! Justice, which would not suffer the Saviour to escape, will never suffer us to be at liberty. It is finished with him, and therefore it shall never be finished for us.' That day, too, the earth had a gleam of sunlight cast over her which she had never known before. Then her hilltops began to glisten with the rising of the sun and though her valleys still are clothed with darkness, and men wander hither and thither and grope in the noonday as in the night, yet that sun is rising, climbing still its heavenly steeps, never to set, and soon shall its rays penetrate through the thick mists and clouds, and every eye shall see him, and every heart be made glad with his light. The words 'It is finished' consolidated heaven, shook hell, comforted earth, delighted the Father, glorified the Son, brought down the Spirit, and confirmed the everlasting covenant to all the chosen seed.

III. And now I come to my last point, upon which very briefly. 'It is finished'! LET US PUBLISH IT.

Children of God, ye who by faith received Christ as your all in all, tell it every day of your lives that 'It is finished.' Go and tell it to those who are torturing themselves, thinking through obedience and mortification to offer satisfaction. Yonder Hindu is about to throw himself down upon the spikes. Stay, poor man! wherefore wouldst thou bleed, for 'It is finished'? Yonder Fakir is holding his hand erect till the nails grow through the flesh, torturing himself with fastings and with self-denials. Cease, cease, poor wretch, from all these pains, for 'It is finished'! In all parts of the earth there are those who think that the misery of the body and the soul may be an atonement for sin. Rush to them, stay them in their madness and say to them, 'Wherefore do ye this? "It is finished."' All the pains that God asks, Christ has suffered, all the satisfaction by way of agony in the flesh that the law demandeth, Christ hath already endured. 'It is finished'! And when ye have done this, go ye next to the benighted votaries of Rome, when ye see the priests with their backs to the people, offering every day the pretended sacrifice of the mass, and lifting up the host on high – a sacrifice, they say – 'an unbloody sacrifice for the quick and the dead' – cry, 'Cease, false priest, cease! for "It is finished"! Cease, false worshipper, cease to bow, for "It is finished"!' God neither asks nor accepts any other sacrifice than that which Christ offered once for all upon the cross. Go ye next to the foolish among your own countrymen who call themselves Protestants, but who are Papists after all, who think by their gifts and their gold, by their prayers and their vows, by their church goings and their chapel goings, by their baptisms and their confirmations, to make themselves fit for God; and say to them, 'Stop, "It is finished." God needs not this of you. He has received enough; why will ye pin your rags to the fine linen of Christ's righteousness? Why will you add your counterfeit farthing to the costly ransom which Christ has paid in to the treasure-house of God? Cease from your pains, your doings, your performances, for "It is finished"; Christ has done it all.' This one text is enough to blow the Vatican to the four winds. Lay but this beneath Popery and like a train of gunpowder beneath a rock, it shall blast it into the air. This is a thunderclap against all human righteousness. Only let this come like a two-edged sword, and your good works and your fine performances are soon cast away. 'It is finished.' Why improve on what is finished? Why add to that which is complete? The Bible is finished, he that adds to it shall have his name taken out of the Book of Life, and out of the holy city: Christ's atonement is finished, and he that adds to that must expect the selfsame doom.

And when ye shall have told it thus to the ears of men of every nation and of every tribe, tell it to all poor despairing souls. Ye find them on their knees, crying 'O God, what can I do to make recompense for my offences?' Tell them, 'It is finished', the recompense is made already. 'O God!' they say, 'how can I ever get a righteousness in which thou canst accept such a worm as I am?' Tell them, 'It is finished', their righteousness is wrought out already; they have no need to trouble themselves about adding to it, if 'It is finished.' Go to the poor despairing wretch, who has given himself up, not for death merely, but for damnation – he who says, 'I cannot escape from sin, and I cannot be saved from its punishment.' Say to him, 'Sinner, the way of salvation is finished once for all.' And if ye meet some professed Christians in doubts and fears, tell them, 'It is finished.' Why, we have hundreds and thousands that really are converted who do not know that 'It is finished.' They never know that they are safe. They do not know that 'It is finished.' They think they have faith today, but perhaps they may become unbelieving tomorrow. They do not know that 'It is finished.' They hope God will accept them, if they do some things, forgetting that the way of acceptance is finished. God as much accepts a sinner who only believed in Christ five minutes ago, as he will a saint who has known and loved him eighty years, for he does not accept men because of any anything they do or feel, but simply and only for what Christ did, and that is finished. Oh! poor hearts! some of you do love the Saviour in a measure, but blindly. You are thinking that you must be this, and attain to that, and then you may be assured that you are saved. Oh! you may be assured of it today – if you believe in Christ you are saved. 'But I feel imperfections.' Yes, but what of that? God does not regard your imperfections, but he covers them with Christ's righteousness. He sees them to remove them, but not to lay them to thy charge. 'Ay, but I cannot be what I would be.' But what if thou canst not? Yet God does not look at thee, as what thou art in thyself, but as what thou art in Christ.

Come with me, poor soul, and thou and I will stand together this morning, while the tempest gathers, for we are not afraid. How sharp that lightning flash! but yet we tremble not. How terrible that peal of thunder! and yet we are not alarmed, and why? Is there anything in us why we should escape? No, but we are standing beneath the cross – that precious cross, which like some noble lightning conductor in the storm, takes to itself all the death from the lightning, and all the fury from the tempest. We are safe. Loud mayest thou roar, O thundering law, and terribly mayest thou flash, O avenging justice! We can look up with calm delight to all the tumult of the elements, for we are safe beneath the cross.

Come with me again. There is a royal banquet spread; the King himself sits at the table, and angels are the servants. Let us enter.

And we do enter, and we sit down and eat and drink, but how dare we do this? Our righteousness are as filthy rags – how could we venture to come here? Oh, because the filthy rags are not ours any longer. We have renounced our own righteousness, and therefore we have renounced the filthy rags, and now today we wear the royal garments of the Saviour, and are from head to foot arrayed in white, without spot or wrinkle or any such thing; standing in the clear sunlight – black, but comely, loathsome in ourselves, but glorious in him; condemned in Adam, but accepted in the Beloved. We are neither afraid nor ashamed to be with the angels of God, to talk with the glorified; nay, nor even alarmed to speak with God himself and call him our friend.

And now last of all, I publish this to sinners. I know not where thou art this morning, but may God find thee out; thou who hast been a drunkard, swearer, thief; thou who hast been a blackguard of the blackest kind; thou who hast dived into the very kennel, and rolled thyself in the mire – if today thou feelest that sin is hateful to thee, believe in him who has said, 'It is finished.' Let me link thy hand in mine, let us come together, both of us, and say, 'Here are two poor naked souls, good Lord, we cannot clothe ourselves'; and he will give us a robe, for 'It is finished.' 'But, Lord, is it long enough for such sinners, and broad enough for such offenders?' 'Yes,' saith he, 'it is finished.' 'But we need washing, Lord! Is there anything that can take away black spots so hideous as ours?' 'Yes,' saith he, 'here is the bath of blood.' 'But must we not add our tears to it?' 'No,' says he, 'no, it is finished, there is enough.' 'And now, Lord, thou hast washed us, and thou hast clothed us, but we would be still completely clean within, so that we may never sin any more; Lord, is there a way by which this can be done?' 'Yes' saith he, 'there is the bath of water which floweth from the wounded side of Christ.' 'And, Lord, is there enough there to wash away my guiltiness as well as my guilt?' 'Ay,' saith he, 'it is finished.' 'Jesus Christ is made unto you sanctification as well as redemption.' Child of God, wilt thou have Christ's finished righteousness this morning, and will thou rejoice in it more than ever thou hast done before?

And oh! poor sinner, wilt thou have Christ or no? 'Ah,' saith one, 'I am willing enough, but I am not worthy.' He does not want any worthiness. All he asks is willingness, for you know how he puts it, 'Whoever will let him come.' If he has given you willingness, you may believe in Christ's finished work this morning. 'Ah!' say you, 'but you cannot mean *me.*' But I do, for it says, *'Ho, every one that thirsteth.'* Do you thirst for Christ? Do you wish to be saved by him? *'Every one* that thirsteth' – not only that young woman yonder, not simply that grey-headed old rebel yonder who has long despised the Saviour, but this mass below, and you in these double tiers of gallery – 'Every one that thirsteth, come ye to the waters, and he that hath no money come.' O that I could 'compel' you to come! Great God, do thou make the sinner willing to be saved, for he wills to be damned and will not come unless thou change his will! Eternal Spirit, source of light, and life, and grace, come down and bring the strangers home! 'It is finished.' Sinner, there is nothing for God to do. 'It is finished'; there is nothing for you to do. 'It is finished', Christ need not bleed. 'It is finished'; you need not weep. 'It is finished', God the Holy Spirit need not tarry because of your unworthiness, nor need you tarry because of your helplessness. 'It is finished'; every stumbling block is rolled out of the road, every gate is opened, the bars of brass are broken, the gates of iron are burst asunder. 'It is finished'; come and welcome, come and welcome! The table is laid, the fatlings are killed; the oxen are ready. Lo! here stands the messenger! Come from the highways and from the hedges; come from the dens and from the kens[1] of London, come, ye vilest of the vile; ye who hate yourselves today, come! Jesus bids you, oh! will you tarry? Oh! Spirit of God, do thou repeat the invitation, and make it an effectual call to many a heart, for Jesus' sake! Amen.

---

[1] ken: (*slang*) a house, esp. disreputable.

16

THE DYING THIEF IN A NEW LIGHT[1]

But the other answering rebuked him, saying, Dost not thou fear God, seeing thou art in the same condemnation? And we indeed justly; for we receive the due reward of our deeds: but this Man hath done nothing amiss. And he said unto Jesus, Lord, remember me when thou comest into thy kingdom.

Luke 23:40–42

A GREAT MANY PERSONS, whenever they hear of the conversion of the dying thief, remember that he was saved in the very article of death, and they dwell upon that fact, and that alone. He has always been quoted as a case of salvation at the eleventh hour; and so, indeed, he is. In his case it is proven that as long as a man can repent he can obtain forgiveness. The cross of Christ avails even for a man hanging on a gibbet, and drawing near to his last hour. He who is mighty to save was mighty, even during his own death, to pluck others from the grasp of the destroyer, though they were in the act of expiring.

But that is not everything which the story teaches us; and it is always a pity to look exclusively upon one point, and thus to miss everything else – perhaps miss that which is more important. So often has this been the case that it has produced a sort of revulsion of feeling in certain minds, so that they have been driven in a wrong direction by their wish to protest against what they think to be a

[1] Sermon No. 1,881. Preached at the Metropolitan Tabernacle on Sunday evening, 23 August 1885.

common error. I read the other day that this story of the dying thief ought not to be taken as an encouragement to death-bed repentance. Brethren, if the author meant – and I do not think he did mean – that this ought never to be so used as to lead people to postpone repentance to a dying bed, he spoke correctly. No Christian man could or would use it so injuriously: he must be hopelessly bad who would draw from God's long-suffering an argument for continuing in sin. I trust, however, that the narrative is not often so used, even by the worst of men, and I feel sure that it will not be so used by any one of you. It cannot be properly turned to such a purpose: it might be used as an encouragement to thieving just as much as to the delay of repentance. I might say, 'I may be a thief because this thief was saved', just as rationally as I might say, 'I may put off repentance because this thief was saved when he was about to die.' The fact is, there is nothing so good but men can pervert it into evil, if they have evil hearts: the justice of God is made a motive for despair, and his mercy an argument for sin. Wicked men will drown themselves in the rivers of truth as readily as in the pools of error. He that has a mind to destroy himself can choke his soul with the Bread of life, or dash himself in pieces against the Rock of ages. There is no doctrine of the grace of God so gracious that graceless men may not turn it into licentiousness.

I venture, however, to say that if I stood by the bedside of a dying man tonight, and I found him anxious about his soul, but fearful that Christ could not save him because repentance had been put off so late, I should certainly quote the dying thief to him, and I should do it with good conscience, and without hesitation. I should tell him that, though he was as near to dying as the thief upon the cross was, yet, if he repented of his sin, and turned his face to Christ believingly, he would find eternal life. I should do this with all my heart, rejoicing that I had such a story to tell to one at the gates of eternity. I do not think that I should be censured by the Holy Spirit for thus using a narrative which he has himself recorded – recorded with the foresight that it would be so used. I should feel, at any rate, in my own heart, a sweet conviction that I had treated the subject as I ought to have treated it, and as it was intended to be used for men *in extremis* whose hearts are turning towards the living God. Oh, yes, poor soul, whatever your age, or whatever the period of life to which you have come, you may now find eternal life by faith in Christ!

> The dying thief rejoiced to see
>   That fountain in his day;
> And there may you, though vile as he,
>   Wash all your sins away.

Many good people think that they ought to guard the gospel; but it is never so safe as when it stands out in its own naked majesty. It wants no covering from us. When we protect it with provisos, and guard it with exceptions, and qualify it with observations, it is like David in Saul's armour: it is hampered and hindered, and you may even hear it cry, 'I cannot go with these.' Let the gospel alone, and it will save; qualify it, and the salt has lost its savour. I will venture to put it thus to you. I have heard it said that few are ever converted in old age; and this is thought to be a statement which will prove exceedingly arousing and impressive for the young. It certainly wears that appearance; but, on the other hand, it is a statement very discouraging to the old. I demur to the frequent repetition of such statements, for I do not find their counterpart in the teaching of our Lord and his apostles. Assuredly our Lord spake of some who entered the vineyard at the eleventh hour of the day; and among his miracles he not only saved those who were dying, but even raised the dead. Nothing can be concluded from the words of the Lord Jesus against the salvation of men at any hour or age. I tell you that, in the business of your acceptance with God, through faith in Christ Jesus, it does not matter what age you now are at. The same promise is to every one of you, 'Today if ye will hear his voice, harden not your hearts'; and whether you are in the earliest stage of life, or are within a few hours of eternity, if now you fly for refuge to the hope set before you in the gospel, you shall be saved. The gospel that I preach excludes none on the ground either of age or character. Whoever you may be, 'Believe on the Lord Jesus Christ, and thou shalt be saved', is the message we have to deliver to you. If we address to you the longer form of the gospel, 'He that believeth and is baptized shall be saved', this is true of every living man, be his age whatever it may. I am not afraid that this story of the dying and repenting thief, who went straight from the cross to the crown, will be used by you amiss; but if you are wicked enough so to use it, I cannot help it. It will only fulfil that solemn Scripture which saith that the gospel is a savour of death unto death to some, even that very gospel which is a savour of life unto life to others.

But I do not think, dear friends, that the only speciality about the thief is the lateness of his repentance. So far from being the only point of interest, it is not even the chief point. To some minds, at any rate, other points will be even more remarkable. I want to show you very briefly that there was a speciality in his case as to *the means of his conversion*; secondly, a speciality in *his faith*; thirdly, a speciality in *the result of his faith while he was here below*; and, fourthly, a speciality in *the promise won by his faith* – the promise fulfilled to him in Paradise.

I. First, then, I think you ought to notice very carefully THE SINGULARITY AND SPECIALITY OF THE MEANS BY WHICH THE THIEF WAS CONVERTED.

How do you think it was? Well, we do not know. We cannot tell. It seems to me that the man was an unconverted, impenitent thief when they nailed him to the cross, because one of the Evangelists says, 'The *thieves* also, which were crucified with him, cast the same in his teeth.' I know that this may have been a general statement, and that it is reconcilable with its having been done by one thief only, according to the methods commonly used by critics; but I am not enamoured of critics even when they are friendly. I have such respect for revelation that I never in my own mind permit the idea of discrepancies and mistakes; and when the Evangelist says 'they' I believe he meant '*they*', and that both these thieves did at their first crucifixion rail at the Christ with whom they were crucified. It would appear that by some means or other this thief must have been converted while he was on the cross. Assuredly nobody preached a sermon to him, no evangelistic address was delivered at the foot of his cross, and no meeting was held for special prayer on his account. He does not even seem to have had an instruction, or an invitation, or an expostulation addressed to him; and yet this man became a sincere and accepted believer in the Lord Jesus Christ.

Dwell upon this fact, if you please, and note its practical bearing upon the cases of many around us. There are many among my hearers who have been instructed from their childhood, who have been admonished, and warned, and entreated, and invited, and yet they have not come to Christ; while this man, without any of these advantages, nevertheless believed in the Lord Jesus Christ and found eternal life. O you that have lived under the sound of the gospel from your childhood, the thief does not comfort you, but he accuses you! What are you doing to abide so long in unbelief? Will you never believe the testimony of divine love? What more shall I say to you? What more can any one say to you?

What do you think must have converted this poor thief? It strikes me that it may have been – it must have been, the sight of our great Lord and Saviour. There was, to begin with, our Saviour's wonderful behaviour on the road to the cross. Perhaps the robber had mixed up with all sorts of society, but he had never seen a Man like this. Never had cross been carried by a Cross-Bearer of his look and fashion. The robber wondered who this meek and majestic Person could be. He heard the women weep, and he wondered in himself whether anybody would ever weep for him. He thought that this must be some very singular Person that the people should stand about him with tears in their eyes. When he heard that mysterious Sufferer say so solemnly, 'Daughters of Jerusalem, weep not for me, but for your children', he must have been struck with wonder. When he came to think, in his death-pangs, of the singular look of pity which Jesus cast on the women, and of the self-forgetfulness which gleamed from his eyes, he was smitten with a strange relenting: it was as if an angel had crossed his path, and opened his eyes to a new world, and to a new form of manhood, the like of which he had never seen before. He and his companion were coarse, rough fellows: this was a delicately formed and fashioned Being, of superior order to himself; yes, and of superior order to any other of the sons of men. Who could he be? What must he be? Though he could see that he suffered and fainted as he went along, he marked that there was no word of complaining, no note of execration, in return for the revilings cast upon him. His eyes looked love on those who glared on him with hate. Surely that march along the *Via Dolorosa* was the first part of the sermon which God preached to that bad man's heart. It was preached to many others who did not regard its teaching; but upon this man, by God's special grace, it had a softening effect when he came to think over it, and consider it. Was it not a likely and convincing means of grace?

When he saw the Saviour surrounded by the Roman soldiery – saw the executioners bring forth the hammers and the nails, and lay him down upon his back, and drive the nails into his hands and feet, this crucified criminal was startled and astonished as he heard him say, 'Father, forgive them; for they know not what they do.' He himself, probably, had met his executioners with a curse; but he heard this man breathe a prayer to the great Father; and, as a Jew, as he probably was, he understood what was meant by such a prayer. But it did astound him to hear Jesus pray for his murderers. That was a petition the like of which he had never heard, nor even dreamed of. From whose lips could it come but from the lips of a divine Being? Such a loving, forgiving, Godlike prayer, proved him to be the Messiah. Who else had ever prayed so? Certainly not David and the kings of Israel, who, on the contrary, in all honesty and heartiness imprecated the wrath of God upon their enemies. Elijah himself would not have prayed in that fashion, rather would he have called fire from heaven on the centurion and his company. It was a new, strange sound to him. I do not suppose that he appreciated it to the full; but I can well believe that it deeply impressed him, and made him feel that his Fellow-Sufferer was a being about whom there was an exceeding mystery of goodness.

And when the cross was lifted up, that thief hanging up on his own cross looked around, and I suppose he could see that inscription written in three languages – 'Jesus of Nazareth, the King of the Jews.' If so, that writing was his little Bible, his New Testament, and he interpreted it by what he knew of the Old Testament. Putting this and that together – that strange Person, incarnate loveliness, all patience and all majesty, that strange prayer, and now this singular inscription, surely he who knew the Old Testament, as I have no doubt he did, would say to himself, 'Is this HE? Is this truly the King of the Jews? This is he who wrought miracles, and raised the dead, and said that he was the Son of God; is it all true, and is he really our Messiah?' Then he would remember the words of the prophet Isaiah, 'He was despised and rejected of men, a Man of sorrows, and acquainted with grief. Surely, he hath borne our griefs, and carried our sorrows.' 'Why,' he would say to himself, 'I never understood that passage in the prophet Isaiah before, but it must point to him. The chastisement of our peace is upon him. Can this be he who cried in the Psalms – "they pierced my hands and my feet"?' As he looked at him again, he felt in his soul, 'It must be he? Could there be another so like to him?' He felt conviction creeping over his spirit. Then he looked again, and he marked how all men down below rejected, and despised, and hissed at him, and hooted him, and all this would make the case the more clear. 'All they that see me laugh me to scorn: they shoot out the lip, they shake the head, saying, He trusted on the Lord that he would deliver him: let him deliver him, seeing he delighted in him.'

Perhaps, this dying thief read the gospel out of the lips of Christ's enemies. They said – 'He saved others.' 'Ah!' thought he, 'did he save others? Why should he not save me?' What a grand bit of gospel that was for the dying thief – 'He saved others!' I think I could swim to heaven on that plank – 'He saved others'; because, if he saved others, he can surely save me.

Thus the very things that the enemies disdainfully threw at Christ would be gospel to this poor dying man. When it has been my misery to read any of the wretched prints that are sent us out of scorn, in which our Lord is held up to ridicule, I have thought, 'Why, perhaps those who read these loathsome blasphemies may, nevertheless, learn the gospel from them!' You may pick a jewel from a dunghill, and find its radiance undiminished; and you may gather the gospel from a blasphemous mouth, and it shall be none the less the gospel of salvation. Perhaps this man learned the gospel from those who jested at our dying Lord; and so the servants of the devil were unconsciously made to be the servants of Christ.

But, after all, surely that which won him most must have been to look at Jesus again, as he was hanging upon the cruel tree. Possibly nothing about the physical person of Christ would be attractive to him, for his visage was more marred than that of any man, and his form more than the sons of men; but yet there must have been in that blessed face a singular charm. Was it not the very image of perfection? As I conceive the face of Christ, it was very different from anything that any painter has yet been able to place upon his canvas. It was all goodness, and kindness, and unselfishness; and yet it was a royal face. It was a face of superlative justice and unrivalled tenderness. Righteousness and uprightness sat upon his brow; but infinite pity and goodwill to men had also there taken up their abode. It was a face that would have struck you at once as one by itself, never to be forgotten, never to be fully understood. It was all sorrow, yet all love; all meekness, yet all resolution; all wisdom, yet all simplicity; the face of a child, or an angel, and yet peculiarly the face of a man. Majesty and misery, suffering and sacredness, were therein strangely combined; he was evidently the Lamb of God, and the Son of Man. As the robber looked, he believed. Is it not singular, the very sight of the Master won him? The sight of the Lord in agony, and shame, and death! Scarcely a word; certainly no sermon; no attending worship on the Sabbath; no reading of gracious books; no appeal from mother, or teacher, or friend; but the sight of Jesus won him. I put it down as a very singular thing, a thing for you and for me to recollect, and dwell upon, with quite as much vividness as we do upon the lateness of this robber's conversion.

Oh, that God of his mercy might convert everybody in this Tabernacle! Oh, that I could have a share in it by the preaching of the word! But I will be equally happy if you get to heaven anyhow; ay, if the Lord should take you there without outward ministries, leading you to Jesus by some simple method such as he adopted with this thief. If you do but get there, he shall have the glory of it, and his poor servant will be overjoyed! Oh, that you would now look to Jesus, and live! Before your eyes he is set forth, evidently crucified among you. Look to him and be saved, even at this hour.

II. But now I want you to think with me a little upon THE SPECIALITY OF THIS MAN'S FAITH, for I think it was a very singular faith that this man exerted towards our Lord Jesus Christ.

I greatly question whether the equal and the parallel of the dying thief's faith will be readily found outside the Scriptures, or even in the Scriptures.

Observe, that this man believed in Christ *when he literally saw him dying the death of a felon,* under circumstances of the greatest personal shame. You have never realized what it was to be crucified. None of you could do that, for the sight has never been seen in our day in England. There is not a man or woman here who has ever realized in their own mind the actual death of Christ. It stands beyond us. This man saw it with his own eyes, and for him to call *him* 'Lord' who was hanging on a gibbet, was no small triumph of faith. For him to ask Jesus to remember him when he came into his kingdom, though he saw that Jesus bleeding his life away, and hounded to the death, was a splendid act of reliance. For him to commit his everlasting destiny into the hands of One who was, to all appearance, unable even to preserve his own life, was a noble achievement of faith. I say that this dying thief leads the way in the matter of faith, for what he saw of the circumstances of the Saviour was calculated to contradict rather than help his confidence. What he saw was to his hindrance rather than to his help, for he saw our Lord in the very extremity of agony and death, and yet he believed in him as the King shortly to come into his kingdom.

Recollect, too, that at that moment when the thief believed in Christ, *all the disciples had forsaken him and fled.* John might be lingering at a little distance, and holy women may have stood farther off, but no one was present bravely to champion the dying Christ. Judas had sold him, Peter had denied him, and the rest had forsaken him; and it was then that the dying thief called him 'Lord', and said, 'Remember me when thou comest into thy kingdom.' I call that splendid faith. Why, some of you do not believe, though you are surrounded with Christian friends – though you are urged on by the testimony of those whom you regard with love; but this man, all alone, comes out, and calls Jesus his Lord! No one else was confessing Christ at that moment: no revival was around him with enthusiastic crowds: he was all by himself as a confessor of his Lord. After our Lord was nailed to the tree, the first to bear witness for him was this thief. The centurion bore witness afterwards, when our Lord expired; but this thief was a lone confessor, holding on to Christ when nobody would say 'Amen' to what he said. Even his fellow-thief was mocking at the crucified Saviour, so that this man shone as a lone star in the midnight darkness. O sirs, dare you be Daniels? Dare you stand alone? Would you dare to stand out amidst a ribald crew, and say, 'Jesus is my King. I only ask him to remember me when he comes into his kingdom?' Would you be likely to avow such a faith when priests and scribes, princes and people, were all mocking at the Christ, and deriding him? Brethren, the dying robber exhibited marvellous faith, and I beg you to think of this next time you speak of him.

And it seems to me that another point adds splendour to that faith, namely, that *he himself was in extreme torture*. Remember, he was crucified. It was a crucified man trusting in a crucified Christ. Oh, when our frame is racked with torture, when the tenderest nerves are pained, when our body is hung up to die by we know not what great length of torment, then to forget the present and live in the future is a grand achievement of faith! While dying, to turn one's eye to Another dying at your side, and trust your soul with him, is very marvellous faith. Blessed thief, because they put thee down at the bottom, as one of the least of saints, I think that I must bid thee come up higher and take one of the uppermost seats among those who by faith have glorified the Christ of God!

Why, see, dear friends, once more, the speciality of this man's faith was that *he saw so much*, though his eyes had been opened for so short a time! He saw the future world. He was not a believer in annihilation, or in the possibility of a man's not being immortal. He evidently expected to be in another world, and to be in existence when the dying Lord should come into his kingdom. He believed all that, and it is more than some do nowadays. He also believed that Jesus would have a kingdom, a kingdom after he was dead, a kingdom though he was crucified. He believed that he was winning for himself a kingdom by those nailed hands and pierced feet. This was intelligent faith, was it not? He believed that Jesus would have a kingdom in which others would share, and therefore he aspired to have his portion in it. But yet he had fit views of himself, and therefore he did not say, 'Lord, let me sit at thy right hand'; or, 'Let me share in the choice things of thy palace'; but he said only, 'Remember me. Think of me. Cast an eye my way. Think of thy poor dying comrade on the cross at thy right hand. Lord, remember me. Remember me.' I see deep humility in the prayer and yet a sweet, joyful, confident exaltation of the Christ at the time when the Christ was in his deepest humiliation.

Oh, dear sirs, if any of you have thought of this dying thief only as one who put off repentance, I want you now to think of him as one that did greatly and grandly believe in Christ; and oh, that you would do the same! Oh, that you would put a great confidence in my great Lord! Never did a poor sinner trust Christ too much. There was never a case of a guilty one, who believed that Jesus could forgive him, and afterwards found that he could not – who believed that Jesus could save him on the spot, and then woke up to find that it was a delusion. No; plunge into this river of confidence in Christ. The waters are waters to swim in, not to drown in. Never did a soul perish that glorified Christ by a living, loving faith in him. Come, then, with all your sin, whatever it may be, with all your deep depression of spirit, with all your agony of conscience. Come along with you, and grasp my Lord and Master with both the hands of your faith, and he shall be yours, and you shall be his.

> Turn to Christ your longing eyes,
> View His bloody sacrifice:
> See in Him your sins forgiven;
> Pardon, holiness, and heaven;
> Glorify the King of kings,
> Take the peace the gospel brings.

I think that I have shown you something special in the means of the thief's conversion, and in his faith in our dying Lord.

III. But now, thirdly, as God shall help me, I wish to show you another speciality, namely, in THE RESULT OF HIS FAITH.

Oh, I have heard people say, 'Well, you see, the dying thief was converted; but then he was not baptized. He never went to communion, and never joined the church!' He could not do either; and that which God himself renders impossible to us he does not demand of us. He was nailed to the cross; how could he be baptized? But he did a great deal more than that; for if he could not carry out the outward signs, he most manifestly exhibited the things which they signified, which, in his condition, was better still.

This dying thief first of all confessed the Lord Jesus Christ; and that is the very essence of baptism. He confessed Christ. Did he not acknowledge him to his fellow-thief? It was as open a confession as he could make it. Did he not acknowledge Christ before all that were gathered around the cross who were within hearing? It was as public a confession as he could possibly cause it to be. Yet certain cowardly fellows claim to be Christians, though they have never confessed Christ to a single person, and then they quote this poor thief as an excuse. Are they nailed to a cross? Are they dying in agony? Oh no; and yet they talk as if they could claim the exemption which these circumstances would give them. What a dishonest piece of business!

The fact is, that our Lord requires an open confession as well as a secret faith; and if you will not render it, there is no promise of salvation for you, but a threat of being denied at the last. The apostle puts it, 'If thou shalt confess with thy mouth the Lord Jesus, and shalt believe in thine heart that God hath raised him from the dead, thou shalt be saved.' It is stated in another place upon this wise – 'He that believeth and is baptized shall be saved' – that is Christ's way of making the confession of him. If there be a true faith, there must be a declaration of it. If you are candles, and God has lit you, 'Let your light so shine before men, that they may see your good works, and glorify your Father which is in heaven.' Soldiers of Christ must, like her Majesty's soldiers, wear their regimentals; and if they are ashamed of their regimentals, they ought to be drummed out of the regiment. They are not honest soldiers who refuse to march in rank with their comrades. The very least thing that the Lord Jesus Christ can expect of us is that we do confess him to the best of our power. If you are nailed up to a cross, I will not invite you to be baptized. If you are fastened up to a tree to die, I will not ask you to come into this pulpit and declare your faith, for you cannot. But you are required to do what you can do, namely, to make as distinct and open an avowal of the Lord Jesus Christ as may be suitable in your present condition.

I believe that many Christian people get into a deal of trouble through not being honest in their convictions. For instance, if a man goes into a workshop, or a soldier into a barrack-room, and if he does not fly his flag from the first, it will be very difficult for him to run it up afterwards. But if he immediately and boldly lets them know, 'I am a Christian man, and there are certain things that I cannot do to please you, and certain other things that I cannot help doing, though they displease you' – when that is clearly understood, after a while the singularity of the thing will be gone, and the man will be let alone; but if he is a little sneaky, and thinks that he is going to please the world and please Christ too, he is in for a rough time, let him depend upon it. His life will be that of a toad under a harrow, or a fox in a dog kennel, if he tries the way of compromise. That will never do. Come out. Show your colours. Let it be known who you are, and what you are; and although your course will not be smooth, it will certainly be not half so rough as if you tried to run with the hare and hunt with the hounds – a very difficult piece of business that.

This man came out, then and there, and made as open an avowal of his faith in Christ as was possible.

The next thing he did was to rebuke his fellow-sinner. He spoke to him in answer to the ribaldry with which he had assailed our Lord. I do not know what the unconverted convict had been blasphemously saying, but his converted comrade spoke very honestly to him. 'Dost not thou fear God, seeing thou art in the same condemnation? And we indeed justly; for we receive the due reward of our deeds: but this Man hath done nothing amiss.' It is more than ever needful in these days that believers in Christ should not allow sin to go unrebuked; and yet a great many of them do so. Do you not know that a person who is silent when a wrong thing is said or done may become a participator in the sin? If you do not rebuke sin – I mean, of course, on all fit occasions, and in a proper spirit – your silence will give consent to the sin, and you will be an aider and abettor in it. A man who saw a robbery, and who did not cry, 'Stop thief!' would be thought to be in league with the thief; and the man who can hear swearing, or see impurity, and never utter a word of protest may well question whether he is right himself. Our 'other men's sins' make up a great item in our personal guilt unless we in anywise rebuke them. This our Lord expects us to do. The dying thief did it, and did it with all his heart; and therein far exceeded large numbers of those who hold their heads high in the church.

Next, *the dying thief made a full confession of his guilt*. He said to him who was hanged with him, 'Dost not thou fear God, seeing thou art in the same condemnation? *And we indeed justly.*' Not many words, but what a world of meaning was in them – 'we indeed justly'. 'You and I are dying for our crimes', said he, 'and we deserve to die.' When a man is willing to confess that he deserves the wrath of God – that he deserves the suffering which his sin has brought upon him – there is evidence of sincerity in him. In this man's case, his repentance glittered like a holy tear in the eye of his faith, so that his faith was bejewelled with the drops of his penitence. As I have often told you, I suspect the faith which is not born as a twin with repentance; but there is no room for suspicion in the case of this penitent confessor. I pray God that you and I may have such a thorough work as this in our own hearts as the result of our faith.

Then, see, *this dying thief defends his lord right manfully*. He says, 'We indeed justly, but this Man hath done nothing amiss.' Was not that beautifully said? He did not say, 'This Man does not deserve to die', but 'This Man hath done nothing amiss.' He means that he is perfectly innocent. He does not even say 'He has done nothing wicked', but he even asserts that he has not acted unwisely or indiscreetly – 'This Man hath done nothing amiss.' This is a glorious testimony of a dying man to one who was numbered with the transgressors, and was being put to death because his enemies falsely accused him. Beloved, I only pray that you and I may bear as good witness to our Lord as this thief did. He outruns us all. We need not think much of the coming of his conversion late in life; we may far rather consider how blessed was the testimony which he bore for his Lord when it was most needed. When all other voices were silent, one suffering penitent spake out, and said – 'This man hath done nothing amiss.'

See, again, another mark of this man's faith. He prays: and *his prayer is directed to Jesus*. 'Lord, remember me when thou comest into thy kingdom.' True faith is always praying faith. 'Behold, he prayeth', is one of the surest tests of the new birth. Oh, friends, may we abound in prayer, for thus we shall prove that our faith in

Jesus Christ is what it ought to be! This converted robber opened his mouth wide in prayer; he prayed with great confidence as to the coming kingdom, and he sought that kingdom first, even to the exclusion of all else. He might have asked for life, or for ease from pain; but he prefers the kingdom; and this is a high mark of grace.

In addition to thus praying, you will see that *he adores and worships Jesus*, for he says, 'Lord, remember me when thou comest into thy kingdom.' The petition is worded as if he felt, 'Only let Christ think of me, and it is enough. Let him but remember me, and the thought of his mind will be effectual for everything that I shall need in the world to come.' This is to impute Godhead to Christ. If a man can cast his all upon the mere memory of a person, he must have a very high esteem of that person. If to be remembered by the Lord Jesus is all that this man asks, or desires, he pays to the Lord great honour. I think that there was about his prayer a worship equal to the eternal hallelujahs of cherubim and seraphim. There was in it a glorification of his Lord which is not excelled even by the endless symphonies of angelic spirits who surround the throne. Thief, thou hast well done!

Oh, that some penitent spirit here might be helped thus to believe, thus to confess, thus to defend his Master, thus to adore, thus to worship; and then the age of the convert would be a matter of the smallest imaginable consequence.

IV. Now, the last remark is this: There was something very special about the dying thief as to OUR LORD'S WORD TO HIM ABOUT THE WORLD TO COME. He said to him, 'Today shalt thou be with me in Paradise.' He only asked the Lord to remember him, but he obtained this surprising answer, 'Today shalt thou be with me in Paradise.'

In some respects I envy this dying thief; for this reason – that when the Lord pardoned me, and pardoned the most of you, who are present, he did not give us a place in Paradise that same day. We are not yet come to the rest which is promised to us. No, you are waiting here. Some of you have been waiting very long. It is thirty years with many of us. It is forty years, it is fifty years, with many others since the Lord blotted out your sins, and yet you are not with him in Paradise. There is a dear member of this church who, I suppose, has known the Lord for seventy-five years, and she is still with us, having long passed the ninetieth year of her age. The Lord did not admit her to Paradise on the day of her conversion. He did not take any one of us from nature to grace, and from grace to glory, in a day. We have had to wait a good while. There is something for us to do in the wilderness, and so we are kept out of the heavenly garden. I remember that Mr Baxter said that he was not in a hurry to be gone to heaven; and a friend called upon Dr John Owen, who had been writing about the glory of Christ, and asked him what he thought of going to heaven. That great divine replied, 'I am longing to be there.' 'Why,' said the other, 'I have just spoken to holy Mr Baxter, and he says that he would prefer to be here, since he thinks that he can be more useful on earth.' 'Oh!' said Dr Owen, 'my brother Baxter is always full of practical godliness, but for all that I cannot say that I am at all desirous to linger in this mortal state. I would rather be gone.' Each of these men seems to me to have been the half of Paul. Paul was made up of the two, for he was desirous to depart, but he was willing to remain because it was needful for the people. We would put both together, and, like Paul, have a strong desire to depart and to be with Christ, and yet be willing to wait if we can do service to our Lord and to his church. Still, I think he has the best of it who is converted, and enters heaven the same night. This robber breakfasted with the devil, but he dined with Christ on earth, and supped with him in Paradise. This was short work, but blessed work. What a host of troubles he escaped! What a world of temptation he missed! What an evil world he quitted! He was just born, like a lamb dropped in the field, and then he was lifted into the Shepherd's bosom straight away. I do not remember the Lord ever saying this to anybody else. I dare say it may have happened that souls have been converted and have gone home at once; but I never heard of anybody that had such an assurance from Christ as this man had: 'Verily, I say unto *thee*'; such a personal assurance: 'Verily I say unto thee, Today shalt thou be with me in Paradise.' Dying thief, you were favoured above many, 'to be with Christ, which is far better', and to be with him so soon!

Why is it that our Lord does not thus emparadise all of us at once? It is because there is something for us to do on earth. My brethren, are you doing it? *Are you doing it?* Some good people are still on earth: but why? But why? What is the use of them? I cannot make it out. If they are indeed the Lord's people, what are they here for? They get up in the morning and eat their breakfast, and in due course eat their dinner, and their supper, and go to bed and sleep; at a proper hour they get up the next morning, and do the same as on the previous day. Is this living for Jesus? Is this life? It does not come to much. Can this be the life of God in man? Oh, Christian people, do justify your Lord in keeping you waiting here! How can you justify him but by serving him to the utmost of your power? The Lord help you to do so! Why, you owe as much to him as the dying thief! I know I owe a great deal more.

What a mercy it is to have been converted while you were yet a boy, to be brought to the Saviour while you were yet a girl! What a debt of obligation young Christians owe to the Lord! And if this poor thief crammed a life full of testimony into a few minutes, ought not you and I, who are spared, for years after conversion, to perform good service for our Lord? Come, let us wake up if we have been asleep! Let us begin to live if we have been half dead. May the Spirit of God make something of us yet: so that we may go as industrious servants from the labours of the vineyard to the pleasures of the Paradise! To our once crucified Lord be glory for ever and ever! Amen.

17

THE BELIEVING THIEF[1]

And he said unto Jesus, Lord, remember me when thou comest into thy kingdom. And Jesus said unto him, Verily I say unto thee, To day shalt thou be with me in paradise.

LUKE 23:42–43

SOME TIME AGO I preached upon the whole story of the dying thief.[2] I do not propose to do the same today, but only to look at it from one particular point of view. The story of the salvation of the dying thief is a standing instance of the power of Christ to save, and of his abundant willingness to receive all that come to him, in whatever plight they may be. I cannot regard this act of grace as a solitary instance, any more than the salvation of Zacchaeus, the restoration of Peter, or the call of Saul, the persecutor. Every conversion is, in a sense, singular: no two are exactly alike, and yet any one conversion is a type of others. The case of the dying thief is much more similar to our conversion than it is dissimilar; in point of fact, his case may be regarded as typical, rather than as an extraordinary incident. So I shall use it at this time. May the Holy Spirit speak through it to the encouragement of those who are ready to despair!

Remember, beloved friends, that our Lord Jesus, at the time he saved this malefactor, was at his lowest. His glory had been ebbing out in Gethsemane, and before Caiaphas, and Herod, and Pilate; but it had now reached the utmost low water mark. Stripped of his garments and nailed to the cross our Lord was mocked by a

---

[1] Sermon No. 2,078. Preached at the Metropolitan Tabernacle on Sunday morning, 7 April 1889.

[2] 'The Dying Thief in a New Light', Sermon No. 1,881, 23 August 1885, p. 233.

ribald crowd, and was dying in agony: then was he 'numbered with the transgressors', and made as the offscouring of all things. Yet, while in that condition, he achieved this marvellous deed of grace. Behold the wonder wrought by the Saviour when emptied of all his glory, and hanged up a spectacle of shame upon the brink of death! How certain is it that he can do great wonders of mercy now, seeing that he has returned to his glory, and sits upon the throne of light! 'He is able to save them to the uttermost that come unto God by him, seeing he ever liveth to make intercession for them.' If a dying Saviour saved the thief, my argument is, that he can do even more now that he liveth and reigneth. All power is given unto him in heaven and in earth; can anything at this present time surpass the power of his grace?

It is not only the weakness of our Lord which makes the salvation of the penitent thief memorable; it is the fact that the dying male-factor saw it before his very eyes. Can you put yourself into his place, and suppose yourself to be looking upon one who hangs in agony upon a cross? Could you readily believe him to be the Lord of glory, who would soon come to his kingdom? That was no mean faith which, at such a moment, could believe in Jesus as Lord and King. If the apostle Paul were here, and wanted to add a New Testament chapter to the eleventh of Hebrews, he might certainly commence his instances of remarkable faith with this thief, who believed in a crucified, derided, and dying Christ, and cried to him as to one whose kingdom would surely come. The thief's faith was the more remarkable because he was himself in great pain, and bound to die. It is not easy to exercise confidence when you are tortured with deadly anguish. Our own rest of mind has at times been greatly hindered by pain of body. When we are the subjects of acute suffering it is not easy to exhibit that faith which we fancy we possess at other times. This man, suffering as he did, and seeing the Saviour in so sad a state, nevertheless believed unto life eternal. Herein was such faith as is seldom seen.

Recollect, also, that he was surrounded by scoffers. It is easy to swim with the current, and hard to go against the stream. This man heard the priests, in their pride, ridicule the Lord, and the great multitude of the common people, with one consent, joined in the scorning; his comrade caught the spirit of the hour, and mocked also, and perhaps he did the same for a while; but through the grace of God he was changed, and believed in the Lord Jesus in the teeth of all the scorn. His faith was not affected by his surroundings; but he, dying thief as he was, made sure his confidence. Like a jutting rock, standing out in the midst of a torrent, he declared the innocence of the Christ whom others blasphemed. His faith is worthy of our imitation in its fruits. He had no member that was free except his tongue, and he used that member wisely to rebuke his brother malefactor, and defend his Lord. His faith brought forth a brave testimony and a bold confession. I am not going to praise the thief, or his faith, but to extol the glory of that grace divine which gave the thief such faith, and then freely saved him by its means. I am anxious to show how glorious is the Saviour – that Saviour to the uttermost, who, at such a time, could save such a man, and give him so great a faith, and so perfectly and speedily prepare him for eternal bliss. Behold the power of that divine Spirit who could produce such faith on soil so unlikely, and in a climate so unpropitious.

Let us enter at once into the centre of our sermon. First, *note the man who was our Lord's last companion on earth*; secondly, *note that this same man was our Lord's first companion at the gate of paradise*; and then, thirdly, let us *note the sermon which our Lord preaches to us from this act of grace*. Oh, for a blessing from the Holy Spirit all the sermon through!

I. Carefully note that THE CRUCIFIED THIEF WAS OUR LORD'S LAST COMPANION ON EARTH. What sorry company our Lord selected when he was here! He did not consort with the religious Pharisees or the philosophic Sadducees, but he was known as 'the friend of publicans and sinners'. How I rejoice at this! It gives me assurance that he will not refuse to associate with *me*. When the Lord Jesus made a friend of me, he certainly did not make a choice which brought him credit. Do you think he gained any honour when he made a friend of you? Has he ever gained anything by us? No, my brethren; if Jesus had not stooped very low, he would not have come to me; and if he did not seek the most unworthy, he might not have come to you. You feel it so, and you are thankful that he came 'not to call the righteous, but sinners to repentance'.

As the great physician, our Lord was much with the sick: he went where there was room for him to exercise his healing art. The whole have no need of a physician: they cannot appreciate him, nor afford scope for his skill; and therefore he did not frequent their abodes. Yes, after all, our Lord did make a good choice when he saved you and me; for in us he has found abundant room for his mercy and grace. There has been elbow room for his love to work within the awful emptinesses of our necessities and sins; and therein he has done great things for us, whereof we are glad.

Lest any here should be despairing, and say, 'He will never deign to look on me', I want you to notice that *the last companion of Christ on earth was a sinner, and no ordinary sinner*. He had broken even the laws of man, for he was a robber. One calls him 'a brigand'; and I suppose it is likely to have been the case. The brigands of those days mixed murder with their robberies: he was probably a freebooter in arms against the Roman government, making this a pretext for plundering as he had opportunity. At last he was arrested, and was condemned by a Roman tribunal, which, on the whole, was usually just, and in this case was certainly just; for he himself confesses the justice of his condemnation. The malefactor who believed upon the cross was a convict, who had lain in the condemned cell, and was then undergoing execution for his crimes. A convicted felon was the person with whom our Lord last consorted upon earth. What a lover of the souls of guilty men is he! What a stoop he makes to the very lowest of mankind! To this most unworthy of men the Lord of glory, ere he quitted life, spoke with matchless grace. He spoke to him such wondrous words as never can be excelled if you search the Scriptures through: 'Today shalt thou be with me in paradise.' I do not suppose that anywhere in this Tabernacle there will be found a man who has been convicted before the law, or who is even chargeable with a crime against common honesty; but if there should be such a person among my hearers, I would invite him to find pardon and change of heart though our Lord Jesus Christ. You may come to him, whoever you may be; for this man did. Here is a specimen of one who had gone to the extreme of guilt, and who acknowledged that he had done so; he made no excuse, and sought no cloak for his sin; he was in the hands of justice, confronted with the death doom, and yet he believed in Jesus, and breathed a humble prayer to him, and he was saved upon the spot. As is the sample, such is the bulk. Jesus saves others of like kind. Let me, therefore, put it very plainly here, that none may mistake me. None of you are excluded from the infinite mercy of Christ, however great your iniquity: if you believe in Jesus, he will save you.

This man was not only a sinner; *he was a sinner newly awakened.* I do not suppose that he had seriously thought of the Lord Jesus before. According to the other Evangelists, he appears to have joined with his fellow thief in scoffing at Jesus: if he did not actually himself use opprobrious words, he was so far consenting thereunto, that the Evangelist did him no injustice when he said, 'The thieves also, which were crucified with him, cast the same in his teeth.' Yet, now, on a sudden, he wakes up to the conviction that the man who is dying at his side is something more than a man. He reads the title over his head, and believes it to be true – 'This is Jesus the King of the Jews.' Thus believing, he makes his appeal to the Messiah, whom he had so newly found, and commits himself to his hands. My hearer, do you see this truth, that the moment a man knows Jesus to be the Christ of God he may at once put his trust in him and be saved? A certain preacher, whose gospel was very doubtful, said, 'Do you, who have been living in sin for fifty years, believe that you can in a moment be made clean through the blood of Jesus?' I answer, 'Yes, we do believe that in one moment, through the precious blood of Jesus, the blackest soul can be made white. We do believe that in a single instant the sins of sixty or seventy years can be absolutely forgiven, and that the old nature, which has gone on growing worse and worse, can receive its death wound in a moment of time, while the life eternal may be implanted in the soul at once.' It was so with this man. He had reached the end of his tether, but all of a sudden he woke up to the assured conviction that the Messiah was at his side, and, believing, he looked to him and lived.

So now, my brothers, if you have never in your life before been the subject of any religious conviction, if you have lived up till now an utterly ungodly life, yet if now you will believe that God's dear Son has come into the world to save men from sin, and will unfeignedly confess your sin and trust in him, you shall be immediately saved. Ay, while I speak the word, the deed of grace may be accomplished by that glorious One who has gone up into the heaven with omnipotent power to save.

I desire to put this case very plainly: *this man, who was the last companion of Christ upon earth, was a sinner in misery*. His sins had found him out: he was now enduring the reward of his deeds. I constantly meet with persons in this condition: they have lived a life of wantonness, excess, and carelessness, and they begin to feel the fire-flakes of the tempest of wrath falling upon their flesh; they dwell in an earthly hell, a prelude of eternal woe. Remorse, like an asp, has stung them, and set their blood on fire: they cannot rest, they are troubled day and night. 'Be sure your sin will find you out.' It has found them out, and arrested them, and they feel the strong grip of conviction. This man was in that horrible condition: what is more, he was *in extremis*. He could not live long: the crucifixion was sure to be fatal; in a short time his legs would be broken, to end his wretched existence. He, poor soul, had but a short time to live – only the space between noon and sundown; but it was long enough for the Saviour, who is mighty to save. Some are very much afraid that people will put off coming to Christ, if we state this. I cannot help what wicked men do with truth, but I shall state it all the same. If you are now within an hour of death, believe in the Lord Jesus Christ, and you shall be saved. If you never reach your homes again, but drop dead on the road, if you will now believe in the Lord Jesus, you shall be saved: saved now, on the spot. Looking and trusting to Jesus, he will give you a new heart and a right spirit, and blot out your sins. This is the glory of Christ's grace. How I wish I could extol it in proper language! He was last seen on earth before his death in company with a convicted felon, to whom he spoke most lovingly. Come, O ye guilty, and he will receive you graciously!

Once more, *this man whom Christ saved at last was a man who could do no good works*. If salvation had been by good works, he could not have been saved; for he was fastened hand and foot to the tree of doom. It was all over with him as to any act or deed of righteousness. He could say a good word or two, but that was all; he could perform no acts; and if his salvation had depended on an active life of usefulness, certainly he never could have been saved.

He was a sinner also, who could not exhibit a long-enduring repentance for sin, for he had so short a time to live. He could not have experienced bitter convictions, lasting over months and years, for his time was measured by moments, and he was on the borders of the grave. His end was very near, and yet the Saviour could save him, and did save him so perfectly, that the sun went not down till he was in paradise with Christ.

This sinner, whom I have painted to you in colours none too black, was *one who believed in Jesus, and confessed his faith*. He did trust the Lord. Jesus was a man, and he called him so; but he knew that he was also Lord, and he called him so, and said, 'Lord, remember me'. He had such confidence in Jesus, that, if he would but only think of him, if he would only remember him when he came into his kingdom, that would be all that he would ask of him. Alas, my dear hearers, the trouble about some of you is that you know all about my Lord, and yet you do not trust him. Trust is the saving act. Years ago you were on the verge of really trusting Jesus, but you are just as far off from it now as you were then. This man did not hesitate: he grasped the one hope for himself. He did not keep his persuasion of our Lord's Messiahship in his mind as a dry, dead belief, but he turned it into trust and prayer, 'Lord, remember me when thou comest into thy kingdom.' Oh, that in his infinite mercy many of you would trust my Lord this morning! You shall be saved, I am sure you shall: if you are not saved when you trust, I must myself also renounce all hope. This is all that we have done: we looked, and we lived, and we continue to live because we look to the living Saviour, Oh, that this morning, feeling your sin, you would look to Jesus, trusting him, and confessing that trust! Owning that he is Lord to the glory of God the Father, you must and shall be saved.

In consequence of having this faith which saved him, *this poor man breathed the humble but fitting prayer*, 'Lord, remember me'. This does not seem to ask much; but as he understood it, it meant all that an anxious heart could desire. As he thought of the kingdom, he had such clear ideas of the glory of the Saviour, that he felt that if the Lord would think of him his eternal state would be safe. Joseph, in prison, asked the chief butler to remember him when he was restored to power; but he forgot him. Our Joseph never forgets a sinner who cried to him in the low dungeon; in his kingdom he remembers the moanings and groanings of poor sinners who are burdened with a sense of sin. Can you not pray this morning, and thus secure a place in the memory of the Lord Jesus?

Thus I have tried to describe the man; and, after having done my best, I shall fail of my object unless I make you see that whatever this thief was, he is a picture of what you are. Especially if you have been a great offender, and if you have been living long without caring for eternal things, you are like that malefactor; and yet you, even you, may do as that thief did; you may believe that Jesus is the Christ, and commit your souls into his hands, and he will save you as surely as he saved the condemned brigand. Jesus graciously says, 'Him that cometh to me I will in no wise cast out.' This means that if *you* come and trust him, whoever you may be, he will for no reason, and on no ground, and under no circumstances, ever cast you out. Do you catch that thought? Do you feel that it belongs to you, and that if *you* come to him, you shall find eternal life? I rejoice if you so far perceive the truth.

Few persons have so much intercourse with desponding and despairing souls as I have. Poor cast down ones write to me continually. I scarce know why. I have no special gift of consolation, but I gladly lay myself out to comfort the distressed, and they seem to know it. What joy I have when I see a despairing one find peace! I have had this joy several times during the week just ended. How much I desire that any of you who are breaking your hearts because you cannot find forgiveness would come to my Lord, and trust him, and enter into rest! Has he not said, 'Come unto me, all ye that labour and are heavy laden, and I will give you rest'? Come and try him, and that rest shall be yours.

II. In the second place, NOTE, THAT THIS MAN WAS OUR LORD'S COMPANION AT THE GATE OF PARADISE. I am not going into any speculations as to where our Lord went when he quitted the body which hung on the cross. It would seem, from some Scriptures, that he descended into the lower parts of the earth, that he might fill all things. But he very rapidly traversed the regions of the dead. Remember that he died, perhaps an hour or two before the thief, and during that time the eternal glory flamed through the underworld, and was flashing through the gates of paradise just when the pardoned thief was entering the eternal world. Who is this that entereth the pearl-gate at the same moment as the King of glory? Who is this favoured companion of the Redeemer? Is it some honoured martyr? Is it a faithful apostle? Is it a patriarch, like Abraham; or a prince, like David? It is none of these. Behold, and be amazed at sovereign grace. He that goeth in at the gate of paradise, with the King of glory, is a thief, who was saved in the article of death. He is saved in no inferior way, and received into bliss in no secondary style. Verily, there are last which shall be first!

Here I would have you notice *the condescension of our Lord's choice*. The comrade of the Lord of glory, for whom the cherub turns aside his sword of fire, is no great one, but a newly-converted malefactor. And why? I think the Saviour took him with him as a specimen of what he meant to do. He seemed to say to all the heavenly powers, 'I bring a sinner with me; he is a sample of the rest.' Have you never heard of him who dreamed that he stood without the gate of heaven, and while there he heard sweet music from a band of venerable persons who were on their way to glory? They entered the celestial portals, and there were great rejoicing and shouts. Enquiring 'What are these?' he was told that they were the goodly fellowship of the prophets. He sighed, and said, 'Alas! I am not one of those.' He waited a while, and another band of shining ones drew nigh, who also entered heaven with hallelujahs, and when he enquired, 'Who are these, and whence came they?' the answer was, 'These are the glorious company of the apostles.' Again he sighed, and said, 'I cannot enter with them.' Then came another body of men white-robed, and bearing palms in their hands, who marched amid great acclamation into the golden city. These he learned were the noble army of martyrs; and again he wept, and said, 'I cannot enter with these.' In the end he heard the voices of much people, and saw a greater multitude advancing, among whom he perceived Rahab and Mary Magdalene, David and Peter, Manasseh and Saul of Tarsus, and he espied especially the thief, who died at the right hand of Jesus. These all entered in – a strange company. Then he eagerly enquired, 'Who are these?'

and they answered, 'This is the host of sinners saved by grace.' Then was he exceeding glad, and said, 'I can go with these.' Yet, he thought there would be no shouting at the approach of this company, and that they would enter heaven without song; instead of which, there seemed to rise a sevenfold hallelujah of praise unto the Lord of love; for there is joy in the presence of the angels of God over sinners that repent.

I invite any poor soul here that can neither aspire to serve Christ, nor to suffer for him as yet, nevertheless to come in with other believing sinners, in the company of Jesus, who now sets before us an open door.

While we are handling this text, note well *the blessedness of the place* to which the Lord called this penitent. Jesus said, 'Today shalt thou be with me in paradise.' Paradise means a garden, a garden filled with delights. The garden of Eden is the type of heaven. We know that paradise means heaven, for the apostle speaks of such a man caught up into paradise, and immediately he calls it the third heaven. Our Saviour took this dying thief into the paradise of infinite delight, and this is where he will take all of us sinners who believe in him. If we are trusting him, we shall ultimately be with him in paradise.

The next word is better still. Note *the glory of the society* to which this sinner is introduced: 'Today shalt thou be with *me* in paradise.' If the Lord said, '*Today* shalt thou be *with me*', we should not need him to add another word; for where he is, is heaven to us. He added the word 'paradise', because else none could have guessed where he was going. Think of it, you uncomely soul; you are to dwell with the Altogether-lovely One for ever. You poor and needy ones, you are to be with him in his glory, in his bliss, in his perfection. Where he is, and as he is, you shall be. The Lord looks into those weeping eyes of yours this morning, and he says, 'Poor sinner, thou shalt one day be with me.' I think I hear you say, 'Lord, that is bliss too great for such a sinner as I am'; but he replies – 'I have loved thee with an everlasting love: therefore with loving-kindness will I draw thee, till thou shalt be with me where I am.'

The stress of the text lies in *the speediness of all this*. 'Verily I say unto thee, Today shalt thou be with me in paradise.' 'Today.' You shall not lie in purgatory for ages, nor sleep in limbo for so many years; but you shall be ready for bliss at once, and at once you shall enjoy it. The sinner was hard by the gates of hell, but almighty mercy lifted him up, and the Lord said, 'Today shalt thou be with me in paradise.' What a change from the cross to the crown, from the anguish of Calvary to the glory of the New Jerusalem! In those few hours the beggar was lifted from the dunghill and set among princes. 'Today shalt thou be with me in paradise.' Can you measure the change from that sinner, loathsome in his iniquity, when the sun was high at noon, to that same sinner, clothed in pure white, and accepted in the Beloved, in the paradise of God, when the sun went down? O glorious Saviour, what marvels thou canst work! How rapidly canst thou work them!

Please notice, also, *the majesty of the Lord's grace* in this text. The Saviour said to him, 'Verily I say unto thee, Today shalt thou be with me in paradise.' Our Lord gives his own will as the reason for saving this man. 'I say.' He says it who claims the right thus to speak. It is he who will have mercy on whom he will have mercy, and will have compassion on whom he will have compassion. He speaks royally, 'Verily I say unto thee.' Are they not imperial words? The Lord is a King in whose word there is power. What he says none can gainsay. He that hath the keys of hell and of death saith, 'I say unto thee, Today shalt thou be with me in paradise.' Who shall prevent the fulfilment of his word?

Notice *the certainty of it*. He says, 'Verily'. Our blessed Lord on the cross returned to his old majestic manner, as he painfully turned his head, and looked on his convert. He was wont to begin his preaching with, 'Verily, verily, I say unto you'; and now that he is dying he uses his favourite manner, and says, 'Verily'. Our Lord took no oath; his strongest asseveration was, 'Verily, verily'. To give the penitent the plainest assurance, he says, 'Verily I say unto thee, Today shalt thou be with me in paradise.' In this he had an absolutely indisputable assurance that though he must die, yet he would live and find himself in paradise with his Lord.

I have thus shown you that our Lord passed within the pearly gate in company with one to whom he had pledged himself. Why should not you and I pass through that pearl-gate in due time, clothed in his merit, washed in his blood, resting on his power? One of these days angels will say of you, and of me, 'Who is this

that cometh up from the wilderness, leaning upon her beloved?'
The shining ones will be amazed to see some of us coming. If you
have lived a life of sin until now, and yet shall repent and enter
heaven, what an amazement there will be in every golden street to
think that you have come there! In the early Christian church
Marcus Caius Victorinus was converted; but he had reached so
great an age, and had been so gross a sinner, that the pastor and
church doubted him. He gave, however, clear proof of having
undergone the divine change, and then there were great acclam-
ations, and many shouts of 'Victorinus has become a Christian!'
Oh, that some of you big sinners might be saved! How gladly
would we rejoice over you! Why not? Would it not glorify God?
The salvation of this convicted highwayman has made our Lord
illustrious for mercy even unto this day; would not your case do
the same? Would not saints cry, 'Hallelujah! hallelujah!' if they
heard that some of you had been turned from darkness to marvellous light? Why should it not be? Believe in Jesus, and it is so.

III. Now I come to my third and most practical point: NOTE
THE LORD'S SERMON TO US FROM ALL THIS.

The devil wants to preach this morning a bit. Yes, Satan asks to
come to the front and preach to you; but he cannot be allowed.
Begone, thou deceiver! Yet I should not wonder if he gets at certain
of you when the sermon is over, and whispers, 'You see you can be
saved at the very last. Put off repentance and faith; you may be
forgiven on your deathbed.' Sirs, you know who it is that would
ruin you by this suggestion. Abhor his deceitful teaching. Do not
be ungrateful because God is kind. Do not provoke the Lord
because he is patient. Such conduct would be unworthy and
ungrateful. Do not run an awful risk because one escaped the
tremendous peril. The Lord will accept all who repent; but how
do you know that you will repent? It is true that one thief was
saved – but the other thief was lost. One is saved, and we may not
despair; the other is lost, and we may not presume. Dear friends, I
trust you are not made of such diabolical stuff as to fetch from the
mercy of God an argument for continuing in sin. If you do, I can
only say of you, your damnation will be just; you will have brought
it upon yourselves.

Consider now the teaching of our Lord; see *the glory of Christ in salvation*. He is ready to save at the last moment. He was just passing away; his foot was on the doorstep of the Father's house. Up comes this poor sinner the last thing at night, at the eleventh hour, and the Saviour smiles and declares that he will not enter except with this belated wanderer. At the very gate he declares that this seeking soul shall enter with him. There was plenty of time for him to have come before: you know how apt we are to say, 'You have waited to the last moment. I am just going off, and I cannot attend to you now.' Our Lord had his dying pangs upon him, and yet he attends to the perishing criminal, and permits him to pass through the heavenly portal in his company. Jesus easily saves the sinners for whom he painfully died. Jesus loves to rescue sinners from going down into the pit. You will be very happy if you are saved, but you will not be one half so happy as he will be when he saves you. See how gentle he is!

> His hand no thunder bears,
> No terror clothes his brow;
> No bolts to drive our guilty souls
> To fiercer flames below.

He comes to us full of tenderness, with tears in his eyes, mercy in his hands, and love in his heart. Believe him to be a great Saviour of great sinners. I have heard of one who had received great mercy who went about saying, 'He is a great forgiver'; and I would have you say the same. You shall find your transgressions put away, and your sins pardoned once for all, if you now trust him.

The next doctrine Christ preaches from this wonderful story is *faith in its permitted attachment*. This man believed that Jesus was the Christ. The next thing he did was to appropriate that Christ. He said, 'Lord, remember me'. Jesus might have said, 'What have I to do with you, and what have you to do with me? What has a thief to do with the perfect One?' Many of you, good people, try to get as far away as you can from the erring and fallen. They might infect your innocence! Society claims that we should not be familiar with people who have offended against its laws. We must not be seen associating with them, for it might discredit us.

Infamous bosh! Can anything discredit sinners such as we are by nature and by practice? If we know ourselves before God we are degraded enough in and of ourselves? Is there anybody, after all, in the world, who is worse than we are when we see ourselves in the faithful glass of the Word? As soon as ever a man believes that Jesus is the Christ, let him hook himself on to him. The moment you believe Jesus to be the Saviour, seize upon him as your Saviour. If I remember rightly, Augustine called this man, "*Latro laudabilis et mirabilis*', a thief to be praised and wondered at, who dared, as it were, to seize the Saviour for his own. In this he is to be imitated. Take the Lord to be yours, and you have him. Jesus is the common property of all sinners who make bold to take him. Every sinner who has the will to do so may take the Lord home with him. He came into the world to save the sinful. Take him by force, as robbers take their prey; for the kingdom of heaven suffereth the violence of daring faith. Get him, and he will never get himself away from you. If you trust him, he must save you.

Next, notice the doctrine of *faith in its immediate power*.

> The moment a sinner believes,
> And trusts in his crucified God,
> His pardon at once he receives,
> Redemption in full through his blood.

'Today shalt thou be with me in paradise.' He has no sooner believed than Christ gives him the seal of his believing in the full assurance that he shall be with him for ever in his glory. O dear hearts, if you believe this morning, you shall be saved this morning! God grant that you, by his rich grace, may be brought into salvation here, on the spot, and at once!

The next thing is, *the nearness of eternal things*. Think of that a minute. Heaven and hell are not places far away. You may be in heaven before the clock ticks again, it is so near. Could we but rend that veil which parts us from the unseen! It is all there, and all near. 'Today', said the Lord; within three or four hours at the longest, 'shalt thou be with me in paradise'; so near is it. A statesman has given us the expression of being 'within measurable distance'. We are all within measurable distance of heaven or hell;

if there be any difficulty in measuring the distance, it lies in its brevity rather than in its length.

> One gentle sigh the fetter breaks,
> We scarce can say, 'He's gone',
> Before the ransomed spirit takes
> Its mansion near the throne.

Oh, that we, instead of trifling about such things, because they seem so far away, would solemnly realize them, since they are so very near! This very day, before the sun goes down, some hearer, now sitting in this place, may see, in his own spirit, the realities of heaven or hell. It has frequently happened, in this large congregation, that some one of our audience has died ere the next Sabbath has come round: it may happen this week. Think of that, and let eternal things impress you all the more because they lie so near.

Furthermore, know that *if you have believed in Jesus you are prepared for heaven.* It may be that you will have to live on earth twenty, or thirty, or forty years to glorify Christ; and, if so, be thankful for the privilege; but if you do not live another hour, your instantaneous death would not alter the fact that he that believeth in the Son of God is meet for heaven. Surely, if anything beyond faith is needed to make us fit to enter paradise, the thief would have been kept a little longer here; but no, he is, in the morning, in the state of nature, at noon he enters the state of grace, and by sunset he is in the state of glory. The question never is whether a deathbed repentance. is accepted if it be sincere: the question is – Is it sincere? If it be so, if the man dies five minutes after his first act of faith, he is as safe as if he had served the Lord for fifty years. If your faith is true, if you die one moment after you have believed in Christ, you will be admitted into paradise, even if you shall have enjoyed no time in which to produce good works and other evidences of grace. He that reads the heart will read your faith written on its fleshy tablets, and he will accept you through Jesus Christ, even though no act of grace has been visible to the eye of man.

I conclude by again saying that *this is not an exceptional case.* I began with that, and I want to finish with it, because so many demi-semi-gospellers are so terribly afraid of preaching free grace too fully. I read somewhere, and I think it is true, that some ministers preach the gospel in the same way as donkeys eat thistles, namely, very, very cautiously. On the contrary, I will preach it boldly. I have not the slightest alarm about the matter. If any of you misuse free-grace teaching, I cannot help it. He that will be damned can as well ruin himself by perverting the gospel as by anything else. I cannot help what base hearts may invent; but mine it is to set forth the gospel in all its fullness of grace, and I will do it. If the thief was an exceptional case – and our Lord does not usually act in such a way – there would have been a hint given of so important a fact. A hedge would have been set about this exception to all rules. Would not the Saviour have whispered quietly to the dying man, 'You are the only one I am going to treat in this way'? Whenever I have to do an exceptional favour to a person, I have to say, 'Do not mention this, or I shall have so many besieging me.' If the Saviour had meant this to be a solitary case, he would have faintly said to him, 'Do not let anybody know; but you shall today be in the kingdom with me.' No, our Lord spoke openly, and those about him heard what he said. Moreover, the inspired penman has recorded it. If it had been an exceptional case, it would not have been written in the Word of God. Men will not publish their actions in the newspapers if they feel that the record might lead others to expect from them what they cannot give. The Saviour had this wonder of grace reported in the daily news of the gospel, because he means to repeat the marvel every day. The bulk shall be equal to sample, and therefore he sets the sample before you all. He is able to save to the uttermost, for he saved the dying thief. The case would not have been put there to encourage hopes which he cannot fulfil. Whatsoever things were written aforetime were written for our learning, and not for our disappointing. I pray you, therefore, if any of you have not yet trusted in my Lord Jesus, come and trust in him now. Trust him wholly; trust him only; trust him at once. Then will you sing with me –

> The dying thief rejoiced to see
> That fountain in his day,
> And there have I, though vile as he,
> Washed all my sins away.

18

OUR LORD'S LAST CRY FROM THE CROSS[1]

And when Jesus had cried with a loud voice, he said, Father,
into thy hands I commend my spirit: and having said thus,
he gave up the ghost.
LUKE 23:46

THESE WERE THE DYING WORDS of our Lord Jesus Christ,
'Father, into thy hands I commend my spirit.' It may be instructive
if I remind you that the words of Christ upon the cross were seven.
Calling each of his cries, or utterances, by the title of a word, we
speak of the seven last words of the Lord Jesus Christ. Let me
rehearse them in your hearing. The first, when they nailed him to
the cross, was, 'Father, forgive them; for they know not what they
do.' Luke has preserved that word. Later, when one of the two
thieves said to Jesus, 'Lord, remember me when thou comest into
thy kingdom,' Jesus said to him, 'Verily I say unto thee, Today
shalt thou be with me in paradise.' This also Luke has carefully
preserved. Farther on, our Lord, in his great agony, saw his mother,
with breaking heart, standing by the cross, and looking up to him
with unutterable love and grief, and he said to her, 'Woman,
behold. thy son!' and to the beloved disciple, 'Behold thy mother!'
and thus he provided a home for her when he himself should be
gone away. This utterance has only been preserved by John.

The fourth and central word of the seven was, 'Eloi, Eloi, lama
sabachthani?' which is, being interpreted, 'My God, my God, why
hast thou forsaken me?' This was the culmination of his grief, the

---

[1] Sermon No. 2,311. Preached at the Metropolitan Tabernacle on Sunday evening,
9 June 1889.

central point of all his agony. That most awful word that ever fell from the lips of man, expressing the quintessence of exceeding agony, is well put fourth, as though it had need of three words before it, and three words after it, as its bodyguard. It tells of a good man, a son of God, *the* Son of God, forsaken of his God. That central word of the seven is found in Matthew and in Mark, but not in Luke or John; but the fifth word has been preserved by John; that is, 'I thirst', the shortest, but not quite the sharpest of all the Master's words, though under a bodily aspect, perhaps the sharpest of them all. John has also treasured up another very precious saying of Jesus Christ on the cross, that is the wondrous word, 'It is finished.' This was the last word but one, 'It is finished', the gathering up of all his lifework, for he had left nothing undone, no thread was left a-ravelling, the whole fabric of redemption had been woven, like his garment, from the top throughout, and it was finished to perfection. After he had said, 'It is finished', he uttered the last word of all, 'Father, into thy hands I commend my spirit', which I have taken for a text tonight; but to which I will not come immediately.

There has been a great deal said about these seven cries from the cross by divers writers; and though I have read what many of them have written, I cannot add anything to what they have said, since they have delighted to dwell upon these seven last cries; and here the most ancient writers, of what would be called the Romish school, are not to be excelled, even by Protestants, in their intense devotion to every letter of our Saviour's dying words; and they sometimes strike out new meanings, richer and more rare than any that have occurred to the far cooler minds of modern critics, who are as a rule greatly blessed with moles' eyes, able to see where there is nothing to be seen, but never able to see when there is anything worth seeing. Modern criticism, like modern theology, if it were put in the garden of Eden, would not see a flower. It is like the sirocco that blasts and burns, it is without either dew or unction; in fact, it is the very opposite of these precious things, and proves itself to be unblest of God, and unblessing to men. Now concerning these seven cries from the cross, many authors have drawn from them lessons concerning *seven duties*. Listen. When our Lord said, 'Father, forgive them', in effect, he said to us, 'Forgive your enemies.' Even when they despitefully use you, and put you to terrible pain, be ready to pardon them. Be like the sandalwood tree, which perfumes the axe that fells it. Be all gentleness, and kindness, and love; and be this your prayer, 'Father, forgive them.'

The next duty is taken from the second cry, namely, that of penitence and faith in Christ, for he said to the dying thief, 'Today shalt thou be with me in paradise.' Have you, like him, confessed your sin? Have you his faith, and his prayerfulness? Then you shall be accepted even as he was. Learn, then, from the second cry, the duty of penitence and faith.

When our Lord, in the third cry, said to his mother, 'Woman, behold thy son!' he taught us the duty of filial love. No Christian must ever be short of love to his mother, his father, or to any of those who are endeared to him by relationships which God has appointed for us to observe. Oh, by the dying love of Christ to his mother, let no man here unman himself by forgetting his mother! She bore you; bear her in her old age, and lovingly cherish her even to the last.

Jesus Christ's fourth cry teaches us the duty of clinging to God, and trusting in God: 'My God, my God'. See how, with both hands, he takes hold of him: 'My God, my God, why hast thou forsaken me?' He cannot bear to be left of God; all else causes him but little pain compared with the anguish of being forsaken of his God. So learn to cling to God, to grip him with a double-handed faith; and if thou dost even think that he has forsaken thee, cry after him, and say, 'Show me wherefore thou contendest with me, for I cannot bear to be without thee.'

The fifth cry, 'I thirst', teaches us to set a high value upon the fulfilment of God's Word. 'After this, Jesus knowing that all things were now accomplished, that the scripture might be fulfilled, saith, I thirst.' Take thou good heed, in all thy grief and weakness, still to preserve the Word of thy God, and to obey the precept, learn the doctrine, and delight in the promise. As thy Lord, in his great anguish said, 'I thirst', because it was written that so he would speak, do thou have regard unto the Word of the Lord even in little things.

That sixth cry, 'It is finished', teaches us perfect obedience. Go through with thy keeping of God's commandment; leave out no command, keep on obeying till thou canst say, 'It is finished.' Work thy life work, obey thy Master, suffer or serve according to his will, but rest not till thou canst say with thy Lord, 'It is finished.' 'I have finished the work which thou gavest me to do.'

And that last word, 'Father, into thy hands I commend my spirit', teaches us resignation. Yield all things, yield up even thy spirit to God at his bidding. Stand still, and make a full surrender to the Lord, and let this be thy watchword from the first even to the last, 'Into thy hands, my Father, I commend my spirit.'

I think that this study of Christ's last words should interest you; therefore let me linger a little longer upon it. Those seven cries from the cross also teach us something about *the attributes and offices of our Master*. They are seven windows of agate, and gates of carbuncle, through which you may see him, and approach him.

First, would you see him as Intercessor? Then he cries, 'Father, forgive them; for they know not what they do.' Would you look at him as King? Then hear his second word, 'Verily I say unto thee, Today shalt thou be with me in paradise.' Would you mark him as a tender Guardian? Hear him say to Mary, 'Woman, behold thy son!' and to John, 'Behold thy mother!' Would you peer into the dark abyss of the agonies of his soul? Hear him cry, 'My God, my God, why hast thou forsaken me?' Would you understand the reality and the intensity of his bodily sufferings? Then hear him say, 'I thirst', for there is something exquisite in the torture of thirst when brought on by the fever of bleeding wounds. Men on the battlefield, who have lost much blood, are devoured with thirst, and tell you that it is the worst pang of all. 'I thirst', says Jesus. See the Sufferer in the body, and understand how he can sympathize with you who suffer, since he suffered so much on the cross. Would you see him as the Finisher of your salvation? Then hear his cry, 'It is finished." Oh, glorious note! Here you see the blessed Finisher of your faith. And would you then take one more gaze, and understand how voluntary was his suffering? Then hear him say, not as one who is robbed of life, but as one who takes his soul, and hands it over to the keeping of another, 'Father, into thy hands I commend my spirit.'

Is there not much to be learnt from these cries from the cross? Surely these seven notes make a wondrous scale of music if we do but know how to listen to them. Let me run up the scale again.

Here, first, you have Christ's fellowship with men, 'Father, forgive them.' He stands side by side with sinners, and tries to make an apology for them: 'They know not what they do.' Here is, next, his kingly power. He sets open heaven's gate to the dying thief, and bids him enter. 'Today shalt thou be with me in paradise.' Thirdly, behold his human relationship. How near of kin he is to us! 'Woman, behold thy son!' Remember how he says, 'Whosoever shall do the will of my Father who is in heaven, the same is my brother, and sister, and mother.' He is bone of our bone, and flesh of our flesh. He belongs to the human family. He is more of a man than any man. As surely as he is very God of very God, he is also very man of very man, taking into himself the nature, not of the Jew only, but of the Gentile, too. Belonging to his own nationality, but rising above all, he is the Man of men, the Son of Man.

See, next, his taking our sin. You say, 'Which note is that?' Well, they are all to that effect; but this one chiefly, 'My God, my God, why hast thou forsaken me?' It was because he bore our sins in his own body on the tree that he was forsaken of God. 'He hath made him to be sin for us who knew no sin', and hence the bitter cry, 'Eloi, Eloi, lama sabachthani?' Behold him, in that fifth cry, 'I thirst', taking, not only our sin, but also our infirmity, and all the suffering of our bodily nature. Then, if you would see his fullness as well as his weakness, if you would see his all-sufficiency as well as his sorrow, hear him cry, 'It is finished.' What a wonderful fullness there is in that note! Redemption is all accomplished; it is all complete; it is all perfect. There is nothing left, not a drop of bitterness in the cup of gall; Jesus has drained it dry. There is not a farthing to be added to the ransom price; Jesus has paid it all. Behold his fullness in the cry, 'It is finished.' And then, if you would see how he has reconciled us to himself, behold him, the Man who was made a curse for us, returning with a blessing to his Father, and. taking us with him, as he draws us all up by that last dear word, 'Father, into thy hands I commend my spirit.'

Now both the Surety and sinner are free.

Christ goes back to the Father, for 'It is finished', and you and I come to the Father through his perfect work. I have only practised two or three tunes that can be played upon this harp, but it is a wonderful instrument. If it be not a harp of ten strings, it is, at any rate, an instrument of seven strings, and neither time nor eternity shall ever be able to fetch all the music out of them. Those seven dying words of the ever-living Christ will make melody for us in glory through all the ages of eternity.

I shall now ask your attention for a little time to the text itself: 'Father, into thy hands I commend my spirit.'

Do you see our Lord? He is dying; and as yet, his face is toward man. His last word to man is the cry, 'It is finished.' Hear, all ye sons of men, he speaks to you, 'It is finished.' Could you have a choicer word with which he should say '*Adieu*' to you in the hour of death? He tells you not to fear that his work is imperfect, not to tremble lest it should prove insufficient. He speaks to you, and declares with his dying utterance, 'It is finished.' Now he has done with you, and he turns his face the other way. His day's work is done, his more than Herculean toil is accomplished, and the great Champion is going back to his Father's throne, and he speaks; but not to you. His last word is addressed to his Father, 'Father, into thy hands I commend my spirit.' These are his first words in going home to his Father, as 'It is finished', is his last word as, for a while, he quits our company. Think of these words, and may they be your first words, too, when you return to your Father! May you speak thus to your Divine Father in the hour of death! The words were much hackneyed in Romish times; but they are not spoilt even for that. They used to be said in the Latin by dying men, '*In manus tuas, Domine, commendo spiritum meum.*' Every dying man used to try to say those words in Latin; and if he did not, somebody tried to say them for him. They were made into a kind of spell of witchcraft; and so they lost that sweetness to our ears in the Latin; but in the English they shall always stand as the very essence of music for a dying saint, 'Father, into thy hands I commend my spirit.'

It is very noteworthy that the last words that our Lord used were quoted from the Scriptures. This sentence is taken, as I daresay most of you know, from the Thirty-first Psalm, and the fifth verse. Let me read it to you. What a proof it is of how full Christ was of the Bible! He was not one of those who think little of the Word of God. He was saturated with it. He was as full of Scripture as the fleece of Gideon was full of dew. He could not speak even in his death without uttering Scripture. This is how David put it, 'Into thine hand I commit my spirit: thou hast redeemed me, O Lord God of truth.' Now, beloved, the Saviour altered this passage, or else it would not quite have suited him. Do you see, first, he was obliged, in order to fit it to his own case, to add something to it? What did he add to it? Why, that word, 'Father'. David said, 'Into thine hand I commit my spirit'; but Jesus says, 'Father, into thy hands I commend my spirit.' Blessed advance! He knew more than David did, for he was more the Son of God than David could be. He was *the* Son of God in a very high and special sense by eternal filiation; and so he begins the prayer with, 'Father'. But then he takes something from it. It was needful that he should do so, for David said, 'Into thine hand I commit my spirit: thou hast re-deemed me.' Our blessed Master was not redeemed, for he was the Redeemer; and he could have said, 'Into thine hand I commit my spirit, for I have redeemed my people'; but that he did not choose to say. He simply took that part which suited himself, and used it as his own, 'Father, into thy hands I commend my spirit.'

Oh, my brethren, you will not do better, after all, than to quote Scripture, especially in prayer. There are no prayers so good as those that are full of the Word of God. May all our speech be flavoured with texts! I wish that it were more so. They laughed at our Puritan forefathers because the very names of their children were fetched out of passages of Scripture; but I, for my part, had much rather be laughed at for talking much of Scripture than for talking much of trashy novels – novels with which (I am ashamed to say it) many a sermon nowadays is larded, ay, larded with novels that are not fit for decent men to read, and which are coated over till one hardly knows whether he is hearing about a historical event, or only a piece of fiction – from which abomination, good Lord, deliver us! So, then, you see how well the Saviour used Scripture, and how, from his first battle with the devil in the wilderness till his last struggle with death on the cross, his weapon was ever, 'It is written.'

Now, I am coming to the text itself, and I am going to preach from it for only a very short time. In doing so, firstly, *let us learn the doctrine* of this last cry from the cross; secondly, *let us practise the duty*; and thirdly, *let us enjoy the privilege.*

I. First, LET US LEARN THE DOCTRINE of our Lord's last cry from the cross. What is the doctrine of this last word of our Lord Jesus Christ? *God is his Father, and God is our Father.* He who himself said, 'Father', did not say for himself, 'Our Father', for the Father is Christ's Father in a higher sense than he is ours; but yet he is not more truly the Father of Christ than he is our Father if we have believed in Jesus. 'Ye are all the children of God by faith in Christ Jesus.'

Jesus said to Mary Magdalene, 'I ascend unto my Father, and your Father; and to my God, and your God.' Believe the doctrine of the Fatherhood of God to his people. As I have warned you before, abhor the doctrine of the universal fatherhood of God, for it is a lie, and a deep deception. It stabs at the heart, first, of the doctrine of the adoption, which is taught in Scripture, for how can God adopt men if they are all his children already? In the second place, it stabs at the heart of the doctrine of regeneration, which is certainly taught in the Word of God. Now it is by regeneration and faith that we become the children of God, but how can that be if we are the children of God already? 'As many as received him, to them gave he power to become the sons of God, even to them that believe on his name: which were born, not of blood, nor of the will of the flesh, nor of the will of man, but of God.' How can God give to men the power to become his sons if they have it already? Believe not that lie of the devil, but believe this truth of God, that Christ and all who are by living faith in Christ may rejoice in the Fatherhood of God.

Next learn this doctrine, that *in this fact lies our chief comfort.* In our hour of trouble, in our time of warfare, let us say, 'Father'. You notice that the first cry from the cross is like the last; the highest note is like the lowest. Jesus begins with, 'Father, forgive them', and he finishes with, 'Father, into thy hands I commend my spirit.' To help you in a stern duty like forgiveness, cry, 'Father'. To help you in sore suffering and death, cry, 'Father'. Your main strength lies in your being truly a child of God.

Learn the next doctrine, *that dying is going home to our Father.* I said to an old friend, not long ago, 'Old Mr So-and-so has gone home.' I meant that he was dead. He said, 'Yes, where else should he go?' I thought that was a wise question. Where else should we go? When we grow grey, and our day's work is done, where should we go but home? So, when Christ has said, 'It is finished', his next word, of course, is 'Father'. He has finished his earthly course, and now he will go home to heaven. Just as a child runs to its mother's bosom when it is tired, and wants to fall asleep, so Christ says, 'Father', ere he falls asleep in death.

Learn another doctrine, that if God is our Father, and we regard ourselves as going home when we die, because we go to him, then *he will receive us.* There is no hint that we can commit our spirit to God, and yet that God will not have us. Remember how Stephen, beneath a shower of stones, cried, 'Lord Jesus, receive my spirit.' Let us, however we may die, make this our last emotion if not our last expression, 'Father, receive my spirit.' Shall not our heavenly Father receive his children? If ye, being evil, receive your children at nightfall, when they come home to sleep, shall not your Father, who is in heaven, receive you when your day's work is done? That is the doctrine we are to learn from this last cry from the cross, the Fatherhood of God and all that comes of it to believers.

II. Secondly, LET US PRACTISE THE DUTY.

That duty seems to me to be, first, *resignation.* Whenever anything distresses and alarms you, resign yourself to God. Say, 'Father, into thy hands I commend my spirit.' Sing, with Faber –

> I bow me to thy will, O God,
> And all thy ways adore;
> And every day I live I'll seek
> To please thee more and more.

Learn, next, the duty of *prayer.* When you are in the very anguish of pain, when you are surrounded by bitter griefs of mind as well as of body, still pray. Drop not the 'Our Father'. Let not your cries be addressed to the air; let not your moans be to your physician, or your nurse; but cry, 'Father'. Does not a child so cry when it has lost its way? If it be in the dark at night, and it starts up in a lone room, does it not cry out, 'Father'; and is not a father's heart touched by that cry? Is there anybody here who has never cried to God? Is there one here who has never said 'Father'? Then, my Father, put thy love into their hearts, and make them tonight say,

'I will arise, and go to my Father.' You shall truly be known to be the sons of God if that cry is in your heart and on your lips.

The next duty is *the committal of ourselves to God by faith*. Give yourselves up to God, trust yourselves with God. Every morning, when you get up, take yourself, and put yourself into God's custody; lock yourself up, as it were, in the casket of divine protection; and every night, when you have unlocked the box, ere you fall asleep, lock it again, and give the key into the hand of him who is able to keep you when the image of death is on your face. Before you sleep, commit yourself to God; I mean, do that when there is nothing to frighten you, when everything is going smoothly, when the wind blows softly from the south, and the barque is speeding towards its desired haven, still make not thyself quiet with thine own quieting. He who carves for himself will cut his fingers, and get an empty plate. He who leaves God to carve for him shall often have fat things full of marrow placed before him. If thou canst trust, God will reward thy trusting in a way that thou knowest not as yet.

And then practise one other duty, that of *the personal and continual realization of God's presence*. 'Father, into thy hands I commend my spirit.' 'Thou art here; I know that thou art. I realize that thou art here in the time of sorrow, and of danger; and I put myself into thy hands. Just as I would give myself to the protection of a policeman, or a soldier, if anyone attacked me, so do I commit myself to thee, thou unseen Guardian of the night, thou unwearied Keeper of the day. Thou shalt cover my head in the day of battle. Beneath thy wings will I trust, as a chick hides beneath the hen.'

See, then, your duty. It is to resign yourself to God, pray to God, commit yourself to God, and rest in a sense of the presence of God. May the Spirit of God help you in the practice of such priceless duties as these!

III. Now, lastly, LET US ENJOY THE PRIVILEGE.

First, let us enjoy the high privilege of *resting in God in all times of danger and pain*. The doctor has just told you that you will have to undergo an operation. Say, 'Father, into thy hands I commend my spirit.' There is every probability that that weakness of yours, or that disease of yours, will increase upon you, and that by and by you will have to take to your bed, and lie there perhaps for many a day. Then say, 'Father, into thy hands I commend my spirit.' Do not fret; for that will not help you. Do not fear the future; for that will not aid you. Give yourself up (it is your privilege to do so) to the keeping of those dear hands that were pierced for you, to the love of that dear heart which was set abroach with the spear to purchase your redemption. It is wonderful what rest of spirit God can give to a man or a woman in the very worst condition. Oh, how some of the martyrs have sung at the stake! How they have rejoiced when on the rack! Bonner's coal-hole, across the water there, at Fulham, where he shut up the martyrs, was a wretched place to lie in on a cold winter's night; but they said, 'They did rouse them in the straw, as they lay in the coal-hole; with the sweetest singing out of heaven, and when Bonner said, "Fie on them that they should make such a noise!" they told him that he, too, would make such a noise if he was as happy as they were.' When you have commended your spirit to God, then you have sweet rest in time of danger and pain.

The next privilege is that of *a brave confidence, in the time of death, or in the fear of death*. I was led to think over this text by using it a great many times last Thursday night. Perhaps none of you will ever forget last Thursday night. I do not think that I ever shall, if I live to be as old as Methuselah. From this place till I reached my home, it seemed one continued sheet of fire; and the further I went, the more vivid became the lightning flashes; but when I came at last to turn up Leigham Court Road, then the lightning seemed to come in very bars from the sky; and at last, as I reached the top of the hill, and a crash came of the most startling kind, down poured a torrent of hail, hailstones that I will not attempt to describe, for you might think that I exaggerated, and then I felt, and my friend with me, that we could hardly expect to reach home alive. We were there at the very centre and summit of the storm. All around us, on every side, and all within us, as it were, seemed nothing but the electric fluid; and God's right arm seemed bared for war. I felt then, 'Well, now I am very likely going home', and I commended my spirit to God; and from that moment, though I cannot say that I took much pleasure in the peals of thunder, and the flashes of lightning, yet I felt quite as calm as I do here at this present moment; perhaps a little more calm than I do in the presence of so many people; happy at the thought that, within a single moment, I might understand more than all I could ever learn on earth, and see in an instant more than I could hope to see if I lived here for a century. I could only say to my friend, 'Let us commit ourselves to God; we know that we are doing our duty in going on as we are going, and all is well with us.' So we could only rejoice together in the prospect of being soon with God. We were not taken home in the chariot of fire; we are still spared a little longer to go on with life's work; but I realize the sweetness of being able to have done with it all, to have no wish, no will, no word, scarcely a prayer, but just to take one's heart up, and hand it over to the great Keeper, saying, 'Father, take care of me. So let me live, so let me die. I have henceforth no desire about anything; let it be as *thou* pleasest. Into thy hands I commend my spirit.'

This privilege is not only that of having rest in danger, and confidence in the prospect of death; it is also full of *consummate joy*. Beloved, if we know how to commit ourselves into the hands of God, what a place it is for us to be in! What a place to be in – in the hands of God! There are the myriads of stars; there is the universe itself; God's hand upholds its everlasting pillars, and they do not fall. If we get into the hands of God, we get where all things rest, and we get home and happiness. We have got out of the nothingness of the creature into the all-sufficiency of the Creator. Oh, get you there; hasten to get you there, beloved friends, and live henceforth in the hands of God!

'It is finished.' You have not finished; but Christ has. It is all done. What you have to do will only be to work out what he has already finished for you, and show it to the sons of men in your lives. And because it is all finished, therefore say, 'Now, Father, I return to thee. My life henceforth shall be to be in thee. My joy shall be to shrink to nothing in the presence of the All in all, to die into the eternal life, to sink my *ego* into Jehovah, to let my manhood, my creaturehood live only for its Creator, and manifest only the Creator's glory.

O beloved, begin tomorrow morning and end tonight with, 'Father, into thy hands I commend my spirit.' The Lord be with you all! Oh, if you have never prayed, God help you to begin to pray now, for Jesus' sake! Amen.

19

THE LAST WORDS OF CHRIST ON THE CROSS[1]

And when Jesus had cried with a loud voice, he said, Father,
into thy hands I commend my spirit: and having said thus,
he gave up the ghost.
LUKE 23:46

Into thine hand I commit my spirit: thou hast
redeemed me, O LORD God of truth.
PSALM 31:5

And they stoned Stephen, calling upon God,
and saying, Lord Jesus, receive my spirit.
ACTS 7:59

THIS MORNING, dear friends, I spoke upon the first recorded word of our Lord Jesus when he said to his mother and to Joseph, 'How is it that ye sought me? wist ye not that I must be about my Father's business!' Now, by the help of the blessed Spirit, we will consider the last words of our Lord Jesus before he gave up the ghost, and with them we will examine two other passages in which similar expressions are used.

The words, 'Father, into thy hands I commend my spirit', if we judge them to be the last which our Saviour uttered before his death, ought to be coupled with those other words, 'It is finished', which some have thought were actually the last he used. I think it

[1] Sermon No. 2,644. Preached at the Metropolitan Tabernacle on Sunday evening, 25 June 1882.

was not so; but, anyhow, these utterances must have followed each other very quickly, and we may blend them together, and then we shall see how very similar they are to his first words as we explained them this morning. There is the cry, 'It is finished', which you may read in connection with our Authorized Version: 'Wist ye not that I must be about my Father's business?' That business was all finished; he had been about it all his life, and now that he had come to the end of his days, there was nothing left undone, and he could say to his Father, 'I have finished the work which thou gavest me to do.' Then if you take the other utterance of our Lord on the cross, 'Father, into thy hands I commend my spirit,' see how well it agrees with the other reading of our morning text, 'Wist ye not that I must be in my Father's house?' Jesus is putting himself into the Father's hands because he had always desired to be there in the Father's house with the Father; and now be is committing his spirit, as a sacred trust, into the Father's hands that he may depart to be with the Father, to abide in his house, and go no more out for ever.

Christ's life is all of a piece, just as the alpha and the omega are letters of the same alphabet. You do not find him one thing at the first, another thing afterwards, and a third thing still later; but he is 'Jesus Christ; the same yesterday, and today, and for ever.' There is a wondrous similarity about everything that Christ said and did. You never need write the name 'Jesus' under any one of his sayings, as you have to put the names of human writers under their sayings, for there is no mistaking any sentence that he has uttered.

If there is anything recorded as having been done by Christ, a believing child can judge whether it is authentic or not. Those miserable false gospels that were brought out did very little if any mischief, because nobody, with any true spiritual discernment, was ever duped into believing them to be genuine. It is possible to manufacture a spurious coin which will, for a time, pass for a good one; but it is not possible to make even a passable imitation of what Jesus Christ has said and done. Everything about Christ is like himself; there is a Christlikeness about it which cannot be mistaken. This morning, for instance, when I preached about the Holy Child Jesus, I am sure you must have felt that there was never such another child as he was; and in his death he was as unique as in his birth, and childhood, and life. There was never another who died as he did, and there was never another who lived altogether as he did. Our Lord Jesus Christ stands by himself; some of us try to imitate him, but how feebly do we follow in his steps! The Christ of God still standeth by himself, and there is no possible rival to him.

I have already intimated to you that I am going to have three texts for my sermon; but when I have spoken upon all three of them, you will see that they are so much alike that I might have been content with one of them.

I. I invite you first to consider OUR SAVIOUR'S WORDS JUST BEFORE HIS DEATH: 'Father, into thy hands I commend my spirit.'

Here observe, first, *how Christ lives and passes away in the atmosphere of the Word of God.* Christ was a grand original thinker, and he might always have given us words of his own. He never lacked suitable language, for 'never man spake like this Man.' Yet you must have noticed how continually he quoted Scripture; the great majority of his expressions may be traced to the Old Testament. Even where they are not exact quotations, his words drop into Scriptural shape and form. You can see that the Bible has been his one Book. He is evidently familiar with it from the first page to the last, and not with its letter only, but with the innermost soul of its most secret sense; and, therefore, when dying, it seemed but natural for him to use a passage from a Psalm of David as his expiring words. In his death, he was not driven beyond the power of quiet thought, he was not unconscious, he did not die of weakness, he was strong even while he was dying. It is true that he said, 'I thirst'; but, after he had been a little refreshed, he cried with a loud voice, as only a strong man could, 'It is finished.' And now, ere he bows his head in the silence of death, he utters his final words, 'Father, into thy hands I commend my spirit.' Our Lord might, I say again, have made an original speech as his dying declaration; his mind was clear, and calm, and undisturbed; in fact, he was perfectly happy, for he had said, 'It is finished.' So his sufferings were over, and he was already beginning to enjoy a taste of the sweets of victory; yet, with all that clearness of mind, and freshness of intellect, and fluency of words that might have been possible to him, he did not invent a new sentence, but he went to the Book of Psalms, and took from the Holy Spirit this expression, 'Into thy hands I commit my spirit.'

How instructive to us is this great truth that the Incarnate Word lived on the Inspired Word! It was food to him, as it is to us; and, brothers and sisters, if Christ thus lived upon the Word of God, should not you and I do the same! He, in some respects, did not, need this Book as much as we do. The Spirit of God rested upon him without measure, yet he loved the Scripture, and he went to it, and studied it, and used its expressions continually. Oh, that, you and I might get into the very heart of the Word of God, and get that Word into ourselves! As I have seen the silkworm eat into the leaf, and consume it, so ought we to do with the Word of the Lord; not crawl over its surface, but eat right into it till we have taken it into our inmost parts.

It is idle merely to let the eye glance over the words, or to recollect the poetical expressions, or the historic facts; but it is blessed to eat into the very soul of the Bible until, at last, you come to talk in Scriptural language, and your very style is fashioned upon Scripture models, and, what is better still, your spirit is flavoured with the words of the Lord. I would quote John Bunyan as an instance of what I mean. Read anything of his, and you will see that it is almost like reading the Bible itself. He had studied our Authorized Version, which will never be bettered, as I judge, till Christ shall come; he had read it till his very soul was saturated with Scripture; and, though his writings are charmingly full of poetry, yet he cannot give us his *Pilgrim's Progress* – that sweetest of all prose poems – without continually making us feel and say, 'Why, this man is a living Bible!' Prick him anywhere, his blood is bibline; the very essence of the Bible flows from him. He cannot speak without quoting a text, for his very soul is full of the Word of God. I commend his example to you, beloved, and, still more, the example of our Lord Jesus. If the Spirit of God be in you, he will make you love the Word of God; and, if any of you imagine that the Spirit of God will lead you to dispense with the Bible, you are under the influence of another spirit which is not the Spirit of God at all. I trust that the Holy Spirit will endear to you every page of this Divine Record, so that you will feed upon it yourselves, and afterwards speak it out to others. I think it is well worthy of your constant remembrance that, even in death, our blessed Master showed the ruling passion of his spirit, so that his last words were a quotation from Scripture.

Now notice, secondly, that *our Lord, in the moment of his death, recognized a personal God*: 'Father, into thy hands I commend my spirit.' God is to some men an unknown God. 'There may be a God', so they say, but they get no nearer the truth than that. 'All things are God', says another. 'We cannot be sure that there is a God', say others, 'and therefore it is no use our pretending to believe in him, and so to be, possibly, influenced by a supposition.' Some people say, 'Oh, certainly, there is a God, but he is very far off! He does not come near to us, and we cannot imagine that he will interfere in our affairs.' Ah! but our blessed Lord Jesus Christ believed in no such impersonal, pantheistic, dreamy, far-off God; but in One to whom he said, 'Father, into thy hands I commend my spirit.' His language shows that he realized the personality of God as much as I should recognize the personality of a banker if I said to him, 'Sir, I commit that money into your hands.' I know that I should not say such a thing as that to a mere dummy, or to an abstract something or nothing; but to a living man I should say it, and I should say it only to a living man. So, beloved, men do not commit their souls into the keeping of impalpable nothings; they do not, in death, smile as they resign themselves to the infinite unknown, the cloudy Father of everything, who may himself be nothing or everything. No, no; we only trust what we know; and so Jesus knew the Father, and knew him to be a real Person having hands, into those hands he commended his departing spirit. I am not now speaking materially, mark you, as though God had hands like ours; but he is an actual Being, who has powers of action, who is able to deal with men as he pleases, and who is willing to take possession of their spirits, and to protect them for ever and ever. Jesus speaks like one who believed that; and I pray that, both in life and in death, you and I may ever deal with God in the same way. We have far too much fiction in religion, and a religion of fiction will bring only fictitious comfort in the dying hour. Come to solid facts, man. Is God as real to thee as thou art to thyself?

Come now; dost thou speak with him 'as a man speaketh unto his friend'? Canst thou trust him, and rely upon him as thou dost trust and rely upon the partner of thy bosom? If thy God be unreal, thy religion is unreal. If thy God be a dream, thy hope will be a dream; and woe be unto thee when thou shalt wake up out of it! It was not so that Jesus trusted. 'Father,' said he, 'into thy hands I commend my spirit.'

But, thirdly, here is a better point still. Observe how *Jesus Christ here brings out the Fatherhood of God*. The Psalm from which he quoted did not say, 'Father'. David did not get as far as that in words, though in spirit he often did; but Jesus had the right to alter the Psalmist's words. He can improve on Scripture, though you and I cannot. He did not say, 'O God, into thine hand I commit my spirit'; but he said, 'Father'. Oh, that sweet word! That was the gem of our thought, this morning, that Jesus said, 'Wist ye not that I must be at my Father's – that I must be in my Father's house!' Oh, yes! the Holy Child knew that he was specially, and in a peculiar sense, the Son of the Highest; and therefore he said, 'My Father'; and, in dying, his expiring heart was buoyed up and comforted with the thought that God was his Father. It was because he said that God was his Father that they put him to death, yet he still stood to it even in his dying hour, and said, 'Father, into thy hands I commend my spirit.'

What a blessed thing it is for us also, my brethren, to die conscious that we are sons of God! Oh, how sweet, in life and in death, to feel in our soul the spirit of adoption whereby we cry, 'Abba, Father'! In such a case as that –

'Tis no longer death to die.

Quoting the Saviour's words, 'It is finished', and relying upon his Father and our Father, we may go even into the jaws of death without the 'quivering lips' of which we sang just now. Joyful, with all the strength we have, our lips may confidently sing, challenging death and the grave to silence our ever-rising and swelling music. O my Father, my Father, if I am in thy hands, I may die without fear!

There is another thought, however, which is perhaps the chief one of all. From this passage, we learn that *our Divine Lord cheer-*

fully rendered up his soul to his Father when the time had come for him to die: 'Father, into thy hands I commend my spirit.' None of us can, with strict propriety, use these words. When we come to die, we may perhaps utter them, and God will accept them; these were the very death-words of Polycarp, and Bernard, and Luther, and Melancthon, and Jerome of Prague, and John Huss, and an almost endless list of saints: 'Into thy hands I commit my spirit.' The Old Testament rendering of the passage, or else our Lord's version of it, has been turned into a Latin prayer, and commonly used among Romanists almost as a charm; they have repeated the Latin words when dying, or, if they were unable to do so, the priest repeated the words for them, attaching a sort of magical power to that particular formula. But, in the sense in which our Saviour uttered these words, we cannot any of us fully use them. We can commit or commend our spirit to God; but yet, brethren, remember that, unless the Lord comes first, we must die; and dying is not an act on our part. We have to be passive in the process, because it is no longer in our power to retain our life. I suppose that, if a man could have such control of his life, it might be questionable when he should surrender it, because suicide is a crime, and no man can be required to kill himself. God does not demand such action as that at any man's hand; and, in a certain sense, that is what would happen whenever a man yielded himself to death. But there was no necessity for our blessed Lord and Master to die except the necessity which he had taken upon himself in becoming the Substitute for his people. There was not any necessity for his death even at the last moment upon the cross, for, as I have reminded you, he cried with a loud voice when natural weakness would have compelled him to whisper or to sigh. But his life was strong within him; if he had willed to do so, he could have unloosed the nails, and come down into the midst of the crowd that stood mocking him. He died of his own free will, 'the Just for the unjust, that he might bring us to God'. A man may righteously surrender his life for the good of his country, and for the safety of others. There have frequently been opportunities for men to do this, and there have been brave fellows who have worthily done it; but, then, all those men would have had to die at some time or other. They were only slightly anticipating the payment of the debt of nature;

but, in our Lord's case, he was rendering up to the Father the sprit, which he might have kept if he had chosen to do so. 'No man taketh it from me', said he concerning his life; 'I lay it down of myself'; and there is here a cheerful willingness to yield up his spirit into his Father's hands.

It is rather remarkable that none of the Evangelists describe our Lord as dying. He did die, but they all speak of him as giving up the ghost, – surrendering to God his spirit. You and I passively die; but he actively yielded up his spirit to his Father. In his case, death was an act; and he performed that act from the glorious motive of redeeming us from death and hell; so, in this sense, Christ stands alone in his death. But, oh, dear brothers and sisters, if we cannot render up our spirit as he did, yet, when our life is taken from us, let us be perfectly ready to give it up. May God bring us into such a state of mind and heart that there shall be no struggling to keep our life, but a sweet willingness to let it be just as God would have it – a yielding up of everything to his hands, feeling sure that, in the world of spirits, our soul shall be quite safe in the Father's hand, and that, until the resurrection day, the life-germ of the body will be securely in his keeping, and certain that, when the trumpet shall sound, spirit, soul, and body – that trinity of our manhood – shall be reunited in the absolute perfection of our being to behold the King in his beauty in the land that is very far off. When God calls us to die, it will be a sweet way of dying if we can, like our Lord, pass away with a text of Scripture upon our lips, with a personal God ready to receive us, with that God recognized distinctly as our Father, and so die joyously, resigning our will entirely to the sweet will of the ever-blessed One, and saying, 'It is the Lord', 'my Father', 'let him do as seemeth him good.'

II. My second text is in the 31st Psalm, at the 5th verse; and it is evidently the passage which our Saviour had in his mind just then: 'Into thine hand I commit my spirit: thou hast redeemed me, O Lord God of truth.' It seems to me that THESE ARE WORDS TO BE USED IN LIFE, for this Psalm is not so much concerning the believer's death as concerning his life.

Is it not very singular, dear friends, that the words which Jesus uttered on the cross you may still continue to use? You may catch up their echo, and not only when you come to die, but tonight, tomorrow morning, and as long as you are here, you may still repeat the text the Master quoted, and say, 'Into thine hand I commit my spirit.'

That is to say, first, *let us cheerfully entrust our souls to God*, and feel that they are quite safe in his hands. Our spirit is the noblest part of our being; our body is only the husk, our spirit is the living kernel, so let us put it into God's keeping. Some of you have never yet done that, so I invite you to do it now. It is the act of faith which saves the soul, that act which a man performs when he says, 'I trust myself to God as he reveals himself in Christ Jesus; I cannot keep myself, but he can keep me; by the precious blood of Christ he can cleanse me; so I just take my spirit, and give it over into the great Father's hand.' You never really live till you do that; all that comes before that act of full surrender is death; but when you have once trusted Christ, then you have truly begun to live. And every day, as long as you live, take care that you repeat this process, and cheerfully leave yourselves in God's hands without any reserve; that is to say, give yourself up to God – your body, to be healthy or to be sick, to be long-lived or to be suddenly cut off – your soul and spirit, give them also up to God, to be made happy or to be made sad, just as he pleases. Give your whole self up to him, and say to him, 'My Father, make me rich or make me poor, give me eyesight or make me blind, let me have all my senses or take them away, make me famous or leave me to be obscure; I just give myself up to thee; into thine hand I commit my spirit. I will no longer exercise my own choice, but thou shalt choose my inheritance for me. My times are in thy hands.'

Now, dear children of God, are you always doing this? Have you ever done it? I am afraid that there are some, even among Christ's professing followers, who kick against God's will; and even when they say to God, 'Thy will be done', they spoil it by adding, in their own mind, 'and my will, too.' They pray, 'Lord, make my will thy will', instead of saying, 'Make thy will my will.' Let us each one pray this prayer every day, 'Into thine hand I commit my spirit.' I like, at family prayer, to put myself and all that I have into God's hands in the morning, and then, at night, just to look between his hands, and see how safe I have been, and then to say to him, 'Lord, shut me up again tonight; take care of me all through the night watches. "Into thine hand I commit my spirit."' Notice, dear friends, that our second text has these words at the end of it: '*Thou hast redeemed me*, O LORD God of truth.' Is not that a good reason for giving yourself up entirely to God? Christ has redeemed you, and therefore you belong to him. If I am a redeemed man, and I ask God to take care of me, I am but asking the King to take care of one of his own jewels – a jewel that cost him the blood of his heart.

And I may still more specially expect that he will do so, because of the title which is here given to him: 'Thou hast redeemed me, O *Lord God of truth.*' Would he be the God of truth if he began with redemption, and ended with destruction – if he began by giving his Son to die for us, and then kept back other mercies which we daily need to bring us to heaven? No; the gift of his Son is the pledge that he will save his people from their sins, and bring them home to glory; and he will do it. So, every day, go to him with this declaration, 'Into thine hand I commit my spirit.' Nay, not only every day, but all through the day. Does a horse run away with you? Then you cannot do better than say, 'Father, into thine hand I commit my spirit.' And if the horse does not run away with you, you cannot do better than say the same words. Have you to go into a house where there is fever; I mean, is it your duty to go there? Then go saying, 'Father, into thine hand I commit my spirit.' I would advise you to do this every time you walk down the street, or even while you sit in your own house. Dr Gill, my famous predecessor, spent very much time in his study; and, one day, somebody said to him, 'Well, at any rate, the studious man is safe from most of the accidents of life.' It so happened that, one morning, when the good man left his familiar armchair for a little while, there came a gale of wind that blew down a stack of chimneys, which crashed through the roof, and fell right into the place where he would have been sitting if the providence of God had not just then drawn him away; and he said, 'I see that we need divine providence to care for us in our studies just as much as in the streets.' 'Father, into thy hands I commit my spirit.' I have often noticed that, if any of our friends get into accidents and troubles, it is usually when they are away for a holiday; it is a curious thing, but

I have often remarked it. They go out for their health, and come home ill; they leave us with all their limbs whole, and return to us crippled; therefore, we must pray God to take special care of friends in the country or by the sea, and we must commit ourselves to his hands wherever we may be. If we had to go into a lazar-house[1], we should certainly ask God to protect us from the deadly leprosy; but we ought equally to seek the Lord's protection while dwelling in the healthiest place or in our own homes.

David said to the Lord, 'Into thine hand I commit my spirit'; but let me beg you to add that word which our Lord inserted, '*Father*'. David is often a good guide for us, but David's Lord is far better; and if we follow him, we shall improve upon David. So, let us each say, '*Father, Father*, into thine hand I commit my spirit.' That is a sweet way of living every day, committing everything to our heavenly Father's hand, for that hand can do his child no unkindness. 'Father, I might not be able to trust thine angels, but I can trust thee.' The psalmist does not say, 'Into the hand of providence I commit my spirit.' Do you notice how men try to get rid of God by saying, 'Providence did this', and 'Providence did that', and 'Providence did the other'! If you ask them, 'What is Providence?' – they will probably reply, 'Well, Providence is –Providence.' That is all they can say. There is many a man who talks very confidently about reverencing nature, obeying the laws of nature, noting the powers of nature, and so on. Step up to that eloquent lecturer, and say to him, 'Will you kindly explain to me what nature is?' He answers, 'Why, nature – well, it is – nature.' Just so, sir; but, then, what *is* nature? And he says, 'Well – well – it is nature'; and that is all you will get out of him. Now, I believe in nature, and I believe in providence; but, at the back of everything, I believe in God, and in the God who has hands – not in an idol that has no hands, and can do nothing – but in the God to whom I can say, '"Father, into thine hand I commit my spirit." I rejoice that I am able to put myself there, for I feel absolutely safe in trusting myself to thy keeping.' So live, beloved, and you shall live safely, and happily; and you shall have hope in your life, and hope in your death.

---

[1] Lazar: one afflicted by a loathsome and pestilential disease like *Lazarus*, the beggar (*Luke* 16.20)

III. My third text will not detain us many minutes; it is intended to explain to us THE USE OF OUR SAVIOUR'S DYING WORDS FOR OURSELVES.

Turn to the account of the death of Stephen, in the 7th chapter of Acts, at the 59th verse, and you will see there how far a man of God may dare to go in his last moments in quoting from David and from the Lord Jesus Christ: 'And they stoned Stephen, calling upon God, and saying, Lord Jesus, receive my spirit.' So here is a text for us to use when we come to die: 'Lord Jesus, receive my spirit.' I have explained to you that, strictly, we can hardly talk of yielding up our spirit, but we may speak of Christ receiving it, and say, with Stephen, 'Lord Jesus, receive my spirit.'

What does this prayer mean? I must just hurriedly give you two or three thoughts concerning it, and so close my discourse. I think this prayer means that, *if we can die as Stephen did, we shall die with a certainty of immortality.* Stephen prayed, 'Lord Jesus, receive my spirit.' He did not say, 'I am afraid my poor spirit is going to die.' No; the spirit is something which still exists after death, something which Christ can receive, and therefore Stephen asks him to receive it. You and I are not going upstairs to die as if we were only like cats and dogs; we go up there to die like immortal beings who fall asleep on earth, and open our eyes in heaven. Then, at the sound of the archangel's trumpet, our very body is to rise to dwell again with our spirit; we have not any question about this matter. I think I have told you what an infidel once said to a Christian man, 'Some of you Christians have great fear in dying because you believe that there is another state to follow this one. I have not the slightest fear, for I believe that I shall be annihilated, and therefore all fear of death is gone from me.' 'Yes,' said the Christian man, 'and in that respect you seem to me to be on equal terms with that bullock grazing over there, which, like yourself, is free from any fear of death. Pray, sir, let me ask you a simple question. Have you any hope?' 'Hope, sir? Hope, sir? No, I have no hope; of course, I have no hope, sir.' 'Ah, then!' replied the other, 'despite the fears that sometimes come over feeble believers, they have a hope which they would not and could not give up.' And that hope is, that our spirit – even that spirit which we commit into Jesus Christ's hands – shall be "for ever with the Lord."'

The next thought is that, *to a man who can die as Stephen did, there is a certainty that Christ is near* – so near that the man speaks to him, and says, 'Lord Jesus, receive my spirit.' In Stephen's case, the Lord Jesus was so near that the martyr could see him, for he said, 'Behold, I see the heavens opened, and the Son of man standing on the right hand of God.' Many dying saints have borne a similar testimony; it is no strange thing for us to hear them say, before they died, that they could see within the pearly gates; and they have told us this with such evident truthfulness, and with such rapture, or sometimes so calmly, in such a businesslike tone of voice, that we were sure that they were neither deceived nor speaking falsehood. They spake what they knew to be true, for Jesus was there with them. Yes, beloved, before you can call your children about your deathbed, Jesus will be there already, and into his hands you may commit your spirit.

Moreover, *there is a certainty that we are quite safe in his hands.* Wherever else we are insecure, if we ask him to receive our spirit, and he receives it, who can hurt us! Who can pluck us out of his hands? Rouse ye, death and hell! Come forth, all ye powers of darkness! What can you do when once a spirit is in the hands of the omnipotent Redeemer? We must be safe there.

Then there is the other certainty, *that he is quite willing to take us into his hands.* Let us put ourselves into his hands now; and then we need not be ashamed to repeat the operation every day, and we may be sure that we shall not be rejected at the last. I have often told you of the good old woman, who was dying, and to whom someone said, 'Are you not afraid to die?' 'Oh, no', she replied, 'there is nothing at all to fear. I have dipped my foot in the river of death every morning before I have had my breakfast, and I am not afraid to die now.' You remember that dear saint, who died in the night, and who had left written on a piece of paper by her bedside these lines which, ere she fell asleep, she felt strong enough to pencil down –

> Since Jesus is mine, I'll not fear undressing,
>   But gladly put off these garments of clay;
> To die in the Lord is a covenant blessing,
>   Since Jesus to glory thro' death led the way.

It was well that she could say it, and may we be able to say the same whenever the Master calls us to go up higher! I want, dear friends, that we should all of us have as much willingness to depart as if it were a matter of will with us. Blessed be God, it is not left to our choice, it is not left to our will, when we shall die. God has appointed that day, and ten thousand devils cannot consign us to the grave before our time. We shall not die till God decrees it.

> Plagues and deaths around me fly,
> Till he please I cannot die;
> Not a single shaft can hit
> Till the God of love sees fit.

But let us be just as willing to depart as if it were really a matter of choice; for, wisely, carefully, coolly, consider that, if it were left to us, we should none of us be wise if we did not choose to go. Apart from the coming of our Lord, the most miserable thing that I know of would be a suspicion that we might not die.

Do you know what quaint old Rowland Hill used to say when he found himself getting very old? He said, 'Surely they must be forgetting me up there'; and every now and then, when some dear old saint was dying, he would say, 'When you get to heaven, give my love to John Berridge, and John Bunyan, and ever so many more of the good Johns, and tell them I hope they will see poor old Rowly up there before long.' Well, there was common sense in that wishing to get home, longing to be with God. To be with Christ is far better than to be here.

Sobriety itself would make us choose to die; well, then, do not let us run back, and become utterly unwilling, and struggle and strive and fret, and fume over it. When I hear of believers who do not like to talk about death, I am afraid concerning them. It is greatly wise to be familiar with our resting place. When I went, recently, to the cemetery at Norwood, to lay the body of our dear brother Perkins there for a little while, I felt that it was a healthy thing for me to stand at the grave's brink, and to walk amid that forest of memorials of the dead for this is where I, too, must go. Ye living men, come and view the ground where you must shortly lie; and, as it must be so, let us who are believers welcome it.

But, what if you are not believers! Ah! that is another matter altogether. If you have not believed in Christ, you may well be afraid even to rest on the seat where you are sitting. I wonder that the earth itself does not say, 'O God, I will not hold this wretched sinner up any longer! Let me open my mouth, and swallow him!' All nature must hate the man who hates God. Surely, all things must loathe to minister to the life of a man who does not live unto God. Oh that you would seek the Lord, and trust Christ, and find eternal life! If you have done so, do not be afraid to go forth to live, or to die, just as God pleases.

20

THE RENT VEIL[1]

Jesus, when he had cried again with a loud voice, yielded
up the ghost. And, behold, the veil of the temple was rent
in twain from the top to the bottom.

MATTHEW 27:50–51

Having therefore, brethren, boldness to enter into the
holiest by the blood of Jesus, by a new and living way,
which be hath consecrated for us, through the veil, that is
to say, his flesh.

HEBREWS 10:19–20

THE DEATH OF OUR LORD JESUS CHRIST was fitly
surrounded by miracles; yet it is itself so much greater a wonder
than all besides, that it as far exceeds them as the sun outshines
the planets which surround it. It seems natural enough that the
earth should quake, that tombs should be opened, and that the
veil of the temple should be rent, when he who only hath
immortality gives up the ghost. The more you think of the death
of the Son of God, the more will you be amazed at it. As much as
a miracle excels a common fact, so doth this wonder of wonders
rise above all miracles of power. That the divine Lord, even though
veiled in mortal flesh, should condescend to be subject to the power
of death, so as to bow his head on the cross, and submit to be laid
in the tomb, is among mysteries the greatest. The death of Jesus is
the marvel of time and eternity, which, as Aaron's rod swallowed
up all the rest, takes up into itself all lesser marvels.

[1] Sermon No. 2,015. Preached at the Metropolitan Tabernacle on Sunday
morning, 25 March 1888.

Yet the rending of the veil of the temple is not a miracle to be lightly passed over. It was made of 'fine twined linen, with cherubims of cunning work'. This gives the idea of a substantial fabric, a piece of lasting tapestry, which would have endured the severest strain. No human hands could have torn that sacred covering; and it could not have been divided in the midst by any accidental cause; yet, strange to say, on the instant when the holy person of Jesus was rent by death, the great veil which concealed the holiest of all was 'rent in twain from the top to the bottom'. What did it mean? It meant much more than I can tell you now.

It is not fanciful to regard it as a solemn act of mourning on the part of the house of the Lord. In the East men express their sorrow by rending their garments; and the temple, when it beheld its Master die, seemed struck with horror, and rent its veil. Shocked at the sin of man, indignant at the murder of its Lord, in its sympathy with him who is the true temple of God, the outward symbol tore its holy vestment from the top to the bottom. Did not the miracle also mean that from that hour the whole system of types, and shadows, and ceremonies had come to an end? The ordinances of an earthly priesthood were rent with that veil. In token of the death of the ceremonial law, the soul of it quitted its sacred shrine, and left its bodily tabernacle as a dead thing. The legal dispensation is over. The rending of the veil seemed to say – 'Henceforth God dwells no longer in the thick darkness of the Holy of Holies, and shines forth no longer from between the cherubim. The special enclosure is broken up, and there is no inner sanctuary for the earthly high priest to enter: typical atonements and sacrifices are at an end.'

According to the explanation given in our second text, the rending of the veil chiefly meant that the way into the holiest, which was not before made manifest, was now laid open to all believers. Once in the year the high priest solemnly lifted a corner of this veil with fear and trembling, and with blood and holy incense he passed into the immediate presence of Jehovah; but the tearing of the veil laid open the secret place. The rent from top to bottom gives ample space for all to enter who are called of God's grace, to approach the throne, and to commune with the Eternal One. Upon that subject I shall try to speak this morning, praying in my inmost soul that you and I, with all other believers, may have boldness actually to enter into that which is within the veil at this time of our assembling for worship. Oh, that the Spirit of God would lead us into the nearest fellowship which mortal men can have with the Infinite Jehovah!

First, this morning, I shall ask you to consider *what has been done*. The veil has been rent. Secondly, we will remember *what we therefore have*: we have 'boldness to enter into the holiest by the blood Jesus'. Then, thirdly, we will consider *how we exercise this grace*: we 'enter by the blood of Jesus, by a new and living way, which he hath consecrated for us, through the veil, that is to say, his flesh'.

I. First, think of WHAT HAS BEEN DONE. In actual historical fact the glorious veil of the temple has been rent in twain from the top to the bottom: as a matter of spiritual fact, which is far more important to us, *the separating legal ordinance is abolished*. There was under the law this ordinance – that no man should ever go into the holiest of all, with the one exception of the high priest, and he but once in the year, and not without blood. If any man had attempted to enter there he must have died, as guilty of great presumption and of profane intrusion into the secret place of the Most High. Who could stand in the presence of Him who is a consuming fire? This ordinance of distance runs all through the law; for even the holy place, which was the vestibule of the Holy of Holies, was for the priests alone. The place of the people was one of distance. At the very first institution of the law when God descended upon Sinai, the ordinance was, 'Thou shalt set bounds unto the people round about'. There was no invitation to draw near. Not that they desired to do so, for the mountain was together on a smoke, and 'even Moses said, I exceedingly fear and quake'. 'The Lord said unto Moses, Go down, charge the people, lest they break through unto the Lord to gaze, and many of them perish.' If so much as a beast touch the mountain it must be stoned, or thrust through with a dart. The spirit of the old law was reverent distance. Moses, and here and there a man chosen by God, might come near to Jehovah; but as for the bulk of people, the command was, 'Draw not nigh hither.' When the Lord revealed his glory at the giving of the law, we read – 'When the people saw it, they removed, and stood afar off.' All this is ended. The precept to keep back is abrogated, and the invitation is, 'Come unto me, all ye that labour and are heavy laden'. 'Let us draw near' is now the filial spirit of the gospel. How thankful I am for this! What a joy it is to my soul! Some of God's people have not yet realized this gracious fact, for still they worship afar off. Very much of prayer is to be highly commended for its reverence; but it has in it a lack of childlike confidence. I can admire the solemn and stately language of worship which recognizes the greatness of God; but it will not warm my heart nor express my soul until it has also blended therewith the joyful nearness of that perfect love which casteth out fear, and ventures to speak with our Father in heaven as a child speaketh with its father on earth. My brother, no veil remains. Why dost thou stand afar off, and tremble like a slave? Draw near with full assurance of faith. The veil is rent: access is free. Come boldly to the throne of grace. Jesus has made thee nigh, as nigh to God as even he himself is. Though we speak of the holiest of all, even the secret place of the Most High, yet it is of this place of awe, even of this sanctuary of Jehovah, that the veil is rent; therefore, let nothing hinder thine entrance. Assuredly no law forbids thee; but infinite love invites thee to draw nigh to God.

This rending of the veil signified, also, *the removal of the separating sin*. Sin is, after all, the great divider between God and man. That veil of blue and purple and fine twined linen could not really separate man from God: for he is, as to his omnipresence, not far from any one of us. Sin is a far more effectual wall of separation: it opens an abyss between the sinner and his Judge. Sin shuts out prayer, and praise, and every form of religious exercise. Sin makes God walk contrary to us, because we walk contrary to him. Sin, by separating the soul from God, causes spiritual death, which is both the effect and the penalty of transgression. How can two walk together except they be agreed? How can a holy God have fellowship with unholy creatures? Shall justice dwell with injustice? Shall perfect purity abide with the abominations of evil? No, it cannot be. Our Lord Jesus Christ put away sin by the sacrifice of himself. He taketh away the sin of the world, and so the veil is rent. By the shedding of his most precious blood we are cleansed from all sin, and that most gracious promise of the new covenant is fulfilled – 'Their sins and their iniquities will I remember no more.' When sin is gone, the barrier is broken down, the unfathomable gulf is filled. Pardon, which removes sin, and justification, which brings righteousness, make up a deed of clearance so real and so complete that nothing now divides the sinner from his reconciled God. The Judge is now the Father: he, who once must necessarily have condemned, is found justly absolving and accepting. In this double sense the veil is rent: the separating ordinance is abrogated, and the separating sin is forgiven.

Next, be it remembered that *the separating sinfulness is also taken away through our Lord Jesus.* It is not only what we have *done*, but what we *are* that keeps us apart from God. We have sin engrained in us: even those who have grace dwelling in them have to complain, 'When I would do good, evil is present with me.' How can we commune with God with our eyes blinded, our ears stopped, our hearts hardened, and our senses deadened by sin? Our whole nature is tainted, poisoned, perverted by evil; how can we know the Lord? Beloved, through the death of our Lord Jesus the covenant of grace is established with us, and its gracious provisions are on this wise: 'This is the covenant that I will make with them after those days, saith the Lord; I will put my laws into their mind, and write them in their hearts.' When this is the case, when the will of God is inscribed on the heart, and the nature is entirely changed, then is the dividing veil which hides us from God taken away: 'Blessed are the pure in heart: for they shall see God.' Blessed are all they that love righteousness and follow after it, for they are in a way in which the Righteous One can walk in fellowship with them. Spirits that are like God are not divided from God. Difference of nature hangs up a veil; but the new birth, and the sanctification which follows upon it, through the precious death of Jesus, remove that veil. He that hates sin, strives after holiness, and labours to perfect it in the fear of God, is in fellowship with God. It is a blessed thing when we love what God loves, when we seek what God seeks, when we are in sympathy with divine aims, and are obedient to divine commands: for with such persons will the Lord dwell. When grace makes us partakers of the divine nature, then are we at one with the Lord, and the veil is taken away.

'Yes,' saith one, 'I see now how the veil is taken away in three different fashions; but still God is God, and we are but poor puny men: between God and man there must of necessity be a separating veil, caused by the great disparity between the Creator and the creature. How can the finite and the infinite commune? God is all in all, and more than all; we are nothing, and less than nothing; how can we meet?' When the Lord does come near to his favoured ones, they own how incapable they are of enduring the excessive glory. Even the beloved John said, 'When I saw him, I fell at his feet as dead.' When we have been specially conscious of the presence and working of our Lord, we have felt our flesh creep, and our blood chill; and then we have understood what Jacob meant when he said, 'How dreadful is this place! This is none other but the house of God, and this is the gate of heaven.' All this is true; for the Lord saith, 'Thou canst not see my face and live.' Although this is a much thinner veil than those I have already mentioned, yet it is a veil; and it is hard for man to be at home with God. But *the Lord Jesus bridges the separating distance.* Behold, the blessed Son of God has come into the world, and taken upon himself our nature! 'Forasmuch then as the children are partakers of flesh and blood, he also himself likewise took part of the same.' Though he is God as God is God, yet is he as surely man as man is man. Mark well how in the Person of the Lord Jesus we see God and man in the closest conceivable alliance; for they are united in one Person for ever. The gulf is completely filled by the fact that Jesus has gone through with us even to the bitter end, to death, even to the death of the cross. He has followed out the career of manhood even to the tomb; and thus we see that the veil, which hung between the nature of God and the nature of man, is rent in the person of our Lord Jesus Christ. We enter into the holiest of all through his flesh, which links manhood to Godhead.

Now, you see what it is to have the veil taken away. Solemnly note that this avails only for believers: those who refuse Jesus refuse the only way of access to God. God is not approachable, except through the rending of the veil by the death of Jesus. There was one typical way to the mercy-seat of old, and that was through the turning aside of the veil; there was no other. And there is now no other way for any of you to come into fellowship with God, except through the rent veil, even the death of Jesus Christ, whom God has set forth to be the propitiation for sin. Come this way, and you may come freely. Refuse to come this way, and there hangs between you and God an impassable veil. Without Christ you are without God, and without hope. Jesus himself assures you, 'If ye believe not that I am he, ye shall die in your sins.' God grant that this may not happen to any of you!

For believers the veil is not rolled up, but rent. The veil was not unhooked, and carefully folded up, and put away, so that it might be put in its place at some future time. Oh, no! But the divine hand took it and rent it front top to bottom. It can never be hung up again; that is impossible. Between those who are in Christ Jesus and the great God, there will never be another separation. 'Who shall separate us from the love of God?' Only one veil was made, and as that is rent, the one and only separator is destroyed. I delight to think of this. The devil himself can never divide me from God now. He may and will attempt to shut me out from God; but the worst he could do would be to hang up a rent veil. What would that avail but to exhibit his impotence? God has rent the veil, and the devil cannot mend it. There is access between a believer and his God; and there must be such free access for ever, since the veil is not rolled up, and put on one side to be hung up again in days to come; but it is rent, and rendered useless.

The rent is not in one corner, but in the midst, as Luke tells us. It is not a slight rent through which we may see a little; but it is rent from the top to the bottom. There is an entrance made for the greatest sinners. If there had only been a small hole cut through it, the lesser offenders might have crept through; but what an act of abounding mercy is this, that the veil is rent in the midst, and rent from top to bottom, so that the chief of sinners may find ample passage! This also shows that for believers there is no hindrance to the fullest and freest access to God. Oh, for much boldness, this morning, to come where God has not only set open the door, but has lifted the door from its hinges; yea, removed it, post, and bar, and all!

I want you to notice that this veil, when it was rent, was rent by God, not by man. It was not the act of an irreverent mob; it was not the midnight outrage of a set of profane priests: it was the act of God alone. Nobody stood within the veil; and on the outer side of it stood the priests only fulfilling their ordinary vocation of offering sacrifice. It must have astounded them when they saw that holy place laid bare in a moment. How they fled, as they saw that massive veil divided without human hand in a second of time! Who rent it? Who but God himself? If another had done it, there might have been a mistake about it, and the mistake might need to be remedied by replacing the curtain; but if the Lord has done it, it is done rightly, it is done finally, it is done irreversibly. It is God himself who has laid sin on Christ, and in Christ has put that sin away. God himself has opened the gate of heaven to believers, and cast up a highway along which the souls of men may travel to himself. God himself has set the ladder between earth and heaven. Come to him now, ye humble ones. Behold, he sets before you an open door!

II. And now I ask you to follow me, dear friends, in the second place, to an experimental realization of my subject. We now notice WHAT WE HAVE: 'Having therefore, brethren, boldness to enter into the holiest'. Observe the threefold 'having'in the paragraph now before us, and be not content without the whole three. *We have 'boldness to enter in'*. There are degrees in boldness; but this is one of the highest. When the veil was rent it required some boldness to look within. I wonder whether the priests at the altar did have the courage to gaze upon the mercy-seat. I suspect that they were so struck with amazement that they fled from the altar, fearing sudden death. It requires a measure of boldness steadily to look upon the mystery of God: 'which things the angels desire to look into'. It is well not to look with a merely curious eye into the deep things of God. I question whether any man is able to pry into the mystery of the Trinity without great risk. Some, thinking to look there with the eyes of their natural intellect, have been blinded by the light of that sun, and have henceforth wandered in darkness. It needs boldness to look into the splendours of redeeming and electing love. If any did look into the holiest when the veil was rent, they were among the boldest of men; for others must have feared lest the fate of the men of Bethshemesh would be theirs. Beloved, the Holy Spirit invites you to look into the holy place, and view it all with reverent eye, for it is full of teaching to you.

Understand the mystery of the mercy-seat, and of the ark of the covenant overlaid with gold, and of the pot of manna, and of the tables of stone, and of Aaron's rod that budded. Look, look boldly through Jesus Christ: but do not content yourself with looking! Hear what the text says: 'Having boldness to *enter in*'. Blessed be God if he has taught us this sweet way of no longer looking from afar, but of entering into the inmost shrine with confidence! 'Boldness to enter in' is what we ought to have.

Let us follow the example of the high priest, and, having entered, *let us perform the functions of one who enters in.* 'Boldness to enter in' suggests that we act as men who are in their proper places. To stand within the veil filled the servant of God with an over-powering *sense of the divine presence.* If ever in his life he was near to God, he was certainly near to God then, when quite alone, shut in, and excluded from all the world, he had no one with him, except the glorious Jehovah. O my beloved, may we this morning enter into the holiest in this sense! Shut out from the world, both wicked and Christian, let us know that the Lord is here, most near and manifest. Oh that we may now cry out with Hagar, 'Have I also here looked after him that seeth me?' Oh, how sweet to realize by personal enjoyment the presence of Jehovah! How cheering to feel that the Lord of hosts is with us! We know our God to be a very present help in trouble. It is one of the greatest joys out of heaven to be able to sing – *Jehovah Shammah* – the Lord is here. At first we tremble in the divine presence; but as we feel more of the spirit of adoption we draw near with sacred delight, and feel so fully at home with our God that we sing with Moses, 'Lord, thou hast been our dwelling place in all generations.' Do not live as if God were as far off from you as the east is from the west. Live not far below on the earth; but live on high, as if you were in heaven. In heaven you will be with God; but on earth he will be with you: is there much difference? He hath raised us up together, and made us sit together in heavenly places in Christ Jesus. Jesus hath made us nigh by his precious blood. Try day by day to live in as great nearness to God, as the high priest felt when he stood for a while within the secret of Jehovah's tabernacle.

The high priest had *a sense of communion with God*; he was not only near, but he spoke with God. I cannot tell what he said,

but I should think that on the special day the high priest un-
burdened himself of the load of Israel's sin and sorrow, and made
known his requests unto the Lord. Aaron, standing there alone,
must have been filled with memories of his own faultiness, and of
the idolatries and backslidings of the people. God shone upon him,
and he bowed before God. He may have heard things which it was
not lawful for him to utter, and other things which he could not
have uttered if they had been lawful. Beloved, do you know what
it is to commune with God? Words are poor vehicles for this fellowship; but what a blessed thing it is! Proofs of the existence of God
are altogether superfluous to those of us who are in the habit of
conversing with the Eternal One. If anybody were to write an essay
to prove the existence of my wife, or my son, I certainly should
not read it, except for the amusement of the thing; and proofs of
the existence of God to the man who communes with God are
much the same. Many of you walk with God: what bliss! Fellowship with the Most High is elevating, purifying, strengthening.
Enter into it boldly. Enter into his revealed thoughts, even as he
graciously enters into yours: rise to his plans, as he condescends
to yours; ask to be uplifted to him, even as he deigns to dwell with
you.

This is what the rent of the veil brings us when we have boldness
to enter in; but, mark you, the rent veil brings us nothing until we
have boldness to enter in. Why stand we without? Jesus brings us
near, and truly our fellowship is with the Father, and with his Son
Jesus Christ. Let us not be slow to take up our freedom, and come
boldly to the throne. The high priest entered within the veil of
blue, and purple, and scarlet, and fine twined linen, with blood,
and with incense, that he might *pray for Israel*; and there he stood
before the Most High, pleading with him to bless the people. O
beloved, prayer is a divine institution, and it belongs to us. But
there are many sorts of prayers. There is the prayer of one who
seems shut out from God's holy temple; there is the prayer of
another who stands in the court of the Gentiles afar off, looking
towards the temple; there is the prayer of one who gets where Israel
stands and pleads with the God of the chosen; there is the prayer
in the court of the priests, when the sanctified man of God makes
intercession; but the best prayer of all is offered in the holiest of

all. There is no fear about prayer being heard when it is offered in the holiest. The very position of the man proves that he is accepted with God. He is standing on the surest ground of acceptance, and he is so near to God that his every desire is heard. There the man is seen through and through; for he is very near to God. His thoughts are read, his tears are seen, his sighs are heard; for he has boldness to enter in. He may ask what he will, and it shall be done unto him. As the altar sanctifieth the gift, so the most holy place, entered by the blood of Jesus, secures a certain answer to the prayer that is offered therein. God give us such power in prayer! It is a wonderful thing that the Lord should hearken to the voice of a man; yet are there such men. Luther came out of his closet, and cried, *Vici* – 'I have conquered.' He had not yet met his adversaries; but as he had prevailed with God for men, he felt that he should prevail with men for God.

But the high priest, if you recollect, after he had communed and prayed with God, *came out and blessed the people*. He put on his garments of glory and beauty, which he had laid aside when be went into the holy place, for there he stood in simple white, and nothing else; and now he came out wearing the breast plate and all his precious ornaments, and he blessed the people. That is what you will do if you have the boldness to enter into the holiest by the blood of Jesus: you will bless the people that surround you. The Lord has blessed you, and he will make you a blessing. Your ordinary conduct and conversation will be a blessed example; the words you speak for Jesus will be like a dew from the Lord: the sick will be comforted by your words; the despondent will be encouraged by your faith; the lukewarm will be recovered by your love. You will be, practically, saying to each one who knows you, 'The Lord bless thee, and keep thee: the Lord make his face shine upon thee, and give thee peace.' You will become a channel of blessing: 'Out of your belly shall flow rivers of living water.' May we each one have boldness to enter in, that we may come forth laden with benedictions!

If you will kindly look at the text, you will notice, what I shall merely hint at, that *this boldness is well grounded*. I always like to see the apostle using a 'therefore': 'Having *therefore* boldness'. Paul is often a true poet, but he is always a correct logician; he is as

logical as if he were dealing with mathematics rather than theology.
Here he writes one of his therefores.

Why is it that we have boldness? Is it not because of our
relationship to Christ which makes us 'brethren'? 'Having
therefore, *brethren*, boldness'. The feeblest believer has as much
right to enter into the holy place as Paul had; because he is one of
the brotherhood. I remember a rhyme by John Ryland, in which
he says of heaven –

> They shall all be there, the great and the small;
> Poor I shall shake hands with the blessed St Paul.

I have no doubt we shall have such a position, and such fellowship.
Meanwhile, we do shake hands with him this morning as he calls
us brethren. We are brethren to one another, because we are
brethren to Jesus. Where we see the apostle go, we will go; yea,
rather, where we see the Great Apostle and High Priest of our
profession enter, we will follow. 'Having therefore, boldness'.

Beloved, we have now no fear of death in the most holy place.
The high priest, whoever he might be, must always have dreaded
that solemn day of atonement, when he had to pass into the silent
and secluded place. I cannot tell whether it is true, but I have read
that there is a tradition among the Jews, that a rope was fastened
to the high priest's foot that they might draw out his corpse in
case he died before the Lord. I should not wonder if their superstition devised such a thing, for it is an awful position for a man
to enter into the secret dwelling of Jehovah. But we cannot die in
the holy place now, since Jesus has died for us. The death of Jesus
is the guarantee of the eternal life of all for whom he died. We
have boldness to enter, for we shall not perish.

Our boldness arises from the perfection of his sacrifice. Read
the fourteenth verse: 'He hath perfected for ever them that are
sanctified.' We rely upon the sacrifice of Christ, believing that he
was such a perfect Substitute for us, that it is not possible for us to
die after our Substitute has died; and we must be accepted, because
he is accepted. We believe that the precious blood has so effectually
and eternally put away sin from us, that we are no longer obnoxious
to the wrath of God. We may safely stand where sin must be

smitten, if there be any sin upon us; for we are so washed, so cleansed, and so fully justified that we are accepted in the Beloved. Sin is so completely lifted from us by the vicarious sacrifice of Christ, that we have boldness to enter where Jehovah himself dwells.

Moreover, we have this for certain, that as a priest had a right to dwell near to God, we have that privilege; for Jesus hath made us kings and priests unto God, and all the privileges of the office come to us with the office itself. We have a mission within the holy place; we are called to enter there upon holy business, and so we have no fear of being intruders. A burglar may enter a house, but he does not enter with boldness; he is always afraid lest he should be surprised. You might enter a stranger's house, without an invitation, but you would feel no boldness there. We do not enter the holiest as housebreakers, nor as strangers; we come in obedience to a call, to fulfil our office. When once we accept the sacrifice of Christ, we are at home with God. Where should a child be bold but in his father's house? Where should a priest stand but in the temple of his God, for whose service he is set apart? Where should a blood-washed sinner live but with his God, to whom he is reconciled?

It is a heavenly joy to feel this boldness! We have now such a love for God, and such a delight in him, that it never crosses our minds that we are trespassers when we draw near to him. We never say, 'God, my dread', but 'God, my exceeding joy'. His name is the music to which our lives are set: though God be a consuming fire we love him as such, for he will only consume our dross, and that we desire to lose. Under no aspect is God now distasteful to us. We delight in him, be he what he may. So you see, beloved, we have good grounds for boldness when we enter into the holiest by the blood of Jesus.

I cannot leave this point until I have reminded you that *we may have this boldness of entering in at all times*, because the veil is always rent, and is never restored to its old place. 'The Lord said unto Moses, Speak unto Aaron thy brother, that he come not at all times into the holy place within the veil before the mercy-seat, which is upon the ark; that he die not'; but the Lord saith not so to us. Dear child of God, you may at all times have 'boldness to enter in'. The veil is rent both day and night. Yea, let me say it, even when thine eye of faith is dim, still enter in; when evidences are dark, still have 'boldness to enter in'; and even if thou hast unhappily sinned, remember that access is open to thy penitent prayer. Come still through the rent veil, sinner as thou art. What though thou hast backslidden, what though thou art grieved with the sense of thy wanderings, come even now! 'Today, if ye will hear his voice, harden not your hearts', but enter at once; for the veil is not there to exclude thee, though doubt and unbelief may make you think it is so. The veil cannot be there, for it was rent in twain from the top to the bottom.

III. My time has fled, and I shall not have space to speak as I meant to do upon the last point – HOW WE EXERCISE THIS GRACE. Let me give you the notes of what I would have said.

Let us at this hour enter into the holiest. Behold the way! We come *by the way of atonement*: 'Having therefore, brethren, boldness to enter into the holiest by the blood of Jesus'. I have been made to feel really ill through the fierce and blasphemous words that have been used of late by gentlemen of the modern school concerning the precious blood. I will not defile my lips by a repetition of the thrice-accursed things which they have dared to utter while trampling on the blood of Jesus. Everywhere throughout this divine Book you meet with the precious blood. How can he call himself a Christian who speaks in flippant and profane language of the blood of atonement? My brothers, there is no way into the holiest, even though the veil be rent, without blood. You might suppose that the high priest of old brought the blood because the veil was there; but *you* have to bring it with you though the veil is gone. The way is open, and you have boldness to enter; but not without the blood of Jesus. It would be an unholy boldness which would think of drawing near to God without the blood of the great Sacrifice. We have always to plead the atonement. As without shedding of blood there is no remission of sin, so without that blood there is no access to God.

Next, the way by which we come is *an unfailing way*. Please notice that word – 'by a *new* way'; this means by a way which is always fresh. The original Greek suggests the idea of 'newly slain'. Jesus died long ago, but his death is the same now as at the moment of its occurrence. We come to God, dear friends, by a way which is always effectual with God. It never, never loses one whit of its power and freshness.

> Dear dying lamb, thy precious blood
> Shall never lose its power.

The way is not worn away by long traffic: it is always new. If Jesus Christ had died yesterday, would you not feel that you could plead his merit today? Very well, you can plead that merit after these nineteen centuries with as much confidence as at the first hour. The way to God is always newly laid. In effect, the wounds of Jesus incessantly bleed our expiation. The cross is as glorious as though he were still upon it. So far as the freshness, vigour, and force of the atoning death is concerned, we come by a new way. Let it be always new to our hearts. Let the doctrine of atonement never grow stale, but let it have dew upon your souls.

Then the apostle adds, it is a *'living way'*. A wonderful word! The way by which the high priest went into the holy place was of course a material way, and so a dead way. We come by a spiritual way, suitable to our spirits. The way could not help the high priest, but our way helps us abundantly. Jesus says, 'I am the way, the truth, *and the life'*. When we come to God by this way, the way itself leads, guides, bears, brings us near. This way gives us life with which to come.

It is *a dedicated way*: 'which he hath consecrated for us'. When a new road is opened, it is set apart and dedicated for the public use. Sometimes a public building is opened by a king or a prince, and so is dedicated to its purpose. Beloved, the way to God through Jesus Christ is dedicated by Christ, and ordained by Christ for the use of poor believing sinners, such as we are. He has consecrated the way towards God, and dedicated it for us, that we may freely use it. Surely, if there is a road set apart for me, I may use it without fear; and the way to God and heaven through Jesus Christ is dedicated by the Saviour for sinners; it is the King's highway for wayfaring men, who are bound for the city of God; therefore, let us use it. 'Consecrated for us'! Blessed word!

Lastly, it is *a Christly way*; for when we come to God, we still come through his flesh. There is no coming to Jehovah, except by the incarnate God. God in human flesh is our way to God; the substitutionary death of the Word made flesh is also the way to the Father. There is no coming to God, except by representation. Jesus represents us before God, and we come to God through him who is our covenant Head, our Representative and Forerunner before the throne of the Most High. Let us never try to pray without Christ; never try to sing without Christ; never try to preach without Christ. Let us perform no holy function, nor attempt to have fellowship with God in any shape or way, except through that rent which he has made in the veil by his flesh, sanctified for us, and offered upon the cross on our behalf.

Beloved, I have done when I have just remarked upon the next two verses, which are necessary to complete the sense, but which I was obliged to omit this morning, since there would be no time to handle them. We are called to take holy freedoms with God. 'Let us draw near', at once, 'with a true heart in full assurance of faith.' Let us do so boldly, for we have a great high priest. The twenty-first verse reminds us of this. Jesus is the great Priest, and we are the sub-priests under him, and since he bids us come near to God, and himself leads the way, let follow him into the inner sanctuary. Because he lives, we shall live also. We shall not die in the holy place, unless he dies. God will not smite us unless he smites him. So, 'having a high priest over the house of God, let its draw near with a true heart in full assurance of faith.'

And then the apostle tells us that we may not only come with boldness, because our high priest leads the way, but because we ourselves are prepared for entrance. Two things the high priest had to do before he might enter: one was, to be sprinkled with blood, and this we have; for 'our hearts are sprinkled from an evil conscience'.

The other requisite for the priests was to have their 'bodies washed with pure water'. This we have received in symbol in our baptism, and in reality in the spiritual cleansing of regeneration. To us has been fulfilled the prayer –

> Let the water and the blood,
> From thy riven side which flowed,
> Be of sin the double cure,
> Cleanse me from its guilt and power.

We have known the washing of water by the Word, and we have been sanctified by the Spirit of his grace; therefore let us enter into the holiest. Why should we stay away? Hearts sprinkled with blood, bodies washed with pure water – these are the ordained preparations for acceptable entrance. Come near, beloved! May the Holy Spirit be the Spirit of access to you now. Come to your God, and then abide with him! He is your Father, your all in all. Sit down and rejoice in him; take your fill of love; and let not your communion be broken between here and heaven.

Why should it be? Why not begin today that sweet enjoyment of perfect reconciliation and delight in God which shall go on increasing in intensity until you behold the Lord in open vision, and go no more out? Heaven will bring a great change in condition, but not in our standing, if even now we stand within the veil. It will be only such a change as there is between the perfect day and the daybreak; for we have the same sun, and the same light from the sun, and the same privilege of walking in the light.

'Until the day break, and the shadows flee away, turn, my beloved, and be thou like a roe or a young hart upon the mountains of Division.' Amen, and Amen.

21

THE MIRACLES OF OUR LORD'S DEATH[1]

Jesus, when he had cried again with a loud voice, yielded up
the ghost. And, behold, the veil of the temple was rent in
twain from the top to the bottom; and the earth did quake,
and the rocks rent; and the graves were opened; and many
bodies of the saints which slept arose, and came out of the
graves after his resurrection, and went into the holy city,
and appeared unto many.

MATTHEW 27:50–53

OUR LORD'S DEATH is a marvel set in a surrounding of marvels.
It reminds one of a Koh-i-noor surrounded with a circle of gems.
As the sun, in the midst of the planets which surround it, far
outshines them all, so the death of Christ is more wonderful than
the miracles which happened at the time. Yet, after having seen
the sun, we take a pleasure in studying the planets, and so, after
believing in the unique death of Christ, and putting our trust in
him as the Crucified One, we find it a great pleasure to examine
in detail those four planetary wonders mentioned in the text, which
circle round the great sun of the death of our Lord himself.

Here they are: *the veil of the temple was rent in twain*; *the earth
did quake*; *the rocks rent*; *the graves were opened*.

I. To begin with the first of these wonders. I cannot, tonight,
enlarge. I have not the strength. I wish merely to suggest thoughts.

[1] Sermon No. 2,059. Preached at the Metropolitan Tabernacle on Sunday evening,
1 April 1888.

Consider THE RENT VEIL, or *mysteries laid open*. By the death of Christ the veil of the temple was rent in twain from the top to the bottom, and the mysteries which had been concealed in the most holy place throughout many generations were laid open to the gaze of all believers. Beginning, as it were, at the top in the deity of Christ, down to the lowest part of Christ's manhood, the veil was rent, and everything was discovered to every spiritual eye.

1. *This was the first miracle of Christ after death.* The first miracle of Christ in life was significant, and taught us much. He turned the water into wine, as if to show that he raised all common life to a higher grade, and put into all truth a power and a sweetness, which could not have been there apart from him. But this first miracle of his after death stands above the first miracle of his life, because, if you will remember, that miracle was wrought in his presence. He was there, and turned the water into wine. But Jesus, as man, was not in the temple. That miracle was wrought in his absence, and it enhances its wonder. They are both equally miraculous, but there is a touch more striking about this second miracle – that he was not there to speak and make the veil rend in twain. His soul had gone from his body, and neither his body nor his soul was in that secret place of the tabernacles of the Most High; and yet, at a distance, his will sufficed to rend that thick veil of fine twined linen and cunning work.

The miracle of turning water into wine was wrought in a private house, amidst the family and such disciples as were friends of the family; but this marvel was wrought in the temple of God. There is a singular sacredness about it, because it was a deed of wonder done in that most awful and mysterious place, which was the centre of hallowed worship, and the abode of God. See! he dies, and at the very door of God's high sanctuary he rends the veil in twain. There is a solemnity about this miracle, as wrought before Jehovah, which I can hardly convey in speech, but which you will feel in your own souls.

Do not forget also that this was done by the Saviour after his death, and this sets the miracle in a very remarkable light. He rends the veil at the very instant of death. Jesus yielded up the ghost, and, behold, the veil of the temple was rent in twain. For thirty years he seems to have prepared himself for the first miracle of his life; he works his first miracle after death in the moment of expiring. As his soul departed from his body our blessed Lord at that same moment laid hold upon the great veil of his Father's symbolical house, and rent it in twain.

2. This first miracle after death stands in such a place that we cannot pass it by without grave thought. *It was very significant, as standing at the head of what I may call a new dispensation.* The miracle of turning water into wine begins his public life, and sets the key of it. This begins his work after death, and marks the tone of it. What does it mean?

Does it not mean that *the death of Christ is the revelation and explanation of secrets?* Vanish all the types and shadows of the ceremonial law – vanish because fulfilled and explained in the death of Christ. The death of the Lord Jesus is the key of all true philosophy: God made flesh, dying for man – if that does not explain a mystery, it cannot be explained. If with this thread in your hand you cannot follow the labyrinth of human affairs, and learn the great purpose of God, then you cannot follow it at all. The death of Christ is the great veil-render, the great revealer of secrets.

It is also the great opener of entrances. There was no way into the holy place till Jesus, dying, rent the veil; the way into the most holy of all was not made manifest till he died. If you desire to approach God, the death of Christ is the way to him. If you want the nearest access and the closest communion that a creature can have with his God, behold, the sacrifice of Christ reveals the way to you. Jesus not only says, 'I am the way', but, rending the veil, he makes the way. The veil of his flesh being rent, the way to God is made most clear to every believing soul.

Moreover, *the cross is the clearing of all obstacles.* Christ by death rent the veil. Then between his people and heaven there remains no obstruction, or if there be any – if your fears invent an obstruction – the Christ who rent the veil continues still to rend it. He breaks the gates of brass, and cuts the bars of iron in sunder. Behold, in his death 'the breaker is come up before them, and the Lord on the head of them.' He has broken up and cleared the way, and all his chosen people may follow him up to the glorious throne of God.

This is significant of the spirit of the dispensation under which we now live. Obstacles are cleared; difficulties are solved; heaven is opened to all believers.

3. *It was a miracle worthy of Christ.* Stop a minute and adore your dying Lord. Does he with such a miracle signalize his death? Does it not prove his immortality? It is true he has bowed his head in death. Obedient to his Father's will, when he knows that the time has come for him to die, he bows his head in willing acquiescence; but at that moment when you call him dead, he rends the veil of the temple. Is there not immortality in him though he died?

And see what *power* he possessed. His hands are nailed; his side is about to be pierced. As he hangs there he cannot protect himself from the insults of the soldiery, but in his utmost weakness he is so strong that he rends the heavy veil of the temple from the top to the bottom.

Behold his *wisdom*, for in this moment, viewing the deed spiritually, he opens up to us all wisdom, and lays bare the secrets of God. The veil which Moses put upon his face Christ takes away in the moment of his death. The true Wisdom in his dying preaches his grandest sermon by tearing away that which hid the supremest truth from the gaze of all believing eyes.

Beloved, if Jesus does this for us in his death, surely, we shall be saved by his life. Jesus who died is yet alive, and we trust in him to lead us into 'the holy places made without hands'.

Before I pass on to the second wonder, I invite everyone here, who as yet does not know the Saviour, seriously to think upon the miracles which attended his death, and judge what sort of man he was who, for our sins, thus laid down his life. He was not suffered by the Father to die without a miracle to show that he had made a way for sinners to draw near to God.

II. Pass on now to the second wonder – THE EARTH DID QUAKE. *The immovable was stirred by the death of Christ.* Christ did not touch the earth: he was uplifted from it on the tree. He was dying, but in the laying aside of his power, in the act of death, he made the earth beneath him, which we call 'the solid globe', itself to quake. What did it teach?

Did it not mean, first, *the physical universe fore-feeling the last terrible shake of its doom?* The day will come when the Christ will appear upon the earth, and in due time all things that are shall be rolled up, like garments worn out, and put away. Once more will he speak, and then will he shake not only the earth, but also heaven. The things which cannot be shaken will remain, but this earth is not one of them: it will be shaken out of its place. 'The earth also and the works that are therein shall be burned up.' Nothing shall stand before him. He alone is. These other things do but seem to be; and before the terror of his face all men shall tremble, and heaven and earth shall flee away. So, when he died, earth seemed to anticipate its doom, and quaked in his presence. How will it quake when he that lives again shall come with all the glory of God! How will you quake, my hearer, if you should wake up in the next world without a Saviour! How will you tremble in that day when he shall come to judge the world in righteousness, and you shall have to face the Saviour whom you have despised! Think of it, I pray you.

Did not that miracle also mean this? – that *the spiritual world is to be moved by the cross of Christ.* He dies upon the cross and shakes the material world, as a prediction that that death of his would shake the world that lieth in the wicked one, and cause convulsions in the moral kingdom. Brothers, think of it. We say of ourselves, 'How shall we ever move the world?' The apostles did not ask that question. They had confidence in the gospel which they preached. Those who heard them saw that confidence; and when they opened their mouths they said, 'The men that have turned the world upside down have come hither unto us.' The apostles believed in shaking the world with the simple preaching of the gospel. I entreat you to believe the same. It is a vast city this – this London. How can we ever affect it? China, Hindustan, Africa – these are immense regions. Will the cross of Christ tell upon them? Yes, my brethren, for it shook the earth, and it will yet shake the great masses of mankind. If we have but faith in it, and perseverance to keep on with the preaching of the Word, it is but a matter of time when the name of Jesus shall be known of all men, and when every knee shall bow to him, and every tongue confess that he is Christ, to the glory of God the Father. The earth did quake beneath the cross; and it shall again. The Lord God be praised for it.

That old world – how many years it had existed I cannot tell. The age of the world, from that beginning which is mentioned in the first verse of the Book of Genesis, we are not able to compute. However old it was, it had to shake when the Redeemer died. This carries us over another of our difficulties. The system of evil we have to deal with is so long-established, hoary, and reverent with antiquity, that we say to ourselves, 'We cannot do much against old prejudices.'

But it was the old, old earth that quivered and quaked beneath the dying Christ, and it shall do so again. Magnificent systems, sustained by philosophy and poetry, will yet yield before what is called the comparatively new doctrine of the cross. Assuredly it is not new, but older than the earth itself. It is God's own gospel, everlasting and eternal. It will shake down the antique and the venerable, as surely as the Lord liveth; and I see the prophecy of this in the quaking of the earth beneath the cross.

It does seem impossible, does it not, that the mere preaching of Christ can do this? And hence certain men must link to the preaching of Christ all the aids of music and architecture, and I know not what beside, till the cross of Christ is overlaid with human inventions, crushed and buried beneath the wisdom of man. But what was it that made the earth quake? Simply our Lord's death, and no addition of human power or wisdom. It seemed a very inadequate means to produce so great a result; but it was sufficient, for the 'weakness of God is stronger than men, and the foolishness of God is wiser than men'; and Christ, in his very death, suffices to make the earth quake beneath his cross. Come, let us be well content in the battle in which we are engaged, to use no weapon but the gospel, no battle axe but the cross. Could we but believe it the old, old story is the only story that is needed to be told to reconcile man to God. Jesus died in the sinner's stead, the just for the unjust, a magnificent display of God's grace and justice in one single act. Could we but keep to this only, we should see the victory coming speedily to our conquering Lord.

I leave that second miracle; wherein you see the immovable stirred in the quaking of the earth.

III. Only a hint or two upon the third miracle – THE ROCKS RENT.

I have been informed that, to this very day, there are at Jerusalem certain marks of rock-rending of the most unusual kind. Travellers have said that they are not such as are usually produced by earthquake, or any other cause. Upon that I will say but little; but it is a wonderful thing that, as Jesus died, as his soul was rent from his body, as the veil of the temple was rent in two, so the earth, the rocky part of it, the most solid structure of all, was rent in gulfs and chasms in a single moment. What does this miracle show us but this – *the insensible startled*?

What! Could rocks feel? Yet they rent at the sight of Christ's death. Men's hearts did not respond to the agonizing cries of the dying Redeemer, but the rocks responded: the rocks were rent. He did not die for rocks; yet rocks were more tender than the hearts of men, for whom he shed his blood.

> Of reason all things show some sign,
> But this unfeeling heart of mine,

said the poet; and he spoke the truth. Rocks could rend, but yet some men's hearts are not rent by the sight of the cross. However, beloved, here is the point that I seem to see here – that obstinacy and *obduracy will be conquered* by the death of Christ. You may preach to a man about death, and he will not tremble at its certainty or solemnity; yet try him with it. You may preach to a man about hell, but he will harden his heart, like Pharaoh, against the judgment of the Lord; yet try him with it. All things that can move man should be used. But that which does affect the most obdurate and obstinate is the great love of God, so strangely seen in the death of the Lord Jesus Christ.

I will not stay to show you how it is, but I will remind you that it is so. It was this which, in the case of many of us, brought tears of repentance to our eyes, and led us to submit to the will of God. I know that it was so with me. I looked at a thousand things, and I did not relent; but when

> I saw One hanging on a tree
> In agonies and blood,

and dying there for me, then did I smite upon my breast, and I was in bitterness for him, as one that is in bitterness for his first-born. I am sure your own hearts confess that the great rock-render is the dying Saviour.

Well, now, as it is with you, so shall you find it with other men. When you have done your best, and have not succeeded, bring out this last hammer – the cross of Christ. I have often seen on pieces of cannon, in Latin words, this inscription, 'The last argument of kings.' That is to say, cannons are the last argument of kings. But the cross is the last argument of God. If a dying Saviour does not convert you, what will? If his bleeding wounds do not attract you to God, what will? If Jesus bears our sin in his own body on the tree, and puts it away, and if this does not bring you to God, with confession of your sin, and hatred of it, then there remains nothing more for you. 'How shall we escape if we neglect so great salvation?' The cross is the rock-render. Brothers and sisters, go on teaching the love of the dying Son of God. Go on preaching Christ. You will tunnel the Alps of pride and the granite hills of prejudice with this. You shall find an entrance for Christ into the inmost hearts of men, though they be hard as adamant; and this will be by the preaching of the cross in the power of the Spirit.

IV. But now I close with the last miracle. These wonders accumulate, and they depend upon each other. The quaking earth produced, no doubt, the rending of the rocks; and the rending of the rocks aided in the fourth wonder. THE GRAVES WERE OPENED. The graves opened, and *the dead revived*. That is our fourth head. It is the great consequence of the death of Christ. The graves were opened. Man is the only animal that cares about a sepulchre. Some persons fret about how they shall be buried. That is the last concern that ever would cross my mind. I feel persuaded that people will bury me out of hatred, or out of love, and especially out of love to themselves. We need not trouble about that. But man has often shown his pride by his tomb. That is a strange thing. To garland the gallows is a novelty, I think, not yet perpetrated; but to pile marble and choice statuary upon a tomb – what is it but to adorn a gibbet, or to show man's great grandeur where his littleness is alone apparent. Dust, ashes, rottenness, putridity, and then a statue, and all manner of fine things, to make you think that the creature that goes back to dust is, after all, a great one. Now, when Jesus died, *sepulchres were laid bare, and the dead were exposed*: what does this mean?

I think we have in this last miracle 'the history of a man'. There he lies dead – corrupt, dead in trespasses and sins. But what a beautiful sepulchre he lies in! He is a churchgoer; he is a dissenter – whichever you please of the two; he is a very moral person; he is a gentleman; he is a citizen; he is Master of his Company; he will be Lord Mayor one day; he is so good – oh, he is so good! yet he has no grace in his heart, no Christ in his faith, no love to God. You see what a sepulchre he lies in – a dead soul in a gilded tomb. By his cross our Lord splits this sepulchre and destroys it. What are our merits worth in the presence of the cross? The death of Christ is the death of self-righteousness. Jesus' death is a super-fluity if we can save ourselves. If we are so good that we do not want the Saviour, why, then, did Jesus bleed his life away upon the tree? The cross breaks up the sepulchres of hypocrisy, formalism, and self-righteousness in which the spiritually dead are hidden away.

What next? *It opens the graves.* The earth springs apart. There lies the dead man: he is revealed to the light. The cross of Christ does that! The man is not yet made alive by grace, but he is discovered to himself. He knows that he lies in the grave of his sin. He has sufficient of the power of God upon him to make him lie, not like a corpse covered up with marble, but like a corpse from which the grave digger has flung away the sods, and left it naked to the light of day. Oh, it is a grand thing when the cross thus opens the graves! You cannot convince men of sin except by the preaching of a crucified Saviour. The lance with which we reach the hearts of men is that same lance which pierced the Saviour's heart. We have to use the crucifixion as the means of crucifying self-righteousness, and making the man confess that he is dead in sin.

After the sepulchres had been broken up, and the graves had been opened, what followed next? *Life was imparted.* 'Many of the bodies of the saints which slept arose.' They had turned to dust; but when you have a miracle you may as well have a great one. I wonder that people, when they can believe one miracle, make any difficulty of another. Once introduce Omnipotence, and difficulties have ceased. So in this miracle. The bodies came together on a sudden, and there they were, complete and ready for the rising. What a wonderful thing is the implantation of life! I will not speak of it in a dead *man*, but I would speak of it in a dead *heart*. O God, send thy life into some dead heart at this moment while I speak! That which brings life into dead souls is the death of Jesus. While we behold the atonement, and view our Lord bleeding in our stead, the divine Spirit works upon the man, and life is breathed into him. He takes away the heart of stone, and gives a heart of flesh that palpitates with a new life. This is the wondrous work of the cross: it is by the death of our Lord that regeneration comes to men. There were no new births if it were not for that one death. If Jesus had not died, we had remained dead. If he had not bowed his head, none of us could have lifted up our heads. If he had not there on the cross passed from among the living, we must have remained among the dead for ever and for ever.

Now pass on, and you will see that those persons who received life, in due time *quitted their graves*. It is written that they came out of their graves. Of course they did. What living men would wish to stay in their graves? And you, my dear hearers, if the Lord quickens you, will not stay in your graves. If you have been accustomed to strong drink, or to any other besetting sin, you will quit it; you will not feel any attachment to your sepulchre. If you have lived in ungodly company, and found amusement in questionable places, you will not stop in your graves. We shall not have need to come after you to lead you away from your old associations. You will be eager to get out of them. If any person here should be buried alive, and if he should be discovered in his coffin before he had breathed his last, I am sure that, if the sod were lifted, and the lid were taken off, he would not need prayerful entreaties to come out of his grave. Far from it. Life loves not the prison of death. So may God grant that the dying Saviour may fetch you out of the graves in which you are still living; and, if he now quickens you, I am sure that the death of our Lord will make you reckon that if one died for all, then all died, and that he died for all, that they which live should not live henceforth unto themselves, but unto him that died for them and rose again.

Which way did these people go after they had come out of their graves? We are told that '*they went into the holy city.*' Exactly so. And he that has felt the power of the cross may well make the best of his way to holiness. He will long to join himself with God's people; he will wish to go up to God's house, and to have fellowship with the thrice-holy God. I should not expect that quickened ones would go anywhere else. Every creature goes to its own company, the beast to its lair, and the bird to its nest; and the restored and regenerated man makes his way to the holy city. Does not the cross draw us to the church of God? I would not wish one to join the church from any motive that is not fetched from the five wounds and bleeding side of Jesus. We give ourselves first to Christ, and then to his people for his dear sake. It is the cross that does it.

> Jesus dead upon the tree
> Achieves this wondrous victory.

We are told – to close this marvellous story – that they went into the Holy City '*and appeared unto many*'. That is, some of them who had been raised from the dead, I do not doubt, appeared unto their wives. What rapture as they saw again the beloved husband! It may be that some of them appeared to father and mother; and I doubt not that many a quickened mother or father would make the first appearance to their children. What does this teach us, but that, if the Lord's grace should raise us from the dead, we must take care to show it? Let us appear unto many. Let the life that God has given us be manifest. Let us not hide it, but let us go to our former friends and. make our epiphanies as Christ made his. For his glory's sake let us have our manifestation and appearance unto others. Glory be to the dying Saviour! All praise to the great Sacrifice!

Oh, that these poor, feeble words of mine would excite some interest in you about my dying Master! Be ready to die for him. And you that do not know him – think of this great mystery – that God should take your nature and become a man and die, that you might not die, and bear your sin that you should be free from it. Come and trust my Lord tonight, I pray you. While the people of God gather at the table to the breaking of bread, let your spirits hasten, not to the table and the sacrament, but to Christ himself and his sacrifice. Amen.

22

MOURNING AT THE SIGHT OF THE CRUCIFIED[1]

And all the people that came together to that sight,
beholding the things which were done, smote their
breasts, and returned.

LUKE 23:48

MANY IN THAT CROWD came together to behold the
crucifixion of Jesus, in a condition of the most furious malice.
They had hounded the Saviour as dogs pursue a stag, and at last,
all mad with rage, they hemmed him in for death. Others, willing
enough to spend an idle hour, and to gaze upon a sensational
spectacle, swelled the mob until a vast assembly congregated
around the little hill upon which the three crosses were raised.
There unanimously, whether of malice or of wantonness, they all
joined in mockery of the victim who hung upon the centre cross.
Some thrust out the tongue, some wagged their heads; others
scoffed and jeered, some taunted him in words, and others in signs,
but all alike exulted over the defenceless man who was given as a
prey to their teeth. Earth never beheld a scene in which so much
unrestrained derision and expressive contempt were poured upon
one man so unanimously and for so long a time. It must have been
hideous to the last degree to have seen so many grinning faces and
mocking eyes, and to have heard so many cruel words and scornful
shouts. The spectacle was too detestable to be long endured of
heaven. Suddenly the sun, shocked at the scene, veiled his face,

---

[1] Sermon No. 860. Preached at the Metropolitan Tabernacle on Sunday morning,
14 March 1869.

and for three long hours the ribald crew sat shivering in midday midnight. Meanwhile the earth trembled beneath their feet, the rocks were rent, and the temple, in superstitious defence of whose perpetuity they had committed the murder of the just, had its holy veil rent as though by strong invisible hands. The news of this, and the feeling of horror produced by the darkness, and the earth tremor, caused a revulsion of feelings; there were no more gibes and jests, no more thrustings out of the tongue and cruel mockeries, but they went their way solitary and alone to their homes, or in little silent groups, while each man after the manner of Orientals when struck with sudden awe, smote upon his breast. Far different was the procession to the gates of Jerusalem from that march of madness which had come out therefrom. Observe the power which God hath over human minds! See how he can tame the wildest, and make the most malicious and proud to cower down at his feet when he doth but manifest himself in the wonders of nature! How much more cowed and terrified will they be when he makes bare his arm and comes forth in the judgments of his wrath to deal with them according to their deserts!

This sudden and memorable change in so vast a multitude is the apt representative of two other remarkable mental changes. How like it is to the gracious transformation which a sight of the cross has often worked most blessedly in the hearts of men! Many have come under the sound of the gospel resolved to scoff, but they have returned to pray. The idlest and even the basest motives have brought men under the preaching, but when Jesus has been lifted up, they have been savingly drawn to him, and as a consequence have smitten upon their breasts in repentance, and gone their way to serve the Saviour whom they once blasphemed. Oh, the power, the melting, conquering, transforming power of that dear cross of Christ! My brethren, we have but to abide by the preaching of it, we have but constantly to tell abroad the matchless story, and we may expect to see the most remarkable spiritual results. We need despair of no man now that Jesus has died for sinners. With such a hammer as the doctrine of the cross, the most flinty heart will be broken; and with such a fire as the sweet love of Christ, the most mighty iceberg will be melted. We need never despair for the heathenish or superstitious races of men; if we can but find occasion to bring the doctrine of Christ crucified into contact with their natures, it will yet change them, and Christ will be their king.

A second and most awful change is also foretold by the incident in our text, namely, the effect which a sight of Christ enthroned will have upon the proud and obstinate, who in this life rebelled against him. Here they fearlessly jested concerning him, and insultingly demanded, 'Who is the Lord, that we should obey him?' Here they boldly united in a conspiracy to break his bands asunder, and cast his cords from them, but when they wake up at the blast of the trump, and see the great white throne, which, like a mirror, shall reflect their conduct upon them, what a change will be in their minds! Where now your quibs and your jests, where now your malicious speeches and your persecuting words? What! Is there not one among you who can play the man, and insult the Man of Nazareth to his face? No, not one! Like cowardly dogs, they slink away! The infidel's bragging tongue is silent! The proud spirit of the atheist is broken; his blusterings and his carpings are hushed for ever!

With shrieks of dismay, and clamorous cries of terror, they entreat the hills to cover them, and the mountains to conceal them from the face of that very Man whose cross was once the subject of their scorn. O take heed, ye sinners, take heed, I pray you, and be ye changed this day by grace, lest ye be changed by and by by terror, for the heart which will not be bent by the love of Christ, shall be broken by the terror of his name. If Jesus upon the cross does not save you, Christ, on the throne shall damn you. If Christ dying be not your life, Christ living shall be your death. If Christ on earth be not your heaven, Christ coming from heaven shall be your hell. O may God's grace work a blessed turning of grace in each of us, that we may not be turned into hell in the dread day of reckoning.

We shall now draw nearer to the text, and in the first place, *analyse the general mourning around the cross*; secondly, we shall, if God shall help us, *endeavour to join in the sorrowful chorus*; and then, ere we conclude, we shall *remind you that at the foot of the cross our sorrow must be mingled with joy.*

I. First, then, let us ANALYSE THE GENERAL MOURNING which this text describes.

'All the people that came together to that sight, beholding the things which were done, smote their breasts, and returned.' They all smote their breasts, but not all from the same cause. They were all afraid, not all from the same reason. The outward manifestations were alike in the whole mass, but the grades of difference in feeling were as many as the minds in which they ruled. There were many, no doubt, who were merely moved with a transient emotion. They had seen the death agonies of a remarkable man, and the attendant wonders had persuaded them that he was something more than an ordinary being, and therefore, they were afraid. With a kind of indefinite fear, grounded upon no very intelligent reasoning, they were alarmed, because God was angry, and had closed the eye of day upon them, and made the rocks to rend; and, burdened with this indistinct fear, they went their way trembling and humbled to their several homes; but perhaps, before the next morning light had dawned, they had forgotten it all, and the next day found them greedy for another bloody spectacle, and ready to nail another Christ to the cross, if there had been such another to be found in the land.

Their beating of the breast was not a breaking of the heart. It was an April shower, a dewdrop of the morning, a hoar frost that dissolved when the sun had risen. Like a shadow the emotion crossed their minds, and like a shadow it left no trace behind. How often in the preaching of the cross has this been the only result in tens of thousands! In this house, where so many souls have been converted, many more have shed tears which have been wiped away, and the reason of their tears has been forgotten. A handkerchief has dried up their emotions. Alas! alas! alas! that while it may be difficult to move men with the story of the cross to weeping, it is even more difficult to make those emotions permanent. 'I have seen something wonderful, this morning', said one who had listened to a faithful and earnest preacher, 'I have seen a whole congregation in tears.' 'Alas!' said the preacher, 'there is something more wonderful still, for the most of them will go their way to forget that they ever shed a tear.' Ah, my hearers, shall it be always so – always so? Then, O ye impenitent, there shall come to your eyes a tear which shall drip for ever, a scalding drop which no mercy shall ever wipe away; a thirst that shall never be abated; a worm that shall never die, and a fire that never shall be quenched. By the love you bear your souls, I pray you escape from the wrath to come!

Others amongst that great crowd exhibited emotion based upon more thoughtful reflection. They saw that they had shared in the murder of an innocent person. 'Alas!' said they, 'we see through it all now. That man was no offender. In all that we have ever heard or seen of him, he did good, and only good: he always healed the sick, fed the hungry, and raised the dead. There is not a word of all his teaching that is really contrary to the law of God. He was a pure and holy man. We have all been duped. Those priests have egged us on to put to death one whom it were a thousand mercies if we could restore to life again at once. Our race has killed its benefactor.' 'Yes', saith one, 'I thrust out my tongue, I found it almost impossible to restrain myself, when everybody else was laughing and mocking at his tortures; but I am afraid I have mocked at the innocent, and I tremble lest the darkness which God has sent was his reprobation of my wickedness in oppressing the innocent.' Such feelings would abide, but I can suppose that they might not bring men to sincere repentance; for while they might feel sorry, that they had oppressed the innocent, yet, perceiving nothing more in Jesus than mere maltreated virtue and suffering manhood, the natural emotion might soon pass away, and the moral and spiritual result be of no great value.

How frequently have we seen in our hearers that same description of emotion! They have regretted that Christ should be put to death, they have felt like that old king of France, who said, 'I wish I had been there with ten thousand of my soldiers. I would have cut their throats sooner than they should have touched him'; but those very feelings have been evidence that they did not feel their share in the guilt as they ought to have done, and that to them the cross of Jesus was no more a saving spectacle than the death of a common martyr. Dear hearers, beware of making the cross to be a commonplace thing with you. Look beyond the sufferings of the innocent manhood of Jesus, and see upon the tree the atoning sacrifice of Christ, or else you look to the cross in vain.

No doubt there were a few in the crowd who smote upon their breasts because they felt, 'We have put to death a prophet of God.

As of old our nation slew Isaiah, and put to death others of the Master's servants, so today they have nailed to the cross one of the last of the prophets, and his blood will be upon us and upon our children.' Perhaps some of them said, 'This man claimed to be Messiah, and the miracles which attended his death prove that he was so. His life betokens it and his death declares it. What will become of our nation if we have slain the Prince of Peace! How will God visit us if we have put his prophet to death!' Such mourning was in advance of other forms; it showed a deeper thought and a clearer knowledge, and it may have been an admirable preparation for the after hearing of the gospel; but it would not of itself suffice as evidence of grace. I shall be glad if my hearers in this house today are persuaded by the character of Christ that he must have been a prophet sent of God, and that he was the Messiah promised of old; and I shall be gratified if they, therefore, lament the shameful cruelties which he received from our apostate race. Such emotions of compunction and pity are most commendable and under God's blessing they may prove to be the furrows of your heart in which the gospel may take root. He who thus was cruelly put to death was God over all blessed for ever, the world's Redeemer, and the Saviour of such as put their trust in him. May you accept him today as your Deliverer, and so be saved; for if not, the most virtuous regrets concerning his death, however much they may indicate your enlightenment, will not manifest your true conversion.

In the motley company who all went home smiting on their breasts, let us hope that there were some who said, 'Certainly this was the Son of God', and mourned to think he should have suffered for their transgressions, and been put to grief for their iniquities. Those who came to that point were saved. Blessed were the eyes that looked upon the slaughtered Lamb in such a way as that, and happy were the hearts that there and then were broken because he was bruised and put to grief for their sakes. Beloved, aspire to this. May God's grace bring you to see in Jesus Christ no other than God made flesh, hanging upon the tree in agony, to die, the just for the unjust, that we may be saved. O come and repose your trust in him, and then smite upon your breasts at the thought that such a victim should have been necessary for your redemption; then may you cease to smite your breasts, and begin to clap your hands for very joy; for they who thus bewail a Saviour may rejoice in him, for he is theirs and they are his.

II. We shall now ask you to JOIN IN THE LAMENTATION, each man according to his sincerity of heart, beholding the cross, and smiting upon his breast.

We will by faith put ourselves at the foot of the little knoll of Calvary: there we see in the centre, between two thieves, the Son of God made flesh, nailed by his hands and feet, and dying in an anguish which words cannot portray. Look ye well, I pray you; look steadfastly and devoutly, gazing through your tears. 'Tis he who was worshipped of angels, who is now dying for the sons of men; sit down and watch the death of death's destroyer. I shall ask you first to smite your breasts, as you remember that *you see in him your own sins.* How great he is! That thorn-crowned head was once crowned with all the royalties of heaven and earth. He who dies there is no common man. King of kings and Lord of lords is he who hangs on yonder cross. Then see the greatness of your sins, which required so vast a sacrifice. They must be infinite sins to require an infinite person to lay down his life in order to their removal. Thou canst never compass or comprehend the greatness of thy Lord in his essential character and dignity, neither shalt thou ever be able to understand the blackness and heinousness of the sin which demanded his life as an atonement.

Brother, smite thy breast, and say, 'God be merciful to me, the greatest of sinners, for I am such.' Look well into the face of Jesus, and see how vile they have made him! They have stained those cheeks with spittle, they have lashed those shoulders with a felon's scourge; they have put him to the death which was only awarded to the meanest Roman slave; they have hung him up between heaven and earth, as though he were fit for neither; they have stripped him naked and left him not a rag to cover him! See here then, O believer, the shame of thy sins. What a shameful thing thy sin must have been; what a disgraceful and abominable thing, if Christ must be made such a shame for thee! O be ashamed of thyself, to think thy Lord should thus be scorned and made nothing of for thee! See how they aggravate his sorrows! It was not enough to crucify him, they must insult him; nor that enough, they must mock his prayers and turn his dying cries into themes for jest, while they offer him vinegar to drink. See, beloved, how aggravated were your sins and mine! Come, my brother, let us both smite upon our breasts and say, 'Oh, how our sins have piled up their guiltiness! It was not merely that we broke the law, but we sinned against light and knowledge; against rebukes and warnings. As his griefs are aggravated, even so are our sins?'

Look still into his dear face, and see the lines of anguish which indicate the deeper inward sorrow which far transcends mere bodily pain and smart. God, his Father, has forsaken him. God has made him a curse for us. Then what must the curse of God have been against us? What must our sins have deserved? If when sin was only imputed to Christ, and laid upon him for awhile, his Father turned his head away and made his Son cry out, 'Lama Sabachthani!' Oh, what an accursed thing our sin must be, and what a curse would have come upon us; what thunderbolts, what coals of fire, what indignation, and wrath from the Most High must have been our portion had not Jesus interposed! If Jehovah did not spare his Son, how little would he have spared guilty, worthless men if he had dealt with us after our sins, and rewarded us according to our iniquities!

As we still sit down and look at Jesus, we remember that his death was voluntary – he need not have died unless he had so willed: here then is another striking feature of our sin, for our sin was voluntary too.

We did not sin as of compulsion, but we deliberately chose the evil way. O sinner, let both of us sit down together, and tell the Lord that we have no justification, or extenuation, or excuse to offer, we have sinned wilfully against light and knowledge, against love and mercy. Let us smite upon our breasts, as we see Jesus willingly suffer, and confess that we have willingly offended against the just and righteous laws of a most good and gracious God. I could gladly keep you looking into those five wounds, and studying that marred face, and counting every purple drop that flowed from hands and feet, and side, but time would fail us. Only that one wound – let it abide with you – smite your breast because you see in Christ your sin.

Looking again – changing, as it were, our standpoint, but still keeping our eye upon that same, dear crucified One – let us see there *the neglected and despised remedy for our sin.* If sin itself, in its first, condition, as rebellion, brings no tears to our eyes, it certainly ought in its second manifestation, as ingratitude. The sin of rebellion is vile; but the sin of slighting the Saviour is viler still. He that hangs on the tree, in groans and griefs unutterable, is he whom some of you have never thought of, whom you do not love, to whom you never pray, in whom you place no confidence, and whom you never serve. I will not accuse you; I will ask those dear wounds to do it, sweetly and tenderly. I will rather accuse myself; for, alas! alas! there was a time when I heard of him as with a deaf ear; when I was told of him, and understood the love he bore to sinners, and yet my heart was like a stone within me, and would not be moved. I stopped my ear and would not be charmed, even with such a master-fascination as the disinterested love of Jesus. I think if I had been spared to live the life of an ungodly man, for thirty, forty, or fifty years, and had been converted, at last, I should never have been able to blame myself sufficiently for rejecting Jesus during all those years.

Why, even those of us who were converted in our youth, and almost in our childhood, cannot help blaming ourselves to think that so dear a friend, who had done so much for us, was so long slighted by us. Who could have done more for us than he, since he gave himself for our sins? Ah, how did we wrong him while we withheld our hearts from him! O ye sinners, how can ye keep the doors of your hearts shut against the Friend of Sinners? How can we close the door against him who cries, 'My head is wet with dew, and my locks with the drops of the night: open to me, my beloved, open to me'? I am persuaded there are some here who are his elect: you were chosen by him from before the foundation of the world, and you shall be with him in heaven one day to sing his praises, and yet, at this moment, though you hear his name, you do not love him, and, though you are told of what he did, you do not trust him. What! shall that iron bar always fast close the gate of your heart? Shall that door still be always bolted? O Spirit of the living God, win an entrance for the blessed Christ this morning! If anything can do it, surely it must be a sight of the crucified

Christ; that matchless spectacle shall make a heart of stone relent and melt, by Jesus' love subdued. O may the Holy Ghost work this gracious melting, and he shall have all the honour.

Still keeping you at the cross foot, dear friends, every believer here may well smite upon his breast this morning as he thinks of *who it was that smarted so upon the cross*. Who was it? It was he who loved us or ever the world was made. It was he who is this day the Bridegroom of our souls, our Best-beloved; he who has taken us into the banqueting house and waved his banner of love over us; he who has made us one with himself, and has vowed to present us to his Father without spot. It is he, our Husband, our *Ishi*, who has called us his *Hephzibah* because his soul delighteth in us. It is he who suffered thus for us. Suffering does not always excite the same degree of pity.

You must know something of the individual before the innermost depths of the soul are stirred; and so; it happens to us that the higher the character and the more able we are to appreciate it, the closer the relation and the more fondly we reciprocate the love, the more deeply does suffering strike the soul. You are coming to his table some of you today, and you will partake of bread: I pray you remember that it represents the quivering flesh that was filled with pain on Calvary. You will sip of that cup: then be sure to remember that it betokens to you the blood of one who loves you better than you could be loved by mother, or by husband, or by friend. O sit you down and smite your breasts that *he* should grieve; that heaven's Sun should be eclipsed; that heaven's Lily should be spotted with blood, and heaven's Rose should be whitened with a deadly pallor. Lament that perfection should be accused, innocence smitten, and love murdered; and that Christ, the happy and the holy, the ever blessed, who had been for ages the delight of angels, should now become the sorrowful, the acquaintance of grief, the bleeding and the dying. Smite upon your breasts, believers, and go your way!

Beloved in the Lord, if such grief as this should be kindled in you, it will be well to pursue the subject, and to reflect upon how unbelieving and how cruel we have been to Jesus since the day that we have known him. What, doth he bleed for me and have I doubted him? Is he the Son of God, and have I suspected his fidelity? Have I stood at the cross foot unmoved? Have I spoken of my dying Lord in a cold, indifferent spirit? Have I ever preached Christ crucified with a dry eye and a heart unmoved? Do I bow my knee in private prayer, and are my thoughts wandering when they ought to be bound hand and foot to his dear bleeding self? Am I accustomed to turn over the pages of the Evangelists which record my Master's wondrous sacrifice, and have I never stained those pages with my tears? Have I never paused spellbound over the sacred sentence which recorded this miracle of miracles, this marvel of marvels? Oh, shame upon thee, hard heart! Well may I smite thee. May God smite thee with the hammer of his Spirit, and break thee to shivers. O thou stony heart, thou granite soul, thou flinty spirit, well may I strike the breast which harbours thee, to think that I should be so doltish[1] in presence of love so amazing, so divine.

Brethren, you may smite upon your breasts as you look at the cross, and mourn that you should have done so little for your Lord. I think if anybody could have sketched my future life in the day of my conversion, and have said, 'You will be dull and cold in spiritual things, and you will exhibit but little earnestness and little gratitude!' I should have said like Hazael, 'Is thy servant a dog, that he should do this great thing?' I suppose I read your hearts when I say that the most of you are disappointed with your own conduct as compared with your too-flattering prophecies of yourselves! What! am I really pardoned? Am I in very deed washed in that warm stream which gushed from the riven side of Jesus, and yet am I not wholly consecrated to Christ? What! in my body do I bear the marks of the Lord Jesus, and can I live almost without a thought of him? Am I plucked like a brand from the burning, and have I small care to win others from the wrath to come? Has Jesus stooped to win me, and do I not labour to win others for him? Was he all in earnest about me, and am I only half in earnest about him? Dare I waste a minute, dare I trifle away an hour? Have I an evening to spend in vain gossip and idle frivolities? O my heart, well may I smite thee, that at the sight of the death of the dear Lover of my soul, I should not be fired by the highest zeal, and be impelled by the most ardent love to a perfect consecration of every

---

[1] doltish: dull, stupid.

power of my nature, every affection of my spirit, every faculty of my whole man? This mournful strain might be pursued to far greater lengths. We might follow up our confessions, still smiting, still accusing, still regretting, still bewailing. We might continue upon the bass notes evermore, and yet might we not express sufficient contrition for the shameful manner in which we have treated our blessed Friend. We might say with one of our hymn writers –

> Lord, let me weep for nought but sin,
>   And after none but thee;
> And then I would – O that I might –
>   A constant weeper be!

One might desire to become a Niobe, and realize the desire of Jeremy, 'O that my head were waters.' Even the holy extravagance of George Herbert does not surprise us, for we would even sing with him the song of GRIEF –

> Oh, who will give me tears? Come, all ye springs,
> Dwell in my head and eyes; come, clouds and rain!
> My grief hath need of all the wat'ry things
> That nature hath produc'd. Let ev'ry vein
> Suck up a river to supply mine eyes,
> My weary weeping eyes; too dry for me,
> Unless they get new conduits, new supplies,
> To bear them out, and with my state agree.
> What are two shallow fords, two little spouts
> Of a less world? The greater is but small.
> A narrow cupboard for my griefs and doubts,
> Which want provision in the midst of all.
> Verses, ye are too fine a thing, too wise,
> For my rough sorrows. Cease! be dumb and mute;
> Give up your feet and running to mine eyes,
> And keep your measures for some lover's lute,
> Whose grief allows him music and a rhyme;
> For mine excludes both measure, tune, and time,
>   – Alas, my God!

III. Having, perhaps, said enough on this point – enough if God bless it, too much if without his blessing – let me invite you, in the third place, to remember that AT CALVARY, DOLOROUS NOTES ARE NOT THE ONLY SUITABLE MUSIC.

We admired our poet when, in the hymn which we have just sung, he appears to question with himself which would be the most fitting tune for Golgotha.

> 'It is finished;' shall we raise
> Songs of sorrow or of praise?
> Mourn to see the Saviour die,
> Or proclaim his victory?
>
> If of Calvary we tell,
> How can songs of triumph swell?
> If of man redeemed from woe,
> How shall notes of mourning flow?

He shows that since our sin pierced the side of Jesus, there is cause for unlimited lamentation, but since the blood which flowed from the wound has cleansed our sin, there is ground for unbounded thanksgiving; and, therefore, the poet, after having balanced the matter in a few verses, concludes with –

> 'It is finished', let us raise
> Songs of thankfulness and praise.

After all, you and I are not in the same condition as the multitude who had surrounded Calvary; for at that time our Lord was still dead, but now he is risen indeed. There were yet three days from that Thursday evening (for there is much reason to believe that our Lord was not crucified on Friday), in which Jesus must dwell in the regions of the dead. Our Lord, therefore, so far as human eyes could see him, was a proper object of pity and mourning, and not of thanksgiving; but now, beloved, he ever lives and gloriously reigns. No charnel house confines that blessed body. He saw no corruption; for the moment when the third day dawned, he could no longer be held with the bonds of death, but he manifested himself alive unto his disciples. He tarried in this world for forty days. Some of his time was spent with those who knew him in the flesh; perhaps a larger part of it was passed with those saints who came out of their graves after his resurrection; but certain it is that he is gone up, as the first-fruit from the dead; he is gone up to the right hand of God, even the Father. Do not bewail those wounds, they are lustrous with supernal splendour. Do not lament his death: he lives no more to die. Do not mourn that shame and spitting –

> The head that once was crowned with thorns,
> Is crowned with glory now.

Look up and thank God that death hath no more dominion over him. He ever liveth to make intercession for us, and he shall shortly come with angelic bands surrounding him, to judge the quick and dead. The argument for joy overshadows the reason for sorrow. Like as a woman when the man-child is born remembereth no more her anguish, for joy that a man is born into the world, so, in the thought of the risen Saviour, who has taken possession of his crown, we will forget the lamentation of the cross, and the sorrows of the broken heart of Calvary.

Moreover, hear ye the shrill voice of the high sounding cymbals, and let your hearts rejoice within you, for in his death our Redeemer conquered all the hosts of hell. They came against him furiously, yea, they came against him to eat up his flesh, but they stumbled and fell. They compassed him about, yea, they compassed him about like bees; but in the name of the Lord did the Champion destroy them. Against the whole multitude of sins, and all the battalions of the pit, the Saviour stood, a solitary soldier fighting against innumerable bands, but he has slain them all. 'Bruised is the dragon's head.' Jesus has led captivity captive. He conquered when he fell; and let the notes of victory drown for ever the cries of sorrow.

Moreover, brethren, let it be remembered that men have been saved. Let there stream before your gladdened eyes this morning the innumerable company of the elect. Robed in white they come in long procession; they come from distant lands, from every clime;

once scarlet with sin and black with iniquity, they are all white and pure, and without spot before the throne for ever; beyond temptation, beatified, and made like to Jesus. And how? It was all through Calvary. There was their sin put away; there was their everlasting righteousness brought in and consummated. Let the hosts that are before the throne, as they wave their palms, and touch their golden harps, excite you to a joy like their own, and let that celestial music hush the gentler voices which mournfully exclaim –

> Alas! and did my Saviour bleed?
> And did my Sovereign die?
> Would he devote that sacred head
> For such a worm as I?

Nor is that all. You yourself are saved. O brother, this will always be one of your greatest joys. That others are converted through your instrumentality is occasion for much thanksgiving, but your Saviour's advice to you is, 'Notwithstanding in this rejoice not, that the spirits are subject unto you; but rather rejoice, because your names are written in heaven.' You, a spirit meet to be cast away, you whose portion must have been with devils – *you* are this day forgiven, adopted, saved, on the road to heaven. Oh! While you think that you are saved from hell, that you are lifted up to glory, you cannot but rejoice that your sin is put away from you through the death of Jesus Christ, your Lord.

Lastly, there is one thing for which we ought always to remember Christ's death with joy, and that is, that although the crucifixion of Jesus was intended to be a blow at the honour and glory of our God – though in the death of Christ the world did, so far as it was able, put God himself to death, and so earn for itself that hideous title, 'a deicidal world', yet never did God have such honour and glory as he obtained through the sufferings of Jesus. Oh, they thought to scorn him, but they lifted his name on high! They thought that God was dishonoured when he was most glorified. The image of the Invisible, had they not marred it? The express image of the Father's person, had they not defiled it? Ah, so they said! But he that sitteth in the heavens may well laugh and have them in derision, for what did they? They did but break the alabaster box, and all the blessed drops of infinite mercy streamed forth to perfume all worlds. They did but rend the veil, and then the glory which had been hidden between the cherubim shone forth upon all lands.

O nature, adoring God with thine ancient and priestly mountains, extolling him with thy trees, which clap their hands, and worshipping with thy seas, which in their fullness roar out Jehovah's praise; with all thy tempests and flames of fire: thy dragons and thy deeps, thy snow and thy hail, thou canst not glorify God as Jesus glorified him when he became obedient unto death. O heaven, with all thy jubilant angels, thine ever chanting cherubim and seraphim, thy thrice holy hymns, thy streets of gold and endless harmonies, thou canst not reveal the Deity as Jesus Christ revealed it on the cross.

O hell, with all thine infinite horrors and flames unquenchable, and pains and griefs and shrieks of tortured ghosts, even thou canst not reveal the justice of God as Christ revealed it in his riven heart upon the bloody tree.

O earth and heaven and hell! O time and eternity, things present and things to come, visible and invisible, ye are dim mirrors of the Godhead compared with the bleeding Lamb. O heart of God, I see thee nowhere as at Golgotha, where the Word incarnate reveals the justice and the love, the holiness and the tenderness of God in one blaze of glory. If any created mind would fain see the glory of God, he need not gaze upon the starry skies, nor soar into the heaven of heavens, he has but to bow at the cross foot and watch the crimson streams which gush from Immanuel's wounds. If you would behold the glory of God, you need not gaze between the gates of pearls, you have but to look beyond the gates of Jerusalem and see the Prince of Peace expire.

If you would receive the noblest conception that ever filled the human mind of the lovingkindness and the greatness and the pity, and yet the justice and the severity and the wrath of God, you need not lift up your eyes, nor cast them down, nor look to paradise, nor gaze on Tophet, you have but to look into the heart of Christ all crushed and broken and bruised, and you have seen it all. Oh, the joy that springs from the fact that God has triumphed after all! Death is not the victor; evil is not master. There are not two rival kingdoms, one governed by the God of good, and the other by the God of evil; no, evil is bound, chained, and led captive; its sinews are cut, its head is broken; its king is bound to the dread chariot of Jehovah-Jesus, and as the white horses of triumph drag the Conqueror up the everlasting hills in splendour of glory, the monsters of the pit cringe at his chariot wheels. Wherefore, beloved, we close this discourse with this sentence of humble yet joyful worship, 'Glory be unto the Father, and to the Son, and to the Holy Ghost: as it was in the beginning is now and ever shall be, world without end. Amen.

23

ON THE CROSS AFTER DEATH[1]

The Jews therefore, because it was the preparation, that the bodies should not remain upon the cross on the Sabbath day (for that Sabbath day was an high day) besought Pilate that their legs might be broken, and that they might be taken away. Then came the soldiers, and brake the legs of the first, and of the other which was crucified with him. But when they came to Jesus, and saw that he was dead already, they brake not his legs: but one of the soldiers with a spear pierced his side, and forthwith came there out blood and water. And he that saw it bare record, and his record is true: and he knoweth that he saith true that ye might believe. For those things were done, that the scripture should be fulfilled, A bone of him shall not be broken. And again another scripture saith, They shall look on him whom they pierced.

JOHN 19:31–37

CRIMINALS WHO WERE CRUCIFIED by the Romans were allowed to rot upon the cross. That cruel nation can hardly be so severely condemned as our own people, who up to a late period allowed the bodies of those condemned to die to hang in chains upon gibbets in conspicuous places. The horrible practice is now abandoned, but it was retained to a time almost, if not quite, within living memory. I wonder whether any aged person here remembers such a horrible spectacle. Among the Romans it was usual, for there are classical allusions to this horror, showing that

[1] Sermon No. 1,956. Preached at the Metropolitan Tabernacle on Sunday morning, 3 April 1887.

the bodies of persons crucified were usually left to be devoured by ravenous birds. Probably out of deference to the customs of the Jews, the authorities in Palestine would sooner or later allow of the interment of the crucified; but they would by no means hasten it, since they would not feel such a disgust at the sight as an Israelite would. The Mosaic law, which you will find in the Book of Deuteronomy, runs as follows: 'If thou hang him on a tree, his body shall not remain all night upon the tree, but thou shalt in any wise bury him that day' (*Deut.* 21:22-23). This alone would lead the Jews to desire the burial of the executed; but there was a further reason. Lest the land should be defiled upon the holy Sabbath of the Passover, the chief priests were importunate that the bodies of the crucified should be buried, and therefore that their deaths should be hastened by the breaking of their legs. Their consciences were not wounded by the murder of Jesus, but they were greatly moved by the fear of ceremonial pollution. Religious scruples may live in a dead conscience. Alas! this is not the only proof of that fact: we could find many in our own day.

The Jews hurried to Pilate, and sought as a boon the merciless act of having the legs of the crucified dashed to pieces with an iron bar. That act was sometimes performed upon the condemned as an additional punishment; but in this instance it was meant to be a finishing stroke, hastening death by the terrible pain which it would cause, and the shock to the system which it would occasion. Ferocious hate of our Lord made his enemies forgetful of everything like humanity: doubtless the more of pain and shame which they could cause to him the better would they be pleased. Not, however, out of cruelty, but out of regard to the ceremonials of their religion, they 'besought Pilate that their legs might be broken, and that they might be taken away.' I have already told you that this breaking of the bones of the crucified was a Roman custom; and of this we have evidence, since there is a Latin word, *crucifragium*, to express this barbarous act. Pilate had no hesitation in granting the desire of the Jews: what would he care about the dead body, since he had already delivered up the living man?

Soldiers go at once to perform the hideous operation, and they commence with the two malefactors. It is a striking fact that the penitent thief, although he was to be in Paradise with his Lord that day, was not, therefore, delivered from the excruciating agony occasioned by the breaking of his legs. We are saved from eternal misery, not from temporary pain. Our Saviour, by our salvation, gives no pledge to us that we shall be screened from suffering in this life. It is true, as the proverb hath it, 'All things come alike to all: there is one event to the righteous, and to the wicked; to the clean, and to the unclean.' Accidents and diseases afflict the godly as well as the ungodly. Penitent or impenitent, we share the common lot of men, and are born to troubles as the sparks fly upward. You must not expect because you are pardoned, even if you have the assurance of it from Christ's own lips, that, therefore, you shall escape tribulation; nay, but from his gracious mouth you have the forewarning assurance that trial shall befall you; for Jesus said, 'These things I have spoken unto you, that in me ye might have peace. In the world ye shall have tribulation.' Suffering is not averted, but it is turned into a blessing. The penitent thief entered into Paradise that very day, but it was not without suffering; say, rather, that the terrible stroke was the actual means of the prompt fulfilment of his Lord's promise to him. By that blow he died that day; else might he have lingered long. How much we may any of us receive by the way of suffering it were hard to guess: mayhap, the promise that we shall be with our Lord in Paradise will be fulfilled that way.

At this point it seemed more than probable that our blessed Lord must undergo the breaking of his bones; but 'he was dead already.' It had pleased him, in the infinite willinghood with which he went to his sacrifice, to yield up his life, and his spirit had therefore departed. Yet one might have feared that the coarse soldiers would have performed their orders to the letter. See, they do not so! Had they conceived a dread of one around whom such prodigies had gathered? Were they, like their centurion, impressed with awe of this remarkable personage? At any rate, perceiving that he was dead already, they did not use their hammer. Happy are we to see them cease from such loathsome brutality. But we may not be too glad; for another outrage will take its place: to make sure that he was dead, one of the four soldiers with a spear pierced his side, probably thrusting his lance quite through the heart. Here we see how our gracious God ordained in his providence that there should be sure evidence that Jesus was dead, and that therefore the sacrifice was slain. Paul declares this to be the gospel, that the Lord Jesus died according to the Scriptures. Strange to say, there have been heretics who have ventured to assert that Jesus did not actually die. They stand refuted by this spear-thrust. If our Lord did not die, then no sacrifice has been presented, the resurrection is not a fact, and there is no foundation of hope for men. Our Lord assuredly died, and was buried: the Roman soldiers were keen judges in such matters, and they saw that 'he was dead already', and, moreover, their spears were not used in vain when they meant to make death a certainty.

When the side of Christ was pierced, there flowed thereout blood and water, upon which a great deal has been said by those who think it proper to dilate upon such tender themes. It was supposed by some that by death the blood was divided, the clots parting from the water in which they float, and that in a perfectly natural way. But it is not true that blood would flow from a dead body if it were pierced. Only under certain very special conditions would blood gush forth. The flowing of this blood from the side of our Lord cannot be considered as a common occurrence: it was a fact entirely by itself. We cannot argue from any known fact in this case, for we are here in a new region. Granted, that blood would not flow from an ordinary dead body; yet remember, that our Lord's body was unique, since it saw no corruption. Whatever change might come over a body liable to decay, we may not ascribe any such change to his frame; and therefore there is no arguing from facts about common bodies so as to conclude therefrom anything concerning our blessed Lord's body. Whether, in his case, blood and water flowed naturally from his holy and incorruptible body, or whether it was a miracle, it was evidently a most notable and remarkable thing, and John, as an eyewitness, was evidently astonished at it, and so astonished at it that he recorded a solemn affirmation, in order that we might not doubt his testimony. He was certain of what he saw, and he took care to report it with a special note, in order that we might believe; as if he felt that if this fact was truly believed, there was a certain convincing power which would induce many to believe on our Lord Jesus as the appointed Saviour. I could enter into many details, but I prefer to cast a veil over this tender mystery. It is scarcely reverent to be discoursing of anatomy when the body of our adorable Lord is before us. Let us close our eyes in worship rather than open them with irreverent curiosity.

The great task before me this morning is to draw truth out of this well of wonders. I shall ask you to look at the events before us in three lights: first, let us see here *the fulfilment of Scripture*; secondly, *the identification of our Lord as the Messiah*; and thirdly, *the instruction which he intends*.

I. I ask you to notice THE FULFILMENT OF SCRIPTURE.

Two things are predicted: not a bone of him must be broken, and he must be pierced. These were the Scriptures which now remained to be accomplished. Last Lord's Day morning we were all of us delighted as we saw the fulfilment of Scripture in the capture of our Lord, and his refusal to deliver himself from his enemies. The theme of the fulfilment of Scripture is worth pursuing yet further in an age when Holy Scripture is treated with so much slight, and is spoken of as having no inspiration in it, or, at least, no divine authority by which its infallibility is secured. You and I favour no such error; on the contrary, we conceive it to be to the last degree mischievous. 'If the foundations be removed, what can the righteous do?' We are pleased to notice how the Lord Jesus Christ and those who wrote concerning him treated the Holy Scriptures with an intensely reverent regard. The prophecies that went before of Christ must be fulfilled, and holy souls found great delight in dwelling upon the fact that they were so.

I want you to notice concerning this case, that *it was singularly complicated*. It was negative and positive: the Saviour's bones must not be broken, and he must be pierced. In the type of the Passover lamb it was expressly enacted that not a bone of it should be broken; therefore not a bone of Jesus must be broken. At the same time, according to Zechariah 12:10, the Lord must be pierced. He must not only be pierced with the nails, and so fulfil the prophecy, 'They pierced my hands and my feet'; but he must be conspicuously pierced, so that he can be emphatically regarded as a pierced one. How were these prophecies, and a multitude more, to be accomplished? Only God himself could have brought to pass the fulfilment of prophecies which were of all kinds, and appeared to be confused, and even in contradiction to each other. It would be an impossible task for the human intellect to construct so many prophecies, and types, and foreshadowings, and then to imagine a person in whom they should all be embodied. But what would be impossible to men has been literally carried out in the case of our Lord. There are prophecies about him and about everything connected with him, from his hair to his garments, from his birth to his tomb, and yet they have all been carried out to the letter. That which lies immediately before us was a complicated case; for if reverence to the Saviour would spare his bones, would it not also spare his flesh? If a coarse brutality pierced his side, why did it not break his legs? How can men be kept from one act of violence, and that an act authorized by authority, and yet how shall they perpetrate another violence which had not been suggested to them? But, let the case be as complicated as it was possible for it to have been, infinite wisdom knew how to work it out in all points; and it did so. The Christ is the exact substance of the foreshadowings of the Messianic prophecies.

Next, we may say of the fulfilment of these two prophecies, that *it was specially improbable*. It did not seem at all likely that when the order was given to break the legs of the crucified, Roman soldiers would abstain from the deed. How could the body of Christ be preserved after such an order had been issued? Those four soldiers are evidently determined to carry out the governor's orders; they have commenced their dreadful task, and they have broken the legs of two of the executed three. The crosses were arranged so that Jesus was hanging in the midst: he is the second of the three. We naturally suppose that they would proceed in order from the first cross to the second; but they seem to pass by the second cross, and proceed from the first to the third. What was the reason of this singular procedure? The supposition is, and I think a very likely one, that the centre cross stood somewhat back, and that thus the two thieves formed a sort of first rank. Jesus would thus be all the more emphatically 'in the midst'. If he was placed a little back, it would certainly have been easier for the penitent thief to have read the inscription over his head, and to have looked to our Lord, and held conversation with him. Had they been placed exactly in a line this might not have been so natural; but the suggested position seems to suit the circumstances. If it were so, I can understand how the soldiers would be taking the crosses in order when they performed their horrible office upon the two malefactors, and came last to Jesus, who was in the midst. In any case, such was the order which they followed. The marvel is that they did not in due course proceed to deal the horrible blow in the case of our Lord. Roman soldiers are apt to fulfil their commissions very literally, and they are not often moved with much desire to avoid barbarities. Can you see them intent upon their errand? Will they not even now mangle that sacred body? Commend me for roughness to the ordinary Roman soldier: he was so used to deeds of slaughter, so accustomed to an empire which had been established with blood and iron, that the idea of pity never crossed his soul, except to be scouted as a womanly feeling unworthy of a brave man. Yet behold and wonder! The order is given to break their legs: two out of the three have suffered, and yet no soldier may crush a bone of that sacred body. They see that he is dead already, and they break not his legs.

As yet you have only seen one of the prophecies fulfilled. He must be pierced as well. And what was that which came into that Roman soldier's mind when, in a hasty moment, he resolved to make sure that the apparent death of Jesus was a real one? Why did he open that sacred side with his lance? He knew nothing of the prophecy; he had no dreams of Eve being taken from the side of the man, and the church from the side of Jesus. He had never heard that ancient notion of the side of Jesus being like the door of the ark, through which an entrance to safety is opened. Why, then, does he fulfil the prediction of the prophet? There was no accident or chance here. Where are there such things? The hand of the Lord is here, and we desire to praise and bless that omniscient and omnipotent Providence which thus fulfilled the word of revelation. God hath respect unto his own word, and while he takes care that no bone of his Son shall be broken, he also secures that no text of Holy Scripture shall be broken. That our Lord's bones should remain unbroken, and yet that he should be pierced, seemed a very unlikely thing; but it was carried out. When next you meet with an unlikely promise, believe it firmly. When next you see things working contrary to the truth of God, believe God, and believe nothing else. Let God be true and every man a liar. Though men and devils should give God the lie, hold you on to what God has spoken; for heaven and earth shall pass away, but not one jot or tittle of his word shall fall to the ground.

Note again, dear friends, concerning this fulfilment of Scripture, that *it was altogether indispensable.* If they had broken Christ's bones, then that word of John the Baptist, 'Behold the Lamb of God', had seemed to have a slur cast upon it. Men would have objected, 'But the bones of the Lamb of God were not broken.' It was especially commanded twice over, not only in the first ordaining of the Passover in Egypt, but in the allowance of a second to those who were defiled at the time of the first Passover. In Numbers, as well as in Exodus, we read that not a bone of the lamb must be broken. How, then, if our Lord's bones had been broken, could we have said, 'Christ our Passover is sacrificed for us', when there would have been this fatal flaw? Jesus must remain intact upon the cross, and he must also be pierced; for else that famous passage in Zechariah, which is here alluded to, 'They shall look on me whom they have pierced', could not have been true of him. Both prophecies must be carried out, and they were so in a conspicuous manner. But why need I say that this fulfilment was indispensable? Beloved, the keeping of every word of God is indispensable.

It is indispensable to the truth of God that he should be true always: for if one word of his can fall to the ground, then all may fall, and his veracity is gone. If it can be demonstrated that one prophecy was a mistake, then all the rest may be mistakes. If one part of the Scripture is untrue, all may be untrue, and we have no sure ground to go upon. Faith loves not slippery places; faith seeks the sure word of prophecy, and sets her foot firmly upon certainties. Unless all the Word of God is sure, and pure 'as silver tried in a furnace of earth, purified seven times', then we have nothing to go upon, and are virtually left without a revelation from God. If I am to take the Bible and say, 'Some of this is true, and some of it is questionable', I am no better off than if I had no Bible. A man who is at sea with a chart which is only accurate in certain places, is not much better off than if he had no chart at all. I see not how it can ever be safe to be 'converted and become as little children' if there is no infallible teacher for us to follow. Beloved, it is indispensable to the honour of God and to our confidence in his Word, that every line of Holy Scripture should be true. It was indispensable evidently in the case now before us, and this is only one instance of a rule which is without exception.

But now let me remind you that although the problem was complicated, and its working out was improbable, yet *it was fulfilled in the most natural manner.* Nothing can be less constrained than the action of the soldiers; they have broken the legs of two, but the other is dead, and they do not break his legs; yet, to make sure that they will be safe in omitting the blow, they pierce his side. There was no compulsion put upon them, they did this of their own proper thought. No angel came from heaven to stand with his broad wings in the front of the cross, so as to protect the Saviour; no awful aegis of mystery was hung over the sacred body of the Lord so that intruders might be driven back with fear. No, the quaternion of soldiers did whatever they wished to do. They acted of their own free will, and yet at the same time they fulfilled the eternal counsel of God. Shall we never be able to drive into men's minds the truth that predestination and free agency are both facts? Men sin as freely as birds fly in the air, and they are altogether responsible for their sin; and yet everything is ordained and foreseen of God.

The foreordination of God in no degree interferes with the responsibility of man. I have often been asked by persons to reconcile the two truths. My only reply is – They need no reconciliation, for they never fell out. Why should I try to reconcile two friends? Prove to me that the two truths do not agree. In that request I have set you a task as difficult as that which you propose to me. These two facts are parallel lines; I cannot make them unite, but you cannot make them cross each other. Permit me also to add that I have long ago given up the idea of making all my beliefs into a system. I believe, but I cannot explain. I fall before the majesty of revelation, and adore the infinite Lord. I do not understand all that God reveals, but I believe it. How can I expect to understand all the mysteries of revelation, when even the arithmetic of Scripture surpasses my comprehension, since I am taught that in the Godhead the Three are One, while in the undivided One I see most manifestly Three? Need I measure the sea? Is it not enough that I am upborne by its waves? I thank God for waters deep enough for my faith to swim in: understanding would compel me to keep to the shallows, but faith takes me to the main ocean. I think it more to my soul's benefit to believe than to understand, for faith brings me nearer to God than reason ever did. The faith which is limited by our narrow faculties is a faith unworthy of a child of God, for as a child of God he should begin to deal with infinite sublimities, like those in which his great Father is at home. These are only to be grasped by faith. To return to my subject: albeit the matter must be as Scripture foreshadowed, yet no constraint nor inducement was put forth; but, as free agents, the soldiers performed the very things which were written in the Prophets concerning Christ.

Dear friends, suffer one more observation upon this fulfilment of Scripture: *it was marvellously complete*. Observe that in these transactions a seal was set upon that part of Scripture which has been most exposed to sceptical derision: for the seal was set first of all upon *the types*. Irreverent readers of Scripture have refused to accept the types: they say, 'How do you know that the Passover was a type of Christ?' In other cases, more serious persons object to detailed interpretations, and decline to see a meaning in the smaller particulars. Such persons would not attach spiritual importance to the law, 'Not a bone of it shall be broken'; but would dismiss it as a petty regulation of an obsolete religious rite. But observe, beloved, the Holy Spirit does nothing of the kind; for he fixes upon a minor particular of the type, and declares that this must be fulfilled. Moreover, the providence of God intervenes, so that it shall be carried out.

Wherefore, be not scared away from the study of the types by the ridicule of the worldly wise. There is a general timidity coming over the minds of many about Holy Scripture, a timidity to which, thank God, I am an utter stranger. It would be a happy circumstance if the childlike reverence of the early fathers could be restored to the church, and the present irreverent criticism could be repented of and cast away. We may delight ourselves in the types as in a very paradise of revelation. Here we see our best Beloved's beauties mirrored in ten thousand delightful ways. There is a world of holy teaching in the books of the Old Testament, and in their types and symbols. To give up this patrimony of the saints, and to accept criticism instead of it, would be like selling one's birthright for a mess of pottage. I see in our Lord's unbroken bones a setting of the seal of God upon the types of Scripture.

Let us go further. I see; next, the seal of God set upon *unfulfilled prophecy*; for the passage in Zechariah is not yet completely fulfilled. It runs thus: 'They shall look upon me whom they have pierced.' Jehovah is the speaker, and he speaks of 'the house of David and the inhabitants of Jerusalem.' They are to look on Jehovah whom they have pierced, and to mourn for him. Although this prophecy is not yet fulfilled on the largest scale, yet it is so far certified; for Jesus is pierced: the rest of it, therefore, stands good, and Israel shall one day mourn because of her insulted King. The prophecy was fulfilled in part when Peter stood up and preached to the eleven, when a great company of the priests believed, and when multitudes of the seed of Abraham became preachers of Christ crucified. Still it awaits a larger fulfilment, and we may rest quite sure that the day shall come when all Israel shall be saved. As the piercing of their Lord is true, so shall the piercing of their hearts be true, and they shall mourn and inwardly bleed with bitter sorrow for him whom they despised and abhorred. The point to mark here is, that a seal is set in this case to a prophecy which yet awaits its largest fulfilment; wherefore, we may regard this as a pattern, and may lay stress upon prophecy, and rejoice in it, and receive it without doubt, come what may.

I have said this much upon the fulfilment of the Word concerning our Lord; let us learn hence a lesson of reverence and confidence in reference to Holy Scripture.

II. But now, secondly, and briefly, THE IDENTIFICATION OF OUR LORD AS THE MESSIAH was greatly strengthened by that which befell his body after death. It was needful that he should conclusively be proved to be the Christ spoken of in the Old Testament. Certain marks and tokens are given, and those marks and tokens must be found in him: they were so found.

The first mark was this: *God's Lamb must have a measure of preservation.* If Christ be what he professes to be, he is the Lamb

353

of God. Now, God's lamb could only be dealt with in God's way. Yes, there is the lamb; kill it, sprinkle its blood, roast it with fire, but break not its bones. It is God's lamb, and not yours, therefore hitherto shalt thou come, but no further. Not a bone of it shall be broken. Roast it, divide it among yourselves, and eat it, but break no bone of it. The Lord claims it as his own, and this is his reserve. So, in effect, the Lord says concerning the Lord Jesus: 'There is my Son; bind him, scourge him, spit on him, crucify him; but he is the Lamb of my Passover, and you must not break a bone of him.' The Lord's right to him is declared by the reservation which is made concerning his bones. Do you not see here how he is identified as being 'the Lamb of God, which taketh away the sin of the world'? It is a mark of identity upon which faith fixes her eyes, and she studies that mark until she sees much more in it than we can this morning speak about, for we have other things to dwell upon.

The next mark of identity must be, that *Jehovah our Lord should be pierced by Israel*. So Zechariah said, and so must it be fulfilled. Not merely must his hands and feet be nailed, but most conspicuously must himself be pierced. 'They shall look upon me whom they have pierced, and they shall mourn for him.' Pierced he must be. His wounds are the marks and tokens of his being the real Christ. When they shall see the sign of the Son of man in the last days, then shall all the tribes of the earth mourn; and is not that sign his appearing as a Lamb that has been slain? The wound in his side was a sure mark of his identity to his own disciples; for he said to Thomas, 'Reach hither thy hand, and thrust it into my side: and be not faithless, but believing.' It shall be the convincing token to all Israel: 'They shall look upon me whom they have pierced, and they shall mourn for him, as one that mourneth for his only son.' To us the opened way to his heart is in his flesh the token that this is the incarnate God of love, whose heart can be reached by all who seek his grace.

But I have not finished this identification; for observe, that when that side was pierced, 'forthwith came there out blood and water.' You that have your Bibles will have opened them already at Zechariah 12. Will you kindly read on till you come to the first verse of the thirteenth chapter, which ought not to have been divided from the twelfth chapter? What do you find there? 'In that day there shall be a fountain opened to the house of David and to the inhabitants of Jerusalem for sin and for uncleanness.' They pierced him, and in that day they began to mourn for him; but more, in that day there was a fountain opened. And what was that fountain but this gush of water and of blood from the riven side of our redeeming Lord? The prophecies follow quickly upon one another; they relate to the same person, and to the same day; and we are pleased to see that the facts also follow quickly upon one another; for when the soldier with the spear pierced the side of Jesus, '*forthwith* came there out blood and water.' Jehovah was pierced, and men repented, and beheld the cleansing fountain within a brief space. The men who saw the sacred fountain opened rejoiced to see in it the attestation of the finished sacrifice, and the token of its cleansing effect.

The identification is more complete if we add one more remark. Take all the types of the Old Testament together, and you will gather this, that *the purification of sin was typically set forth by blood and water.* Blood was conspicuous always, you have no remission of sin without it: but water was exceedingly prominent also. The priests before sacrificing must wash, and the victim itself must be washed with water. Impure things must be washed with running water. Behold how our Lord Jesus came by water and by blood; not by water only, but by water and blood. John who saw the marvellous stream never forgot the sight; for though he wrote his Epistles, I suppose, far on in life, the recollection of that wondrous scene was fresh with him. Though I suppose he did not write his Gospel until he was a very old man, yet when he came to this passage it impressed him as much as ever, and he uttered affirmations which he was not at all accustomed to use: 'He that saw it bare record, and his record is true: and he knoweth that he saith true.' In solemn form he thus, after a manner, gave his affidavit before God's people, that he did really behold this extraordinary sight. In Jesus we see One who has come to atone and to sanctify. He is that High Priest who cleanses the leprosy of sin by blood and water. This is one part of the sure identification of the great Purifier of God's people, that he came both by water and by blood, and poured out both from his pierced side. I leave these identifications to you. They are striking to my own mind, but they are only part of the wonderful system of marks and tokens by which it is seen that God attests the man Christ Jesus as being in very deed the true Messiah.

III. I must close by noticing, thirdly, THE INSTRUCTION INTENDED FOR US in all these things.

The first instruction intended for us must be only hinted at, like all the rest. *See what Christ is to us.* He is the Paschal Lamb, not a bone of which was broken. You believe it. Come, then, and act upon your belief by feeding upon Christ; keep the feast in your own souls this day. That sprinkled blood of his has brought you safety: the Destroying Angel cannot touch you or your house. The Lamb himself has become your food; feed on him; remove your spiritual hunger by receiving Jesus into your heart. This is the food whereof if a man eat he shall live for ever. Be filled with all the fullness of God, as you now receive the Lord Jesus as God and man. 'Ye are complete in him.' Ye are 'perfect in Jesus Christ'. Can you not say of him: 'He is all my salvation, and all my desire'? 'Christ is all and in all.' Do not merely learn this lesson as a doctrine, but enjoy it as a personal experience. Jesus our Passover is slain, let him be eaten. Let us feast on him, and then be ready to journey through the wilderness, in the strength of this divine meat, until we come to the promised rest.

What next do we learn from this lesson but this? See *man's treatment of Christ.* They have spit upon him, they have cried, 'Crucify him, crucify him', they have nailed him to the cross, they have mocked his agonies, and he is dead; but man's malice is not glutted yet. The last act of man to Christ must be to pierce him through. That cruel wound was the concentration of man's ill-treatment of Jesus. His experience at the hands of our race is summed up in the fact that they pierced him to the heart. That is what men have done to Christ: they have so despised and rejected him that he dies, pierced to the heart. Oh, the depravity of our nature! Some doubt whether it is *total* depravity. It deserves a worse adjective than that. There is no word in human language which can express the venom of the enmity of man to his God and Saviour: he would wound him mortally if he could. Do not expect that men will love either Christ or you, if you are like him. Do not expect that Jesus will find room for himself in the inn, much less that he will be set on the throne by guilty, unrenewed men. Oh, no! Even when he is dead they must insult his corpse with a spear-thrust. One soldier did it, but he expressed the sentiment of the age. This is what the world of sinners did for him who came into the world to save it.

Now, learn, in the next place, *what Jesus did for men*. Beloved, that was a sweet expression in our hymn just now –

> Even after death his heart
> For us its tribute poured.

In his life he had bled for us: drop by drop the bloody sweat had fallen to the ground. Then the cruel scourges drew from him purple streams; but as a little store of life-blood was left near his heart, he poured it all out before he went his way. It is a materialistic expression, but there is something more in it than mere sentiment – that there remains among the substance of this globe a sacred relic of the Lord Jesus in the form of that blood and water. As no atom of matter ever perishes, that matter remains on earth even now. His body has gone into glory, but the blood and water are left behind. I see much more in this fact than I will now attempt to tell. O world, the Christ has marked thee with his blood and he means to have thee! Blood and water from the heart of God's own Son have fallen down upon this dark and defiled planet, and thus Jesus has sealed it as his own, and as such it must be transformed into a new heaven and a new earth, wherein dwelleth righteousness. Our dear Lord, when he had given us all he had, and even resigned his life on our behalf, then parted with a priceless stream from the fountain of his heart: 'forthwith came there out blood and water.' Oh, the kindness of the heart of Christ, that did not only for a blow return a kiss, but for a spear-thrust returned streams of life and healing!

But I must hurry on. I can see in this passage also *the safety of the saints*. It is marvellous how full of eyes the things of Jesus are; for his unbroken bones look backward to the Paschal lamb, but they also look forward throughout all the history of the church to that day when he shall gather all his saints in one body, and none shall be missing. Not a bone of his mystical body shall be broken. There is a text in the Psalms which saith of the righteous man – and all righteous men are conformed unto the image of Christ – 'He keepeth all his bones: not one of them is broken.' I do rejoice in the safety of Christ's elect; he shall not permit a bone of his redeemed body to be broken.

> For all the chosen seed
> Shall meet around the throne,
> Shall bless the conduct of his grace,
> And make his glories known.

A perfect Christ there shall be in the day of his appearing, when all the members of his body shall be joined to their glorious Head, who shall be crowned for ever. Not one living member of Christ shall be absent; 'Not a bone of him shall be broken.' There shall be no lame, maimed Christ, no half-wrought redemption; but the purpose that he came to accomplish shall be perfectly achieved to the glory of his name.

I have not quite done, for I must add another lesson. *We see here the salvation of sinners.* Jesus Christ's side is pierced to give to sinners the double cure of sin, the taking away of its guilt and power; but, better than this, sinners are to have their hearts broken by a sight of the Crucified. By this means also they are to obtain faith. 'They shall look upon me whom they have pierced, and they shall mourn for him.' Beloved, our Lord Jesus came not only to save sinners, but to seek them: his death not only saves those who have faith, but it creates faith in those who have it not. The cross produces the faith and repentance which it demands. If you cannot come to Christ *with* faith and repentance, come to Christ *for* faith and repentance, for he can give them to you. He is pierced on purpose that you may be pricked to the heart. His blood, which freely flows, is shed for many for the remission of sins. What you have to do is just to look, and, as you look, those blessed feelings which are the marks of conversion and regeneration shall be wrought in you by a sight of him. Oh, blessed lesson! Put it into practice this morning. Oh, that in this great house many may now have done with self and look to the crucified Saviour, and find life eternal in him! For this is the main end of John's writing this record, and this is the chief design of our preaching upon it: we long that you may believe.

Come, ye guilty, come and trust the Son of God who died for you. Come, ye foul and polluted, come and wash in this sacred stream poured out for you. There is life in a look at the Crucified One. There is life at this moment for every one of you who will look to him. God grant you may look and live, for Jesus Christ's sake! Amen.

24

JOSEPH OF ARIMATHÆA[1]

Joseph of Arimathæa, an honourable counsellor, which also
waited for the kingdom of God, came, and went in boldly
unto Pilate, and craved the body of Jesus. And Pilate
marvelled if he were already dead: and calling unto him the
centurion, he asked him whether he had been any while dead.
And when he knew it of the centurion, he gave the body to
Joseph. And he bought fine linen, and took him down, and
wrapped him in the linen, and laid him in a sepulchre which
was hewn out of a rock, and rolled a stone unto
the door of the sepulchre.

MARK 15:43-46

IT WAS A VERY DARK DAY with the church of God and with
the cause of Christ, for the Lord Jesus was dead, and so the sun of
their souls had set. 'All the disciples forsook him, and fled.' 'Ye
shall be scattered, every man to his own, and shall leave me alone',
were the sad words of Jesus, and they had come true. He was dead
upon the cross, and his enemies hoped that there was an end of
him, while his friends feared that it was even so. A few women
who had remained about the cross, true to the very last, were found
faithful unto death, but what could they do to obtain his sacred
body and give it honourable burial? That priceless flesh seemed to
be in danger of the fate which usually awaited the bodies of
malefactors: at any rate, the fear was that it might be hurled into
the first grave that could be found to shelter it. At that perilous

---

[1] Sermon No. 1,789. Preached at the Metropolitan Tabernacle on Sunday
morning, 6 July 1884.

moment Joseph of Arimathæa, a city of the Jews, of whom we never heard before, and of whom we never hear again, suddenly made his appearance. He was the very man needed for the occasion, a man of influence, a man possessing that kind of influence which was most potent with Pilate – a rich man, a counsellor, a member of the Sanhedrin, a person of weight and character. Every evangelist mentions him and tells us something about him, and from these we learn that he was a disciple, 'a good man and a just . . . who also himself waited for the kingdom of God'. Joseph had been retiring, and probably cowardly, before; but now he came to the cross, and saw how matters stood, and then went in boldly unto Pilate, craved the body of Jesus, and obtained it. Let us learn from this that God will always have his witnesses. It matters not though the ministry should forsake the truth, though they that should be leaders should become apostate, the truth of God will not fail for lack of friends.

It may be with the church as when a standard-bearer fainteth and the host is ready to melt with dismay; but there shall be found other standard-bearers, and the banner of the Lord shall wave over all. As the Lord liveth, so shall his truth live: as God reigneth, so shall the gospel reign, even though it be from the cross. 'Tell it out among the heathen that the Lord reigneth *from the tree.*' Such is a singular version of a verse in the Psalms [96:10], and it contains a glorious truth. Even while Jesus hangeth on the cross in death he is still keeping possession of the throne, and he shall reign for ever and ever.

Let this be remembered for your encouragement in the cloudy and dark day. If you live in any place where the faithful fail from among men, do not wring your hands in grief and sit down in despair, as though it was all over with the cause you love. The Lord liveth, and he will yet keep a faithful seed alive in the earth. Another Joseph of Arimathæa will come forward at the desperate moment: just when we cannot do without him the man will be found. There was a Joseph for Israel in Egypt, and there was a Joseph for Jesus on the cross. A Joseph acted to him a father's part at his birth, and another Joseph arranged for his burial. The Lord shall not be left without friends. There was a dark day in the Old Testament history when the eyes of Eli, the servant of God, had failed him; and worse still, he was almost as blind mentally as physically; for his sons made themselves vile, and he restrained them not. It seemed as if God must forsake his Israel. But who is this little boy who is brought in by his mother? This tiny child who is to be left in the sanctuary to serve his God as long as he liveth? This pretty little man who wears the little coat which his mother's hands have lovingly made for him? Look, ye that have eyes of faith; for the prophet Samuel is before you, the servant of the Lord, by whose holy example Israel shall be led to better things, and delivered from the oppression which chastised the iniquities of Eli's sons.

God hath today somewhere, I know not where, in yon obscure cottage of an English village, or in a log hut far away in the backwoods of America, or in the slums of our back streets, or in our palaces, a man who in maturer life shall deliver Israel, fighting the battles of the Lord. The Lord hath his servant making ready, and when the time shall come, when the hour shall want the man, the man shall be found for the hour. The Lord's will shall be done, let infidels and doubters think what they please. I see in this advent of Joseph of Arimathæa exactly at the needed time, a well of consolation for all who have the cause of God laid upon their hearts. We need not worry our heads about who is to succeed the pastors and evangelists of today: the apostolical succession we may safely leave with our God.

Concerning this Joseph of Arimathæa, the honourable counsellor, I want to speak this morning, praying that I may speak to your souls all along. As I have already said, we hear no more of Joseph than what is recorded here. He shines out when he is wanted, and then suddenly he disappears: his record is on high. We need not mention the traditions about him, for I think that even the quotation of legends has an evil tendency, and may turn us aside from the pure, unadulterated Word of God. What have you and I to do with tradition? Is not the Scripture enough? There is probably no truth in the silly tales about Joseph and Glastonbury; and if there were, it could be of no consequence to us; if any fact had been worthy of the pen of inspiration, it would have been written, and because it is not written, we need not desire to know. Let us be satisfied to pause where the Holy Spirit stays his pen.

I shall use Joseph of Arimathæa this morning in four ways: first, as *our warning* – he was a disciple of Jesus, 'but secretly for fear of the Jews'; secondly, for *our instruction* – he was at last brought out by the cross concerning which holy Simeon had declared that by the death of the Lord Jesus the thoughts of many hearts should be revealed; thirdly, for *our arousing* – there was an occasion for Joseph to come forward, and there is occasion now for all the timid to grow brave; and lastly, for *our guidance* – that we may, if we have been at all bashful and fearful, come forward in the hour of need and behave ourselves as bravely as Joseph of Arimathæa did on the eve before the Paschal Sabbath.

I. First, then, I desire to look at Joseph of Arimathæa as OUR WARNING. He was a disciple of Christ, but secretly, for fear of the Jews: we do not advise any one of you to imitate Joseph in that. Fear which leads us to conceal our faith is an evil thing. Be a disciple by all means, but not secretly: you miss a great part of your life's purpose if you are. Above all, do not be a disciple secretly because of the fear of man, for the fear of man bringeth a snare. If you are the slave of such fear it demeans you, belittles you, and prevents your giving due glory to God.

> Fear him, ye saints, and you will then
> Have nothing else to fear.

Be careful to give honour to Christ and he will take care of your honour.

Why was it that Joseph of Arimathæa was so backward? Perhaps it was owing to *his natural disposition*. Many men are by nature very bold; some are a little too much so, for they become intrusive, self-assertive, not to say impudent. I have heard of a certain class of persons who 'rush in where angels fear to tread'. They are fearless because they are brainless. Let us avoid fault in that direction. Many, on the other hand, are too retiring: they have to screw their courage up even to say a good word for the Saviour whom they love. If they can do so they fall into the rear rank; they hope to be found among the victors when they divide the spoil, but they are not over ambitious to be among the warriors while they are braving the foe. Some of these are true-hearted notwithstanding their timidity. It was found in the martyr days that certain of those who endured most bravely at the stake were naturally of a fearful mind. It is noted by Foxe that some who boasted of how well they could bear pain and death for Christ turned tail and recanted; while others who in prison trembled at the thought of the fire, played the man in death, to the admiration of all that were round about them.

Still, dear friends, it is not a desirable thing if you are troubled with timidity to foster it at all. Fear of man is a plant to be rooted up, and not to be nurtured. I should set that plant, if I could, where it would get but little water, and no sunshine, and meanwhile I would beg a cutting from a better tree. Would it not be well often to brace ourselves with such a hymn as this –

> Am I a soldier of the cross,
> A follower of the Lamb?
> And shall I fear to own his cause,
> Or blush to speak his name?

> Must I be carried to the skies
> On flowery beds of ease;
> While others fought to win the prize,
> And sail'd through bloody seas?

If you know that your temptation lies in the direction of fear, watch and strive against it, and school yourselves evermore to dauntless courage by the help of the Holy Spirit.

I am afraid, too, that what helped to intimidate Joseph of Arimathœa was the fact that *he was a rich man*. A sad truth lies within our Lord's solemn exclamation, 'How hardly shall they that have riches enter into the kingdom of God.' Riches do not strengthen the heart, or make men daring for the good cause. Albeit wealth is a great talent which may be well used by the man who has entered into the kingdom of heaven, yet it brings with it snares and temptations, and when a man has not yet entered into the kingdom it is, in many ways, a terrible hindrance to his entrance. 'It is easier for a camel to go through the eye of a needle, than for a rich man to enter into the kingdom.' The fishermen of the Galilean Lake readily left their boats and their fishing tackle; but Joseph of Arimathæa was a rich man, and was therefore slow to leave all for Christ's sake. The tendency of great possessions is seen in the case of the young man who turned away in sorrow from the Lord Jesus, when put to the unusual test of selling all he had. Strong swimmers have saved their lives when the ship has struck upon a rock, by casting aside every weight; while others have gone straight down to the bottom because they have bound their gold around their waists. Gold sinks men as surely as lead. Take care, any of you that are well to do in this world, that you do not permit the liberality of God to be a cause of disloyalty to him.

Beware of the pride of life, the lust for rank, the desire to hoard, for any of these may prevent your service of your Lord. Riches puff men up, and prevent their stooping to find the pearl of great price. A poor man enters a humble village sanctuary where Christ is preached, and he finds eternal life, another man under concern of soul in the same village does not like to go down to the poor conventicle, and remains unblest. He keeps away because he puts to himself the question, 'What will the people say if the squire goes to hear the gospel? What a stir there will be if the son of a lord is converted!' Joseph of Arimathæa's wealth made him unduly cautious; and possibly, without his knowing it, prevented his casting in his lot with the common sort of people who followed the Lord Jesus. His heart was for the prize, but the heavy weight of his substance hindered him in his race; it was an instance of abounding grace that he was helped to run well at the last.

Possibly, too, he may have been checked by the fact that *he was in office, and that he was honourable in it.* It needs great grace to carry human honour; and, truth to tell, it is not particularly much worth carrying when you have it. For what is fame but the breath of men's nostrils? Poor stuff to feed a soul upon! If a man could so live as to gain universal plaudits, if he could write his name athwart the sky in letters of gold, what of it all? What is there in the applause of a thoughtless multitude? The approbation of good men, if it be gained by persevering virtue, is better to be desired than great riches; but even then it may become a temptation; for the man may begin to question rather, What will people say? than,

What will God say? and the moment he falls into that mood he has introduced a weakening element into his life. The 'Well done, good and faithful servant', of the Master's own lip is worth ten thousand thunders of applause from senators and princes. Honour among men is, at best, a peril to the best. Joseph was honoured in council, and this is apt to make a man prudently slow. The tendency of office is towards caution rather than enthusiasm. I would have those placed in high positions remember this, and candidly judge themselves as to whether their shrinking from the public avowal of Christ may not be a cowardice unworthy of the position in which the Lord has placed them.

It seems clear that all the earthly things which men covet may not be so desirable as they appear to be; and that which men would give their eyes to procure, they might, if their eyes were opened, think far less of.

I would lovingly enquire of you at this time (for the sermon is meant to be personal all the way through) if any of you who love my Lord and Master are doing so secretly because of the fear of men. You have never openly confessed your faith, and why not? What doth hinder your taking up a decided position on the Lord's side? Are you wealthy? Are you honourable? Do you occupy an enviable position in society? And are you such a mean-spirited creature that you have become proud of these glittering surroundings, like a child that is vain of its new frock? Are you so craven that you will not cast in your lot with the followers of truth and righteousness because they are persons of low degree? Are you really so base? Is there no holy chivalry in you? Can it be so, that, because God has dealt so well with you, and trusted you so generously, you will repay him by denying his Son, violating your conscience, and turning your back on truth; and all for the sake of being in the fashion?

I know it may seem hard to receive the cold shoulder in society, or to have the finger of scorn pointed at you; but to bow before this selfish dread is scarcely worthy of a man, and utterly disgraceful to a Christian man. 'Oh, but I am so retiring in disposition.' Yes, but do not indulge it, I pray you; for, if all were of such a mind, where were the noble advances of truth, her reformations, her revivals? Where would have been our Luther, or our Calvin, or our Zwingli? Where would have been our Whitefield, or our Wesley, if they had thought it to be the main object of desire to walk at ease along the cool sequestered vale of life? Come forth, my brother, for the truth and for the Lord. Recollect that what is right for you would be right for the rest of us: if you do not join the Christian church, for instance, every one of us might also neglect that duty, and where would be the visible church of Christ, and how would the ordinances of our holy faith be kept up as a witness among the sons of men? I charge all concealed believers to think over the inconsistency of their concealment and to quit that cowardly condition.

I feel sure that Joseph of Arimathæa was a great loser by his secrecy; for you see, he did not live with Jesus, as many other disciples did. During that brief but golden period in which men walked and talked, and ate and drank with Jesus, Joseph was not with him. He was not among the twelve: as possibly he might have been if he had possessed more courage and decision. He lost many of those familiar talks with which the Lord indulged his own after the multitudes had been sent away. He missed that sacred training and strengthening which fitted men for the noble lives of primitive saints. How many opportunities he must have missed, too, of working for the Master and with the Master! Perhaps we hear no more of him because he had done no more. Possibly that one grand action which has redeemed his name from forgetfulness, is all that is recorded because it really was all that was worth recording. Joseph must have been a weaker, a sadder, a less useful man for having followed Christ afar off. I would to God that such reflections as these would fetch out our beloved, truly faithful, and honourable Christian men, who hitherto have hidden away among the stuff, and have not come to the front to stand up for Jesus.

II. Secondly, having viewed Joseph of Arimathæa as a warning, I shall go on to speak of him as a lesson for OUR INSTRUCTION.

Joseph did come out after all; and so will you, my friends. If you are honest and sincere, you will have to avow your Lord sooner or later. Do you not, think it would be better to make it sooner rather than later? The day will come when that shame which you are now dreading will be yours. As surely as you are a sincere believer, you will have to encounter that reproach and derision which now alarm you: why not face them at once and get it over? You will have to confess Christ before many witnesses, why not begin to do so at once? What is the hardship of it? It will come easier to you, and it will bring you a larger blessing, and it will be sweeter in the recollection afterwards, than if you keep on postponing it. What was it that fetched Joseph of Arimathæa out? *It was the power of the cross!* Is it not a remarkable thing that all the life of Christ did not draw out an open avowal from this man? Our Lord's miracles, his marvellous discourses, his poverty, and self-renunciation, his glorious life of holiness and benevolence, all may have helped to build up Joseph in his secret faith, but it did not suffice to develop in him a bold avowal of faith. The shameful death of the cross had greater power over Joseph than all the beauty of Christ's life.

Now let us see, you timid, backward ones, whether the cross will not have the same influence over you today. I believe it will if you carefully study it. I am sure it will if the Holy Spirit lays it home to your heart. I suppose that to Joseph of Arimathæa Christ's death on the cross seemed such *a wicked thing* that he must come out on behalf of one so evil entreated. He had not consented to the deed of the men of the Sanhedrin when they condemned Jesus to death; probably he and Nicodemus withdrew themselves from the assembly altogether; but when he saw that the crime was actually committed, and that the innocent man had been put to death, then he said, 'I cannot be a silent witness of such a murder. I must now side with the Holy and the Just.' Therefore he came out, and was found the willing servant of his crucified Master. Come what may of it, he felt that he must own himself to be on the right side, now that they had maliciously taken away the life of the Lord Jesus. It was late, it was sadly late, but it was not too late.

Oh, secret disciple, will you not quit your hiding place? Will you not hasten to do so? You who are quiet and retiring, when you hear the name of Jesus blasphemed, as it is in these evil days, will you not stand up for him? When you hear his deity denied, when his headship in the church is given to another, when his very person is by lewd fellows of the baser sort set up as the target of their criticism, will you not speak up for him? Will you not be shocked by such evil conduct into an open avowal? His cause is that of truth and righteousness, and mercy and hope for the sons of men, therefore he must not be abused while you sit by in silence. Had others favoured him you might, perhaps, have been somewhat excused for holding back; but you cannot keep back without grievous sin now that so many deride him. Jesus is worthy of all honour, and yet they heap scorn upon him: will you not defend him? He is your Saviour and Lord; oh, be not slow to own that you are his. The cross laid bare the heart of Joseph; he loathed the wickedness which slew the Holy and the Just, and therefore he girded himself to become the guardian of his sacred body.

But, next, it may have been in part *the wonderful patience of the Master's death* which made Joseph feel he could not hide any longer. Did he hear him say, 'Father, forgive them; for they know not what they do'? Did he mark him when those blessed lips said, 'I thirst'? Do you think he observed the ribaldry and scorn which surrounded the dying Lord? And did he feel that the stones would cry out if he did not show kindness to his best friend? Since Jesus spake not for himself, but was dumb as a sheep before her shearers, Joseph is bound to open his mouth for him. If Jesus answered not, but only breathed out prayers for his murderers, the honourable counsellor must acknowledge him. The sun has owned him, and veiled his face in sackcloth! The earth has owned him, and trembled to her very heart at his sufferings! Death has owned him, and yielded up the bodies which the sepulchre had hitherto detained! The temple has owned him, and in its horror has rent its veil, like a woman that is utterly broken in heart by the horrors she has seen! Therefore Joseph must own him, he cannot resist the impulse. Oh, brethren, if you have been backward, let some such motive lead you unto the forefront of the host.

Then there were all *the wonders of that death* which he saw, and to which I have already alluded. They sufficed to convince the centurion that this was a righteous man. They convinced others that he was the Son of God; and he who was already a disciple of Christ must have been greatly confirmed in that conviction by what he saw around the cross. The time was come when he must boldly act as Christ's disciple. Have there been no wonders of conversion around you? no answers to prayer? no providential deliverances? Should not these lead the secret ones to declare themselves?

I do not suppose he fully understood *the design of our Lord's death;* he had some knowledge of it, but not such a knowledge as we have now that the Spirit of God has appeared in all his fullness, and taught us the meaning of the cross. Oh, listen, sirs, ye that are not upon his side openly, ye that have never worn his livery, nor manifestly entered on his service. He died for you! Those wounds were all for you; that bloody sweat, of which you still may see the marks upon the countenance of the Crucified, was all for you. For you the thirst and fever, for you the bowing of the head, and the giving up of the ghost; and can you be ashamed to own him? Will you not endure rebuke and scorn for his dear sake who bore all this for you? Now speak from your soul and say, 'He loved me, and gave himself for me.' If you cannot say that, you cannot be happy; but if you can, then what follows? Must you not love him, and give yourself for him? The cross is a wondrous magnet, drawing to Jesus every man of the true metal. It is as a banner lifted on high, to which all who are loyal must rally. This fiery cross, carried through all lands, will rouse the valiant and speed them to the field. Can you see your Lord suffering to the death for you, and then turn your backs? I pray you may no longer hesitate, but may at once cry, 'Set down my name among his followers; for I will fight it out even to the end, till I hear him say –

Come in, come in;
Eternal glory thou shalt win.'

Thus much by way of instruction taken from the life of Joseph of Arimathæa. If the cross does not bring a man out, what will? If the spectacle of dying love does not quicken us into courageous affection for him, what can?

III. So I have to mention, in the third place, something for OUR AROUSING. Perhaps you are saying in your heart that the season in which Joseph lived was one which imperatively demanded that he should leave his hiding place and should go in to Pilate, but that you are under no such constraint. Hearken, friends, many people are not true to their occasions, whatever they may be; they do not consider that they have come to the kingdom for such a time as this. The Lord Jesus is not hanging on a cross today needing to be buried; but other stern necessities exist, and call for your exertions. This hour's necessities imperiously demand that every man who is right at heart should acknowledge his Lord and do him service. Every man that loves Christ should at this hour prove it by his actions.

A buoy off the Mumbles in South Wales bears a bell which is meant to warn mariners of a dangerous rock. This bell is quiet enough in ordinary weather; but when the winds are out, and the great waves rush in towards the shore, its solemn tones are heard for miles around as it swings to and fro in the hands of the sea. I believe there are true men who are silent when everything is calm, who will be forced to speak when the wild winds are out. Permit me to assure you that a storm is raging now, and it is growing worse and worse.

If I rightly read the signs of the times, it is meet that every bell should ring out its warning note lest souls be lost upon the rocks of error. You that have fallen behind because the fighting did not seem to require you, must quit your positions of ease. I summon you in the Master's name to the war. The Lord hath need of you. If you come not to his help against the mighty a curse will light upon you. Ye must either be written across the back as *craven cowards*, or else you will today solemnly espouse the cause of Jesus. Shall I tell you why?

I will tell you why Joseph was wanted, and that was, just because *Christ's enemies had at last gone too far.* When they hunted him about and took up stones to stone him they went a very long way; when they said he had a devil and was mad they went much too far; when they asserted that he cast out devils by Beelzebub, the prince of the devils, that was a piece of blasphemy; but now, now they have overstepped the line most fatally; they have actually taken the King of Israel and nailed him up to a cross, and he is dead; and therefore Joseph cannot stand it any longer. He quits their company and joins himself to the Lord Jesus. See how far men are going in these days. In the outside world we have infidelity of so gross, so brutish, a character, that it is unworthy of the civilization, much less of the Christianity, of our age. Now, ye fearful ones, come out, and refuse to be numbered with the unbelieving world.

Besides, in the outward Christian church we see men who, having already taken away every doctrine that we hold dear, are now assailing the inspiration of God's own Word. They tell us plainly that they do not believe what the Scriptures say further than they choose to do. The Bible to them is a fine book, but rather out of date.

Now, if you can be quiet, I cannot. The citadel of Christendom is now attacked. Let no brave man shrink from its defence. If you can hold your tongues, and see the faith rent to pieces, I cannot. Why, it is enough to make every man gird on his weapon and rush to the fight. Years ago, when they talked of the French invading England, an old lady grew very indignant, and threatened deadly resistance. When she was asked what the women of England could do, she said they would rise to a man. I have no doubt whatever that they would do their best in any such emergency. Every iron in the fire place, whether it be poker or shovel, would be grasped to defend our hearths and homes; and just so now, when error knows no bounds, we must stand up for the defence of the truth. Since they push error to extremes, it becomes us to hold by every particle of the faith. I will not, for my own part, give up a corner of my creed for any man. Even if we might have been prepared to modify expressions had the age been different, we are not in that mood now. A generation of vipers shall have a naked file to bite at. We will modify nothing. If truth bears a stern aspect we will not veil it. If there be an offence in the cross we will not conceal it.

This shall be my answer to those who would have us attune ourselves to the spirit of the age – I know no Spirit but one, and he is unchanging in every age. Your extravagance of doubt shall have no influence over us except to make us bind the gospel more closely to our hearts. If we gave you an inch you would take a mile, and so no inch shall be given you. Our resolve is to live for the Book as we read it, for the gospel as we rest in it, for the Lord as he made atonement, for the kingdom as it ruleth over all. I beg every trembling Christian to take heart, put on his Lord's livery, and advance to the fray. Come out now, if you never did before! Come out, if there is any manliness in you, in these days of blasphemy and rebuke.

> Ye that are men, now serve him,
>   Against unnumber'd foes;
> Your courage rise with danger
>   And strength to strength oppose.

When Joseph of Arimathæa revealed himself as our Lord's disciple, *our Lord's friends had mostly fled* – we might almost say they had all departed. Then Joseph said, 'I will go in and beg for the body.' When everybody else runs away, then the timid man grows brave; and often have I noticed it, that when there has been a wide desertion from the faith, then the feeble have become strong. Those poor souls who had said, 'Ye hardly know whether we are the people of God at all, we are so unworthy', have crept out of their dens and have waxed valiant in fight, putting to flight the armies of the aliens. A sister was asked to tell her experience before the church, and she could not do it; but as she went away she turned round and said, 'I cannot speak for Christ, but I could die for him.' 'Come back', said the minister, you are welcome here!' They do gloriously, those hidden ones, in days whereof we are apt to fear that no witness for the truth will remain alive. Oh, that you who live where religion is declining may be all the more resolved to serve the Lord Jesus faithfully!

And then, you know, in Joseph's time *the people that were true to the Lord Jesus were such a feeble company*. Those that were not absolutely poor – the women that could minister to him of their substance – were nevertheless unable to go in unto Pilate and beg for the Lord's body. He would not have received them, and if he would they were too timid to have sought an interview, but Joseph is rich, and a counsellor, and therefore he seemed to say, 'These dear good women need a friend; they cannot get that precious body down from the cross alone. I will go to the Roman governor. Together with Nicodemus, I will provide the linen and the spices, and the women shall help us take Jesus down from the tree and lay him in my new tomb, and swathe his limbs in linen and spices, so as to embalm him honourably.' Some of you live in country towns where those who are faithful to God are very poor, and have not much ability among them. If anything should move you to be the more decided, it should be that fact. It is a brave thing to help a feeble company; any common people will follow at the heels of success, but the true man is not ashamed of a despised cause when it is the cause of truth. You who have talent and substance should say, 'I will go and help them now. I cannot leave the Master's cause to this feeble folk. I know they do their best, and as that is little, I will join them and lay myself out to aid them for my great Master's sake.'

Can you not see my drift? My only desire this morning is to induce any of you who have for a moment faltered to 'stand up, stand up for Jesus', and everywhere, in every place as wisdom may suggest, avow his dear and sacred name. Perhaps you are flowers that cannot bloom till the light is darkened, like the night-blooming cereus or the evening primrose. Now is your hour. The evening is already come: Bloom, my dear friends, and fill the air with the delightful fragrance of your love. When other flowers are closed, take care to open to the dew. In these dark hours shine out, ye stars! The sun has gone, else might ye lie hid; but now let us see you! Joseph and Nicodemus had never been seen in the daylight when Jesus was alive; but when the sun was set through his death, then their radiance beamed at its full. Oh, my hesitating brother, now is your time and your hour: boldly avail yourself of it, for our great Master's sake!

IV. Lastly, there is something in this subject for OUR GUIDANCE. Somebody says, 'Well, what do you mean by my coming out? I can see what Joseph did: what am I to do? I do not live at Arimathæa, and there is no Pilate in these days.'

Joseph in owning his Lord *put himself under personal risk.* A Christian slave, whose master was executed for being a Christian, went to the judge, and begged the body of his master that he might bury it. The judge replied, 'Wherefore do you wish for your master's body?' 'Because he was a Christian, and I am one.' Upon this confession he was himself condemned to die. It might have been so with Pilate; for the Jewish rulers must have hated Joseph and longed for his death. He had been backward a long time, but now he put his life in his hand, and went in boldly to Pilate. We read, 'He craved the body of Jesus', but, as a commentator well says, he was not a craven, though he craved the body. He simply asked for it, begged for it, implored to have it, and the procurator yielded to his wish. Now, do you think that if it were needful for you to jeopardize your best earthly interests for Christ, you could do it? Could you lose your character for culture and courage by avowing the old faith in these apostate days? Can you leave all for Jesus? Should it rend the fondest connection, should it break up the brightest prospects, could you take up the cross and follow your Lord? It is due to him who died for you that you should count the cost, and reckon it little enough for his dear sake if you may but do him honour.

Remember, again, that this good man, Joseph of Arimathæa, when he took the body of Jesus, brought upon himself *ceremonial pollution*. It may seem little enough to you, but to a Jew it was a great deal, especially during the Passover week. He handled that blessed body, and defiled himself in the judgment of the Jews. But, oh, I warrant you he did not think it any defilement to touch the blessed person of his Lord, even when the life was gone out of that matchless frame. Nor was it any pollution. It was an honour to touch that holy thing, that body prepared of God. Yet they will say to you, if you come out for Christ and unite with his people, that you lower yourself. They will point at you, give you some opprobrious name, and charge you with fanaticism. Take upon yourself this blessed shame, and say, as David did, 'I will be yet more vile.' Dishonour for Christ is honour, and shame for him is the very top of all glory. You will not stand back, I trust, but you will come forward and avow your faith, though you thus become as the offscouring of all things.

And then, this man having risked his life, and given up his honour was content to be *at great cost for the burial of Christ*. He went and bought the fine linen, and that rock-hewn sepulchre which it was the ambition of every Israelite to possess, he cheerfully resigned, that the Lord might lie there. Now, whenever you do own Christ, own him practically. Do not keep back your purse from him, or think that you are to say, 'I am his', and do nothing for him. I was reading the story of a good old deacon in Maine, in America, who came in to a meeting after there had been a missionary collection. The minister there and then asked 'our good brother

Sewell' to pray. Sewell did not pray, but thrust his hand in his pocket and stood fumbling about. 'Bring the box', he said; and when the box came, and he had put his money into it, the minister said, 'Brother Sewell? I did not ask you to give anything, I only wished you to pray.' 'Oh', said he, 'I could not pray till I had first given something.' He felt obliged first to do something for the great mission work, and having done that he could pray for it.

Oh, that all Christ's people felt the justice of that course of conduct! Is it not most natural and proper? Joseph could not, when the Saviour wanted burying, have been true to him without burying him. And now that the Saviour does not want burying, but wants in all his living power to be preached among the sons of men, if we love him we must do all that lieth in us to spread the knowledge of his name. Come out then, come out then, ye that are hidden among the stuff! Some of you strangers from the country, who have lived in the village, and attended the services, but never joined the church, do not let another Sunday dawn till you have sent in your name to be classed with the people of God. And any of you that have come often to the Tabernacle, and say that nobody has spoken to you, just you speak to somebody and own what the Lord has done for you.

Joseph of Arimathæa, where are you? Come forward, man! Come forth; your time has come! Come forth *now*! If you have followed Christ secretly, throw secrecy to the winds! Henceforth be bravest of the brave, among the bodyguard of Christ, who follow him whithersoever he goeth. Have no fear nor thought of fear, but count it all joy if you fall into manifold trials for his name's sake, who is King of kings and Lord of lords, to whom be glory for ever and ever. Amen.

25

A ROYAL FUNERAL[1]

And after this Joseph of Arimathæa, being a disciple of
Jesus, but secretly for fear of the Jews, besought Pilate that
he might take away the body of Jesus: and Pilate gave him
leave. He came therefore, and took the body of Jesus. And
there came also Nicodemus, which at the first came to Jesus
by night, and brought a mixture of myrrh and aloes, about
an hundred pound weight. Then took they the body of Jesus
and wound it in linen clothes with the spices, as the manner
of the Jews is to bury. Now in the place where he was
crucified there was a garden; and in the garden a new
sepulchre, wherein was never man yet laid. There laid they
Jesus therefore because of the Jews' preparation day; for
the sepulchre was nigh at hand.

JOHN 19:38–42

LET US GO TO THIS GRAVE, but not to weep there; nay, not to
shed so much as a single tear. The stone is rolled away, our Lord's
precious body is not there, for Christ has risen from the dead. It
may be that, like Mary at the sepulchre, we shall see a vision of
angels; but if not, we may behold a company of comforting truths
which still linger about the empty tomb of our ascended Lord.

We are expressly told, in Holy Scripture, that our Lord was
buried. It was evidently not sufficient for us merely to be told that
he died; we must also know that he was buried. Why was this?
Was it not, first, that we might have a certificate of his death? We
do not bury living men; and the Lord Jesus would not have been
buried if the centurion had not certified that he was certainly dead.

[1] Sermon No. 2,390. Preached at the Metropolitan Tabernacle on Sunday evening,
7 October 1888.

The Roman officer had probably seen Christ's heart pierced by the soldier's spear, when blood and water flowed forth from his side.

At any rate, when his men went to execute the *coup de grâce*, which finished the lives of the other two, by the breaking of their legs, they were so certain that he who hung in the middle was really dead that they brake not his legs. Christ's being given up for burial, was Pilate's certificate that he had not merely pretended to die, but that it was a real death, and that his body had no life remaining in it. This is an essential point, for if Jesus did not die, he has made no atonement for sin. If he died not, then he rose not; and if he rose not, then your faith is vain, ye are yet in your sins. The sepulchre, therefore, occupies a very important place in the story of the death of Jesus.

Again, was he not buried to fulfil a type which he had himself chosen? Like as Jonah was three days and three nights in the belly of the fish, in the heart of the sea, even so was the Son of man to lie for that time in the bowels of the earth. The casting of the runaway prophet into the sea quieted the angry waves; the tempest fell asleep when he was given up as a victim; and Christ's being cast into the sea of death has quieted the storm of almighty wrath; we sail today as on a sea of glass, because Christ was buried in those awful billows.

He must fulfil the type of Jonah, or else he spoke not aright concerning himself when he said, 'An evil and adulterous generation seeketh after a sign and there shall no sign be given to it, but the sign of the prophet Jonah.'

Further, was not our Lord buried to make his battle with death and his triumph over it more complete? He has conquered death; but he has also burst open the castle of death, that is the grave. He has bearded the lion in his den, the Douglas in his hall. In this matchless duel, he has set himself to fight, not only with death, but with death and the grave combined; and hence the paean of victory is not merely, 'O death, where is thy sting?' but it is also, 'O grave, where is thy victory?' Christ's victory is altogether complete. He hath led captivity captive, because he became a captive. He has vanquished all death's allies, as well as death itself, by going down into the grave, and rending its bars asunder.

Beside all this, did not our Lord die, and condescend to be buried, to sweeten the grave for his people? Rightly did we sing just now concerning the tomb –

> There the dear flesh of Jesus lay,
> And left a long perfume.

Unless the Lord should speedily come, as he may – God grant that he may! – we shall fall asleep, and these bodies of ours will be committed to the silence of the grave. We must not dare to dread the sepulchre; where Christ has been, we may safely and honourably go. As I told you, the other day, he left the fine linen to be the furniture of our last bed; he left the napkin rolled up by itself, that weeping friends might dry their tears thereon; he left, beside, the myrrh and aloes, about one hundred pounds' weight, which Nicodemus brought. I never heard that they were taken away from the tomb; Jesus left them there, and they still shed their sweet fragrance throughout the graves of all his saints. We are not going to a noisome vault, but to a perfumed chamber, hung with the fine linen sheets that encompassed the Christ, and odorous with the spices that shed their sweetness upon him. To die, is now our gain; to sleep in Jesus, is to be blest indeed.

I may add, also, that I think our Lord was buried so that, from his tomb, he might leap to his throne. He goes to the lowest depths that thence he may rise to the loftiest heights. You, too, believer, may go as low as the grave, but you can never go any lower, and when you are at your lowest, you are then on your way to your highest. Your Lord stooped to conquer, so must you. You will have won the victory over death when you lie, stark and cold, upon your last bed. The adversary may think that he has defeated you –

> When silent is your pleading tongue
> And blind that piercing eye,

and inactive that once diligent hand, but it is not so; you shall then have broken loose from everything that hinders you from entering upon your highest service for your Lord, and you shall have entered that holy place where you shall see his face, and serve him day and night in his glorious temple.

I like to think of Jesus as going down into the lowest parts of the earth, when I remember that he that descended is the same who also ascended. This should encourage us to feel that, sink as we may, lower and yet lower still, we shall rise all the higher because of that sinking, and shall enter still more completely into fellowship with Christ both in his sufferings and in his glory. It was needful, then, my brother, that there should be a new tomb in the garden close by Golgotha, and that our Lord should lie there. It is a very wonderful thing that he, whose face is the light of heaven, whose hands are sceptred with the government of the universe, and whose very feet are sandalled with the stars, should yet bear the image of death upon his pale countenance, and should lie there lifeless, to be handled by others, and to be wrapped as any other dead man might be, in fine linen and sweet spices.

But my subject at this time is concerning the wonderful working of God with regard to the burial of Jesus. The providence of God began with the body of Christ from the very first, even from his conception; and it followed him right to the last, even to his burial. You see the holy Child in the manger, and you notice how all things round about minister strangely to him. Throughout his life, all things worked together for his good; not to screen him from suffering, but to cause him to suffer, and to make him triumphant through those sufferings. And when he came to die, I see the finger of God displayed at every part of that dread tragedy; but now that he is dead, will that kind providence forsake him? Ah, no!

I want to stop here, and say to you who anxiously ask, 'What will become of me when I die? I am so very poor and needy' – never think about that matter; you have enough to do to trust God till you die. As to what is to become of your body when you are dead, never fret about that. It is wonderful how God does take care of the very dust and ashes of his chosen, how, sometimes, they receive in death respect and honour which they never thought would have come to them, and after they have passed away, their children and their household are blessed of God for their sake. The God of the living forsakes not his saints in dying, or after death. As Ruth would cleave to Naomi, and said, 'Where thou diest, I will die, and there will I be buried', so, with greater faithfulness, does God cleave to his people; he will see them buried, and take care of their children after they are gone. This is his comforting promise, 'Leave thy fatherless children, I will preserve them alive; and let thy widows trust in me.'

Now let me remind you how God took care of the Firstborn among many brethren. Jesus is dead, and in the hands of wicked men; the executioners have him in their charge, those same executioners, who just now broke the legs of the two thieves, have hold of Christ; but that precious body must be preserved, not a bone of him must be broken, no disrespect must be paid to that immaculate Being. Death and hell would have revelled in insulting Christ's body if they could. As Achilles dragged Hector by the heels round the walls of Troy, so would Satan have liked that men should have mauled the dead body of Christ. He would have cast him to the dogs or to the kites if he could have had his way; but so it must not be. Many a man who has been a prince has been buried with the burial of an ass; but this great Saviour, whom men despised, must have a royal funeral: how is he to have it? That is the point I wish to bring to your notice now; and, before I have finished my discourse, I hope I shall be able to prove to you that everything required for Christ's burial was supplied.

I. The first requisite was, SOMEONE TO OBTAIN THE BODY.
The law has executed Jesus, though wrongfully, and his body therefore belongs to the executioner, or, at any rate, to the law. Who is to rescue that precious body from the clutches of the law? Ah! you may look your eyes out, but you cannot see the man who can accomplish this task; yet God knows where he is. There is one Joseph, who has an estate at Arimathæa, a wealthy man, a member of the Sanhedrin, 'an honourable counsellor'. He appears upon the scene, and he is the right man to do what is required, for he is a *secret disciple*. He has great respect for that dead body; for he had great regard for Jesus while he was alive. As we look Joseph up and down, we say, 'Yes, if he will do his best, he is the very man for this emergency.' He is under great arrears of obligation to his Lord, whom he scarcely owned in his lifetime; yet he is a real disciple. Joseph, if thou canst do anything in this matter, we give thee this solemn charge, go and get the body of Christ.

He was, besides, *an official, and influential*; therefore he could gain an entrance where a private person could not; and what was still more to the point with such a man as Pilate, he was *a rich man*, for in those days, in the courts, everything went by favour. The poor man's cause might be just, yet he could not secure a hearing; but the gold in a rich man's hand would speak more loudly than the most convincing arguments upon a poor man's tongue. So this secret disciple is the one to beg the body of Jesus, because he is an honourable counsellor, and also because he is rich. If he is willing to undertake the task, he is the man to accomplish it.

But my heart misgives me, for Joseph has been secretly a disciple, and therefore I conclude that he must be *very timid*. During the last two years or so, he has been really a follower of Christ, and yet he has kept in the council. He has been a member of the Sanhedrin, yet he has not spoken out against its evil deeds. Ah, me! I am afraid that he will not be able to go and speak to Pilate. But note, brethren, what Mark tells us about him: 'Joseph of Arimathæa went in *boldly* unto Pilate, and craved the body of Jesus.' God can make a coward bold as a lion in the day when he needs him; and this good man, full of honour, and abounding in wealth, said, 'I will go to Pilate.' Why! this cruel vacillating governor will put a man to death if he aggravates him; who knows how this interview may end? But Joseph says, 'I will go to Pilate.' He obtains admittance, and he asks for the body of Jesus. Pilate exclaims, 'Why, he is not dead yet!' 'Yes, he is', answers Joseph, 'I have seen him die.' When the centurion comes, he certifies that he is dead. Pilate cannot imagine what Joseph can want with a dead man's bones, but he says, 'You may have his body. Take him down, you may have him.' So Joseph comes back to the cross; he has proved that he was the very man for this work. We should never have thought of him, but God had him in reserve for the hour of need, and brought him to the front at the right moment.

Now you see Joseph hurrying away from Pilate's hall to the hill of Calvary, where the crosses are still standing. He has, in his hand, the order signed by the governor, he shows it to the officer in charge, and he is a man of such prominence, so well known as an honourable counsellor, an official gentleman, and a person of wealth, that everybody is ready to help him. He himself is probably first and foremost in raising the ladder, helping to pull out the great nails, and to let down the blessed body. He is the man for this work, for *he is objectionable to nobody.* He has been a counsellor, so that those on the side of the Sanhedrin do not object to him. The holy women stand watching him, but they have no fears as to his action; they know him, for he has probably done them many a kindness privately in days gone by; and they know that he has been a secret disciple of the Lord. He has brought with him fine white linen, which he was well able to buy, he reverently takes the body of Jesus down from the cross, and tenderly wraps it round with the costly winding-sheets which he has purchased; and so this trying business is finished without interference from anyone.

I hope that these details do not seem trivial to you, for nothing is trivial that concerns our Lord and his cause. In the tabernacle and the temple, even the nails had to be duly prepared; and I think that, in this matter of providing a suitable person to go and get the body of Jesus out of the hand of the legal custodian, we ought to admire the wonderful goodness of God. Depend upon it, if, at any other time, there should be some great and terrible task to be accomplished, God will find the man to do it. If one shall be wanted, by and by, at peril of his life to bear witness for Christ, the right person will be found; and until this chapter of divine providence shall come to an end in our Lord's eternal glory, there shall never be a crisis, however crucial, but the man shall be found whom God wants, or the woman who is to occupy the place which the Lord has for her to fill.

Thus, Joseph has obtained the body of Jesus from the hands of Pilate, and he may do what he will with it; that is the first point.

II. The next requisite is, SOMEONE TO BURY THE BODY.

We do not want one man to carry away that body, and lay it in the grave, for such a person as Jesus should have an honourable funeral. Now see what happens; There is another man, also a counsellor, 'a ruler of the Jews', 'a master of Israel', yet another secret disciple who had come to Jesus by night; he appears just at this very moment: 'There came also Nicodemus, which at the first came to Jesus by night.' Now we have two mourners for our Master's funeral. James and John – where are you? They cannot hear my question. Peter and Bartholomew, where are you? They are too far away; they cannot hear me. Who will follow the body of Jesus to the grave? Who will be chief mourner? There are some gracious women, brave enough to stand afar off, and willing enough, if beckoned, to come and join the sad *cortège* that attends the corpse to the tomb. But how honourable to Christ was it that the first two and the chief mourners on that sorrowful occasion should be two members of the Sanhedrin, Joseph of Arimathæa and Nicodemus, two men of note, two reputable individuals who were held in honour even among the Jews who crucified Christ!

First, let me say of these two men who attended the burial of our Lord, that *they did him honour*. Thus was fulfilled Isaiah's prophecy, 'He made his grave with the wicked, and with the rich in his death; because he had done no violence, neither was any deceit in his mouth.' All the while until Christ had paid the dreadful price of our redemption, he was despised and rejected of men; but as soon as ever he could say, 'It is finished', and the debt was fully paid, he must not be despised and rejected any more. Now, rich men must come and do him homage; and accordingly Joseph and Nicodemus came. It may seem only a little thing, but it indicates the turn of the tide, just as the floating of a straw may do. Jesus is no longer derided, nor even attended alone by the poorest and most obscure of Galileans; but Joseph from Arimathæa, and Nicodemus, a ruler of the Jews, attend the funeral of the great Lord and Saviour of men, and so pay such honour as they can to his dead body.

While they thus did him honour, *they received from him much more honour*. Ah, my brethren, it was a great privilege that was accorded to these two men! I stand and wonder how it was that this position was allotted to two who had kept so long behind the scenes. They had lost – they had lost – I cannot tell you how much they had lost, two, perhaps three years of constant fellowship with Christ, and of instruction from his own dear lips; they had lost incalculably. They were at the tail end of all Christ's disciples; Mary Magdalene was in front of them, the woman that was a sinner was far ahead of them, they were right in the rear rank; yet their Master, in the splendour of his grace, gives them this privilege even while he himself lies dead, to them is accorded the high honour of handling his blessed flesh, and laying him in the tomb. I am afraid that some of you secret Christians, who never come out boldly for Christ, will not have such an honour as this. If the Lord ever uses you at all, it will be in some sad business, such as a funeral; and even that will be an honour to you, if you are permitted to attend him in his death though you have not shared the glory of his life. You lose – oh! you lose incalculable boons by not avowing your discipleship. Yet I pray that there may come a time, and that it may come at once, when even you will come out, and do what you can for your Lord, saying to yourself, 'Now is the hour when even I, timid as I am, must avow him.' When soul-murder is in your streets, when heresy is in your pulpits, when apostasy is in your churches, you are recreant to the last grain of your spiritual manhood if you who love Christ do not come out boldly on his side, and declare that you belong to him. If you never have confessed him before men, and you neglect this opportunity, wherein there is the greatest and most urgent of need, I fear that you will never own him at all.

Joseph of Arimathæa and Nicodemus were both wanted for this sad task; and though we should never have thought of inviting them to perform it, yet they were the only two men connected with Christ who were exactly fitted for the office; and, as I have said, they thus honoured Christ, and he thus honoured them. I should also say, brethren, that among all the disciples, there were *no more sincere mourners for Christ then these two men.* I think that I hear Joseph fetch a deep sigh, and say, 'Ah! Nicodemus, how wicked I have been, for I have not kept with Christ as I ought to have done! I ought to have gone with him to prison and to death; instead of that, I have been among the ungodly, rich and honoured.' 'Ah!' says Nicodemus, 'and I went to him by night, and he talked so sweetly to me, but I have been hiding away ever since. I feel ashamed to touch this blessed bleeding hand; I realize that it is a high honour to be allowed to handle these dear feet, and to wrap the linen all about them, but I do not deserve such an honour, I am sure'; and they would stop, and weep, and sigh again, to think of how they had ill-treated their Lord, by what they may have thought was modesty, but which conscience now tells them was nothing else than shameful cowardice.

And I do not think that, out of all Christ's followers, there were any who would be *more tender with that blessed body*, for they were gentlemen. They were not countrymen or fishermen, used to handling and being handled roughly; they were of tenderer mould, and when they looked on that dear form, how gently would they treat it! Being also men of property, they would have many servants able to help them in all sorts of ways. In his wonderful interment, our Lord Jesus could not have been better attended, nor have been buried by men who would have performed the mournful duty with more solemn feelings, more hushed reverence. They loved him, yet felt that they had acted in an unloving manner towards him, and now also felt that the best they could possibly do was all too little for the blessed One who had sealed the forgiveness of their cowardice by permitting himself to be entrusted to their hands. I can see great love about this dead Christ, and great pity, and great kindness, that even his lifeless body should be giving life to the faith and hope of Joseph and Nicodemus, and should be firing them with fresh ardour. While they looked upon his corpse, they must have been compelled to resolve that never more would they be ashamed of him whom they had helped to lay in the grave.

So far we have, in imagination, brought our Lord Jesus Christ into the hands of two most suitable persons to bury him.

III. The next requisite is, THE MATERIALS NECESSARY FOR THE BURIAL.

The manner of the Jews is to bury the body wrapped in fine white linen; where is that? I do not believe that Peter has a yard of it anywhere, I hardly think that James and John have anything much finer than fishermen's coats, and so forth. *Fine linen* – let it be the best that can be bought, let it be white as snow, for wrapping around this perfect body; but where is it to be obtained? Joseph has it; he is a man of wealth, who can get anything that is wanted, and he has brought with him the best winding-sheets in which to wrap the Saviour's body.

But we must also have *mixed spices in abundance*, fifty pounds' weight at the least. 'Oh!' says Nicodemus, 'I have brought one hundred pounds' weight with me, and if I could have found a conveyance, and more spices had not been superfluous, I would have brought many hundred pounds' weight of myrrh and aloes, well mingled according to the art of apothecary, with which to surround that blessed form.'

See, my brothers, Christ wanted for nothing when he was dead; do you think that he will want for anything while he is alive? 'Ah! but our little church, our poor cause, is wanting money badly, and we are going to get up a bazaar.' What! and you have not thought about going to your Lord for what you lack? The fact is, the church of God has been looking to the devil to find funds for the Lord's work, instead of seeking aid from the Lord himself. It is a pity that we cannot come back to him who, even when he was dead, had a hundred pounds' weight of myrrh and aloes brought to him. Cannot we trust him for all that is required for his service? It will be a better and a brighter day for the church when she believes that, if Christ wants myrrh and aloes, he can get them. Does not the Lord say, 'The silver is mine, and the gold is mine . . . Every beast of the forest is mine, and the cattle upon a thousand hills . . . If I were hungry, I would not tell thee: for the world is mine, and the fullness thereof'? Let us go forth to fight the Lord's battles without any doubts concerning the commissariat of his army. He can provide, and he will provide; only let us trust him, and not go down to Egypt for help, nor lean upon an arm of flesh.

As Nicodemus gave so freely to the dead Christ, how generously ought you and I to give to our living Lord! If we have anything in the world, let us give it all up to Christ. Even if we have nothing left but a grave, which we have provided for our own funeral, yet let us surrender that, as Joseph did when he gave up his new tomb that his Lord and Master might lie therein.

Thus, you see, that all that is needed for Christ's burial is there already. So I leave that part of our subject, and go on to the next.

IV. Another requisite is, A PLACE WHEREIN TO BURY THE BODY. We have the body, Pilate has given us that; we have the spices and the fine linen; and we have the two men ready to bury the body; now we want a tomb.

It would be very convenient, and also very important, if we could get *a sepulchre near at hand*; because, you see, if the body of Christ had to be carried a long way to be buried, the Jews would say, 'Ah!

they changed it on the road; they took it a mile or two out of the city, and the Christ who rose from the dead is not the Christ that was buried.' But here, just at the bottom of this rocky scarp which is called Golgotha, there is a garden, and in that garden there is a tomb. Mark the providence of God in this matter, for that tomb belongs to Joseph, and there the Saviour's body is lovingly laid. He did not, and he could not, lack a tomb when it was required; when the time came for him to be buried, the sepulchre was there already prepared, hewn out of the rock.

It would be also a great advantage if it could be *a new tomb*, wherein never was anybody buried; for if they buried him in an old tomb, the Jews would say that he had touched the bones of some prophet or other holy man, and so came to life. Ah! well, Joseph's is a new tomb; there are no bones there, for nobody has ever been buried there before.

It would seem, too, to be the proper thing for our Lord to have *a tomb in a rock*. You cannot fitly put him in sand who is himself the Rock of Ages. Nay, let our Lord Jesus, with that grand immutable love and eternal faithfulness of his, let him lie in the solid rock. There it is, all ready for him, just the very kind of tomb that is wanted for him who is the Rock of our salvation.

If it should also be *a tomb in a garden*, there would be a touch of familiar beauty about that arrangement. One likes that the very surroundings of Christ's grave should be instructive. I cannot stop to tell you about all the beauty and the instruction which cluster around a garden; the gardens of Scripture especially are most fruitful subjects, and our Lord's garden-tomb might suggest to us a most profitable theme for meditation.

Thus, Christ's tomb is the very thing we would wish for him. In no second-hand grave, in no town fosse, in no pauper's grave dug out of the earth, but in a rich man's sepulchre, worthy of a king, it is there that the Christ must lie. See how God provides for his Son, and learn how he will provide for you. If he provides for his Son when dead, he will provide for you while living; therefore be you comforted whatever your condition may be.

V. There is one more difficulty, and perhaps it is the worst of all, for it concerns THE TIME FOR THE BURIAL. You see, it is very late in the afternoon, and besides, it is the 'preparation' for a very important Sabbath, and these good people cannot do any work on the Sabbath, their consciences will not permit them to do so, for they are strict Jews. But it so happened that they obtained the body just in time to wrap it round about with the spices and with the linen, and then we are told, 'There laid they Jesus therefore because of the Jews' preparation day; for *the sepulchre was nigh at hand.*' To me, it is a very pretty thought that, when there was so little time, the place of burial was so near. It would have taken all the lingering twilight to have carried Jesus far, but the right place was near. Providence knew all about the difficulty, and provided for it.

Next, they could not take much time with the body, and *the ceremony was the more fitting for Christ's rising.* Beloved, whenever you cannot do anything for your Lord as you would like to do it, do the best you can, and you may depend upon it that you have done just what ought to be done. 'Oh, no!' they say, 'Oh, no! we would have liked to have wrapped him up much more leisurely, and more delicately; we would have made a finished work of embalming that precious body.' Listen: nothing more was wanted. Jesus was not going to be in the sepulchre long. God's Holy One could not see corruption. He did not need to be embalmed, for he was to be up again so soon, and therefore a hurried burial was quite sufficient.

Listen again: there is another thing worth mentioning. *The incompleteness brought them early to the sepulchre.* If they do not finish their task of love on the evening of the crucifixion, they will be there early in the morning, when the Sabbath is over, to complete it. That was precisely what was wanted, that, as soon as the Master was risen, on that first day of the week, they should be there to see him; but they would not have been there to see him, perhaps, if they had not come, as the holy women did, with more spices to finish the work which had been, comparatively speaking, so roughly and hurriedly done on that dread evening.

It was all right; and I drew much comfort and joy out of this fact when I was thinking it over. I said to myself, 'Sometimes, I am so oppressed with the care of the many things entrusted to me that I cannot study my sermon as I would like.' Perhaps it is all the better for that; the Master does not want studied sermons. It may be also that it suits the hearer all the better. If you cannot bury Christ as you would like to because there is not time, when you have done the best that you could, and sorrowed over it, you have done the very thing that your Lord wants you to do. Rest you content with that, and just say to yourself, 'He takes the will for the deed, and all my blunderings and mistakes he overlooks because I did it all out of love for his dear name.'

I have talked thus to you about Christ's dead body. Oh, that I had an opportunity of speaking to you about him as the living Lord! But as I cannot, for our time is gone, I would ask you just to stoop down, and in faith and love to kiss those wounds, admire that pierced hand, that other hand, that nailed foot, that other foot, that side with the spear gash, and that dear face with closed eyes, and then say, 'He bore all this for me; what have I done for him?' God bless you! Amen.